Homo Academicus

Homo Academicus

Pierre Bourdieu

Translated by Peter Collier

Stanford University Press
Stanford, California

Stanford University Press
Stanford, California
© 1984 Les Editions de Minuit, except for
    Preface and Postscript © 1988 Pierre Bourdieu
English translation © 1988 by Polity Press, Cambridge
    in association with Basil Blackwell, Oxford
Originally published in French 1984 by
    Les Editions de Minuit
Originating publisher of English edition:
    Polity Press, Cambridge
First published in the U.S.A. by
    Stanford University Press, 1988
Printed in Great Britain
Cloth ISBN 0-8047-1466-5
Paper ISBN 0-8047-1798-2
Last figure below indicates year of this printing:
99 98 97 96 95 94 93 92 91 90

378.12
B 76

91-2312
19069599

Contents

Contents

List of Graphs, Classifications and Tables

TABLES

Acknowledgements

I wish to thank all those who were kind enough to help me by answering queries, providing documents and information, or reading one or other of the preliminary versions of this text. I hope that they will find in it a faithful echo of their suggestions and criticisms. The preliminary readings which I was able to solicit, from a larger and more varied circle than usual, have helped considerably, at least in my eyes, to guarantee the scientific quality of this study. My first readers also helped me to overcome my anxieties over publication, inasmuch as the corrections or confirmations that they were able to suggest, from very different points of view, seem to free my analysis from the limitations inherent in the fact of holding a position in the space being analysed.

I would like to express my particular thanks to Yvette Delsaut, who participated in every phase of the work, from the gathering of source material and the researching of information to the processing and analysis of the data. Without her this study would not have been what it is.

Translator's Note

I wish to express my gratitude to Pierre Bourdieu for reading my translation with great care, for making many valuable suggestions, and for writing especially for this English edition a preface, a postscript and a note on the analysis of correspondences. I also wish to thank John Thompson for his advice and encouragement. I have endeavoured to be true to the spirit as well as the letter of the original: any shortcomings which have escaped the friendly vigilance of both author and editor are entirely my own responsiblity.

Peter Collier
Cambridge

Preface to the English Edition

It is history which is the true unconscious.
Emile Durkheim, The Evolution of Educational Thought

This analysis of the academic world is the end product of the critical reflection on scientific practice which I have never ceased to conduct as part of the very process of my research, since the time when, as a young ethnologist, I took my own native region as the object of my ethnological observation.[1] Thus my sociological analysis of the academic world aims to trap *Homo Academicus*, supreme classifier among classifiers, in the net of his own classifications. It is a comic scenario, that of Don Juan deceived or The Miser robbed, and there are those who, hoping to feel endangered or to make others feel threatened, prefer to treat it in tragic terms. I for my part think that the experience whose results this book presents is perhaps not so different from that attributed by David Garnett to the hero of his short story *A Man in the Zoo*, where the young man, as the result of a quarrel with his girlfriend, writes in despair to the director of the zoo to offer him a mammal missing from his collection, that is, himself, so that he is placed in a cage, next to the chimpanzee, with a notice saying: 'Homo sapiens. This specimen is the gift of John Cromantie, Esquire. Visitors are requested not to tease the man with personal remarks.'

The sociologist who chooses to study his own world in its nearest and most familiar aspects should not, as the ethnologist would, domesticate the exotic, but, if I may venture the expression, exoticize the domestic, through a break with his initial relation of intimacy with modes of life and thought which remain opaque to him because they are too familiar. In fact the movement towards the originary, and the ordinary, world should be the culmination of a movement towards alien and extraordinary worlds. But it hardly ever is: in Durkheim as in Lévi-Strauss, there is no prospect of subjecting to analysis the 'forms of classification' employed by the scholar, and seeking in the social structures of the academic world (which Durkheim had none the less analysed superbly in his *The Evolution of Educational Thought*) the sources of the categories of professorial understanding. And yet, social science may expect to derive its most decisive progress from a constant effort to undertake a sociological critique of sociological reasoning – that is, to establish the social derivation not only of the categories of thought which it consciously or unconsciously deploys, such as those pairs of antithetical terms which so often inform the scientific construction of the social world, but also of the concepts which it uses, and which are often no more than commonsense notions introduced uncritically into scholarly discourse (like the notion of 'profession', which is tacitly repudiated in this study[2]), or of the problems which it elects to study, which not infrequently are nothing but more or less skilfully disguised versions of the latest 'social problems' ('poverty' or 'hooliganism', 'under-achievement in school' or 'the senior citizen', etc.).

One cannot avoid having to objectify the objectifying subject. It is by turning to study the historical conditions of his own production, rather than by some form or other of transcendental reflection, that the scientific subject can gain a theoretical control over his own structures and inclinations as well as over the determinants whose products they are, and can thereby gain the concrete means of reinforcing his capacity for objectification. Only a sociological self-analysis of this kind, which owes and concedes nothing to self-indulgent narcissism, can really help to place the scholar in a position where he is able to bring to bear on his familiar world the detached scrutiny which, with no special vigilance, the ethnologist brings to bear on any world to which he is not linked by the inherent complicity of being involved in its social game, its *illusio*, which creates the very value of the objectives of the game, as it does the value of the game itself.

In making a scientific analysis of the academic world, one takes as one's object an institution which has been socially licensed as entitled to operate an objectification which lays claim to objectivity and universality. Far from leading to a nihilistic attack on science, like certain so-called 'postmodern' analyses, which do no more than add the flavour of the month dressed with a soupçon of 'French radical chic' to the age-old irrationalist rejection of science, and more especially of social science, under the aegis of a denunciation of 'positivism' and 'scientism', this sort of sociological experimentation applied to sociological study itself aims to demonstrate that sociology *can* escape from the vicious circle of historicism or sociologism, and that in pursuit of this end it need only make use of the knowledge which it provides of the social world in which science is produced, in order to try to gain control over the effects of the social determinisms which affect both this world, and, unless extreme caution is exercised, scientific discourse itself. In other words, far from destroying its own foundations when it brings to light the social determinants which the logic of the fields of production brings to bear on all cultural productions, sociology claims an epistemological privilege: that conferred by the fact of being able to reinvest in scientific practice its own scientific gains, in the form of a sociological increase in epistemological vigilance.

What scientific profit can there be in attempting to discover what is entailed by the fact of belonging to the academic field, that site of permanent rivalry for the truth of the social world and of the academic world itself, and by the fact of occupying a determined position within it, defined by a certain number of properties, an education and training, qualifications and status, with all their concomitant forms of solidarity or membership? Firstly, it provides an opportunity for conscious neutralization of the probabilities of error which are inherent in a position, understood as a point of view implying a certain angle of vision, hence a particular form of insight and blindness. But above all it reveals the social foundations of the propensity to theorize or to intellectualize, which is inherent in the very posture of the scholar feeling free to withdraw from the game in order to conceptualize it, and assuming the objective, which attracts social recognition as being scientific, of arriving at a sweeping overview of the world, drafted from an external and superior point of view. There is patent bad faith in refusing to credit science, when it encroaches on the world of the scholar, with the qualities readily granted to structuralist objectivism when it handles the 'savage mind', assumed to be inaccessible to itself; none the less, this should not prevent us from asking if the will to know is not surreptitiously motivated in the present case by a special kind of will to power, which is displayed in the fact of attempting to adopt towards rivals, reduced to the state of objects, a point of view which they are unable or unwilling to adopt towards themselves. But in the event the declared intention of the enterprise is hardly relevant, since the enterprise functions as a mechanism generating 'problem situations', as Popper would say. The tendency to forget to programme into the complete theory of the world analysed the gap between the theoretical and the practical experience of this world is compensated for by the inevitably reflexive view imposed by the sociological analysis of the social conditions of sociological analysis: the objective analysis, or even the objectivist or structuralist analysis, of the structures of a world in which the scientist responsible for the work of objectification is himself ensconced, and of which he has an initial representation which is capable of surviving objective analysis, will then reveal its own limits in its turn by calling attention, for instance, to its own individual or collective defence mechanisms, which often take the form of an operation of negation, and through which the agents aim to maintain in being, for themselves and for others, representations of the social world which clash with the representation constructed by science through a totalization which ordinary existence precludes, in spirit and in letter. Objective analysis obliges us to realize that the two approaches, structuralist and constructivist (by which I mean a kind of phenomenology of one's initial experience of the social world and of the contribution which this experience makes towards one's construction of that world), are two complementary stages of the same procedure. If the agents do indeed contribute to the construction of these structures, they do so at every stage within the limits of the structural constraints which affect their acts of construction both from without, through determinants connected with their position in the objective structures, and from within, through the mental structures – the categories of professorial understanding – which organize their perception and appreciation of the social world. In other words, although they are never more than particular angles of vision, taken from points of view which the objectivist *analysis situs* constitutes as such, the partial and partisan views of the agents engaged in the game, and the individual or collective struggles through which they aim to impose these views, are part of the objective truth of this game, playing an active part in sustaining or transforming it, within the limits set by the objective constraints.

It is understandable that a book aiming to account for this sort of initiatory itinerary orientated towards that reappropriation of the self which, paradoxically, is only accessible through objectification of the familiar world, is bound to be read differently by readers who are part of this world as opposed to those who are outsiders. And this is so despite the fact that this text, given its object, has the singularity of providing its own context – contrary to what usually happens, in the international (and also the intergenerational) circulation of ideas, where texts are transmitted without the context of their production and use, and count on receiving a so-called 'internal' reading which universalizes and eternalizes them while derealizing them by constantly relating them to the sole context of their reception.[3] It could be supposed that, contrary to the native reader who understands only too well in one sense, but who may be inclined to resist objectification, the foreign reader, because (at least at first sight) he has no direct stake in the game which is described, will be less inclined to offer resistance to the analysis. All the more so since, as it happens in the theatre that one may laugh unwittingly at the portrait of one's own foibles, the foreign reader can always elude the challenges implicit in situations or relations which he *does* find familiar, by isolating only the most blatantly exotic, but perhaps also the least significant, characteristics of academic traditions thus dismissed as archaisms, thereby managing all the better to keep his distance.[4] In fact, *mutatis mutandis*, the foreign reader finds himself faced with the same alternative as the native reader (and the sociologist himself): he can use the objectification of a world in which he participates at least by analogy (as witness the international solidarity between holders of equivalent positions in the different national fields) in order to reinforce the defence mechanisms of his bad faith, by accentuating the differences which particularize the species *homo academicus gallicus*; or, alternatively, he may use it to lay the foundations of a self-analysis, either by concentrating on the invariants of the genus *homo academicus*, or, better still, by educating himself with what he may discover about himself through the objectification, however harsh at first sight, of one of the positions of *homo academicus gallicus* which is homologous to his own position in his own field. In order to foster the second kind of reading, the only one, I believe, which reflects the epistemological intentions of this book, one would need either to offer a constructed set of transformational rules enabling systematic transfers to be made from one historical tradition to another,[5] or at least, more modestly, to suggest starting points for the transposition of the analyses, those, for instance, which concern the rhetorical strategies of teachers' judgements, the pairs of adjectives which structure professorial understanding, or the objective and subjective bases of that management of one's own and other people's time which ensures the maintenance of the hierarchy of power, that is, if I may make a slight modification to Leibniz's famous definition of time, 'the order of successions' on which depends the perpetuation in time of the social order.[6]

The scientific virtue (and perhaps also the ethical value) of the notion of the field resides no doubt in the fact that this notion tends to exclude those partial and unilateral objectifications of the unconscious of other people, whether rivals or opponents, which characterize the 'sociology of intellectuals', and which differ from the folk-sociology of intellectual gossip only in their claims to the 'ethical neutrality' of science, which render them guilty of a veritable abuse of symbolic power. Thus for instance when in *The Opium of the Intellectuals* (a classic of the genre) Raymond Aron undertakes to lay bare the reasons behind the arguments of his opponents of the day, and describes the social determinants of the ethical or political stances of those he calls intellectuals (excluding himself, of course, from the stigmatized class), that is, Jean-Paul Sartre, Simone de Beauvoir and the other 'left-wing intellectuals', Aron makes no attempt to ask himself from what point of view he operates this sovereign objectification (no more than does Simone de Beauvoir herself in the diametrically opposite article which she devotes, at roughly the same time and with the same lack of moral hesitation, to 'right-wing thought')[7]: trapped within the lights of his self-interest, he is entirely blind, as blind as those whose blindness he denounces, to the space within which he is situated, yet within which may be defined the objective relation which connects him to them, and which is the source both of his insights and of his oversights.

The construction of the field of production, substituting for a polemic where prejudice is disguised as analysis a polemic where scientific reason challenges itself, that is, challenges its own limits, implies a break with naïve and self-indulgent objectifications unaware of their sources. It can only be an unjustifiable abstraction (which could fairly be called reductive) to seek the source of the understanding of cultural productions in these productions themselves, taken in isolation and divorced from the conditions of their production and utilization, as would be the wish of *discourse analysis*, which, situated on the border between sociology and linguistics, has nowadays relapsed into indefensible forms of internal analysis. Scientific analysis must work to relate to each other two sets of relations, the space of works or discourses taken as differential stances, and the space of the positions held by those who produce them. This means for instance that any one particular work produced by an academic on the subject of the events of May 1968 only yields its significance if, using the principle of intertextuality, it is set in the space of the works dealing with this subject, within which its symbolically pertinent properties are defined, and if this space is related to the homologous space of the positions held by their authors in the academic field. Any reader familiar with this literature will be able to verify, if they refer to the diagram on p. 276, how this functions as an instrument of analysis: the differences observed in the distribution of power and prestige among the authors correspond to the differences, intentional or not, which they display not only in their overall judgement of the events but also in their way of expressing them. The hypothesis that there is an almost perfect homology between the space of the stances (conceived as a space of forms, styles and modes of expression as much as of contents expressed) and the space of the positions held by their authors in the field of production finds its most remarkable confirmation in the fact, which will be blindingly obvious to all observers familiar with the details of what happened in the universities in 1968, that the distribution in the academic field – constructed by considering *exclusively* the most typically academic characteristics of the different professors (the institution they belong to, their academic qualifications, etc.) – corresponds very closely to the distribution in terms of political positions or trade-union affiliations and even stances adopted during the events of May 1968. Thus it is that the Director of the Ecole Normale Supérieure, Robert Flacelière, who made a very firm stand against the student movement, is surrounded on the diagram by the names of the professors who signed motions in support of his action, whereas those who took up positions favourable to the movement are all situated in the opposite area. This means that it is not, as is usually thought, political stances which determine people's stances on things academic, but their positions in the academic field which inform the stances that they adopt on political issues in general as well as on academic problems. The margin of autonomy which ultimately devolves to the specifically political sources of the production of opinions then varies according to the degree to which the interests directly associated with their position in the academic field are directly concerned or, in the case of the dominant agents, threatened.

But one could go further and reintroduce into the model not only the political stance but also the works themselves, considered in their most visibly social properties, like their genre or their place of publication, and in their topic as well as their form: thus we see, for instance, that the distribution of works according to their degree of conformity to academic norms corresponds to the distribution of their authors according to their possession of specifically academic power. And to give a more concrete idea of this relation I need only mention the astonishment of a certain young American visitor, at the beginning of the seventies, to whom I had to explain that all his intellectual heroes, like Althusser, Barthes, Deleuze, Derrida and Foucault, not to mention the minor prophets of the moment, held marginal positions in the university system which often disqualified them from officially directing research (in several cases, they had not themselves written a thesis, at least not in canonical form, and were therefore not allowed to direct one).

If we linger a while over the case of these philosophers, who are the most likely to be familiar to Anglo-Saxon readers, we see that knowing the structure of the overall space in which they are situated enables us to put ourselves so to speak *in their place* in the social space, through a genuinely 'participant objectification' which has nothing reductively polemical about it, and to reconstruct the point of view from which their intellectual project was defined. As may be seen from the diagram, they were caught in a dual relation with the worlds of philosophy and the social sciences. Their relation to the temporally dominant pole of institutionalized philosophy, which, frozen in the motionless time of lectures informed by the eternal recurrence of the topics set for competitive examinations, is personified by the university professors who control the organs of reproduction of the corps, agencies entrusted with the selection of teachers for secondary education, such as the *agrégation* competitive examination, or for higher education, such as the Comité Consultatif des Universités, the Universities Consultative Committee. In their relation with the philosophical high priests of the Sorbonne, who, like most of them, are products of the 'great lay seminary', the Ecole Normale Supérieure, which is the apex of the whole academic hierarchy, they appear like religious heretics, or, in other words, rather like freelance intellectuals installed within the university system itself, or at least, to venture a Derridean pun, encamped on the margins or in the marginalia of an academic empire threatened on all sides by barbarian invasions (that is, of course, as seen by the dominant fraction). More or less totally deprived of, or liberated from, the powers and privileges but also the tasks and the responsibilities of the ordinary professor (examining the entrance examinations, supervising theses, etc.) they have strong connections with the intellectual world, and especially with the avant-garde reviews (*Critique, Tel Quel*, etc.) and with journalism (especially the *Nouvel Observateur*): Michel Foucault is no doubt the most representative of this position, since, until the end of his life, and even when he became professor at the Collège de France (after this enquiry was completed), he remained almost entirely bereft of specifically academic and even scientific powers, and therefore of the clientele which these powers afford, even if because of his fame he wielded considerable power over the press and, through it, over the whole field of cultural production. The marginal nature of this position, even more striking in the cases of Althusser or Derrida, who held minor posts (tutor or *caïman* – 'alligator', in Ecole Normale slang – at the Ecole Normale Supérieure), is obviously not unconnected with the fact that all these heretics with a vocation to become heresiarchs, beyond the differences, the divergencies, and sometimes the conflicts which separate them, share a sort of *anti-institutional mood* homologous in its form to that of a considerable fraction of students: they are inclined to react impatiently to the discrepancy between their already considerable fame in the outside world, that is, outside the university and also outside France, and the subaltern status which is accorded them inside the French university world, in collusion with their contempt and their rejection, by an institution which, when they were adolescents, had attracted and even consecrated them.[8]

If it was necessary to start by considering the case of the most obscure pole, it is because that is the one most likely to escape the foreign observer or the superficial analyst (not to mention the polemicist whose home ground it is), although it no doubt played a decisive part – and not just as a foil, but also as the opponent who had to be constantly fought in order to assert the right to exist or at least to subsist – in the same way that the old Sorbonne did, when faced with the *Annales* team, in the constitution or the reinforcement of the ethical or political dispositions which will define the general trend of the works. It remains the case that it is above all in relation to the other pole, that of the all-conquering social sciences, which are incarnated by Lévi-Strauss, who rehabilitates these disciplines traditionally despised by the philosophy teachers from the École Normale, and who establishes them as the paragon of intellectual achievement, under the heading of *anthropologie*, that it is necessary to redefine these philosophical projects which had initially been constituted between 1945 and 1955, both with reference to the phenomenological and existential tradition and the figure of the philosopher as endowed by Sartre with exemplary stature, and also, and above all, against it. The adoption, instead of the banal and restrictive term 'ethnology', of the term 'anthropology', which, borrowed from the Anglo-Saxon tradition, is also laden with all the prestige of a great philosophical past (it is in this period that Foucault translates and publishes Kant's *Anthropology*), symbolizes the formidable challenge that the social sciences, through their most eminent representatives, offer to philosophy, which previously was all-powerful. This challenge comes out into the open in the confrontation between Lévi-Strauss and Sartre, in the first real protest against its undivided rule over the whole intellectual field for a quarter of a century. Indeed, although Sartre and Merleau-Ponty also had to take the social sciences into account during the preceding generation, they were in an incomparably easier situation, since, because of the extreme decadence of the Durkheimian school and the very inferior status of an empirical sociology still in its infancy and 'compromised', in those highly politized times, by its American origins, they were confronted with only a 'scientistic' psychology (albeit with the exception of Piaget) and a psychoanalysis with no influence (despite the presence at the Sorbonne of Lagache, a fellow student of Sartre and Merleau-Ponty at the École Normale).

Henceforth, as the final diagram clearly shows,[9] it is the social sciences as a whole or even as a mutually supportive autonomous bloc (the arts faculties become faculties of the arts and social sciences) which hold the symbolically dominant position, confronting the representatives of philosophy, threatened with an entirely new situation not only in its position of dominant discipline but also in its intellectual identity and its research programmes: this is the case in linguistics, a truly dominant discipline, with Benveniste and the virtual presence of Jakobson (living abroad but consecrated by Lévi-Strauss), and, albeit less importantly, Martinet; in 'anthropology', with Lévi-Strauss, backed up by Dumézil; in history, with Braudel, long since consecrated by the long discussion that Sartre had devoted to his *Méditerranée*, working to lay the institutional foundations of a renovated and integrated social science, with the 6th section of the Ecole Pratique des Hautes Etudes, its prestigious scientific council (including Lévi-Strauss, Aron, Le Bras, Friedmann), its research centres in full development, its reviews (including *Les Annales*, inherited from Marc Bloch and Lucien Febvre, and *L'Homme*, founded by Lévi-Strauss, which supplants the ageing *Temps modernes*, relegated to the status of purveyor of partisan, Parisian literary essays), and, soon, its Parisian stronghold, the Maison des Sciences de l'Homme; in psychoanalysis with Lacan, who, socially and symbolically allied to Lévi-Strauss and to Merleau-Ponty, has great importance in the field (although he was not included in the correspondence analysis, and therefore not in the diagram, because he did not hold an official position in the university – the refusal to permit him to lecture at the Ecole Normale Supérieure had been at the root of the revolt against Flacelière); in sociology itself which, although relegated to the bottom division of the major new intellectual powers, manages, through Raymond Aron and his polemics with Sartre or the new philosophical currents (*D'une sainte famille à l'autre*), to command the respect of a generation of philosophers who had still been brought up to write essays on the themes launched, between the two wars, by the *Introduction to the Philosophy of History*.

One might also pause for a moment to consider the case of Roland Barthes, which shows us more clearly than others the relation of twofold difference which is characteristic of the avant-garde of the seventies: not being one of the institutional elite (he is neither *normalien* nor *agrégé*, nor a 'philosopher'), and, doubtless moved by the obscure sentiment of revenge felt by the outsider, he is able to engage with the ordinary professors (represented in this instance by Picard) in public controversy which their feelings of statutory dignity prohibit in the more consecrated of the young heresiarchs;

and he can also display towards the great masters, who accumulate both ordinary and extraordinary claims to his gratitude, an unambiguous reverence, which others grant only in much more subtle or perverse forms. Condensing in his social being the tensions or contradictions inherent in the awkward position of the marginal academic institutions (like the Ecole des Hautes Etudes 'après Braudel', or, at other times, Nanterre or Vincennes), which try to convert a twofold opposition, often linked to a double privation, into a willed transcendence, and which, as places of transit for some and as terminus for others, cause divergent trajectories to meet momentarily, Roland Barthes represents the peak of the class of essayists, who, having nothing to oppose to the forces of the field, are condemned, in order to exist, or subsist, to float with the tides of the external or internal forces which wrack the milieu, notably through journalism. He calls to mind the image of a Théophile Gautier whom a contemporary described- as 'a spirit floating on every breeze, quivering at every touch, able to absorb every impression and to retransmit it in turn, but needing to be set in motion by a neighbouring spirit, always eager to borrow a watchword, which so many others would then come to seek from him': like the good Théo, who was accused of lacking 'character' by his friend Flaubert who failed to see that his very inconsistency was the source of his importance, and who inspired someone else to remark that he adopted in turns the Chinese, the Greek, the Spanish, the medieval, the sixteenth-century, the Louis XIII, the Louis XIV, the rococo and the romantic styles, Roland Barthes gives instantaneous expression to all the changes in the forces of the field while appearing to anticipate them, and in this respect it is sufficient to follow his itinerary, and his successive enthusiasms, to discover all the tensions which were applied to the point of least resistance of the field, where what is called fashion continually flowers.

It is clear that the relation of twofold opposition would inevitably be experienced very differently according to the position occupied in the field and the previous trajectory, as we have just seen in the case of Roland Barthes, and according to the specifically philosophical capital which could be invested in the effort to overcome the tension it engendered. Those who, like Althusser and above all Foucault, had been led by their rejection of what has been called the 'philosophy of the subject', and of the 'humanism' associated with existentialist ideas, towards a tradition of epistemology and of history of science represented by Gaston Bachelard, Georges Canguilhem and Alexandre Koyré (among others), were predisposed, with that touch of ostentatious extravagance needed to signal their distance from the 'positivism' of the scholars ('Man is dead. . .'),[10] to identify with the 'subjectless philosophy', which Lévi-Strauss, loyal in this to the Durkheimian tradition, had just reaffirmed, giving it a modernist air by referring to a notion of the unconscious which reconciled Freud revised by Lacan, Saussure summarized by Jakobson, and, if not the old Durkheim, still excluded from the very closed circle of distinguished philosoophers, at least Marcel Mauss, easier to adapt at the cost of some bold reinterpretations to the new intellectual regime (Merleau-Ponty, who played an important part in the transition between the two intellectual generations because of his particularly open and comprehensive attitude towards the social sciences, notably biology, psychology and linguistics, had written an article entitled 'From Mauss to Lévi-Strauss'). Thus through a strange ruse of intellectual reason it happened that the Durkheimian philosophy of man became rehabilitated, with the more acceptable face of an anthropology legitimated by linguistics, in opposition to the 'philosophy of the subject' that an earlier generation of *normaliens*, that of Sartre, Aron and Nizan, had set up in the thirties in opposition to this 'totalitarian' philosophy of the Durkheimians, among others.

But, let there be no mistake about it, the acknowledgement of the social sciences implies no unconditional surrender. Although each philosopher in his own way betrays his deference to or dependence on the social sciences – if only, like Derrida, by choosing them as the target of his criticism, or by borrowing their themes (for instance the criticism of the use of pairs of adjectives in literary criticism) – the philosophers constantly mark (and not least in their style, as with Foucault, who indulges in set-pieces of rhetorical elegance, or with Derrida, who imports into the philosophical field the procedures and effects which are used in *Tel Quel* circles) their statutory distance from the ordinary practitioners of the 'so-called social sciences', as Althusser liked to put it (and thus, not surprisingly, they elicit quite a different reaction from those who read them and expect to find in their reading a demonstration of the dignity which they invest in their writing). And they deploy all the resources of their culture in order to transfigure, perhaps above all in their own eyes, the 'historicist' philosophy which they borrow from social science along with many of its themes, its problems and its mode of thought.

Thus it is that Foucault finds in Nietzsche an acceptable philosophical sponsor for the socially improbable combination of artistic
transgression and scientific invention that he achieves and for the
screen-concepts which, like that of genealogy, help to provide a
cover for an ambitious enterprise in social history or genetic
sociology. Similarly, as I have shown in the case of the analysis
which he devoted to the *Critique of Judgement*, Derrida knows
how to suspend 'deconstruction' just in time to prevent it tipping
over into a sociological analysis bound to be perceived as a vulgar
'sociologistic reduction', and thus avoids deconstructing himself
qua philosopher.[11]

In addition to all this argument, which cannot take the place of
genuine genetic sociology of the works themselves, perceived from
the particular points of view (specified by the secondary social,
religious or sexual characteristics of the different producers) in which
they were elaborated, we could not understand the critical liberty
which gives these works a family resemblance and which makes
them much more than variously successful reconversions of the
philosophical enterprise, if we failed to see that this critical liberty
is rooted in the especially intense experience of an especially dramatic
crisis. The previously dominant disciplines, philology, literary history
and even philosophy, whose intellectual foundations are threatened
by their new rivals, disciplines like linguistics, semiology, anthropology, or even sociology, find that the social foundations of their
academic existence are also under siege from the criticisms welling
up on all sides, usually in the name of the social sciences and on
the initiative of teachers from these disciplines, against the archaic
nature of their contents and their pedagogial structures. This double
criticism frequently awakens touching reactions of traditionalist
conservatism in those professors who did not have the instinct and
the boldness to recycle themselves in time, and in particular among
those whom I call the 'oblates'[12] and who, consigned from childhood
to the school institution (they are often children of the lower or
middle classes or sons of teachers), are totally dedicated to it. These
reactions are bound to exacerbate the revolt of those who are by
their capital and dispositions led to break simultaneously with
institutionalized philosophy and the philosophical institution. The
break, which sometimes takes on the aspect of a civil war, is
accomplished in fact, well before 1968, between the professors who
remained attached to the traditional definition of their discipline and

the social foundations of its existence in terms of a social body (like the *agrégation*), and the members of the new avant-garde who managed to find in the resources inherent in membership of a prestigious discipline the means necessary to operate a successful reconversion and who are perceived as traitors or renegades by the guardians of orthodoxy – who, like themselves, are products of the 'great seminary'. All the more so because these modernists, despite being called by a precocious and often dramatic consecration to fulfil the highest academic destinies, found that they were relegated, often with their own connivance, to awkward positions which predispose them to feel and express, whether in direct or in transposed forms, a crisis of the academic institution of which their very position in the institution is proof enough. A crisis affecting an institution which has the function of inculcating and imposing forms of thought must weaken or ruin the social foundations of thought, bringing in its wake a crisis of faith, a veritable, practical *epoche* of doxa, which encourages and facilitates the appearance of a reflexive awareness of these foundations. If the experience and the expression of this crisis took a more radical form in France than elsewhere, it is because, owing to the particularly archaic nature of an educational system hypnotized by illusory images of its grandeur, those consecrated by a bankrupt institution were obliged, if they were to be worthy of the ambitions which it had inculcated in them, to break with the derisory and henceforth untenable roles which it assigned to them, and were led to invent new ways of playing the part of the teacher (all based on adopting a reflexive distance from practice and from the ordinary definition of their functions), by lending him the strange features of an intellectual master of reflection who reflects on himself and in so doing, helps to destroy himself qua master.[13]

Because of their self-critical dispositions and their impatience with authority, and especially with the power wielded in the name of science, these self-destructive masters were prepared to harmonize their rhythms with the movements which pulsated through the ethical and political avant-garde of the student world. The students of bourgeois origins who have become academically downclassed, and who populate the arts faculties, especially in the new disciplines, are victims of verdicts which, like those of the school, appeal to reason and science in order to block off the paths leading (back) to power. They are spontaneously inclined to denounce science, power, the power of science, and above all perhaps a power which, like the

triumphant technocracy of the moment, appeals to science in order
to legitimate itself. Moreover, the new 'student life' which is created
in the faculties suddenly invaded by an incomparably more numerous
and more diversified clientele than in the past, in terms both of
social origins and of gender (it is around 1970 that girls become as
numerous as boys in the arts faculties) forms a social experiment
through which, as in bohemian circles in the nineteenth century, a
new bourgeois 'life-style' developed, making room for values excluded
from the old, pre-war, neo-Kantian university and still not admitted
in the disciplines professed by the boarding schools leading to the
'schools for the elite' – that is, desire, pleasure and 'anti-repressive'
dispositions. All these are themes which will be strongly orchestrated
by all the philosophical avant-garde,[14] from Deleuze to Foucault,
via Derrida and even Althusser (with his 'ideological state apparatuses'), not to mention the minor heresiarchs, more closely 'tuned
in' to the new vulgate.[15]

I have made no concessions in writing this book, but I trust that
it bears no malice, for it comprises, as the reader will have guessed,
a considerable proportion of self-analysis by proxy, as well as a
distance, no doubt encouraged by sociology but first affirmed in the
fact of abandoning philosophy for the social sciences – and that,
obviously, at a time when, thanks to Lévi-Strauss's rehabilitation of
ethnology, it became possible to do so without stooping too low
. . . And the special place held in my work by a somewhat singular
sociology of the university institution is no doubt explained by the
peculiar force with which I felt the need to gain rational control
over the disappointment felt by an 'oblate' faced with the annihilation
of the truths and values to which he was destined and dedicated,
rather than take refuge in feelings of self-destructive resentment.

1

A 'Book for Burning'?

Historians don't want to write a history of historians. They are quite happy to plunge endlessly into limitless historical detail. But they themselves don't want to be counted as part of the limitless historical detail. They don't want to be part of the historical order. It's as if doctors didn't want to fall ill and die.
Charles Péguy, L'Argent, suite

In choosing to study the social world in which we are *involved*, we are obliged to confront, in *dramatized* form as it were, a certain number of fundamental epistemological problems, all related to the question of the difference between practical knowledge and scholarly knowledge, and particularly to the special difficulties involved first in *breaking* with inside experience and then in reconstituting the knowledge which has been obtained by means of this break. We are aware of the obstacles to scientific knowledge constituted as much by excessive proximity as by excessive remoteness, and we know how difficult it is to sustain that relation of a proximity broken and restored, which requires much hard work, not only on the object of our research, but also on ourselves as researchers, if we are to reconcile everything we can know only as insiders, and everything we cannot or do not wish to know as long as we do remain insiders. But we are perhaps less aware of the problems which arise when we attempt to transmit scientific knowledge of the object, especially through the medium of writing. These problems are particularly apparent in the case of *exemplification*. This rhetorical strategy, which is commonly employed to 'make things clear', but by persuading the reader to draw on his own experience, that is, to smuggle subjective information into his reading, almost inevitably results in reducing to the realm of ordinary knowledge those scientific constructs which had been painstakingly wrested from it.[1] Likewise, we have only to introduce proper names – and how can this be altogether avoided, when one of the objectives in this milieu is to 'make a name for oneself'? – to reinforce the reader's inclination to reduce to a concrete individual, seen confusedly, the constructed individual who exists as such only within the theoretically constructed space of the relations of identity and difference obtaining between the explicitly defined set of his properties, and the specific sets of properties, defined according to the same principles, which character-ize other individuals. But, however vigorous our effort to eschew all the overtones which operate constantly, albeit implicitly, within ordinary reasoning, those of gossip, insult and slander, or those of the satire and the broadsheet (which, although nowadays very prone to masquerade as analysis, exploit every possible anecdote, barb and witticism, for the sheer pleasure of drawing blood or showing off), however systematically we may abstain (as we do here) from referring to matters which are none the less common knowledge – the overt involvement of academics with journalism, not to mention the secret relationships (and family affairs) that historians will make it their duty to discover – we will none the less still be open to the suspicion of undertaking an act of *denunciation* for which the reader is in fact responsible. It is the reader, reading between the lines, more or less consciously filling in the gaps in the analysis, or quite simply 'putting himself in their shoes', as the saying goes, who transforms the sense and the value of the intentionally censored report of the scientific investigation. Since the sociologist cannot describe everything that he knows (including matters which those readers most eager to denounce his 'denunciations' often know better than he does, albeit on an entirely different level), he is in danger of appearing to surrender to the well-known strategies of polemic, insinuation, allusion, hint and veiled innuendo – all those procedures which are especially dear to academic rhetoric. And yet the anonymous history to which the sociologist is reduced is no more representative of historical truth than the anecdotal narrative of the actions and attitudes of individual agents, famous or unknown, to which both old- and new-style history so easily surrender: the effects produced by the structural necessity of the field can be accomplished only through personal relationships, based on the apparent contin-gency of socially expressed coincidences of mutual encounter and acquaintance and on the sympathies and antipathies inspired by a shared *habitus*.[2] And how can we not regret that it is *socially impossible* to expound and explain what I believe to be the real logic of historical action and the true philosophy of history by making full use of the advantages inherent in the relation of belonging, which would enable us to combine information gathered by the objective techniques of scientific enquiry with the profound intuitions gained from personal familiarity?

Thus sociological knowledge is always liable to be led back to superficial perception by the self-centred reading which focuses on anecdotes and individual details and which, if not checked by a formal language, reduces to their ordinary meaning words shared by scholarly and ordinary language. This almost inevitably partial reading generates a false understanding, based on ignorance of everything which defines specifically scientific knowledge as such, that is, the very structure of the explanatory system: it dismantles what scientific construction had created, mingling what had been separated, and in particular confusing *constructed* individuals (whether a person or an institution), which exist only in the network of relations elaborated by scientific study, with empirical individuals directly accessible to ordinary intuition. It dissolves everything that distinguishes scientific objectification either from ordinary knowledge or from the pseudo-scholarly knowledge which – as is patent in most essays on intellectuals, essays which demystify less than they suffer mystification – is almost always based on what we might call 'the Thersites principle', Thersites being the envious footsoldier in Shakespeare's *Troilus and Cressida*, determined to rubbish the mighty, or, closer to historical reality, 'The Marat principle', remembering that Marat was also, or even first and foremost, an unsuccessful physician.[3] The partial insight facilitated by this *reductive* drive, fuelled by resentment, leads to a naïvely finalist view of history which, unable to plumb the hidden principles of social practices, falls back on anecdotal denunciations of those apparently responsible, and finally overestimates the importance of the supposed authors of the 'conspiracies' denounced, by seeing them as the cynical authors of every despicable action.[4]

Moreover, those who frequent the borderland between scholarly and ordinary knowledge – essayists, journalists, academic journalists and journalistic academics – have a vital stake in blurring the frontier and denying or eliminating what separates scientific analysis from partial objectifications, imputing to single individuals, or to a lobby, effects which in fact implicate the whole structure of the field – as we have seen in the case of the director of a certain television book programme,[5] or with the members of the Ecole des Hautes Etudes[6] associated with the *Nouvel Observateur*.[7] They can if they so desire indulge even here in a reading guided by idle curiosity, interpreting examples and individual cases in a perspective of snobbish gossip or critical infighting, if they wish to reduce the systematic and relational mode of explanation which is characteristic of science to the most ordinary procedure of polemical reduction, to *ad hoc* explanation using *ad hominem* arguments.

The reader can find in appendix 3 an analysis of the process (virtually a judicial procedure) through which journalistic notoriety is conferred. The main effect of this analysis is to denounce the naïvety of all personal denunciations which, on the pretext of treating the game objectively, are still fully implicated in the game, in so far as they attempt to enlist the appearance of objectivity in the service of interests linked with a position in the game: the source of the technique of the literary hit parade is neither an individual agent (Bernard Pivot, in the instance quoted), however influential and skilful he may be, nor a specific institution (such as a television programme or a magazine), nor even the totality of journalistic media able to influence the field of cultural production, but rather the set of the objective relations which constitute this field, and particularly those in force between the producers' field of production and the field of general production. The logic discovered by scientific analysis easily overruns the individual (or collective) intentions (or conspiracies) and desires of even the most lucid and powerful agents cited in the search for 'those responsible'. None the less, it would be quite wrong to derive from these analyses an argument for the dissolution of responsibilities in the network of objective relations in which each agent is involved. Against those who would use the formulation of social laws, converted into destiny, as an alibi for fatalistic or cynical resignation, we must remember that scientific explanation, which gives us the means to understand and even to exonerate, is also what may allow us to make changes. A greater understanding of the mechanisms which govern the intellectual world *should not* (and I choose these equivocal words with care) have the effect of 'releasing the individual from the embarrassing burden of moral responsibility', as Jacques Bouveresse fears.[8] On the contrary, it should teach him to place his responsibilities where his liberties are really situated and resolutely to refuse the infinitesimal acts of cowardice and laxness which leave the power of social necessity intact, to fight in himself and in others the opportunist indifference or conformist ennui which allow the social milieu to impose the slippery slope of resigned compliance and submissive complicity.

It is well known that no groups love an 'informer', especially perhaps when the transgressor or traitor can claim to share in their own highest values. The same people who would not hesitate to acclaim the work of objectification as 'courageous' or 'lucid' if it is applied to alien, hostile groups will be likely to question the credentials of the special lucidity claimed by anyone who seeks to analyse his own group. The sorcerer's apprentice who takes the risk of looking into native sorcery and its fetishes, instead of departing to seek in tropical climes the comforting charms of exotic magic, must expect to see turned against him the violence he has unleashed. Karl Kraus was well placed to formulate the law according to which objectification is all the more likely to be approved and acclaimed as 'courageous' in 'family circles', the more distant in social space are the objects to which it applies; and indeed, in the editorial of the first issue of his journal, *Die Fackel*, he says that anyone who rejects the pleasure and easy profits of long-distance criticism, in order to investigate his immediate neighbourhood, which everything bids him hold sacred, must expect the torments of 'subjective persecution'. Thus we have been tempted to adopt the title, *A Book for Burning*, which Li Zhi, a renegade mandarin, gave to one of those self-consuming works of his which revealed the rules of the mandarins' game. We do so, not in order to challenge those who, despite their readiness to denounce all inquisitions, will condemn to the stake any work perceived as a sacrilegious outrage against their own beliefs,[9] but simply to state the contradiction which is inherent in divulging tribal secrets and which is only so painful because even the partial publication of our most intimate details is also a kind of public confession.[10]

Sociology is not much given to creating illusions that enable the sociologist to imagine himself for one moment in the role of a liberating hero. None the less, by mobilizing all available scientific expertise in an attempt to objectify our social milieu, far from exerting reductive violence or totalitarian imperialism – as is sometimes claimed, especially when the sociologist's study is applied to those who wish to objectify without being objectified – he offers a potential liberty; and he can at least hope that his treatise on the academic passions will be for others what it has been for him, a means of *socio-analysis*.

THE WORK OF CONSTRUCTION AND ITS EFFECTS

When faced with the challenge of studying a world to which we are
linked by all sorts of specific investments, inextricably intellectual
and 'temporal', our first automatic thought is to escape; our concern
to escape any suspicion of prejudice leads us to attempt to negate
ourselves as 'biased' or 'informed' subjects automatically suspected
of using the weapons of science in the pursuit of personal interests,
to abolish the self even as knowing subject, by resorting to the most
impersonal and automatic procedures, those, at least in this perspective
(which is that of 'normal science'), which are the least questionable.
(Here we can see the attitude of resignation which so often underpins
the choice of hyperempiricism; and also the genuinely political
ambition – in the specific sense – which is dissimulated by scientistic
neutralism, the ambition to resolve confused debates, through
scientific work and in the name of science, to offer oneself as referee
or judge, to negate oneself as subject involved in the field, but only
to resurface 'far from the madding crowd', with the irreproachable
appearance of an objective, transcendent subject.)

There is no escaping the work of constructing the object, and the
responsibility that this entails. There is no object that does not imply
a viewpoint, even if it is an object produced with the intention of
abolishing one's viewpoint (that is, one's bias), the intention of
overcoming the partial perspective that is associated with holding a
position within the space being studied. But our very operations of
research, by obliging us to articulate and *formalize* the implicit criteria
of ordinary experience, have the effect of rendering *possible* the logical
verification of their own premises. Indeed, it goes without saying that
the series of successive choices, spread moreover over several years,
which, in the case of the enquiry into the power structure of the arts
and social sciences faculties in 1967, led us for instance to draw up the
list of individuals studied by determining the world of pertinent
properties which would characterize them, that is the population of
the most 'powerful' or the most 'important' academics, was not
accomplished with perfect epistemological transparency or entire
theoretical lucidity.[11] Only someone who has never undertaken
empirical research could believe or claim the contrary, and we cannot
be sure that the kind of opacity which the successive operations have
for us (where there is a proportion of what is called 'intuition', that
is, a more or less verifiable form of pre-scientific knowledge of the

object directly concerned, and also of the scholarly knowledge of analogous objects) is not the true source of the indispensable creativity of empirical research: when we act without entirely knowing what we are doing, we make it possible to discover in what we have done something of which we were previously unaware.

This scholarly construction is achieved through the slow and difficult accumulation of different indices, whose relevance is suggested from first hand knowledge of the different positions of power (for instance, the Universities Consultative Committee,[12] or the board of examiners for the *agrégation*),[13] and of people considered 'powerful', or even properties commonly designated or denounced as indices of power. The 'physiognomy', globally and approximately apprehended, of the 'powerful' and of power thus gradually gives way to an analytical series of the distinctive characteristics of the holders of power and of the different forms of power, whose significance, but also importance, become clarified, during the process of research, through the statistical relations which link them to each other. Far from being, as certain 'initiatory' representatives of the 'epistemological break' would have us believe, a sort of simultaneously inaugural and terminal act, the renunciation of first-hand intuition is the end product of a long dialectical process in which intuition, formulated in an empirical operation, analyses and verifies or falsifies itself, engendering new hypotheses, gradually more firmly based, which will be transcended in their turn, thanks to the problems, failures and expectations which they bring to light.[14] The logic of research is an intermeshing of major or minor problems which force us to ask ourselves at every moment what we are doing and permit us gradually to understand more fully what we are seeking, by providing the beginnings of an answer, which will suggest new, more fundamental and more explicit questions.

But it would be extremely dangerous to be satisfied with this 'learned ignorance'. And I would go so far as to say that the principal virtue of the scientific work of objectification (on condition, of course, that we know how to analyse its results) consists in its allowing us to objectify objectification. Indeed, for the researcher anxious to know what he is doing, the code changes from an instrument of analysis to an object of analysis: the objectified product of the work of codification becomes, under his self-reflexive gaze, the immediately readable trace of the operation of construction of the object, the grid which has been mapped out to construct the datum, the more or less coherent system of categories of perception which have produced the object of scientific analysis, in this particular case, the world of 'important academics' and their properties. The set of properties identified unites on the one hand the world of criteria (or properties), which, apart from the *proper name*, the most precious of all properties in the case of 'a famous name', are in fact utilizable and utilized in ordinary practice to *identify* or even to classify academics (which is corroborated by the fact that we are dealing for the most part with published information, and especially with the formulas used for self-introduction), and, on the other hand, a series of characteristics which practical experience of the university field leads us to consider as pertinent and thus to establish as constituent properties.

In addition, our self-reflexive scrutiny of the very operation of coding reveals everything which separates the constructed code, which usually only duplicates socially identified codifications like school certificates or the socio-professional categories of INSEE statistical surveys[15] from the practical and implicit schemata of ordinary perception; and, in so doing, it reveals all the implications which an awareness of that difference has for the adequate understanding of scientific study and its object. Indeed, if it is true that any code, as much in the sense of information theory as in the legal sense, supposes a consensus on the finite set of properties chosen as pertinent (juridical formulas, says Weber, 'take into account exclusively the unequivocal general characteristics of the case in point'), and on a set of formal relations between these properties, it would be tendentious to ignore the distinction between cases where the scientific coding duplicates a coding already existing in social reality, and cases where it produces a new criterion from scratch, thus assuming that the question of the pertinence of this criterion has been resolved, whereas it could be an object of conflict – as, more generally, it would be tendentious to gloss over the question of the social conditions and effects of the codification. One of the most important properties of any property, which is abolished when we mingle criteria constructed by the researcher with socially recognized criteria, is in fact its degree of codification, just as one of the most significant properties of a field is the degree to which its social relations are objectified in public codes.

In fact it is clear that the different properties chosen to construct the identity of different academics are very unequally used in ordinary experience to perceive and appreciate the pre-constructed individuality of these same agents, and above all very unequally objectified, therefore very unequally present in the written sources. The frontier between the institutionalized properties, which are therefore identifiable in official documents, and properties which are not objectified, or mostly not, is relatively fluid, and is bound to change according to situations and periods (any particular scientific criterion, a socio-professional category, for instance, can become a political criterion in certain political conjunctures): thus one moves through decreasing degrees of objectification, from the formal titles used when introducing oneself (for example, on official letterheads, identity cards, visiting cards, etc.) such as university posts ('professor at the Sorbonne'), or positions of power or authority ('dean' or 'member of the Institute'), which *official* terms of reference, known and recognized by all, are often associated with terms of address ('professor', 'dean', etc.), to properties which are little used in official classifications of ordinary existence, although they are institutionalized, like the direction of a laboratory, membership of the University Supreme Council or of examiners' boards for *concours*,[16] and finally to all those indices, often impenetrable for the foreigner, which define what is called 'prestige', that is, one's position in strictly intellectual or scientific hierarchies. In this case the researcher is constantly faced with an alternative: either to introduce classifications which are more or less artificial or even arbitrary (or, at the very least, always liable to be denounced as such), or to bracket out hierarchies which, even if they do not exist in an official, public, objectified state, are constantly at issue and operative in the very constitution of objectivity. In fact, as we shall see, the same is true of all criteria, even the most 'self-evident', such as purely 'demographic' indices, which allow their authorized users to view their science as a 'natural' science.[17] But what we find when we choose indices of 'intellectual' or 'scientific prestige' – is that the questions of criteria which the researcher is led to formulate about his object, that is, the problems of legitimate membership and of hierarchization and, more precisely, the problems of power and of the principles defining and hierarchizing power, are problems which are already inherently formulated in *the object itself*.

Thus the work of construction of the object determines a finite set of *pertinent properties*, established hypothetically as *effective variables*, whose variations are associated with the variations of the phenomenon observed, and it thereby defines the population of *constructed individuals*, themselves characterized by the possession of these properties to varying degrees. These logical operations produce a set of effects which must be articulated to avoid recording them unwittingly in the form of an affirmation (which constitutes the cardinal error of objectivist positivism). In the first place, the objectification of the non-objectified (for example, scientific prestige), as we have just seen, tends to create an effect of officialization of a quasi-judicial kind: thus the establishment of classes of international celebrity founded on the number of references or the elaboration of an index of journalistic participation are operations absolutely analogous to those achieved from within the field by the producers of hit parades.[18] This effect cannot be overlooked in the test case of properties which are officially or tacitly excluded from all taxonomies, whether official and institutionalized or unofficial and informal, such as religious denomination or sexual preference (heterosexuality or homosexuality), although they can intervene in practical judgements and be associated with variations visible in observed reality (it is no doubt this kind of information which people have in mind when they denounce the 'police investigation' tendencies of sociological enquiry).

In order to illustrate the effects of scholarly codification, especially the homogenization of the status accorded to different properties which are very unequally objectified in real life, we need only consider the mode and degree of existence *qua groups* of the populations identified by the different criteria, which vary from age-groups or sexual groupings (despite the appearance of a feminist consciousness and movement), to sets such as *normaliens*[19] or *agrégés*,[20] which are characteristic of two different modes of collective existence: the title of *normalien* underwrites a network of practical solidarity maintained by a minimum of institutional support (graduate association, annual newsletter, annual dinner of matriculation years); the title of *agrégé*, which implies no real solidarity linked to any common experience, underwrites an organization, the Société des Agrégés, oriented towards defending the value of the diploma and all the values dependent on it, and mandated with the power to speak and act for the group as a whole, to express and defend its interests (in negotiations with government institutions, for instance).

The effects of institutionalization and homogenization which operate through simple codification, and of the elementary form of recognition which it instinctively accords to unequally acknowledged criteria, operate as if they were laws. In so far as they operate unbeknown to the researcher, they lead him to conclude 'in the name of science' what is not conclusive in reality: indeed, the degrees of recognition granted in practice to the different properties vary considerably according to the agents (and also according to situations and periods), and certain properties which some might advance and lay public claim to, such as the fact of writing for the *Nouvel Observateur* (not an imaginary case), will be perceived by others, situated in different positions in their world, as stigmata, entailing exclusion from that world. Cases of perfect inversion like this, where one person's pedigree can become another's mark of infamy, one's coat of arms another's insult, and vice versa, are there to remind us that the university field is, like any other field, the locus of a struggle to determine the conditions and the criteria of legitimate membership and legitimate hierarchy, that is, to determine which properties are pertinent, effective and liable to function as capital so as to generate the specific profits guaranteed by the field. The different sets of individuals (more or less constituted into groups) who are defined by these different criteria have a vested interest in them. In proffering these criteria, in trying to have them acknowledged, in staking their own claim to constitute them as legitimate properties, as specific capital, they are working to modify the laws of formation of the prices characteristic of the university market, and thereby to increase their potential for profit.

Thus there exists quite objectively a plurality of rival principles of hierarchization, and the values which they determine are incommensurate, or even incompatible, because they are associated with mutually conflicting interests. One cannot simply, as believers in indices doubtless would, conflate participation in the Universities Consultative Committe or the board of examiners of the *agrégation* with the fact of being published by Gallimard or of writing for the *Nouvel Observateur*, and a pseudo-scholarly construction conflating these indices would only reproduce the polemical amalgam designated by the semi-scholarly notion of 'mandarin'. A number of the criteria used by scientific construction as instruments of knowledge and analysis, even those most neutral and 'natural' in appearance, like age, also function in the reality of practices as principles of division and hierarchization (we only have to think of the classificatory and often polemical use of oppositions – old/young, palaeo/neo, former/recent, etc.) and thereby also become an object of conflict. That is to say that we can only avoid claiming that the truth of the university field is one or other of the more or less rationalized representations which are engendered in the struggle for classification, and especially the semi-scholarly representations which scholarly circles give of themselves, if we include in our study the process of classification effected by the researcher, and the relationship between that and the classificatory attributions indulged in by the agents (and by the researcher himself, once he is not directly involved in research).

Indeed, it is because it does not clearly operate the break between these two discourses that in this domain, as elsewhere, sociology so often tends to offer semi-scholarly taxonomies, which it calls 'typologies', mingling indigenous labels, often closer to the stigma or the insult than the concept, with 'scholarly' notions, constructed on the basis of a more or less informed analysis. Organized around several typical characters, these 'typologies' are neither really concrete – although they are no doubt derived, like the 'characters' described by moralists, from familiar figures of first-hand experience or from more or less polemical categoremes – nor really constructed, although they resort to terms current in the jargon of the American *social scientists*, such as *local* or *parochial* or *cosmopolitan*. Being the product of a realist intention, that of describing *typical* individuals or groups, they combine, in disordered fashion, different principles of opposition, mingling criteria as heteroclite as age, relations to political power or to science, etc. For instance, we have *the locals* (including *the dedicated*, 'strongly committed to the institution', *the true bureaucrat, the homeguard* and *the elders*) and the *cosmopolitans* (including *the outsiders* and *the empire builders*), whom Alvin W. Gouldner distinguishes according to their attitudes towards the institution *(faculty orientations)*, their investment in professional competence and their internal or external orientation;[21] or again, according to Burton Clark, who sees in them the representatives of different 'cultures', *the teacher*, devoted to his students, *the scholar-researcher*, 'chemist or biologist totally committed to his laboratory', *the demonstrator*, a sort of instructor bent on transmitting technical competence, and finally *the consultant*, 'who spends as much time in the air as on the campus';[22] or finally – although we might continue at length in this vein – the six types distinguished by John W. Gustad, *the scholar*, who considers himself 'not as an employee but as a free citizen of the academic community', *the curriculum adviser, the individual entrepreneur, the consultant*, 'always off campus', *the administrator* and *the cosmopolitan*, 'oriented towards the outside world'.[23]

It is hardly necessary to point out all the cases where the concept-as-insult and the semi-scholarly stereotype – like that of the *jet sociologist* – become transformed into semi-scientific 'types' –

consultant, outsider – and all the subtle indices where the position of the analyst in the space being analysed is betrayed. In fact these typologies gain credence inasmuch as, being the product of classificatory schemes current in the milieu under consideration, they operate as series of *real divisions*, analogous to those operated by ordinary intuition, of a domain of objective relations thus reduced to a *population* of university lecturers, and prevent us from conceptualizing the university field, either as such or in the relations which, at different times in its history and in different national contexts, link it with the field of political power on the one hand, and the intellectual and scientific field on the other. If these typologies, unfortunately very common and perfectly representative of what often passes for sociology, warrant our interest, it is because, through retranslating things into a language of scholarly appearance, they can lead people – and not only their authors – to believe that they are providing access to a superior level of knowledge and reality, whereas ultimately they are telling us less than we would learn from a direct description by a good inside informer. The classifications engendered by a disguised application of the principles of vision normally used for the needs of practice 'are like those that someone would give who tried to classify clouds by their shapes', as Wittgenstein says.[24] But appearances are often superficially convincing, and these objectless descriptions, which have in their favour the logic of ordinary experience and the façade of scientificity, are better placed to satisfy common expectations than are scientific constructions, which both directly confront the individuality of the particular case seized in all its complexity, and are much more distant from the immediate representation of the real given by ordinary language or its semi-scholarly retranslation.

Thus social science cannot break with common criteria and classifications and disentangle itself from the struggles of which they are both end and means, unless it takes them explicitly as its object instead of letting them slyly infiltrate scientific discourse. The milieu which it must study is the object and, to a certain extent at least, the product of rival, sometimes hostile representations, which all claim the status of truth and thereby the right to exist. Any position adopted towards the social world orders and organizes itself from a certain position in the world, that is to say from the viewpoint of the preservation and augmentation of the power associated with this position. Thus it is that, in a milieu which depends as much for its very reality as the university field does on the representation which its agents have of it, these agents can exploit the plurality of principles of hierarchization and the low degree of objectification of symbolic capital, in an attempt to impose their vision and modify their position inside that space, as far as their symbolic power allows, by modifying the representation which others (and they themselves) can have of this position. There is nothing more revealing, from this point of view, than the forewords, exordia, preambles or prefaces, which often disguise behind the appearance of a methodologically indispensable methodological premise their more or less skilful attempts to translate into scientific virtues the necessities and above all the limits inherent in a position and a trajectory, at the same time as depriving inaccessible virtues of their enchantment. Thus we may see the scholar whom we readily call 'narrowly specialized', and who cannot be unaware of this (it must have been pointed out to him a thousand times, in a thousand ways, in the cruelly euphemistic language of academic judgement, and first of all, perhaps, through those magisterial verdicts which grant him only 'solid scholarship'), working to discredit the flights of 'brilliant' essayists and 'ambitious' theorists; as for the latter, they will rely on the rhetoric of irony to praise the erudition which delivers such 'precious material' for their reflection, and only if they felt really threatened in the hegemonic position which they allocate themselves would they overtly express their arrogant contempt for the petty and sterile caution of 'positivist' hacks.[25]

In short, as we can see in polemical exchanges, which are the high spots of a constant process of symbolic competition, practical knowledge of the social world, and especially of adversaries, obeys a *reductionist* tendency; it resorts to classifactory epithets which designate or identify groups, and groups of properties, in an eclectic perspective, and do not admit awareness of the principles on which they are based. And we would have to be quite ignorant of all this logic to suppose that a technique like that used by 'judges', which consists in interrogating a group of agents, treated as experts, on the problems under discussion – for instance, the relevant criteria for defining university power or a hierarchy of prestige – might evade the question of which agencies can be authorized to legitimate the agencies of legitimation. Indeed, we have only to put this technique to the test to see that it reproduces the very logic of the game which it is supposed to referee: the different 'judges' – and the same judge at different moments – deploy different or even incompatible criteria, thus reproducing (but only imperfectly, because in an *artificial situation*) the logic of classificatory judgements produced by the agents in ordinary existence. But, above all, the slightest attention to the relations between the categoremes selected and the properties of those who formulate them shows that we anticipate the nature of the judgements obtained if we anticipate the criteria of selection of the 'judges', that is to say the spatial position, still unknown at the moment of research, which motivates their judgements.

Does this mean that the sociologist has no choice but to use the technical yet also symbolic force of science to set himself up as a judge of the judges, and impose a judgement which can never be entirely free from the presuppositions and prejudices associated with his position in the field which he claims to objectify, or to renounce his claim to objectivist absolutism and be satisfied with a perspectivist recording of the viewpoints at issue (including his own)? In fact, his freedom in the face of the social determinisms which affect him is proportionate to the power of his theoretical and technical methods of objectification, and above all, perhaps, to his ability to use them on himself, so to speak, to objectify his own position through the objectification of the space within which are defined both his position and his primary vision of his position, and positions opposed to it; it is proportionate to his capacity simultaneously to objectify the very intention of objectifying, to take a sovereign, absolute view of the world, and especially of the world which he belongs to, and to work at excluding from scientific objectification everything that it might owe to the ambition to dominate by means of the weapons of science; finally, it is proportionate to his capacity to orientate the effort of objectification towards the dispositions and interests which the researcher himself owes to his trajectory and to his position and also towards his scientific practice, towards the presuppositions which this entails in its concepts and problematics, and in all the ethical or political aims associated with the social interests inherent in a position within the scientific field.[26]

When research comes to study the very realm within which it operates, the results which it obtains can be immediately reinvested in scientific work as instruments of reflexive knowledge of the conditions and the social limits of this work, which is one of the principal weapons of epistemological vigilance. Indeed, perhaps we can only make our knowledge of the scientific field progress by

using whatever knowledge we may have available in order to discover
and overcome the obstacles to science which are entailed by the fact
of holding a determined position in the field. And not, as is so often
the case, to reduce the *reasons* of our adversaries to *causes*, to social
interests. We have every reason to think that the researcher has less
to gain, as regards the scientific quality of his work, from looking
into the interests of others, than from looking into his own interests,
from understanding what he is motivated to see and not to see. And
thus we can suggest, without any suspicion of moralizing, that
scientific benefit could only be obtained in this case by renouncing
social benefit, and particularly by resisting any tendency to use
science or scientific effects to attempt to achieve a social triumph in
the scientific field. Or, in other words, that we may well have some
chance of contributing to the science of power if we renounce the
attempt to turn science into an instrument of power, above all in
the world of science.

Nietzschean genealogy, the Marxist critique of ideologies, the sociology
of knowledge – all the perfectly legitimate procedures which tend to
relate cultural productions to social interests – have usually been led
astray as a result of the dual strategy deriving from the temptation to
use the science of conflict in the conflict itself. This sort of illicit use of
social science (or of the authority which it can bestow) finds an exemplary
illustration, exemplary in its naïvety, in an article where Raymond
Boudon passes off as a scientific analysis of the intellectual field in France
a denunciation of 'extra-scientific' success, which (barely) disguises its
chauvinist plea, which amounts to making a virtue out of obscurity.[27] A
description which contains no critical reflection on the position from
which it is articulated can have no other principle than the interests
associated with the unanalysed relation that the researcher has with his
object. Thus it is hardly surprising if the fundamental thesis of the article
is nothing but a social strategy aiming to discredit the national hierarchy
of celebrities by reproaching it with being purely French, that is
linked to 'singularities' and particularities, automatically identified as
anachronistic – harping on the theme of the literary turn of mind – and
by taking this hierarchy, tacitly designated as different from the
international hierarchy (the only scientific one), and therefore as extra-
scientific, to compare it unfavourably with a hierarchy presumed scientific,
because international, that is, American.[28] Strikingly enough, this
scientistic declaration receives not the slightest trace of empirical
verification. For this would force us to admit, for instance, as we shall
see, that an important fraction of the producers who dominate what, in

an article published some time ago,[29] I called the restricted field or restricted market (and which Raymond Boudon, forever concerned with the external trappings of scientific appearances, calls 'Market I', without acknowledging his source) are also the best known on the general production market, or to discover that the highest scores as regards foreign translations or mentions in the *Citation Index*, which has nothing typically French about it, are generally obtained by the best-known researchers in the most extra-scientific sectors of the national market – except for the most traditional disciplines, like ancient history or archaeology, which are not as 'literary' as all that.

In constructing the finished, finite set of the properties which function as effective forces in the struggle for specifically university power, and which are possessed to diverse degrees by the set of effective agents, the sociologist produces an objective space, defined in a methodical and unambiguous (and therefore reproducible) way, and irreducible to the sum of all partial representations of agents. Thus the 'objectivist' construction which is the condition of the break with intuitive vision and with all hybrid discourse mingling the semi-concrete and the semi-constructed, the label and the concept, is also what enables us to reintegrate into our knowledge of the object the pre-scientific representations which are an integral part of the object. We cannot in fact dissociate the intention to establish the structure of the university field, a space with several dimensions, constructed on the basis of the whole set of the powers which can prove effective at any particular moment in competitive struggles, from the intention to describe the logic of the struggles which derive their principle from this structure and aim to preserve or transform it by redefining the hierarchy of powers (and therefore of criteria). Even when it does not take the organized form of rivalry between consciously militant or tacitly loyal groups, the struggle, whose criteria and the properties they imply are both end and means, is an ineluctable fact which the researcher is bound to integrate into his model of reality instead of artificially attempting to exclude it by setting himself up as arbiter or as 'impartial observer', as a judge of last appeal who would alone be competent to produce the *right order* able to reconcile everyone by finding a place for everything. He needs to transcend the alternatives of the objectivist vision of objective classification – of which the search for a single scale and for cumulative indices is a caricatural illustration – and the subjectivist or, even better, *perspectivist* vision, which would settle for recording the diversity of hierarchies, treated as so many incommensurable viewpoints. In fact, like the social field taken as a whole, the university field is the locus of a classification struggle which, by working to preserve or transform the state of the power relations between the different criteria and between the different powers which they designate, helps create the classification, such as it may be objectively grasped at a given moment in time; but the representation which the agents have of the classification, and the force and the orientation of the strategies which they may deploy to maintain or subvert it, depend on their position in the objective classifications.[30] Scientific work, therefore, aims to establish an adequate knowledge both of objective relations between the different positions and the necessary relations which are established, through the mediation of the systems of dispositions of their occupants, between these positions and the respective dispositions which they adopt, that is to say between the point occupied in the space and their viewpoint of that same space, which is part of reality and of the development of that space. In other words, the 'classification' produced by scientific work through the delineation of *regions* in the space of positions is the objective ground of the classificatory strategies through which the agents aim to preserve or modify the space. Among these strategies we must include the constitution of groups mobilized to ensure the defence of the interests of their members.

The need to integrate the two visions, objectivist and perspectivist, requiring us to work at attempting to objectify objectification, to create a theory of the effect of theory, is necessary for another, no doubt fundamental, reason, as much from the theoretical as from the ethical or political viewpoint: the scholarly construction of the 'objective' space of agents and of operative properties tends to replace a global and confused perception of the population of the 'powerful' with an analytic and reflexive perception, thus destroying the vagueness and the mist of imprecision and uncertainty which constitute our everyday world. To understand 'objectively' the world in which we live without understanding the logic of this understanding, and what differentiates it from practical understanding, is to prevent oneself from understanding what makes the world livable in and viable, that is to say the very vagueness of practical understanding. As in the case of the exchange of gifts, the objectivist approach, which is unaware of its own truth, denies the condition which makes practice possible, that is, a misconstrual of the model which would explain that practice. And only the satisfactions that a reductivist vision offers those of reductivist mood could lead us to forget to introduce into the model of reality the distance between experience and the objectivist model, which corresponds to the truth of experience as we know it.

There are no doubt few worlds which provide so much scope, or even so much institutional support, for the game of self-deceit and for the gap between the representation experienced and the true position occupied in a social field or space; the tolerance granted to this gap doubtless reveals the inner truth of a milieu which authorizes and encourages all forms of *splitting the ego*, in other words all ways of making the confusedly perceived objective truth coexist with its negation, thus permitting those most lacking in symbolic capital to survive in this struggle of each against all, where everyone depends on everyone else, at once his competitor and client, his opponent and judge, for the determination of his own truth and value, that is, of his symbolic life and death.[31] For it is obvious that these individual systems of defence would hardly have any social effectiveness unless they met with the complicity of those who are led by their occupation of an identical or homologous position to recognize in these vital errors and illusions of survival the expression of an effort to persevere in a social identity which they recognize as their own.

Many more or less institutionalized representations and practices can indeed only be understood in terms of *collective defence mechanisms* through which the agents find a way to avoid the excessively harsh questioning that the rigorous application of their explicit criteria, such as those of science or erudition, would provoke. Thus it is that the multiplicity of scales of evaluation, scientific or administrative, academic or intellectual, offers a multiplicity of paths to salvation and of forms of excellence, allowing everyone, with the complicity of everyone else, to disguise truths known to all.[32] The scientific report should take account of the effect of vagueness which the indeterminacy of the criteria and the principles of hierarchization engender in objectivity itself: the indeterminacy, for instance, of criteria such as place of publication or the number of foreign colloquia or visiting lectures is due to the fact that there is, for each science, a complex and contentious hierarchy of reviews and publishers, of foreign countries and colloquia, and also that those who refuse to participate may appear difficult to distinguish from those who are not invited. In short, it would be a serious blow to objectivity not to write into the theory the objective imprecision of the hierarchies which the model, constructed on the basis of an (indispensable) survey of the indicators of scientific status, aims precisely to overcome. And we must ask ourselves if the very plurality of hierarchies, and the coexistence of practically incommensurate forces, scientific prestige and university power, internal recognition and external renown, are not the effect of a sort of anti-trust law both written into the structures and at the same time tacitly recognized as a protection against the consequences of a strict application of the norms officially professed.

We can see another instance of this in the paradoxical fact that this milieu which claims allegiance to science proposes practically no institutionalized signs of scientific prestige as such. No doubt we can invoke the Institute,[33] and the gold medal of the CNRS,[34] but the former distinction seems to consecrate politico-moral attitudes as much as scientific accomplishments, while the latter is absolutely exceptional. And it is in the same perspective, that is to say as a concession imposed by the need to subscribe to and insure against the specific risks of the profession of researcher, that we should interpret the tendency of so many scientific committees to function like bipartite committees, or the strategies familiar to occupants of subordinate positions inside the academic or scientific fields which consist in using the ability to universalize offered by political or trade-union rhetoric in order to treat homologies of position as identity of condition (in accordance, for instance, with the pattern of the 'three Ps', père, patron, professeur [i.e. father, manager, professor], which was such a success in 1968) and thus to establish more or less strained identifications, in the name of the solidarity, which is never insignificant, of all the subordinates in all the fields, between positions and stances as far apart as those of the Renault car worker on the assembly line and the temporary researcher[35] at the CNRS, between the struggle against accelerated production rhythms and the rejection of purely scientific criteria. We would also need to note methodically all the cases where politicization functions as a compensatory strategy allowing an escape from the specific laws of the academic or scientific market, for instance all forms of political criticism of scientific studies which allow scientifically outmoded producers to give themselves – and to give their peers – the illusion that they transcend what transcends them: the state of historical Marxism – such as it may be observed in the reality of the social uses which are made of it – would not be comprehensible if we failed to see that often, with all its references to the 'people' and the 'popular', it has that function of last resort which allows the least scientifically capable to set themselves up as scientific judges.

EMPIRICAL INDIVIDUALS AND EPISTEMIC INDIVIDUALS

If we have had to try to clarify, through a self-reflexive detachment from the operations of research and from the object which they have produced, the principles of production which have been *deployed*, it is because this logical work, as long as it is successful, can contribute to reinforcing the logical and sociological control of writing and its effects and giving greater efficacity to warnings against readings which tend to ruin the work of construction. For it is in fact only if we know 'what the sociologist does', to use Saussure's terms, that we can adequately read the product of his operations.

The risks of misunderstanding in the transmission of scientific discourse on the social world depend, in a very general way, on the fact that the reader tends to make the utterances of the language of construction function as they would function in ordinary usage. This is quite clear in the case where the reader, ignorant of Weber's distinction, perceives as sociological value-judgements 'references to values' inherent in the object of study:[36] when, for example, he speaks of a 'second-class faculty', of a 'subordinate discipline' or of the 'lower echelons' of the university space, the sociologist is only recording a *fact of evaluation* which he attempts to explain by relating it to the ensemble of the social conditions of its existence, and he can even see in it the explanatory principle of the form of the *value-judgements* destined to 'refute' it (for example, the protests which it can provoke, if incorrectly read). But it is only a minor form of misunderstanding,since it is blatant, and blatantly evident. And the most dangerous effect of this reading, as we can see in the case of named individuals, consists in substituting the logic of ordinary knowledge for the logic of scientific knowledge.

Scientific discourse demands a scientific reading, capable of reproducing the operations of which it is itself the product. However, the words of scientific discourse, and especially those designating persons (named individuals) or institutions (such as the Collège de France),[37] are exactly the same as those of ordinary discourse, of fiction or history, whereas the referents of these two species of discourse are separated by all the distance which is introduced by the scientific break and by construction. Thus, in everyday life, the proper name merely *identifies*, and, acting in the same way as what logicians call an indicator, it is in itself virtually insignificant ('Smith' does not signify 'a blacksmith') and gives virtually no information about the person designated (unless it is an aristocratic or famous name or if it is ethnically specific). As a label capable of being arbitrarily applied to any object, it says that the object designated is different, without specifying *in what respect* it differs; as an instrument of *recognition*, and not of *cognition*, it singles out an *empirical individual*, generally apprehended as singular, that is to say, different, but without analysing the difference. The constructed individual, on the contrary, is defined by a finite set of explicitly defined properties which differ through a series of identifiable differences from the set of properties, constructed according to the same explicit criteria, which characterize other individuals; more precisely, it identifies its referent not in ordinary space, but in a space constructed of differences produced by the very definition of the finite set of effective variables.[38] Thus, strictly speaking, the constructed Lévi-Strauss processed and produced by scientific analysis does *not* have the same referent as the proper name which we use in daily life to designate the author of *Tristes tropiques*; in an ordinary utterance, 'Lévi-Strauss' is a signifier to which may be applied the infinite universe of predicates corresponding to the various differences which may distinguish the French ethnologist not only from all other professors but from all other human beings, and which we will bring into being, in each case, as a function of the principle of implicit permanence which will be imposed on us by the needs or the exigencies of practice. Sociological construction is distinguished from other possible constructions – those of psychoanalysis, for example – by the finite list of the effective properties, of the active variables, which it includes and, concomitantly, by the infinite list of the properties which it excludes, at least provisionally, as irrelevant. Variables such as eye or hair colour, blood group or height are bracketed out, so to speak, and it is as if the constructed Lévi-Strauss had none. But, as is shown by the diagram of the analysis of correspondences, where he is distinguished by the position which he occupies in a constructed space, the epistemic space is characterized by the system of differences, of uneven intensity and unevenly linked to each other, established between the finite set of his relevant properties in the theoretical domain considered, and the whole set of finite sets of properties attached to the set of other constructed individuals. In short, he is defined by the position which he occupies in the space which his properties have helped to construct (and which also partly helps to define it). As opposed to the doxic Lévi-Strauss, who is inexhaustible, the epistemic individual contains nothing evading conceptualization; but this self-transparency is the corollary of reduction, and any progress in this theory as *viewpoint*, as principle of selective vision, will have to stem from the invention of categories and operations able to reconcile the theory with properties provisionally excluded (for instance, those which the psychoanalyst would construct).[39]

The spatial diagram uses one of the properties of ordinary space, the reciprocal externality of the objects distinguished, to reproduce the logic of a strictly theoretical space of differentiation, that is, the logical efficacity of a set of principles of differentiation (the factors of the analysis of correspondences) allowing us to distinguish between individuals who have been constructed through the statistical treatment of properties determined by the application to different empirical individuals of a common definition, that is, of a common viewpoint, concretized in a set of identical criteria.[40] And the best illustration of what marks the difference between the epistemic and the empiric individual is the way in which at a certain point of the analysis we can observe the fusion of more than one pair of empirical individuals (Raymond Polin and Frédéric Deloffre,[41] for example). They become *indistinguishable* (they had the same co-ordinates on the first two axes) from the viewpoint of the analyst at that moment, which was written into the list of variables chosen at that stage of research.[42]

This example, which I have chosen deliberately, poses the problem of the effect of reading and of the danger of regression into ordinary knowledge as simple recognition. A naïve reading of the diagram tends to dissolve what constitutes precisely the scientific virtues of its construction: in this theoretical space of differences, a space constructed from a finite – and relatively restricted – set of explicitly defined variables, such a reading can 'recognize' the set of differences noted empirically in everyday experience, since these do in fact provide its principle, even including differences noted empirically which had not been introduced into the viewpoint originally adopted for the construction, such as differences in political attitudes, particularly in May 1968, or, as could no doubt be verified, in styles and works. Thus any reader endowed with the practical sense of placing which is acquired through prolonged exposure to the regularities and rules of that milieu will recognize himself easily (too easily, if we forget the conditions of construction) in the epistemic space constructed with a rigour and a self-transparency which are completely excluded from ordinary experience. This feeling of certainty is understandable if we realize that, like a well-drafted map or plan, the diagram is a model of 'reality' as we know it or, more accurately, as it is revealed to us, in ordinary existence, in the (veiled) guise of distance observed, respected, denied by transgression or condescension, etc.: in its forms of hierarchies and precedences, of affinities or incompatibilities – of style, character, etc. – of sympathies or antipathies, of complicities or hostilities; and, in this way, it can function as the objectified, *codified* form of the practical patterns of perception and action which orientate the practices of the agents best adjusted to the immanent necessity of their domain. In truth, the multi-dimensional space shown by the diagram claims to be an isomorphic representation of the university field: a true image of this structured space, it establishes between each agent and each property of the two spaces a one-to-one correlation, such that the set of relations between the agents and the properties of the two spaces show the same structure. The structure revealed by this research is the true principle of the nature, which is essentially relational, of each element and its operations, and notably of the strategies of the agents, and thereby of the development of the elements and the structure of the relations which define them.

After these analyses, we understand better that scientific discourse on the social world is problematic, and reaches crisis-point in the case of a discourse bearing directly on the very game which its author finds himself playing, and wagering on. If it is difficult, if not impossible, to prevent utterances from containing proper names, or individual examples from assuming a polemical value, it is because the reader almost inevitably substitutes for the epistemic subject and object of the discourse the practical subject and object, converting a neutral utterance on a constructed agent into a performative denunciation, or, as the saying goes, into an *ad hominem* polemic.[43] The writer occupies a position in the space described: he knows it and he knows that his reader knows it. He knows that the latter will tend to relate the constructed vision he offers to the position he occupies in the field, and to reduce it to a viewpoint like any other; he knows that he will see in the slightest nuances of the writing – a *but*, a *perhaps* or, simply, the tense of a verb – indices of bias; he knows that he is likely to notice, amid all the efforts expended to produce a neutral language stripped of all personal resonance, only the effect of greyness, judging that it is a high price to pay for what is, after all, never more than a form of autobiography. And it is probable that the effort of the enquiring subject to negate himself as empirical subject, to disappear behind the anonymous record of his operations and his results, is doomed in advance to failure: thus the use of circumlocution which would substitute for the proper name the (partial) enumeration of pertinent properties, apart from guaranteeing only an appearance of anonymity, resembles one of the classic procedures of university polemics, which is to designate opponents only by allusions, insinuations or undertones understood solely by those initiated in the code, that is to say, more often than not solely by the opponents attacked. Scientific neutralization can thus help to charge discourse with that extra violence which is added to the discreet polemics of academic hatred by the methodical erasure of all external signs of violence. In short, just as the proper name constituted by general terms, 'Prairie Trail', 'Black Bear', 'Bear's Back-fat', 'Wagtail Fish',[44] does not in practice, whatever Lévi-Strauss says, function as a classificatory act conferring on the bearer of the name the properties designated by the general terms which it combines, so the circumlocution (Professor of Ethnology at the Collège de France) intended to show that the *agent* thus designated is not the *individual* Claude Lévi-Strauss has very little chance, unless a deliberate warning is issued, of being read as other than a euphemistic substitute for Claude Lévi-Strauss. And the concepts constructed to designate the regions of the theoretical space of pertinent positions, in this particular case, the classes of individuals defined by the tenure of the same region of constructed space (thanks to the analysis of correspondences), have every likelihood of suffering the same fate, either by being overshadowed, in the reading, by the institutions which they partially overlap (Collège de France, Ecole des Hautes Etudes, Sorbonne, etc.), or by functioning as simple *labels*, similar to the impressionistic notions which are current in everyday life, especially in polemics, and which are taken up more or less unthinkingly by the authors of 'typologies'.

Because, among other reasons, the rigorous use of techniques of analysis of the most refined data, such as the analysis of correspondences, would suppose a perfect mastery of the mathematical principles which underlie them, and of the sociological effects which they produce by their more or less conscious application to social data, there is no doubt that, despite all the warnings issued by their 'inventors', a good deal of users (and readers) find it difficult to assign their veritable epistemological function to the notions devised in order to name the factors, or the divisions which these determine: indeed, these units are not strictly defined logical classes, separated by clearly marked frontiers whose numbers possess *all* the pertinent characteristics, that is to say, a number of attributes all necessary, and all to the same degree, to determine belonging (in such a way that the possession of certain properties cannot be compensated for by the possession of certain others). The set of agents collected in the same region of space is united by what Wittgenstein calls a 'family resemblance', in a sort of common physiognomy, often close to that apprehended in a confused and *implicit* way by 'first-hand' intuition. And the properties which contribute to the characterization of these sets are united by a complex network of statistical relations which are also relations of *intelligible affinity* – rather than of logical similarity – which the analyst must *render explicit* as completely as possible and condense in a designation at once stenographic, mnemotechnic and suggestive.

There too, the choices of writing are rendered difficult by ordinary usage, and especially by the tradition which consists in using concepts in '-ism' as slogans or as sanitized insults, that is, usually, as proper names designating empirical individuals or groups. The designation of a class by a concept is thus reduced to an act of *nomination*, obeying the ordinary logic of this kind of operation. To give a name, one single name, to an individual or group of individuals, as we see in the *nickname*, which unlike the ordinary proper name is not in itself insignificant, and which functions in the manner of the proper name according to Lévi-Strauss, is to adopt one of the possible viewpoints towards them and claim to impose it as the single, legitimate viewpoint. What is at stake in the symbolic struggle is the monopoly of legitimate nomination, the dominant viewpoint which, in gaining recognition as the legitimate viewpoint, causes its truth as a specific, situated, dated viewpoint to be misconstrued.[45] Thus, to escape the danger of polemical recuperation, we might think of designating each of the sectors of the space by a plurality of concepts designed to remind us that each of the regions of the space can, by definition, only be conceptualized and expressed in its relation to the others, and also to remind us that, in practice – which the theory must incorporate – each sector becomes the object of different or even antagonistic nominations, according to the viewpoint from which it is perceived: to give to an individual or a group the name which it gives itself ('the emperor', 'the nobility') is to *recognize* it, accept it as dominant, accept its viewpoint, agree to adopt towards it the viewpoint of perfect coincidence which it adopts towards itself; but we can also give it another name, the name given it by others and especially its enemies ('the usurper'), and which it rejects as insult, calumny, defamation. Or we can even give it is *official* name, conferred by an official authority, recognized as legitimate, that is, by the state, holder of the monopoly of legitimate symbolic violence (the socio-professional categories of the INSEE). In this particular case, the sociologist, both judge and plaintiff, has little chance of seeing his monopoly of nomination recognized. In any case, there is every likelihood that his designations will also function in ordinary logic and that the reader will interpret them as hostile, as alien, and therefore insulting, if they are applied to himself and his own group, but will adapt and exploit them for his own purposes, still using them as insults and polemical attacks, when they are objectifying others, the *out-group*.

To struggle to defeat these readings, to prevent anyone from reducing the instruments of generalized objectification to the weapons of partial objectification, our constant aim should be to choose systematic circumlocution (despite the threat to communication, which prefers simple and stable appellations), leading to a complete enumeration of the relevant properties, or to choose the most 'synoptic' concept, the one most capable of instantly evoking the system of relations which characterize it objectively, that is to say from the viewpoint of the outside observer,[46] and combine them with the epistemic polyonomy which would effectively express the different ways in which the same set can be defined in its *objective* relation to other sets; without forgetting to refer to empirical polyonomy – that is, the diversity of the names really used to designate the same individuals or the same groups, and thereby the diversity of aspects with which a person or a group appears to other persons and other groups – which should remind us that the struggle for the imposition of a legitimate viewpoint is part of objective reality.[47]

We would need, I believe, an unshakeably positivist confidence to see in these questions of scientific writing the complacent survival of a 'literary' disposition. The concern to control his discourse, that is the reception of his discourse, imposes on the sociologist a scientific rhetoric which is not necessarily a rhetoric of scientificity: he needs to inculcate a scientific reading, rather than belief in the scientificity of what is being read – except in so far as the latter is one of the tacit conditions of a scientific reading. Scientific discourse is distinct from the discourse of *fiction* – from the novel, for instance, which passes itself off more or less openly as a feigned and fictitious discourse – in that, as John Searle remarks, it *means* what it says, it takes seriously what it says and accepts responsibility for it, that is, if the case arises, for its mistakes.[48] But the difference is not only situated, as Searle believes, at the level of illocutionary intentions. A survey of all the features of discourse designed to signify the doxic modality of utterances, that is to inspire belief in the truth of what is said, or on the other hand to point out that it is only a pretence, would no doubt show that the novel can resort to a rhetoric of veracity while scientific discourse can conform to a rhetoric of scientificity destined to produce a fiction of science, superficially matching the picture that the upholders of 'normal science' have, at a given moment, of a discourse which is socially accredited as being responsible for what it proposes.

If socially accredited scientificity is such an important objective, it is because, although truth has no intrinsic force, there is an intrinsic force of belief in truth, of belief which produces the appearance of truth. In the struggle between different representations, the representation socially recognized as scientific, that is to say as true, contains its own social force, and, in the case of the social world, science gives those who hold it, or who appear to hold it, a monopoly of the legitimate viewpoint, of self-fulfilling prophecy. It is because it contains the possibility of this specifically social force that science, in the case of the social world, is *necessarily contested*, and that the threat of attack which it contains is bound to provoke defensive strategies, especially from the holders of temporal power and those who are their homologues and their allies in the field of cultural production. The most common of these defensive strategies consists in reducing the epistemic viewpoint, at least partly liberated from social determinism, to a simple doxic viewpoint, by relating it to the position of the researcher in the field. But those who do so ignore the fact that this strategy of disqualification entails a recognition of the very intention which defines the sociology of scientific knowledge, and the fact that it could only be justified if it challenged scientific discourse in the name of a more rigorous scientific knowledge of the limits associated with the conditions of its production.[49]

The importance of the social issues which are linked, in the case of the social sciences, to the social effects of scientificity explains the fact that the rhetoric of scientificity can play such a decisive part in these sciences. Any discourse with scientific pretensions towards the social world must take into account the state of representations of scientificity and the norms to be respected in practice in order to produce a *scientific effect* and thereby acquire symbolic efficacity and the social profits associated with conformity to scientific appearances. Thus any such discourse is bound to be situated in the space of possible discourses on the social world, and is bound to receive a part of its properties from the objective relations which unite it to them, especially to their style. And it is within the framework of this relation, in ways largely independent of the wishes and the knowledge of the authors, that its *social value*, its status as science, as fiction or as fiction of science, is defined. The art we call realist, in painting as in literature, is only ever that art which is able to produce an impression of reality, that is to say an impression of conforming to reality; similarly, the discourse we call scientific is likely to be the one which produces an impression of scientificity based on at least apparent conformity to the norms by which we recognize science. It is according to this logic that the style which we call literary or scientific plays a determining role: just as, in other times, professional philosophy in the process of establishing itself affirmed its claims to rigour and profundity, especially in the case of Kant, through stylistic precision, in opposition to the facility and frivolity of fashionable society, or as, contrariwise (as Wolf Lepenies has so well demonstrated), Buffon compromised his claims to scientificity through excessive attention to fine writing, so too any sociologists whose exaggerated concern with linguistic finesse might threaten their status as scientific researchers can resist this, more or less consciously, by rejecting literary elegance and draping themselves in the trappings of scientificity (graphs, statistical tables, even mathematical formalism, etc.).

In fact, positions adopted in the space of styles correspond closely to positions in the university field. Thus it is that, faced with the alternative of writing too well, which can procure literary benefit but undermines the impression of scientificity, or of writing badly, which can produce an impression of rigour or profundity (as in philosophy) but to the detriment of social success, geographers, historians and sociologists adopt strategies which, transcending individual differences, are related to their respective positions. Placed in a central position in the field of the arts and social science faculties, therefore halfway between the two systems of demands, the historians, while accepting the compulsory attributes of scientificity, generally take considerable care over their writing. If the geographers and sociologists are related in showing more indifference to literary qualities, the former display the humility of disposition which suits their station by adopting the neutral style which is equivalent, in the order of expression, to the empiricist abdication to which they most commonly resign themselves. As for the sociologists, they often betray their claim to hegemony (inherent right from the start in the Comtean classification of the sciences) by borrowing alternatively or simultaneously from the most powerful rhetorics in the two fields in relation to which they are forced to situate themselves, the mathematical, often used as an external sign of scientificity, or the philosophical, often reduced to lexical display.[50]

Knowledge of the social space within which scientific practice is accomplished, and the world of options, stylistic or other, with reference to which its choices are defined, does not lead us to repudiate scientific ambition and reject all possibility of knowing and of stating facts, but rather to reinforce, through awareness and the vigilance it encourages, our capacity to know reality scientifically. Indeed, it leads to a much more radical questioning than all the cautionary advice and safety regulations assigned by 'methodology' to 'normal science', and which make it possible to obtain scientific respectability at a low cost: 'reliability' (*le sérieux*), in science as elswhere, is a typically social virtue, and it is no coincidence that it is attributed to those who, in their lifestyle as in the style of their studies, provide guarantees of the predictability and measurability characteristic of 'dependable', settled people. This is the case for all the bureaucrats of normal science who, settled in science as in an official residence, are careful to take seriously only what deserves to be, that is, especially, themselves, to heed only what counts and what can be counted on. The social character of these demands is seen in the fact that they concern more or less exclusively the external display of scientific virtue: do not the greatest symbolic profits of science accrue to those kinds of scientific pharisees who know how to deck themselves with the most visible signs of scientificity, for example by mimicking the procedures and the languages of the most advanced sciences? Ostentatious conformity to the formalist requirements of normal science (significance tests, calculation of error, bibliographical references, etc.), and the superficial respect of minimal prescriptions, necessary but not sufficient, those thoroughly social virtues with which all the holders of social authority in the domains of science automatically identify, have more than the simple effect of ensuring that the directors of the major scientific bureaucracies have a scientific respectability out of all proportion to their real contribution to science. Institutionalized science tends to establish as its model of scientific activity a routine practice where the most scientifically decisive operations can be accomplished without reflection or critical control, since the apparent flawlessness of the visible procedures – often entrusted to assistants – deflects any questioning likely to challenge the respectability of the scientist and his science. This is why, far from being a scientistic form of the claim to absolute knowledge, a social science armed with a scientific knowledge of its social determinations constitutes the strongest weapon against 'normal science' and against positivist *self-confidence*, which represents the most formidable social obstacle to the progress of science.

Marx suggested that, every now and then, some individuals managed to liberate themselves so completely from the positions assigned to them in social space that they could comprehend that space as a whole, and transmit their vision to those who were still prisoners of the structure. In fact, the sociologist can affirm that the representation which he produces through his study transcends ordinary visions, without thereby laying claim to such absolute vision, able fully to grasp historical reality as such. Taken from an angle which is neither the partial and partisan viewpoint of agents engaged in the game, nor the absolute viewpoint of a divine spectator, the scientific vision represents the most systematic totalization which can be accomplished, in a given state of the instruments of knowledge, at the cost of as complete as possible an objectification both of the historical moment and of the work of totalization. In this way it marks a genuine step along the path leading to the *focus imaginarius* spoken of by Kant, this imaginary focus from which the perfected *system* could be discovered but which a properly scientific intention

can only posit as the ideal (or regulative idea) of a practice which
can only hope to approach ever closer to it in so far as it has
renounced all hope of reaching it immediately.

Thus we return to our point of departure, that is to say to the
work on himself that the researcher must accomplish to try to
objectify everything that links him to his subject, and which the
reader must duplicate on his own behalf in order to master the social
principles of the more or less unhealthy interest which he may take
in his reading. Unless he wants to run the risk of universalizing an
individual viewpoint and of delivering up a more or less rationalized
form of the unconscious determined by his position in the social
space, he must unwrap in succession all the boxes within which the
researcher and the greater part of his readers are enclosed, and all
the more surely the less they wish to know; that is, he must evoke
the structure of the field of power and the relation which the
university field taken as a whole maintains with it, analyse – as far
as the empirical data permit – the structure of the university field
and the position which the different faculties occupy within it, and,
finally, analyse the structure of each faculty and the position that
the different disciplines occupy within it. Thus (in chapter 3) we
will be able to allow the return, albeit in profoundly modified
form, of the question which lay behind our research into the
foundations and forms of power in the arts and social science faculties
on the eve of 1968, only when (in chapter 2) we have better defined
the position of the initial object inside the interlocking social spaces
and, thereby, the position of the researcher who himself participates
in these different spaces with the insights and blind spots they imply.
Having sketched the structure of the university field as a whole and
the structure of the field of the arts and social science faculties which,
because of their central position in the university field and because
of the very division between the humanities and the social sciences,
allow us to see with striking clarity the tensions, caused by the
strengthening of science and scientists, which rack the whole
university field and each of its faculties, we will then be able to ask
relevant questions of history, and attempt to grasp the determinants
and the object of certain transformations, of which the state of the
structure observed represents one moment. The increase in the
population of students and the concomitant increase in the population
of lecturers have profoundly modified the power relations at the
heart of the university field and at the heart of each faculty, especially

in the relations between the professional grades and between the disciplines, themselves unequally affected by the transformation of hierarchical relations, and this has happened in spite of all the actions which have been objectively orchestrated (without being intentionally co-ordinated) by the professors trying to ensure the defence of their corps (chapter 4). The morphological changes here (as also in the literary field) are the medium whereby history, which mechanisms of reproduction tend to resist, invests the fields, which are *open* spaces obliged to draw from outside the resources necessary for their functioning, and are thereby liable to become the locus of that collision of independent causal series which creates the event, that is, the quintessentially historical (chapter 5).

This attempt to sketch a structural history of recent developments in the educational system presents a problem of writing which touches on the use of tenses, and beyond that on the epistemological status of discourse. Should we, because of the relative specificity of the documents and enquiries used, and because of their clearly declared limitations in social space and time, refrain from endowing our discourse with the generality which is conveyed by the transhistoric present of the scientific utterance? That would be equivalent to repudiating the very project of any intellectual enterprise attempting to 'immerse itself' in historical singularity in order to sort out the transhistorical invariants (abandoning the privilege of timeless generalities to essayists or anthologists who are embarrassed by no historical reality other than their reading or their personal experience). Unlike 'the discursive tenses' (often a present) which according to Benveniste 'suppose a speaker and a listener and in the former the intention to influence the latter in some way', but just like the aorist, 'the supreme historical tense' which according to Benveniste again 'objectifies the event by detaching it from the present' and 'excludes all autobiographical linguistic form',[51] the omnitemporal present of scientific discourse marks the objectifying distance without referring to a situated and dated past. On these lines it is suitable for the scientific report, when this presents *structural invariants* which can be observed as such in very different historical contexts and still function in the same world as *constants*, everywhere operative. Incidentally, it is this presence in the present – that is, what matters now – which makes of sociology an eventful or, as the Anglo-Saxons say, a *controversial* science, and all the more so the more advanced it is. It is clear that if we are more ready to grant the historian the objectivity and neutrality of the scientist it is because we are generally more indifferent to the games and the objectives in which he is involved; always remembering that chronological distance in the chronological present is not a good measure of historical distance, that is, the distance which converts into history, into the past historic, and not forgetting that belonging to the present as *news*, that is to say, as a universal agency of objects and ideas which can be chronologically past or present but which are effectively a *live issue*, thus practically *made present* in the moment considered, is what defines the divide between the 'ever-living and ever-burning' present and the past, 'dead and buried' like the social worlds for which it was once still a live issue, new and up to date, active and reactive.

Thus the present seems necessary for the description of all the mechanisms or processes which, despite superficial changes – as regards vocabulary, notably president instead of dean, UER[52] instead of faculty, etc. – are still part of our historic present because they still exercise their effects. To take an extreme case, it is certain that we can still use the present to discuss the principle of clarification dear to Thomas Aquinas, as long as, in the unchanging time of university life, dissertations and so many other forms of discourse are organized according to the triadic divisions and subdivisions of scholastic thought. Even the ahistorical model of the quintessential historical event, the crisis as synchronization of different social times, can be written in the omnitemporal present as the unique accomplishment of a series of omnitemporal effects whose conjunction produces a historical conjuncture.

The present is valid also for everything which is true at the moment of the enquiry and is still true at the moment of reading, or which can be understood by using the patterns and mechanisms established on the basis of the enquiry. Thus it is that the distance of nearly twenty years between the moment of study and the moment of publication allows everyone, using the changes which have occurred in the meantime and those which they portend, to verify whether the proposed model – and in particular the analysis of the transformations of the power relations between academic disciplines and professional grades – allows us to explain phenomena which, being subsequent to the enquiry and difficult to grasp in a methodical way, are only alluded to here. I am thinking of the appearance of new forms of power, particularly that of the unions, which tend to force to its ultimate conclusions the process initiated by the transformation of the mode of recruitment of lecturers and assistant lecturers, by giving the products of the new mode of recruitment control over the appointment of the new subordinate teachers – which can lead in certain cases to the *de facto* elimination of the prime categories of the old mode of recruitment, that is the *normaliens* or the *agrégés*.[53] And how can we not see that the contradiction between the new mode of recruitment and the previous mode of career promotion, which, being protected by the past which it aims to maintain, tends to confine in subordinate positions the products of the new mode of recruitment, is the principle behind a number of claims, pressures and transformations, which, helped especially by political change, attempt to abolish the differences associated with the initial differences of the school and university trajectory (by abolishing either the differences between grades or the differences between the diplomas which give access to these grades).

Finally, we should underline the various precautions needed to avoid misreadings of these analyses, yet at the same time we should elaborate them to the point where we convert them into *ad hoc* responses, that is to say in more than one case into *ad hominem* arguments: indeed, everything leads us to believe that readings of our scientific reconstructions of variations and invariants will vary, as does experience of real history, according to the reader's relation to the past and the present of the academic institution. To understand in this case is difficult only because we understand far too well, in a manner of speaking, and because we *do not wish* to see or know what it is we understand. Thus it is that the easiest thing can also be the most extraordinarily difficult because, as Wittgenstein says, 'The problem of *understanding* language is connected with the problem of the Will'. Sociology, which of all sciences is the best placed to know the limits of the 'intrinsic force of the true idea', knows that the force of the resistances which will be opposed to it will be very exactly commensurate with the 'problems of the will' which it has managed to overcome.[54]

2

The Conflict of the Faculties

The class of the higher faculties (in a manner of speaking the right wing of the parliament of knowledge) defends the statutes of the government; however, in a free constitution, as any which respects the truth must be, there must also exist an opposition audience (the left), for, without the severe scrutiny and objections of the latter, the government would not be sufficiently informed of what can be helpful or harmful to it.

I. Kant, The Conflict of the Faculties

As *authorities*, whose position in social space depends principally on the possession of cultural capital, a subordinate form of capital, university professors are situated rather on the side of the subordinate pole of the field of power and are clearly opposed in this respect to the managers of industry and business. But, as holders of an institutionalized form of cultural capital, which guarantees them a bureaucratic career and a regular income, they are opposed to writers and artists: occupying a temporally dominant position in the field of cultural production, they are distinguished by this fact, to differing degrees according to the faculties, from the occupants of the less institutionalized and more heretical sectors of the field (and especially from the 'independent' or 'freelance' writers and artists, as opposed to those who belong to the university).[1]

Although the comparison is difficult because of the problems posed by the differentiation of the two populations under consideration (and especially because of their partial overlap), we may use a comparison with the regular contributors to 'intellectual' reviews like *Les Temps modernes* or *Critique*, to establish the fact that university professors, similar in this to senior civil servants, are more likely than writers and intellectuals (who have relatively high rates of bachelorhood and divorce and a low average number of children) to display the different indices of social integration and respectability (low rate of bachelorhood, high number of children, high number of decorations, of titles of reserve officer, etc.), and all the more so as one ascends the social hierarchy of the faculties (science, arts, law, medicine).[2]

To this collection of converging indications, we may add the data provided by Alain Girard's enquiry into social success, where we see that writers impute their success to charismatic factors (talent, intellectual qualities, vocation) in 26 per cent of cases, against 19.1 per cent for professors, who for their part regularly invoke the role of their family origins (11.8 as against 7.5 per cent), of their teachers (9.1 as against 4.4 per cent) and of their wives (1.7 as against 0.3 per cent). 'They are pleased to pay homage to their teachers. A general homage to all of their teachers, at the different teaching levels, or homage to one of them more especially, who singled them out, or awoke their vocation, or perhaps later supervised them and helped their research. A feeling of gratitude and sometimes almost of veneration or fervour towards their teachers can be detected in reading their answers. In the same spirit, they also recognize, more often than others, the influence of their family, who from childhood gave them a respect for moral or intellectual qualities, which facilitated the accomplishment of their careers. They are ready to admit that they felt they were following a vocation, and, finally, more often than many others, they evoke the harmony which reigns in the bosom of their family and the support they have always had from their wives'.[3]

In fact, more than indices of social integration and support for the dominant order, we should take into account indicators of the distance, variable for different societies and periods, between the academic field and, on the one hand, the field of economic or political power, as well as the intellectual field on the other hand. Thus the autonomy of the university field grew constantly throughout the nineteenth century: as Christophe Charle shows, the professor in higher education evolves from being the dignitary appointed by the political authorities and committed to politics, which he was in the first half of the century, to becoming a select and specialized teacher, cut off from the world of social dignitaries by a professional activity incompatible with political life, and animated by a specifically academic ideal; at the same time he tends to distance himself from the intellectual field, as we can plainly see in the case of professors of French (notably Lanson) who, by becoming professional and by equipping themselves with a specific methodology, tend to break the traditional relation between criticism and fashionable society.

We must, however, beware of pushing too far a comparison, intended only to establish a 'position', between the population of professors, taken as a whole, and any particular fraction of the dominant class. Indeed, like the field of the institutions of higher education (that is to say the whole set of the faculties and the *grandes écoles*) whose structure reproduces in specifically academic logic the structure of the field of power (or, in other words, the oppositions between the fractions of the dominant class) to which it gives access, the professors of the different faculties are distributed between the pole of economic and political power and the pole of cultural prestige according to the same principles as the different fractions of the dominant classes: indeed, we see an increase in the frequency of the most characteristic properties of the dominant fractions of the dominant class as we move from the science faculties to the arts faculties, and from these to the faculties of law and medicine (while the possession of distinctive marks of academic excellence, such as success in the *concours général*, tends to vary in inverse proportion to the social hierarchy of the faculties). In fact, everything seems to indicate that dependency on the field of political or economic power varies in the same direction, whereas dependency on the norms specific to the intellectual field – which, especially since the Dreyfus affair, require independence from the temporal powers, and the adoption of political positions of a totally new kind, that is to say at once external and critical – is incumbent above all on the professors of the arts faculties and social science faculties, but in a very unequal way according to their position in this space.

> The statistical analysis whose results are presented below was applied to a random sample ($N=405$), whose rate varies between 45 and 50 per cent according to the faculties, of tenured professors in the Paris faculties (excluding the faculty of pharmacy) recorded in the *Annuaire de l'Education nationale* [*National Education Directory*] for the year 1968.[4] Although the collection of data, begun in 1967, at the same time as a set of in-depth interviews with professors of science and literature, was then interrupted, to be completed, grosso modo, in 1971, we wanted to describe the state of the university field on the eve of 1968 for the purposes of comparison with the enquiry into power in the faculties of arts and social sciences (which had been conducted at that time and whose results are presented below) and also because we were convinced that at this critical moment,

when the most ancient traditions of the corps still survive while we see the signs of forthcoming transformations, in particular all the effects of the morphological changes in the student population and the teaching body, it contained the seeds both of the reactions by the various categories of professors to the crisis of May 1968, and the limits to those institutional transformations which have been effected by reforms subsequent to the crisis.[5]

In order to accomplish this kind of 'prosopography' of the university professors, we collected for each professor of the sample all of the information provided from written sources and from various enquiries already made for other purposes, usually administrative, on our behalf (the reader will find in appendix 1 a critical account of the operations of data collation and the sources used) or carried out by us specifically to complement or verify the information obtained from other sources (in-depth interviews and telephone enquiries to professors in the sample). For all questions of opinion, we had to depend principally and exclusively on written sources, for several reasons. Firstly, as we came to realize during our interviews, a very large proportion of the professors interviewed refused to classify themselves in political terms and rejected or refuted, with different arguments, any attempt to pin down the positions they adopted with regard to political or trade-union matters.[6] Then, it was evident that there was no question, whether on positions of power held (such an eminent object of protest in 1968) or on positions adopted towards the reforms or their consequences, which was not affected by the relation created by the enquiry and thus interpreted as a criticism, as a continuation of earlier attacks on 'mandarins' (to which several of the professors interviewed alluded spontaneously). In short, to avoid distortions as completely as possible, as well as dissimulations and misrepresentations, at the same time as the suspicion or the accusation of establishing a sectarian and inquisitorial police file which the sociologist and his 'filing cards' generally incur in intellectual and artistic milieux, we decided to restrict ourselves exclusively to information deliberately and consciously publicized or intended for publication (such as the information deliberately and consciously revealed during various investigations intended for the preparation of directories of researchers with which we have been associated). This procedure was all the more necessary since we wished to be able to publish diagrams using proper names as we had done for other milieux. Thus we collected all the relevant indicators on:

1 the principal social determinants of the opportunities of access to the positions held, that is to say the determinants of the formation of the *habitus* and of academic success, the economic capital and above all the inherited cultural and social capital: the social origins (father's

profession, mention in the *Bottin mondain* [society directory]),[7] geographical origins, original religion of the family;[8]

2 educational determinants, which are the educational retranslation of the preceding determinants (educational capital): school attended (*lycée* or private school,[9] in Paris or the provinces, etc.) and educational success (*concours général*)[10] during secondary education; establishment attended for higher education (Paris, provinces, abroad) and the qualifications acquired;[11]

3 the capital of academic power: membership of the Institute, of the Universities Consultative Committee (CCU), tenure of positions such as dean or director of UER [Unit of Education and Research = university institute], director of institute, etc. (membership of board of examiners for the national competitive examinations, for entrance to the ENS, for the *agrégation*, etc., which was used for the enquiry in the arts faculties only, could not be taken into account for the whole set of the faculties because of the non-comparability of the positions concerned);[12]

4 capital of scientific power: direction of a research unit, of a scientific review, teaching in an institution of training for research, membership of the directorate of the CNRS, of committees of the CNRS, of the Higher Council for Scientific Research;

5 the capital of scientific prestige: membership of the Institute, scientific distinctions, translations into foreign languages, participation in international congresses (the number of mentions in the *Citation Index*, too variable from faculty to faculty, was not usable, nor was the editorship of scientific reviews or collections);[13]

6 the capital of intellectual renown: membership of the Académie Française[14] and mention in *Larousse*,[15] appearances on television, writing for newspapers, weeklies or intellectual reviews, publication in paperback, membership of editorial committees of intellectual reviews;[16]

7 the capital of political or economic power: mention in *Who's Who*, membership of ministerial cabinets,[17] of planning committees, teaching in 'establishment' schools [ENA, Polytechnique, HEC, etc. (Tr.)[18]], decorations of various kinds;[19]

8 'political' dispositions in the widest sense: participation in the congresses of Caen and Amiens, signature of diverse petitions.

DETACHMENT AND INTEGRATION

The structure of the university field reflects the structure of the field of power, while its own activity of selection and indoctrination contributes to the reproduction of that structure. Indeed, it is in and through its functioning as a space of differences between positions (and thereby between the dispositions of those holding them) that, escaping the control of any individual or collective consciousness and will, the reproduction of the space of the different positions which constitute the field of power is effected.[20] As is clearly shown in the diagram of the analysis of correspondences, the differences separating the faculties of the professors show a structure homologous to that of the field of power overall: the temporally subordinate faculties, the science faculty and, to a lesser extent, the arts faculty, contrast with the socially dominant faculties, more or less indistinguishable in this respect, the faculty of law and the faculty of medicine, through a whole set of economic, cultural and social differences, where we recognize the essential features of what creates the opposition, at the heart of the field of power, between the subordinate fraction and the dominant fraction.

This principal opposition is apparent even from reading the statistical tables setting out the distribution of the various more or less direct indices of economic and cultural capital. The same hierarchy – science, arts, law, medicine – which can be observed when we distribute professors of the different faculties according to social origin, recorded in terms of the father's profession (the respective proportions of professors originating in the dominant classes being 58.0, 66.0, 77.0, 85.5 per cent), can be found when we consider other indicators of social position, like attendance at a private educational establishment, except for an inversion in the case of law and medicine (9.5, 12.5, 30.0, 23.0 per cent). And we note that the proportions of the various fractions – themselves hierarchized according to economic capital and cultural capital – from which the professors of the various faculties originate vary to the same degree: the proportion of sons of professors is greatest for arts professors (23.3 per cent) and least for professors of medicine (10.0 per cent), while the professors of medicine (except the *fondamentalistes*[21]) and above all the professors of law are most often the offspring of members of liberal professions, and of managers or executives in the public or private sectors.[22]

In fact, a finer analysis shows that the individuals classified in the same category show different properties according to their faculties. Thus, in addition to the fact that they are much less uncommon than in law or medicine, the professors of the arts and science faculties who are of working-class origins have their own path to success, the Ecole Normale d'instituteurs;[23] on the contrary, in the faculties of law or medicine, they have nearly all been educated in private junior schools. The same opposition could be found among the professors whose families were in the teaching profession (who are much more strongly represented in arts and science). Hence it is impossible to determine, within the limits of the information available (and also of the populations concerned, whose numbers are always very small), whether, in the case of individuals of the same origins whose practices and representations vary according to their faculty and discipline, we should inpute these differences to *secondary* differences of origin or to the effect of differences in trajectory (such as the degree of improbability of the careers considered) or, as is no doubt the most common occurrence, to a combination of the two effects.

Note Concerning the Following Tables

The tables given below show the distribution according to the faculties – science, arts, law and medicine – of a certain number of indicators of inherited or acquired capital (in its different forms). Given the method used, which is that of the prosopography (cf. appendix 1, 'the sources used'), some of the individuals who have been classified in the category of 'no reply' (NR) may have the properties concerned. We have not tried to present the distribution according to discipline taught (which, in the analysis of correspondences, intervenes only as an illustrative variable). In fact the indispensable groupings present many uncertainties. Should we have linked mechanics to mathematics or to fundamental physics, genetics to natural science or biochemistry? Should classical Arabic philology be classified with the teaching of foreign languages and literature, like English or German philology, or with ancient literature and philology? And does demography, which is taught in arts faculties, belong to philosophy (as the official annuals show it), to geography or to the social sciences? As far as law is concerned, which is more legitimate: to classify the teaching of the history of political thought or the history of economic thought in the section containing the history of law, or to classify it with public law, or with economics? Things are no clearer in medicine, and it is not always possible to distinguish between clinical practitioners and surgeons. We could multiply examples. It transpires that each of these decisions would have necessitated an extended enquiry in the appropriate milieu. We preferred therefore to stick to the major administrative divisions into science, arts, law and medicine, which, however vast and conventional they may be, correspond none the less, at the time of our enquiry, to a reality of university life.

Table 1. Demographic indicators and indicators of inherited or acquired capital

	Science (N=120)	Arts (N=120)	Law (N=87)	Medicine (N=70)	Total (N=405)
Sex					
Men	91.4	91.7	96.6	100.0	94.0
Women	8.6	8.3	3.4	—	6.0
Date of birth					
Before 1900	2.3	3.3	2.3	1.6	2.5
1900–1904	13.4	8.3	9.2	15.9	11.5
1905–1909	11.0	15.0	13.8	21.8	14.6
1910–1914	21.9	20.0	21.8	25.9	22.0
1915–1919	14.3	10.8	9.2	15.9	12.5
1920–1924	21.9	23.4	21.8	14.5	21.0
1925–1929	7.9	12.5	16.2	2.9	10.4
1930 or after	5.6	5.9	3.5	1.5	4.5
NR (no reply)	1.7	0.8	1.2	—	1.0
Marital status					
Unmarried	4.1	4.2	6.1	—	3.9
Married	89.3	92.5	92.5	98.5	92.4
Divorced	2.5	0.8	—	1.5	1.3
Widowed	4.1	2.5	1.4	—	2.4
Number of children					
Unmarried	4.1	4.2	6.1	—	3.9
No children	6.4	10.0	8.3	5.9	7.7
1 child	19.6	15.0	11.6	10.4	14.9
2 children	23.6	21.6	20.7	24.4	22.5
3 children	19.6	25.0	20.7	23.1	22.1
4 children	17.2	12.5	19.7	21.6	17.2
5 children or more	9.5	10.9	12.8	12.9	11.2
NR	—	0.8	—	1.7	2.4
Place of birth					
Paris and suburbs	29.3	37.5	19.5	51.2	33.3
Elsewhere	69.9	62.5	79.3	45.9	65.7
NR	0.8	—	1.2	2.9	1.0

Continued

Table 1. (continued) Demographic indicators and indicators of inherited or acquired capital

	Science (N=120)	Arts (N=120)	Law (N=87)	Medicine (N=70)	Total (N=405)
Place of residence					
Paris 16,17,8,7+ Neuilly[a]	6.4[b]	13.4	36.9	58.6	24.0
Paris 5,6,13,14	25.1[b]	28.3	18.7	28.6	25.3
Paris, other districts	7.2[b]	10.0	12.9	5.7	8.9
Suburbs 78 and 92 (except Neuilly)	9.5[b]	18.3	21.9	4.3	13.9
Other	7.2[b]	15.8	5.9	2.8	8.7
Religion					
Jewish	15.6	3.3	5.9	7.3	8.4
Protestant	6.3	9.2	10.5	5.9	7.9
Practising Catholic	7.8	19.2	21.8	41.6	20.0
Other	70.3	68.3	62.0	45.2	63.7
Father's socio-professional category					
Agricultural labourer or industrial worker	8.6	10.0	3.5	1.5	6.7
Clerk, craftsman, middle management, primary teacher	33.6	30.0	19.5	11.4	25.7
Engineer, industrialist, senior management	25.8	23.4	27.6	32.8	26.7
Officer, magistrate, liberal professions, administrative executive	12.5	13.3	37.9	42.8	23.5
Professor, intellectual	19.5	23.3	11.5	10.0	17.2
NR	—	—	—	1.5	0.2
Who's Who	40.6	46.7	60.9	50.0	48.4
Bottin mondain [French society directory]	1.6	1.7	12.6	37.1	10.1
Decorations					
Legion of Honour	28.9[b]	25.8	41.4	61.4	36.3
Order of Merit	11.7[b]	3.3	8.1	8.6	7.9

Notes to table 1

[a]The Paris postal districts are ranked from the most fashionable residential areas downwards. [Tr.]
[b]These figures have only a nominal significance because of the high proportion of professors for whom the information was unobtainable (over 40 per cent).

Table 2. Indicators of educational capital

	Science	Arts	Law	Medicine	Total
Private secondary schooling					
Private	9.5	12.5	29.9	22.9	22.1
Public only	78.5	81.7	68.9	75.6	77.0
ENI [teacher-training college]	8.7	5.0	—	—	4.2
NR [No reply]	3.3	0.8	1.2	1.5	1.7
Lycée					
Top Paris *lycées*	22.7	39.2	10.4	11.5	22.9
Other Paris *lycées*	27.4	22.4	12.7	41.2	24.9
Provincial or foreign *lycée*	39.7	30.0	52.6	24.3	37.5
Private school (Paris)	1.6	3.4	3.5	12.9	4.4
Private school (provincial)	4.7	4.2	19.6	2.9	7.4
NR	3.9	0.8	1.2	7.2	2.9
Higher education					
Paris	86.7	87.5	63.2	88.6	82.4
Provincial only	13.3	12.5	36.8	5.7	16.7
NR	—	—	—	5.7	0.9
Studies overseas					
Yes	7.8	8.4	10.4	4.5	7.9
No	85.1	91.6	89.6	91.0	89.1
NR	7.1	—	—	4.5	3.0
Concours général					
Prizewinner	10.1	14.1	6.8	5.7	9.8

Table 3. Indicators of capital of academic power

	Science	Arts	Law	Medicine	Total
Consultative Committee	27.4	34.2	26.4	41.4	31.6
Academic Palms	26.6	51.7	40.2	15.7	35.0
Institute Institute	10.2	3.3	5.7		
National Academy of Medicine				12.9	8.1
Dean of faculty	11.7	17.5	32.2	20.0	19.3
Director of UER [university institute]	15.2	34.2	31.1	14.3	22.7

Table 4. Indicators of capital of scientific power and prestige

	Science	Arts	Law	Medicine	Total
CNRS committees	33.6	37.5	9.2	10.0	25.4
Direction of CNRS lab	22.6	15.0	10.3	8.6	15.3

Teaching in intellectual
  schools ['intellectual'
  grandes écoles e.g. ENS]
	17.2	39.2	5.7	2.9	18.8

Conferences 1 to 3	24.2	30.8	51.7	28.6	32.8
4 or more	46.9	31.7	26.4	37.1	36.3
None	28.9	37.5	21.9	34.3	30.9
CNRS medal	2.4	0.8	—	1.4	1.2
Translations Yes	15.6	25.0	16.1	8.6	17.3
No	84.4	75.0	83.9	91.4	82.7

Table 5. Indicators of capital of intellectual renown

	Science	Arts	Law	Medicine	Total
Paperbacks	4.7	30.0	20.7	5.7	15.8
Articles in *Le Monde*	3.9	15.0	11.5	5.7	9.1
Articles in reviews and weeklies	2.3	21.7	14.9	2.8	10.9
Television broadcasts	5.5	15.0	1.1	10.0	8.1

Table 6. Indicators of capital of political or economic power

	Science	Arts	Law	Medicine	Total
Public bodies	14.8	16.7	41.4	65.7	29.9
Sixth [five-year] plan	0.8	0.9	5.7	4.3	2.5
Teaching in 'establishment' schools	12.5	8.3	28.7	1.4	12.8

The indices of economic or social capital presently held by members of the different faculties are distributed according to the same pattern, whether in the case of living in a fashionable neighbourhood, Paris postal districts 16, 17, 18, 7 and Neuilly (6.4, 13.4, 36.9 and 58.6 per cent respectively), or being mentioned in the *Bottin mondain* [society directory] (1.6, 1.7, 12.6, 37.1 per cent), or having a family of three or more children (46.3, 48.4, 53.2, 57.6 per cent) which doubtless has a close correlation with economic capital (and also with social capital, at least potentially), although it also obviously expresses attributes which are related to other factors, like religion and, in particular, active membership of the Roman Catholic Church, whose incidence follows the same pattern (7.8, 19.2, 21.8, 41.6 per cent).[24] These few indices, being very sparse and indirect, cannot give an exact idea of the economic differences between science and arts professors and professors of law and above all medicine, who add to the income earned from their post of professor and head of clinical department the profits derived from private practice.[25] It is still the case that, as regards the salary itself, we note strong differences between the faculties, because of the fact that differences in career patterns imply considerable differences in the sum of salary acquired throughout active life: in this respect, the arts faculties seem the most underprivileged, because of the fact that appointment to the posts of assistant lecturer (*assistant*) and lecturer (*maître-assistant*)[26] is particularly late (at age 31 and 37 on average, as opposed to 25 and 32 in science and 28 and 34 in law in 1978), as is appointment to the grades of senior lecturer (*maître de conférences*) and professor (*professeur*) (43 and 50 as opposed to 34 and 43 in law, 35 and 44 in science).[27] As a result, the average duration of an A-grade post (senior lecturer or professor) is particularly short, that is, in 1978, 25 years as opposed to 29 in medicine (where appointment to senior lecturer is at 39 and to professor at 49), 33 in science and 34 in law.[28]

But it is important to note that all the indices of political and economic power, such as participation in public bodies (ministerial cabinets, Constitutional Court, Economic and Social Council, Council of State, Financial Inspectorate) or committees for the Five-Year Plan, vary in the same direction, whereas the proportion of prizewinners in the *concours général*, which is a good index of educational success in secondary education,[29] and the different indicators of investment in research and of scientific acclaim vary in the inverse direction. Thus we discover that the university field is organized according to two antagonistic principles of hierarchization: the social hierarchy, corresponding to the capital inherited and the economic and political capital actually held, is in opposition to the specific, properly cultural hierarchy, corresponding to the capital of scientific authority or intellectual renown. This opposition is inherent in the very structures of the university field which is the locus of confrontation between two competing *principles of legitimation*: the first, which is specifically temporal and political, and which demonstrates in the logic of the university field the dependence of that field on the principles operative in the field of power, becomes increasingly dominant as we ascend the specifically temporal hierarchy extending from the science faculties to the faculties of law or medicine; the other, which is founded on the autonomy of the scientific and intellectual order, becomes increasingly dominant as we move from law or medicine to science.

The fact that the very oppositions which may be observed at the heart of the field of power between the field of economic power and the field of cultural power are thus to be found at the heart of a field orientated towards cultural production and reproduction no doubt explains why the opposition observed between the two poles of this field has something so absolute about it, and why it affects all aspects of existence, characterizing two lifestyles so profoundly differentiated in their economic and cultural foundations, but also on the ethical, religious and political planes.

Although the actual objective of the enquiry naturally tended to privilege the properties more specifically linked to the university and to university life, we find, among the information obtained, indirect indices of the profoundest and most general dispositions which underlie their whole lifestyle. Thus it is that we can see in bachelorhood or divorce on the one hand, and in the size of the family on the other, which contribute quite strongly to produce the principal opposition of the field, an index not only of social integration but also of *integration into the social order*, in short, a measure of what one might call the taste for order.

Indeed, rather than decipher one by one the different statistical relations, such as that which links the rate of divorce (an index of weak family integration) with having few children (a presumed index of weak family integration and above all of weak integration into the social order), we should try to grasp as a whole all the insights into social significance offered by the whole set of indices associated with the dominant pole of the academic field – large family and Legion of Honour, right-wing voting and teaching of law, Roman Catholicism and private schooling, fashionable residential area and *Bottin mondain*, studies at Sciences Po [School of Political Science[30]] or the ENA and teaching in such 'establishment schools', bourgeois origins and participation in public bodies or committees for the Five-Year Plan – or, less clearly, because they are defined above all negatively, all the indices associated with the subordinate pole – left-wing opinions and graduation from the Ecole Normale Supérieure, Jewish identity or status as 'oblate'[31] of state education. If these sets of traits inspire a feeling of coherence and necessity, it is because commonsense intuition recognizes in them the spontaneous coherence of practices or properties produced by a single generating and unifying principle. It is this coherence at a practical level which we must attempt to reconstitute in words, while guarding against the temptation, thus encouraged, to convert the objectively systematic, but non-verbalized and still less systematized, products of the *habitus*

Graph 1 The space of the faculties: analysis of correspondences: plane of the first and second axes of inertia – properties *Note* The illustrative variables are in italics.

into an explicitly totalized system, into a coherent ideology.

What is revealed or betrayed in the first set of indices is doubtless what the ordinary language of the dominant would call reliability (*le sérieux*), a taste for order, which is a way of taking oneself seriously and taking the given world seriously, of identifying unreservedly with the status quo, a way of life which is at the same time an assumption of duty. As for the other set, what it evokes through its lacks or lacunae, which are also a rejection, is detachment, that is the opposite of integration, the rejection of everything which enforces respect for the status quo, or which enhances integration into the normal world of orderly, respectable people – ceremonies, rituals, *idées reçues*, traditions, honours, Legion of Honour ('Honours dishonour', as Flaubert said), traditions and manners, in short, everything which profoundly ties the maintenance of social order to the most insignificant practices of social custom, with all the discipline which they impose, the hierarchies which they evoke, the vision of social divisions which they imply.[32] It is easy to see the relations which link this opposition to the opposition between left and right, in mythological terms even more than in political terms.

We should remember what sets scientific research, that free enquiry which has no limits beyond its own, against not only a normative discipline like law but also against the scientifically guaranteed art of medicine, entrusted with putting science into practice, and also imposing an order, the Medical Order, that is to say a morality, a lifestyle and a life ideal, as was evident in the case of abortion, in the name of an authority which is not only that of science but also that of the 'capable' and the 'notable', predisposed by their position and their dispositions to define the good, and standards of goodness (we know the remarkable frequency of participation by professors of medicine in public bodies, in committees and, more generally, in politics, and the role of consultant to governments and international bodies played by jurists, notably by specialists in international law, commercial law or public law).[33] A support for science which is confined within the limits of social or even religious propriety is consonant with the hostile relationship which the Roman Catholic bourgeoisie has always had with science. It has long tended to channel its children into private education, which upholds the moral order, the family, especially large and upper-class families, their honour, their morale and morality, and, thereby, the reproduction of *well-bred sons*, sons of doctors or magistrates who are appointed doctors and magistrates, legitimate heirs, or rather, legitimated heirs, seeking their inheritance as worthy successors, grateful and gratified. These two relationships, so totally opposed to science and to power respectively, are linked to diametrically opposite past and present positions in the field of power: those science and arts professors who have their origins in the lower or middle classes and owe their entry into the upper classes entirely to their academic success, like those from families in the teaching profession, are very strongly inclined to reinvest totally in the institution which has so well rewarded their previous investments, and are very little inclined to seek power other than university power. On the contrary, the law professors, three-quarters of whom are of bourgeois origin, are more likely than science or arts professors to combine functions of authority in the university with positions of power in the political world or even in the business world. In short, we have to go beyond the old oppositions which divided the whole nineteenth century, Homais and Bournisien, scientism and clericalism,[34] in order to understand what creates the vital affinity between the ethical dispositions and the intellectual dispositions associated with the positions held in this space, organized according to a dual system of economic capital and intellectual capital and the relations correlative with these two sorts of capital, in which Jews and practising Catholics inhabit the two polar extremes, with the Protestants in the median position: the affinity between the heretical or critical attitudes displayed by the holders of socially subordinate and intellectually dominant positions and the critical breaks associated with academic practice, especially in the social sciences; affinity between the upholders of orthodoxy and order (it is surely no coincidence that these positions of order give such an important place to the sons of officers), of right-thinking and right-wing support for a social world so obviously modelled on expectations that it seems self-evidently natural, and the inseparably bourgeois and Catholic negation of science, of the worrying, critical or heretical questions and interrogations which so often orientate organic scientists – particularly those of the Ecole Polytechnique – towards regions of thought where physics and metaphysics, biology and spiritualism, archaeology and theosophy intermingle.

Athough it is homologous to the field of power, the academic field has its own logic, and the conflicts between class fractions change their significance entirely when they take on the specific form of a 'conflict of faculties', to use Kant's terms. If the two poles of the university field are fundamentally opposed according to their degree of dependence on the field of power and the inhibitions imposed or temptations proposed, the most heteronomous positions are never entirely free of the specific demands of a field officially orientated towards the production and reproduction of knowledge, and the most autonomous positions are never entirely free of the external necessities of social reproduction. This autonomy is affirmed notably in the existence of a second opposition revealed in the analysis of correspondences, and which is based, in this case, on the purely internal criteria of success specific to the university field, establishing, at the heart of each of the sectors defined by the first factor, a stark opposition, strongly connected with social origins, between the holders of the different kinds of specific capital and the others. Thus to those, most usually of humble and provincial origins (and it is also in this sector that we find the women), who are on the side of the insecure, because often elective, power conferred by membership of the committees of the CNRS, and of the purely academic power over reproduction of the university body, afforded by membership of the Universities Consultative Committee, are opposed the holders of the different kinds of specific capital, whether that of scientific prestige (with the gold medal of the CNRS) or intellectual prestige, more or less monopolized by the arts and social science professors (with books translated or in paperback, membership of editorial committees of scholarly or intellectual reviews, publication of articles in *Le Monde*, frequent appearances on television). In fact, these differences in academic achievement (which are obviously connected with age) are so closely associated with social differences that they seem to be the retranslation into a specifically academic logic of initial differences of incorporated capital (the *habitus*) or of objectified capital which are associated with different social or geographical origins. They seem to be the result of a gradual transformation of inherited advantages into 'earned' advantages effected through an outstandingly successful school career (crowned by success in the *concours général*) and by a flawless student career, especially at each moment of increasingly difficult choice between sections, options, institutions (including attendance at the most prestigious secondary schools, the *lycées* Louis-Le-Grand or Henri IV).

Knowing that the different faculties are distributed according to a chiastic structure, homologous to the structure of the field of power, with at one pole the scientifically dominant but socially subordinate faculties, and, at the other, the scientifically subordinate but temporally dominant faculties, we shall better understand that the principal opposition concerns the place and the significance that the different categories of professors spend in practice (and above all in their time-economy) on scientific activity, and the very idea that they have of scholarship. The common terms 'research', 'teaching', 'laboratory direction', etc., designate very different realities, and are no doubt all the more deceptive today since the generalization of a scientific model, under the combined effects of fashion and the homogenizing constraints of research administration, has led the whole body of teachers in higher education to pay homage to science by borrowing terms from the natural sciences to designate realities often very far from scientific reality (I am thinking of the notion of laboratory).[35]

Thus it is that, without even mentioning law or the more traditional arts subjects where new terminology often barely conceals old realities, the medical faculties often undertake, in the name of research, activities which are very distant from what the science faculties call research. For example, one professor, who was asked to say how much time he devoted to research compared to other things, was able to reply: 'Much less, unfortunately, because I have so little time. Research is above all a work of direction, guiding people, finding funds, finding the right people, much more than work as such. I don't actually do the research myself, I help other people do it, but I don't do it personally, or at least relatively little, unfortunately.' And another professor, also at the faculty of medicine, commented: 'As for research, I don't actually do any myself; given my age, I direct it, I supervise it, I apply for funds to subsidize it; and, as for teaching, I do that too, in any case I have to do a minimum of three hours' lecturing a week, so I am involved in teaching, with those lectures, and also with the departmental meetings which we hold at least once a week, where we study the particularly difficult cases, and that is part of our research as well as . . . it is part of research and teaching, as well as clinical care.' The indications are that in cases like this one, which is not uncommon, the 'patriarchal head', who sacrifices his so-called personal research to the search for the means of research for researchers whom he can only direct in the bureaucratic sense of the term in so far as he sabotages his ability to direct them in their scientific work, can find in the blurring of roles a means of disguising appearances, for himself and for others, by disguising as a research post a post of administrative director or scientific administrator.[36]

The work of accumulation and preservation of the social capital necessary to retain a vast clientele and provide it with the social benefits expected from a 'head', participation in committees, commissions, boards of examiners, etc., supposes a great expenditure in time, and therefore competes with the scientific work which is the (necessary) condition of the accumulation and the maintenance of the specifically scientific capital (itself always more or less contaminated by the statutory powers).[37] Success in this enterprise of accumulation also supposes a talent for good investment – the value of a clientele depending on the social status of the clients – and also skill and tact – in short, that social sense which is no doubt particularly linked to previous membership of the milieu and to the precocious acquisition of adequate information and dispositions. Thus it is that the enlightened director must be able to display tolerance and liberalism, which are in any case implied by the official definition of the institution, and sacrifice the political (or scientific) homogeneity of his clientele to their social status and their number (which, as J. Nettelbeck notes,[38] enabled left-wing candidates to be appointed to professorships, even in law).

This sort of contamination of specifically scientific authority by the statutory authority founded on the arbitrariness of the institution is a fundamental principle of the functioning of the faculties of law and medicine (and also, of course, the most socially important arts subjects). This can be seen primarily in the fact that the return on social capital, whether inherited or acquired through university interactions, increases the further we move from the pole of research, and consequently, as is attested by the fact that it contributes more and more to determining trajectories (and therefore to the tacit conditions of access to the dominant positions), the more it becomes an increasing part of the composition of that mixture of variable proportions of technical and social qualifications which comprises the statutory competence of the professor. We know that the existence of great dynasties of jurists and doctors, which presupposes much more than a simple professional inheritance linked to the effects of the transmission of cultural capital, is not a myth. But, in addition to that, the choice of an influential 'head' is never more decisive than in the medical careers, where the professor is, more obviously than anywhere else, a protector, entrusted with furthering the careers of his clients, before being a master, entrusted with fostering the academic or intellectual training of his pupils or disciples.[39]

What also becomes apparent from the social logic of the recruitment to this body is the nature of the best-hidden, and perhaps the most categorically required, entrance fee: nepotism is not only a strategy of reproduction destined to keep within the family the possession of a rare position; it is a way of preserving something more essential, which forms the basis of the very existence of the group, the primordial *illusio*[40] without which there would be no stakes to play for, nor even any game. The express and explicit consideration of family origins is only the declared form of the strategies of co-optation which rely on indices of support for the group's values and the value of the group (as in the 'conviction' or 'enthusiasm' encouraged by the boards of examiners), as well as on the imponderables of practice and even manners and behaviour, in order to determine those who are *worthy of admission to the group*, to become members of the group, to constitute the group. Indeed, the group only exists durably as such, that is to say as something transcending the set of its members, in so far as each of its members is so disposed as to exist through and for the group or, more accurately, in conformity with the principles which underpin its existence. The real fee for admission to the group, what is known as 'team spirit' (or, in its various instances, the 'legal', 'philosophical' or 'polytechnical' spirit, etc.), that is, the visceral form of recognition of everything which constitutes the existence of the group, its identity, its truth, and which the group must reproduce in order to reproduce itself, only appears indefinable because it is irreducible to the technical definitions of competence officially required for membership of the group. And, if social heredity plays such an important part in the reproduction of all those professional bodies which are implicated in the reproduction of the social order, it is because, as we see in the case of the crises which introduce a profound change in the social composition of the new entrants, what is unconditionally demanded by this kind of highly selective club is learnt less by educational apprenticeship than by previous and external experiences, and is inherent in the professional body, in the guise of durable dispositions which are constitutive of an ethos, of a corporeal *hexis*, of a style of expression and thought, and of all those 'indefinable somethings', pre-eminently physical, which we call 'spirit'.[41]

As I have shown elsewhere, using *agrégation* reports, co-optation techniques always aim to select 'the man', the whole person, the *habitus*. Here is evidence on the *agrégation* in law: 'There's no explicit syllabus: no marking scheme, nor even necessarily any marking; you have to judge the man, not add up marks. Each board of examiners may decide on its criteria and methods. Experience shows the wisdom of this "impressionism", safer and surer than the deceptive accuracy of figures.'[42] Use of co-optation, based on an overall intuition of the whole person, is never more mandatory than in the case of professors of medicine. It is indeed enough to think of the qualities required of the 'great surgeon' or the 'supremo' of a hospital department who must exercise, often with great urgency, an *art* which, like that of a military leader, implies total mastery of the conditions of its practical accomplishment, that is to say a combination of self-control and confidence able to inspire confidence and dedication in others. What the co-optation technique must discover and what the teaching must transmit or reinforce in this case is not knowledge, not a package of scientific knowledge, but skill or, more exactly, the art of applying knowledge, and applying it aptly in practice, which is inseparable from an overall manner of acting, or living, inseparable from a *habitus*. This is what we are told by the defenders of a purely clinical medical education and practice: 'It was a rather scholastic education . . .: we learnt things as a series of little problems. . . . For a major thing like typhoid fever, we worried relatively little about the purely biological problem. Of course, we knew that it was caused by Eberth's bacillus but, once we knew that, that was more or less enough. The medicine we studied was a medicine of symptoms helping us to make a diagnosis; it wasn't the physiopathological medicine the Americans like, which is an excellent thing, which needs doing. . . . But it is a great pity to sacrifice to this physiopathological medicine the clinical medicine which we were so good at, which helped us to diagnose, and which consequently was an essentially practical medicine.' The post of *externe* [junior hospital doctor][43] was the privileged mode of this 'in-service' training, learning from experience or object-lessons. That was the training ground for that great class of 'good average doctors' who 'had had practical experience with patients, and had been in contact with good supervisors', and who, without being 'absolutely first-rate, very bright doctors', like the elite of the *internes* [resident hospital doctors], 'did know their job'. Through being on emergency call, the *externes* could gain the experience 'of syndromes which require an urgent decision' and 'go through with the *interne* the elaboration of the elements of the diagnosis, the X-rays, the hesitations, etc., the meeting with the surgeon called in for advice . . . and this contact with them allowed real improvisation' (a clinical practitioner, 1982). The demonstration of skill displayed by the master had little in common with the didactic lesson given by the professor, since it required neither the same competence nor, above all, the same conception of knowledge. This entirely traditional, almost artisanal, apprenticeship, which proceeded pragmatically, demanded less a theoretical knowledge than an investment of the whole person in a relationship of trust in the head or the *interne*, and, through them, in the institution and the 'art of medicine' ('And afterwards, we took part in the operation, we helped the *interne* either as his first or his second assistant, and we were very satisfied').

The comparison thus brings to light differences which assign limits to the comparison. And, in fact, between the clinical practitioners and the mathematicians, or even between the jurists and the sociologists, lies all the distance that separates two different modes of production and reproduction of knowledge and, more generally, two systems of values and two lifestyles or, in other words, between two ways of envisaging the successful man. As a responsible and respectable member of the elite, committed to an inextricably dual technical and social role implying a whole set of administrative and political responsibilities, the professor of medicine owes his success to his social capital, to relations of birth or marriage, at least as much as to his cultural capital; and also to dispositions such as reliability, respect for his masters and respectability in his private life (illustrated notably by the social status of the spouse and by a large number of offspring), docility in the face of the hyper-scholastic routines necessary to prepare for the competitive examination for resident hospital doctors ('Learn everything by heart – intelligence can wait', according to one informant), or even rhetorical skill, which all guarantee support for primarily social values and virtues.[44]

The differential importance of professional heredity according to faculties and disciplines can be explained (apart from the direct effects of nepotism) if one sees in it a form of *seniority in the profession*, enabling agents born into the milieu to have a considerable advantage in the competition – other things, including age, being equal – because they possess to a higher degree certain properties explicitly or implicitly demanded of new entrants: firstly, the symbolic capital attached to a proper name and capable, just like a famous brand name in business, of guaranteeing a lasting relationship with a captive clientele; then, the specific cultural capital whose possession no doubt constitutes an advantage all the more powerful if the capital common to the field considered, whether faculty or discipline, is less *objectified*, less *formalized*, and if it is more completely reducible to the dispositions and the experience constitutive of an *art* which can only be acquired in the long term, and at first hand.[45] The fact that the social origins of professors and the age of appointment to professorships tend to become lower as we move from the faculties of medicine and law to the arts and above all to the science faculties (or the fact that the professors of economics and the medical researchers are younger and less often born into the milieu than the lawyers and the clinical practitioners) can no doubt be explained *in part* by the fact that the degree to which the procedures and processes of production and acquisition of knowledge are objectified in instruments, methods and techniques – instead of existing only in a personally internalized state – varies to the same degree: the outsiders, and notably those among them who lack inherited capital, have more chance and earlier opportunities in competing with the insiders, if the capacities and dispositions required place less emphasis, both for the production and for the reproduction of knowledge (in particular for the acquisition of productive capacities), on experience in all its forms and on intuitive knowledge arising from a long process of familiarization, and if these capacities and dispositions are more formalized, therefore more likely to be rationally, that is equitably, transmitted and acquired.[46]

But the opposition between the two *faculties*, between scientific competence and social competence, can also be found at the heart of each of the temporally dominant faculties (and even within the arts and social science faculties, which from this point of view occupy an intermediate position). Thus it is that the faculty of medicine alone duplicates, in a manner of speaking, the whole space of the faculties (and even the field of power):[47] although it is not possible to summarize all its aspects in a few sentences, the complex and multidimensional opposition between the clinical practitioners and the biologists in the medical faculties (moreover different enough in their social and educational origins from the biologists in the science faculties) can be described as the opposition between an *art*, guided by the 'experience' culled from the example of their elders, and acquired over a period of time through attention to individual cases, and a *science*, which is not satisfied with the external appearances which prompt diagnosis, but seeks to grasp the underlying causes.[48]

This opposition, which gives rise to two quite different concepts of medical practice, the first concentrating on the clinical relation between patient and doctor, the famous 'one-to-one consultation', basis of any defence of 'liberal' medicine, and the second, privileging laboratory tests and pure research. This is further complicated by the fact that the artistic and the scientific change their meaning and value according to whether they are made to play a leading or a subordinate role. The clinical practitioners would be satisfied with research directly orientated towards their requirements, and the imperatives of economic profitability have been invoked in order to confine or maintain the *'fondamentalistes'* (medical researchers) in the purely technical function of applied research, consisting essentially in putting into practice, at the request of the clinical practitioners, tried and tested methods of analysis, rather than setting themselves *long-term* problems to solve, which the clinical practitioners often find irrelevant and incomprehensible. As for the medical researchers, who used to be socially subordinate, those of them who are best placed to invoke the authority of science (that is to say the specialists in molecular biology, who are on the way up, rather than the anatomists, who are on the way down) tend more and more, in the name of the advances in therapy made possible by science, to claim their right to conduct a pure research totally liberated from the functions of a merely technical service, and, comforted by the prestige of their scientific discipline, become the defenders of a modern medicine, liberated from the routine which they detect behind the 'clinical' vision and the ideology of the 'one-to-one consultation'. In this struggle, the medical researchers seem to be on the side of the future, that is to say of science, and in fact the most prestigious among them, whom even the most fervent defenders of the traditional image of medicine place above the ordinary clinical practitioners, pose a threat to the previously perfectly unified and simply hierarchized representation of the professorial body.

The medical researchers present social and educational properties which place them between the science professors and the clinical professors. Thus, although they are very similar to the other categories of professors of medicine if we look at their fathers' generation (apart from a slightly larger proportion of sons of the petty bourgeoisie), they seem closer to the scientists if we look at their grandfathers' generation: the chances of belonging to a family whose place in the bourgeoisie, measured by the profession of the paternal grandfather, goes back at least two generations, are only 22 per cent for the medical researchers, as opposed to 42.5 per cent for the clinical practitioners, 54.5 per cent for the surgeons (and 39 per cent for the whole set of professors of medicine) and 20 per cent for the science professors. The medical researchers no doubt come from less established and wealthy families, and, unlike the clinical practitioners and the surgeons, they do not benefit from two separate sources of income, salary and private patients. They reside far less often in fashionable neighbourhoods, are far less often cited in *Who's Who* and the *Bottin mondain* – and it is remarkable that, like the scientists, they include a relatively large proportion of Jews. These social differences are sufficient, in a world which is socially very homogeneous and very concerned to retain its homogeneity, to form the basis of two socially distinct and antagonistic groups, as witness among other indices the fact that most of our informants, and no doubt the whole set of the professors, seem to overestimate these differences: 'It's the ones who are slightly mad who go in for research: it's the young men from poor backgrounds who choose research, instead of concentrating on what people call a good career' (interview with medical researcher, 1972). At all events, everything leads us to believe that these differences are translated into political oppositions, the medical researchers tending to be situated on the left while the clinical practitioners and above all the surgeons, whose specifically scientific prestige is low – although it fluctuates acording to public opinion at large, depending on the success of transplants, for instance – and who are the spearhead of all conservative movements, tend to be situated on the right (these two categories seem to have rallied massively to the 'non-aligned' trade union the Syndicat Autonome, created in May 1968 on the lines of those in the arts and science faculties, which holds all the positions of administrative power).

No doubt this opposition, although its constituent elements may differ according to the fields, constitutes an invariant in the field of cultural production, for which the religious field provides the paradigm, with its opposition between orthodoxy and heresy. Just as we shall see within the arts and social science faculties an opposition between the orthodoxy of the canonical professors who have travelled the royal road of competitive examinations, and the moderate heresy of the marginal or eccentric researchers and professors who often reach the winning-post by cross-country routes, so within the medical faculties we can distinguish between the defenders of a medical order inseparable from a social order and

based on the competitive examination and its sacred rites, which
guarantee the reproduction of the professional body, and the heretical
innovators, as for instance the instigators of the reform of medical
studies, who entered through the back door, that is, often, from
abroad (especially the United States), and who, since they lack the
social titles conferring access to the socially dominant positions, have
found in more or less prestigious marginal institutions, the Museum
of Natural History, the Science Faculty, the Pasteur Institute or the
Collège de France, the possibility of pursuing a research career with
more scientific than social success.[49] This sort of antinomy between
science and social respectability, between the deviant, precarious
career of the researcher and the more limited but safer trajectory of
the professor, can be related to differences objectively inherent in
their institutional positions, in their dependence on or independence
from the temporal powers, and also to differences in the dispositions
of the agents, more or less inclined towards or condemned to accept
conformity or innovation (simultaneously scientific and social),
submission or transgression, the management of established knowledge or the critical renovation of academic orthodoxy.

SCIENTIFIC COMPETENCE AND SOCIAL COMPETENCE

The reader will have recognized, in the different forms of opposition
between the faculties (or the disciplines) which are temporally
dominant, and the faculties (or disciplines) which are oriented more
towards scientific research, the distinction made by Kant between
two sorts of faculties: on the one hand, the three 'higher faculties'
(in temporal terms), that is the faculty of theology, the faculty of
law and the faculty of medicine, which, being able to provide the
government with 'the strongest and most durable influence on the
people', are the most directly controlled by the government, the
least autonomous from it at the same time as the most directly
entrusted with creating and controlling customary practice and the
ordinary exponents of knowledge, priests, judges, doctors; on the
other hand, the 'lower faculty', which, having no temporal power,
is abandoned to 'the scholar's own reason', that is to say, to its own
laws, whether of historical and empirical knowledge (history,
geography, grammar, etc.) or of pure, rational knowledge (pure
mathematics or pure philosophy). On the side of what constitutes

in Kant's terms 'as it were the right wing of the parliament of knowledge' is authority; on the left is the freedom to examine and to object.[50] The faculties which are dominant in the political order have the function of training executive agents able to put into practice without questioning or doubting, within the limits of a given social order, the techniques and recipes of a body of knowledge which they claim neither to produce nor to transform; on the contrary, the faculties which are dominant in the cultural order are destined to arrogate to themselves, in their need to establish a rational basis for the knowledge which the other faculties simply inculcate and apply, a freedom which is withheld from executive activities, however respectable these are in the temporal order of practice.

The competence of the doctor or jurist is a technical competence guaranteed by the law, which confers the authority and the authorization to use a more or less scientific knowledge: the subordination of the medical researchers to the clinical practitioners expresses this subordination of knowledge to social power, which lays down its functions and limits. And the operation effected by Kant's higher faculties is partly akin to social magic, which, as in initiation ceremonies, tends to consecrate a competence which is inextricably social and technical. The genealogy of the concept of clinical medicine established by Michel Foucault clearly reveals this dual dimension of medical competence, technical and social; it describes the progressive institution of social necessity which underpins the social importance of professors of medicine and distinguishes their art from all the technical skills which confer no particular social authority (like that of the engineer). Medicine is a practical science whose truth and success interest the whole nation, and clinical medicine 'figures as a structure essential to the scientific coherence but also the social rationale' of the medical order, 'as the point of contact where the art of healing is integrated into the social order' (as one past reformer said).[51] And we could show in the same logic that the very exercise of the clinical act implies a form of symbolic violence: clinical competence, a system of patterns of perception which are codified to varying degrees, and are more or less completely personified by the medical agents, cannot function practically, that is be adequately applied to the specific case – in an operation analogous to the act of jurisprudence for the judge – except by relying on indices provided by the patients, bodily indices (like swelling or red patches) and verbal indices (like information on the frequency, duration and localization of the visible bodily indices or on the frequency and duration of pain, etc.), which for the most part, have to be *solicited by clinical enquiry*. But this work of establishing symptoms which leads to a (true or false) diagnosis is accomplished, as Aaron Cicourel has shown, in a dissymmetrical social relation where the expert is able to impose his own cognitive presuppositions on the indices delivered by the patient, without having to worry about any discrepancy between the tacit assumptions of the patient and his own explicit or implicit assumptions about clinical signs which might generate misunderstandings and mistakes in diagnosis, and, thereby, without posing as such the (fundamental) problem of the *translation of the spontaneous clinical discourse* of the patient into the codified clinical discourse of the doctor (with, for instance, a 'red patch', shown or described, becoming an 'inflammation'). Another question which is pre-eminently repressed is that of the cognitive effects of the time spent acquiring information, the limitations of the cognitive repertory of the expert (the questions not asked) or limitations to his skill in deploying his knowledge, which may derive from lack of experience but also and above all from the haste or the presuppositions (reinforced by *leading questions*) generated by an emergency.

In a general fashion, the progression of academic disciplines within each faculty corresponds to the substitution of an academic necessity which is socially arbitrary for a social necessity which is academically arbitrary (and culturally arbitrary).[52] Although academic knowledge tends to gain social recognition, and thereby also social efficacity, both of which increase as scientific values become more generally recognized (especially as a result of technological change and the activities of the education system), it can only receive its social force from the outside, in the form of a delegated authority able to use socially grounded academic necessity to legitimate its 'arbitrary' social values. But this statutory authority is able to maintain the same circular relation of legitimation with an art like clinical practice, or with scholarly traditions such as theology, law or even the history of literature or of philosophy, whose fundamentally social necessity resides in the last analysis in the 'common opinion of scholars', itself rooted not only in a rational need for coherence and compatibility with facts, but in the social necessity of a system of objectively orchestrated dispositions and the more or less objectified and codified 'arbitrary' cultural values which express it. We know that the ideological constructions which artistic or political individuals or groups can produce, to give their 'choices' in the most diverse domains – political, aesthetic, ethical – the appearance of coherence, appear in fact as combinations of logically disparate elements which only cohere through the integrating force of common dispositions or positions; so that disciplines, like history or philosophy, art or literature, which grant autonomy to constructions that cannot contain intrinsically either their whole explanation or their whole *raison d'être*, or which, like aesthetics, ethics or the philosophy of law, tend to show as grounded in the coherence of reason things which in fact are based on belief or, in short, on the *orthodoxy* of a group, simply reproduce the specific effect of these constructions which resides precisely in the illusion of their purely rational genesis, free from any determination.[53]

The scope provided for everything contributing to the social cohesion of the group of scholars, and notably all the forms of co-optation (whose extreme form is nepotism) designed to ensure the durable homogeneity of the *habitus*, tends to increase as we move from physicists or mathematicians to clinical practitioners or jurists. This is no doubt to some extent because the need to ground in the social unity of the group the intellectual unity of the *communis doctorum opinio* is all the more pressing when their specifically academic coherence is more uncertain and when the *social responsibility* of the body is greater.[54] As we can see particularly well in the case of the jurists, a body of 'authorities' cannot present itself in a state of disarray, as intellectuals may, without compromising its capital of authority, and, just as it must erase from its 'written judgement' the contradictions which are the visible traces of the conflicts that gave rise to it and the questions which might allow its true functions to be discovered, it must make a pre-emptive dismissal of all those who could threaten the order of the body of the guardians of order.

We should examine at this stage the tacit contracts of delegation which form the basis of the authority of the different faculties, hedging their liberties round with limits which are all the stricter as the social responsibility accorded to them is greater. We should also analyse the ways in which the privileged users of the institutions of higher education – that is to say the members of the dominant class – represent the functions of these institutions. As is clearly shown by an analysis of the answers to the national consultation on education in 1969, the propensity to privilege the social functions of the university over its specifically academic functions, to grant priority for instance to 'training the nation's administrators' rather than to advancing the frontiers of knowledge, increases when we move from the members of the subordinate fractions (intellectuals, etc.) to the members of the dominant fractions (executives, etc.); and it is the same when we move from the professors of the science faculties to the professors of the legal and medical faculties. Thus it is that the degree of *coincidence* of the functions which the professors assign to their pedagogical action with the functions attributed to it by the privileged receivers of this action tends to increase proportionally (and so thereby does the improbability of any sort of secession through which the professors might finally exploit their relative autonomy in order to satisfy their own interests). The suspicion that the dominant fractions always feel, and sometimes show, above all in the period after 1968, towards the faculties, as places of the 'corruption of youth', is above all addressed to the faculties of arts and social sciences and, secondarily, to the science faculties, much less 'safe' than the *grandes écoles*, in the words of one company director in an interview, because of the effects of 'contamination'. It is as if they were ready to break the contract of delegation if ever the possibility arose that fulfilling the technical functions of technical training might threaten or compromise the fulfilment of social functions.

In the light of these analyses, it is easier to understand the true significance of the political differences between the faculties which we are able to establish on the basis of information published or obtained directly from a proportion (varying greatly according to the faculty) of the professors. Although they are most often unfamiliar with politics and in any case little inclined to make public declarations on such matters, the professors of science (even if they are often not union members) seem to lean slightly to the left. Despite their popular image, the professors of the arts and social science faculties are no doubt overall less left-wing than the science professors, that is to say they are more often on the centre-right or on the right than on the left – despite the fact that, where public declarations are concerned (as in petitions, or declarations in favour of candidates for election), the left-wing minority is much more strongly represented, therefore much more visible (*a fortiori* if we refer to the whole teaching body, including lecturers and assistant lecturers), which is understandable if we know that the social impetus to make a public declaration of political position is all the stronger, in this state of the history of the intellectual field, the nearer one is to the 'intellectual' pole of the university field, that is, the nearer to the left. While they are often enough inclined to political indifference, like all those who take the social order for granted, and are rarely attracted to the eccentricity of public demonstrations, the professors of medicine, apart from the medical researchers, are nearly all situated at the centre or on the right. As for the professors of law, who invest more strongly in politics than the professors of medicine, but who are no doubt less massively concentrated on the right, they are more inclined to take up a public position on political problems, especially perhaps when they belong to the left-wing minority.[55]

This analysis implies and introduces a reflection on what we should understand by the political opinion of an agent and on the conditions of grasping and measuring it, that is to say on the relation between a political opinion which we might call private (as expressed between friends or in the privacy of the voting booth) and a public political opinion. We know, and we have been able to confirm it by questioning our respondents' students or colleagues on the political opinions of any particular group of professors, that opinions on the political opinions of others vary, within certain limits, as a function of the political opinions of those 'judging' them (therefore of the systems of explicit or implicit criteria which are used to distribute agents between right and left, which criteria the right and the left also disagree about), but also according to a definition, most often implicit, of what constitutes 'true', 'authentic' political opinion, that is, in what circumstances such an opinion 'really' reveals itself.[56] In fact, if we admit that political opinion is opinion displayed in the form of a manifest expression (according to Plato's dictum: 'I call belief a statement' [*Thaetetus*, 190a]), we see that public opinion as such will be defined in the relation between ethical dispositions or specifically political inclinations and the market where the opinion expressed is on offer. We nearly always forget the variations resulting from the market effect (of which the enquiry effect, variable according to the social characteristics of the enquiry, is an aspect), and especially, for any determined group, the gap between the tendencies which appear in private opinions, uttered in confidence among friends or, in the relation of the enquiry, under cover of anonymity and adulterated by various forms of euphemism ('centre' being put for 'right', for instance), and those tendencies which appear in opinions publicly professed, in demos and manifestos, and which are liable to impose themselves as the normality or the norm of a group, as modal or modish opinion, to which one feels bound to conform, even in silence and in secret. Paying attention to this gap is essential if we are to avoid interpreting as sudden retractions or abrupt conversions those public expressions of opinion which, like taking sides in times of crisis, in the context of a general increase in the tendency to publicize opinion, are partly attributable to market effects.[57]

The analysis of a random sample of members of the Syndicat National de l'Enseignement Supérieur [National Union of Higher Education] in 1969 establishes that, for professors of science, arts, medicine and law respectively, the rates of membership are 15, 30, 6 (nearly all from the medical researchers) and 1 per cent. The rates of participation in the 'non-aligned' Syndicat Autonome, more right-wing, no doubt vary in the opposite direction.[58] (In May 1983, the teachers affiliated to the SNESup were distributed thus among the different faculties: law 1.2 per cent, medicine 3 per cent and pharmacy 1.2 per cent; arts 26.1 per cent, of which 1.9 from sociology, 1.1 from education, 1.3 from psychology, 1.9 from philosophy, 4.8 from literature, 2.7 from history, 2.5 from geography, 1.6 from linguistics, 7.8 from languages; science had 56.3 per cent, of which 16 from mathematics, 16.4 from physics, 1.6 from geology, 7.1 from chemistry, 15.2 from biology and 1 from mechanical and civil engineering). Our analysis of the results of the AEERS[59] national consultation in 1969 even enables us to suggest, despite the limits inherent in any random sample, that the opinions on the education system publicly expressed by the professors of the different faculties, whether for example on the introduction of trade-union or political liberty into the university system or on the mode of recruitment of professors, are also strictly homologous to the positions of their faculty within the system of the institutions of higher education (it being understood that opinions on the university system and its transformations are never determined directly by social origins and define themselves in the relation between a disposition and a position: thus it is that the 'lucky survivors' who owe everything to the system are, all things being otherwise equal, among the most unconditional defenders of the system and its hierarchies).

The opposition established by Kant between the two categories of faculties, the first subject to the temporal order which they serve, the second free of all social discipline and limitations, finds its culmination, and reaches its limits, in the relation between the juridical disciplines and the social sciences which, in allowing the liberty or even the irresponsibility characteristic of the temporally lower faculties into the private terrain of the higher faculties, have gradually come to challenge their monopoly of legitimate thought and discourse on the social world: on the one hand we have knowledge in the service of order and power, aiming at the rationalization, in both senses, of the given order; on the other hand we have knowledge confronting order and power, aiming not at putting public affairs in order but at analysing them as they are, at analysing the nature of social order and the state, by reducing the established order and the state, through historical comparison or speculative transposition, to the status of merely a special case in the gamut of realized or realizable possibilites.[60] This is an operation less andoyne than it might seem, since it supposes a withholding of ordinary support for the status quo, which, for the guardians of order, is already a critical break, or even evidence of irresponsibility.

Note on the factor analysis of correspondences[61]

The basis of the method is the table of deviations (in the case of a two-by-two table) between the result observed and the result which would be obtained in the hypothetical case of random distribution, where all the statistical units behaved according to the general average, the rows and columns of the table being reciprocally proportional. The analysis of correspondences represents these deviations visually in factorial planes which weight them according to their distance from χ^2 (chi-square): positive deviations (where the results observed are more frequent than the results expected), negative deviations (where they are less frequent) or zero deviations (where they are equal). This weighting enables us to detect strong links between phenomena which are relatively infrequent but not negligible.

The analysis is applied here not to a contingency table showing interrelated responses to two different questions, but to the associations between categories of responses to the various questions of an enquiry. Each statistical unit does or does not possess a certain number of attributes (coded as presence/absence 0–1), and we take into consideration both the deviations between individuals and those between variables: a positive deviation from the randomized positions of two individuals signifies that they often present the same characteristics or absence of characteristics; conversely, two attributes will be positively associated when they are the simultaneous property of more than one individual. The characteristic of a negative deviation from their randomized positions in the case of individuals will be a certain regularity observed when the presence of characteristics for one individual corresponds to their absence in another. This logic is transposable to the space of the response categories. The situation of random distribution is then defined by the lack of such regularities. The associations of characteristics and/or of individuals form in the factorial planes a system of relations where the redundancy of the categories of analysis (frequent in sociology, where we often use indicators which are highly correlated with each other, such as the profession and qualifications of the father, of the mother, of the grandfather, of the grandmother and of the spouse) does not entail any fatal statistical error.

The associations of attributes are distributed in the domain of the factorial planes according to the following rules:

1 A positive deviation from random distribution (in other words, an attraction between two categories) is represented in spatial terms as a conjunction between characteristics. For instance, in graph 2 (p. 80), we note the conjunction of the points 'preparatory class in *lycée* Henri IV', 'ENS board of examiners', '*agrégation* board of examiners', etc. This conjunction or attraction between two attributes is all the stronger as the angle (that is, the angle formed by the two points whose apex is situated at the origin of the graph) is more acute, and as the points are further away from the centre. As a result, the connection between the points 'director of research team', 'no preparatory class' and 'contemporary history' will be weaker than the previously mentioned connection.

2 A negative deviation, or repulsion, between two response categories is translated as a spatial opposition: as, for example, the attributes 'father professor in higher education' and 'EPHE 6th section'. The discrepancy between the values expected and the values observed between two categories is all the stronger as the angle is more obtuse and as the points are further from the centre.

3 Finally, a situation of random distribution between two categories is translated as a square, or right angle.

The points situated in the centre of the graph have no strongly positive or negative associations with the pertinent elements of the plane. Thus, in the case of matrimonial status, 'married' is represented by a point situated at the centre of the graph and is not a distinguishing sign for any of the groups.

The analysis of correspondences is presented as a succession of factorial planes (cf. graph 2, p. 80, axes 2 and 3, and graph 3, p. 82, axes 1 and 3). There is a simple correspondence between each axis and a table of approximation. The first of these tables, and therefore the first of these axes, is the 'best possible approximation' of the table of deviations. The second table is the 'best correction' made to this first approximation. In sociological terms, this means that the structure of the strongest deviations is better accounted for by the first two axes. The later axes account for other, weaker effects. The last factors only account for those irregularities which are virtually uninterpretable.

The plane described by axes 1 and 2 structures the data according to two principles which we can resume as follows (cf. our interpretation on pp. 75–84): on the one hand, along the first axis, there is the opposition between specifically academic power and the other forms of power, and on the other hand, along the second axis, there is the opposition between the prestigious professors and the younger professors, who lack institutional distinctions. The third axis modulates this play of oppositions by distinguishing between the more obscure specialists and those from the 'main establishment'. We should note that in the plane formed by axes 1 and 3 the distinctions ('Legion of Honour', 'honorary doctorate') are now situated in the centre of the graph; they no longer have any function in the play of oppositions expressed.

This hierarchy of the factorial axes enables us to represent visually in the first planes the strongest oppositions and attractions contained in our data. This method indicates the importance of the information used in each plane.

Apart from the structure of the relations, the analysis of correspondences evaluates the importance of the contributions of the characteristics, and/or of the individuals, to the formation of an axis (that is, to the constitution of the system of attractions and oppositions of the graph). The identification of these important points enables us to decipher rapidly the essential features of the contrasts, and where appropriate designate an axis: thus on pp. 48–51 an interpretation of axis 1 of graph 1 is suggested through the opposition established between the whole set of the attributes associated with the temporally dominant pole of the university field (grouped on the right) and those which are associated with the subordinate pole. These designations must be treated with care, since they are only the theoretical shorthand of a graphical system. (This would tend to argue against the use of a different factorial analysis: the search to reveal a hidden factor like intelligence, for instance.)

To reconstitute the variables and interpret the response categories in relation to each other is another technique which would help interpretation. If the variables are quantitative, or at least ordinal (age, number of translations), the order of the response categories can be respected in an axis (age in the second axis) or in a plane (axes 1 and 2, for the number of translations). This technique can be applied to the qualitative variables. Thus the reconstitution of the 'father's profession' is easy to read: in the first axis, the professorial body is opposed to the other professions, while the second axis orders them according to a more classic social hierarchy.

3

Types of Capital and Forms of Power

Whatever you do, you must not stop trying for the Academy;
it so happens that a fortnight tomorrow I am dining with Leroy-
Beaulieu, without whom no election can be arranged, and I am
going with him afterwards to an important meeting; I had
already mentioned your name in his presence, but, naturally
enough, he already knew perfectly well who you were. He did
raise one or two objections. But in the event he needs the support
of my group for the forthcoming election, and I intend to return
to the attack; I will tell him quite openly of our connection, I
will not hide from him the fact that, if you stand for election,
I shall ask all my friends to vote for you ... and he knows
that I do have friends. I calculate that, if I manage to obtain
his support, your chances would be quite considerable.

M. Proust, À la recherche du temps perdu

Because of their position in the space of the faculties, between the
'society' pole represented by the faculties of law and medicine, and
the 'scientific' pole represented by the faculties of science, the arts
faculties (in 1967) are no doubt a privileged vantage-point for
observing the struggle between the two kinds of university power
which, at the two poles of the field, tend to impose themselves more
or less uncontested: in the case of medicine, as in that of law, the
predominance of academic power, founded on the accumulation of
positions allowing the control of other positions and their holders,
is so accentuated that the pure researchers, that is, the medical
researchers, appear somewhat 'out of place' and are rejected into
another order, that of the science faculties, where they are moreover
less recognized, apart from the odd exception, than the pure scientists;

in the case of the science faculties, on the contrary, scientific prestige, founded on successful investment in the activity of research alone, tends to make the subordinate power exercised in the very place of non-power by the vice-chancellors, deans or other academic administrators look like a compensatory substitute (although one can always find a few contrary cases of administrators with scientific reputations).

The characteristic of the arts and social science faculties lies in the fact that the relations between their different principles of hierarchization are more balanced. Indeed, on the one hand these faculties participate in the scientific field, and therefore in the logic of research, and the intellectual field[1] – with the consequence that intellectual renown constitutes the only kind of capital and profit which is specifically their own; on the other hand, as institutions entrusted with the transmission of legitimate culture and invested because of this with a social function of consecration and conservation, they are places of specifically social powers, which have as much right as those of the professors of law and medicine to contribute to the most basic structures of the social order. In short, the arts and social science faculties are divided up according to the same principle which divides up the space of the faculties as a whole: the opposition between the agents and institutions which are orientated mostly towards research and scholarly goals or the intellectual field and specifically cultural goals, and those which are orientated more towards the reproduction of the cultural order and the body of reproducers, and towards the interests associated with the exercise of a temporal power within the cultural order. This opposition is thus homologous to that which is established at the heart of the university field as a whole between the faculties dominant within the cultural order and the faculties dominant within the strictly temporal order.

We could thus observe and describe, at this more restricted level, the relations between the structure of the space of the positions constitutive of the field, and the struggles aiming to maintain or to subvert this structure, that is to say between the 'objective' classification, constructed by taking as criterion all of the properties mobilized within the field, and the struggle for classification, which aims to conserve or transform this classification by conserving or transforming the hierarchy of the criteria of classification.[2]

Since we admit that, because of the strongly hierarchical and centralized organization of French universities, the most 'powerful' professors of arts and social sciences are likely with only a few exceptions to belong to the Paris faculties, we have chosen as initial population for the enquiry into power the whole set of tenured professors in the major Paris institutions of higher education in 1967, the Collège de France (except for the scientists), the Sorbonne, the faculty of Nanterre, the Ecole Pratique des Hautes Etudes (4th, 5th and 6th sections), the Ecole des Arts et Métiers [School of Applied Arts], the Ecole des Langues Orientales and the Ecole des Chartes [School of Palaeography] (which would tend to exclude 'freelance' or non-university intellectuals – Lacan, for example). Institutions like the Museum of Natural History, the Observatory, the Bureau of Longitudes, the INRA and the Palace of Discovery are excluded because of the fact that they have no tenured professors in the arts or social sciences. At the Ecole des Chartes (which has a very small professorial body) and at the School of Oriental Languages, only one professor (who actually taught at the Ecole Pratique des Hautes Etudes) possessed the necessary properties (whose definition may be found below). The faculty of Nanterre, which had a very strong proportion of senior lecturers, has a very weak representation. To codify the principal membership of those professors attached to more than one of the institutions chosen for the basic population, we adopted the conventional social hierarchy, assigning for example to the Collège de France or to the Sorbonne those who belong both to either the Collège de France or the Sorbonne and to the Ecole des Hautes Etudes – this operation implying, undeniably, an expression of opinion on the hierarchy which is itself one of our subjects of debate. It follows that the Ecole des Hautes Etudes is reduced to those who teach only there, which does not do justice to one of the rarest properties of the institution, as much in the 4th section, specializing in religious studies, as in the 5th section, with its philological and historical studies, and its close links with both the Sorbonne and the Collège de France, or in the 6th section, which, as a result of institutional loyalty, investment in research and also its privileged relations with journalism and publishing, manages to produce symbolic effects and practices irreducible to those of its professorial body proper.

Within the base population of the tenured holders of at least one post in the Paris university institutes in 1967, we chose the whole set of the professors defined by at least one of the following properties, chosen because efficient for varying reasons and to varying degrees in the field: membership of the Institute, of the *agrégation* board of examiners, of the Universities Consultative Committee (academic power), of the CNRS committee of 1963 and 1967 (scientific power), of an editorial committee, of an intellectual review – or the editorship of a publisher's series (intellectual renown) – or a score of more than five references in the *Citation Index* (academic prestige).[3] This mode of selection, founded on objective indicators of the possession of powers that are different in their strength, their mode of exercise and their effects (including the most objectified of the indices of symbolic capital such as scientific prizes or presence in the *Citation Index*), seems infinitely safer than all forms of the 'reputational' method, the worst of which is no doubt *snowball* sampling, which is often employed in this kind of research; indeed, apart from the fact that the choice of the initial core predetermines subsequent choices, and therefore the final population, it privileges one form of power over others, the one that is based on the fact of being known and recognized.

The method of selection used to construct the population studies was designed to produce a small-scale but correctly proportioned model of the university field as a space of positions perceived through the properties of the agents who hold its attributes or attributions and who struggle, with arms and powers capable of producing visible effects, to take or defend them, to preserve them unchanged or to transform them. In contrast to random sampling, which would dissolve the structures (especially since a structurally determining position can be represented by a very small number of people, and sometimes, as is often the case in the fields of cultural production, by a single person), this mode of selection enables us to characterize the positions of power through the properties and the powers of their holders. The fact that, to construct the ensemble of the relations constitutive of this space, we are obliged to resort to information attached to individuals in no way implies that we adopt an implicit or explicit theory of power as a substance personally possessed by certain individuals that the enquiry has set out to identify (*Who governs?*) or even to show up or censure (the 'heads' or the 'mandarins'). Indeed, since the various kinds of specific power attached to the various positions are weakly institutionalized, they are difficult to dissociate from the holders of the positions considered. Unless we are to limit ourselves to purely theoretical propositions, we can only give a scientific representation of the structure of objective relations, which is the source of all the powers ordinarily perceived and experienced as substances or essences attached to things or people, if we base our study on an analysis of the distribution of all the pertinent properties which are attached to individuals; that is, those properties effective in a given operational space: the sum of each of the attributes of the members of an institution (for instance, the total number of graduates of the Ecole Normale Supérieure or of members of the Institute) defines the *social weight of the institution* which, in its turn, characterizes each of its members generically and specifically – because the more their position in the institution depends on the possession or non-possession of a property, the more that property helps characterize the position of the institution.[4]

It goes without saying that the composition of the constructed population depends on the criteria – that is, on the powers – which we have chosen: the omission of an index of intellectual renown such as membership of the editorial committee of an intellectual review or the editorship of a publisher's series would have eliminated the most intellectual fraction of academics – and often those most famous because of this; likewise, the introduction of a criterion like the fact of writing for *Le Nouvel Observateur*, which would no doubt be violently rejected by the holders of the most typical attributes of university power, would have introduced some of those journalist-academics who, despite the contempt in which the more academically successful affect to hold them, are invested with the power of celebration and criticism afforded by privileged access to the daily and weekly press and are thereby able to exercise quite real effects within the field itself.[5] If, at all events, it appears proven that we have introduced, within the limits of available information, all the relevant criteria, that is those able to determine differences significant in view of the goal pursued and to show up the distribution of powers constitutive of the structure of the university field at the moment considered, it remains the case that research discovers and reproduces uncertainties which are inherent in reality itself:[6] struggles for the imposition of the principle of legitimate hierarchization do in fact cause the dividing-line between those who belong and those who do not to be constantly discussed and disputed, therefore shifting and fluctuating, at every moment and above all according to the moment.[7] Thus it is that, through an effect of the logic of individual careers (and especially of age) or transformations in the field (and especially its relations with journalism), a person who, a few years earlier, would have held a dominant position can be found absent (which is the case notably of Pierre Renouvin, who disappears from the space when he abandons his positions of university power in 1964) or relegated to the lower edges of the space (like Ernest Labrousse, who, after abdicating his positions of academic power, finds himself reduced to his scientific prestige),[8] while conversely another who has not been chosen because he had none of the determining properties would have been chosen a few years later.[9]

THE STRUCTURE OF THE SPACE OF THE POWERS

We see immediately that the population thus constituted is distinguished from the whole set of the tenured professors of the Paris establishments of higher education in the arts, from within which it has been selected via systematic differences, the different categories of professors having rates of representation that much higher as they hold positions placed higher in the field: the Collège de France and the Sorbonne are much more strongly represented, whereas the share of the Ecole Pratique des Hautes Etudes and above all of Nanterre is much smaller than in the source population; likewise for the disciplines – classical literature and philology, modern history and social science, and, to a lesser degree, philosophy, are overrepresented, contrary to modern literature and languages, and geography. The chances of acceding to the different forms of power – here amalgamated – are closely linked to age. They also vary with the different indices of inherited cultural and social capital; with social origins, the proportion of sons of farm workers, industrial workers and office workers being smaller in the population of the 'powerful', whereas the proportion of sons of primary teachers, craftsmen and tradesmen and above all the sons of businessmen is much greater; or with academic capital, measured in terms of graduation from the Ecole Normale Supérieure and the age of passing the *agrégation*. The relations would no doubt be clearer if we could distinguish between the two major categories of power; indeed, the overrepresentation of professors of the Sorbonne, like that of literature and philology or philosophy, or of sons of primary or secondary teachers, increases as we move towards the professors whose profile is weighted towards the side of specifically academic power; the title of *normalien* being, it would seem, the universal standard which provides access, in association with different dispositions, to both forms of power.[10]

The field of arts and social science is organized around a principal opposition between two kinds of power. Specifically academic power is founded principally on control of the instruments of reproduction of the professorial body – the board of examiners for the *agrégation*, the Universities Consultative Committee (which appoints tenured professors) – that is, on the possession of a capital acquired within the university, particularly at the Ecole Normale, and held principally by professors at the university – the Sorbonne – especially in the canonical disciplines. These professors are most often themselves children of teachers in secondary or higher education, but above all of teachers in primary education. This kind of power prevails almost exclusively throughout the (French) university system. To this socially codified power is opposed a collection of powers of different kinds, encountered especially among the social science specialists: the scientific power or authority displayed through the direction of a research team, scientific prestige measured through the recognition accorded by the scientific field, above all abroad (through citations and translations), intellectual renown, more or less institutionalized, with membership of the Académie Française and mention in the *Larousse*, publication in a paperback series (Gallimard's 'Idées' or Seuil's 'Points') conferring a kind of classic status, membership of the editorial committee of intellectual reviews, and finally connections with the popular media, television and widely read weeklies (*Le Nouvel Observateur*), which is the index both of a power of consecration and criticism and of a symbolic capital of renown.[11]

The second principle of division opposes on the one hand the older professors, and those best provided with strictly academic titles of consecration, such as membership of the Institute (and, secondarily, of the Académie Française), or scientific titles, such as citations or translations, or purely social titles, such as an entry in *Who's Who*, the Legion of Honour or the Order of Merit, and on the other hand younger professors, who are defined above all negatively, by their lack of institutionalized signs of prestige and by the possession of inferior forms of academic power. This opposition is also operative between university institutions, with the Collège de France on one side – and in particular the specialists in classical disciplines, notably ancient history and archaeology – and on the other the Ecole des Hautes Etudes and the faculty of Nanterre. Similarly the opposition is operative between professors, some endowed with greater scientific power – through membership of the committees of the CNRS – others either orientated towards academic reproduction – through membership of the *agrégation* board of examiners – or possessing a certain renown but bereft of academic power. The opposition corresponds to systematic differences in inherited capital: the degree of social success in all its forms tends to increase with social proximity to the Parisian bourgeoisie; sons of businessmen, engineers or officers on one side, and, on the other, sons of faculty professors, often born in Paris or in the large provincial cities, and to a considerable degree education in private schools, are clearly opposed to the sons of small farmers, workmen or office employees, often born in small provincial towns, the median area being held by professors from intermediate regions of the geographical and social space.[12]

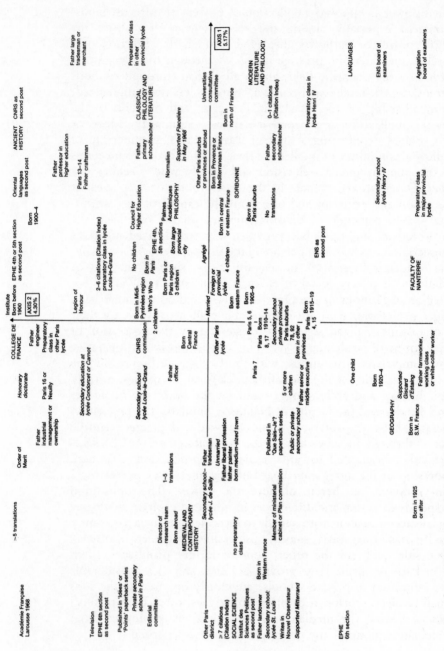

Graph 2 The space of the arts and social science faculties: analysis of correspondences: plane of the first and second axes of inertia – properties

Note The corresponding plane for individuals has been placed in appendix 4. The illustrative variables

As for the third factor, it opposes the main university *Establishment*, formed by 'eminent academics' and 'major heads' mostly installed at the Sorbonne, who dominate a whole discipline and who often combine the control of internal reproduction (teaching at the Ecole Normale, membership of the *agrégation* board, of the Universities Consultative Committee, of the ENS entrance examination board) with strong external recognition (television, publication in Gallimard's 'Idées' paperback series, translations), to the negative set of the obscure, who are often specialists in very circumscribed subjects (notably in ancient history) and alien as much to society fame as to internal power (that is, scholars from the Collège de France as well as specialists in marginal subjects within the university, economists, social psychologists, who seem alien to the 'milieu' as much in their university career – they are less often *normaliens* – as in their social origins – they are more often sons of tradesmen and born abroad) (cf. p. 82).

The space defined by the first two axes is organized into regions corresponding to classes of positions and dispositions which are opposed in very different ways: the region of academic power in its (almost) pure form (east south-east in figure 2) unites the ordinary professors of the most ordinary subjects (with, at the very bottom of the hierarchy, all the modern variants of the classic disciplines, modern languages, modern literature and philology) and especially a number of professors known for the violence of their reactions to the May 1968 movement, or for their public support for one of the major targets of student protest, Robert Flacelière, director of the Ecole Normale Supérieure. It is opposed as much in the (north-east) sector of strictly internal prestige, consecrated by the Institute, where we find above all the great scholars, as it is in the (west south-west) sector of external renown and of young or minor masters, above all sheltered by the 6th section of the Ecole des Hautes Etudes; and it has almost nothing in common with the upper (northern) spheres of great scientific prestige (Dumézil, Benveniste, Dupont-Sommer) which, in the case of specialists in social science and history (north-west), are associated with intellectual prestige (Lévi-Strauss, Aron, Perroux, Braudel or Duby) (cf. Appendix 4, p. 276).

It is obviously a study of the works themselves, and of their themes and their styles that would most plainly reveal the gap which separates the great scholars from the ordinary professors. The place of publication, although it has not been chosen for the final analysis because it would characterize too limited a proportion of the population, no doubt constitutes a good indicator of this opposition: on the one hand,

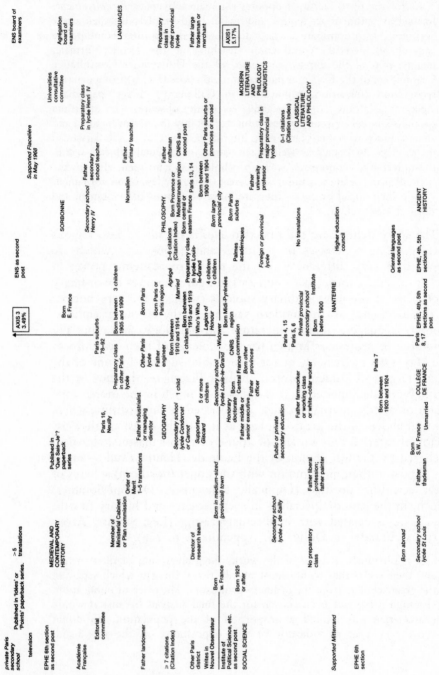

Graph 3 The space of the arts and social science faculties: analysis of correspondences: plane of the first and third axes of inertia – properties *Note* The illustrative variables are in italics.

Klincksieck, a long-established publisher founded in the nineteenth century by German booksellers, with its concentration of scholars and works of highly specialized, very high-powered scholarship; on the other hand, Les Belles Lettres, a publisher founded at the beginning of the twentieth century, born of the reaction of the French university to Germanic influence, which attracts work concerned more with traditional French elegance than with erudition. To give a reasonably non-tendentious idea of the culture prescribed by official teaching, we might evoke in their own idiom these works which 'skilfully resolve problems and convey essentials in a limpid, attractive form', these grammarians who are suspicious of the 'terminological extremes of modern linguistics' and who 'are a little wary of the cumbersome academic apparatus' of the new, imported fields of study, these commentators who aim only at 'a better understanding of the text and thus to increase literary pleasure', these professors who feel profoundly nonconformist because their lectures are a 'firework-display of cleverness and wit' (all the passages quoted are taken from obituary notices).

The privilege accorded to specialists in social science as opposed to scholars is due no doubt to the importance of the *Citation Index*, which contributes very strongly to the determination of the first factor and which privileges the different subjects and the different researchers all the more, the more they are orientated towards social science and the American tradition. The importance of the link with the mass media (journalism, television) can be seen in the fact that nine of the thirty people cited in the hit parade of the magazine *Lire* (April 1981) are to be found in the sectors both of academic and of intellectual prestige.

Although they are temporally – and temporarily – dominant, the holders of the positions of power most strictly founded on the institution and limited to the institution, such as boards of examiners for higher competitive examinations or the Universities Consultative Committee, are subordinate from the viewpoint of strictly academic acclaim and especially from the viewpoint of intellectual renown (they are virtually never translated); crowned with scholastic glory (they have often been prizewinners in the *concours général*, or placed first in the entrance examination for the Ecole Normale or the *agrégation*), they are the ultimate product of the dialectic of acclaim and recognition which drew into the heart of the system those most inclined and able to reproduce it without distortion. In general terms, they are all the more determinedly attached to the institution, the more heavily dependent is their particular competence on the institutional conditions of its exercise – as in the case of philology or language teaching in general – and the more they owe to the institution, as is the case with the 'oblates' of humble origins, or those born into the school milieu (as sons of primary teachers).[14]

THE ORDINARY PROFESSORS AND THE REPRODUCTION OF THE CORPS

Academic capital is obtained and maintained by holding a position enabling domination of other positions and their holders, such as all the institutions entrusted with controlling access to the corps – boards of examiners for the entrance exam to the Ecole Normale Supérieure, for the *agrégation* or the doctorate, the Universities Consultative Committee: this power over the agencies of reproduction of the university body ensures for its holders a statutory authority, a kind of function-related attribute which is much more linked to hierarchical position than to any extraordinary properties of the work or the person, and which acts not only on the constantly renewed audience of students but also on the clientele of the doctoral candidates, from whom the assistant lecturers are usually appointed, and who are placed in a relation of wide-ranging and prolonged dependency.[15]

We may take from an interview with a group of informants this portrait of the ideal-typical incarnation of such a power of reproduction which, in this extreme case, is almost entirely independent of the scientific value of the work produced. 'X is a graduate of the School of Athens, but who did not keep up his archaeology for long. He preferred to move into the history of literature, with a penchant for the popular. But he is on all the university councils, on the Consultative Committee, on the CNRS, everywhere that decisions are taken. He was elected to the CNRS again last year with an amazing number of votes. . . . He has no intellectual prestige, yet he has power. . . . He's well known, even if what he produces is feeble – he's the Barbara Cartland of Greek studies in France. . . . He wrote a literary history of Greece. It's a popular work, made up of literary passages, padded out with trendy remarks. X aims at the ordinary reading public. It's not a work on Greek literature, but, as its title suggests, a literary history of Greece. That says it all. . . . What's happened to X makes you stop and think. Nobody ever thought he was any good. How could someone so useless get so near to the top? His book is the most pathetic in the whole Erasmus series. It has absolutely nothing to say. He got into the Ecole Normale at his first shot. He was placed first in the *agrég*. That must have helped in those days. He's published a lot. He works quickly, because he hardly ever stops to take thought. He makes up his mind without bothering with any complexities' (interview, classics department, 1971). No doubt this is an extreme case. But its characteristics can be found elsewhere: 'Y has kept his intellectual prestige but it's a special kind. The fact that he doesn't do research – mind you, we do challenge him on this, people do quite often now, but only over the last seven or eight years.... I remember saying it in 1963: my colleagues hit the roof! "What do you mean! Don't you call his geographical abstracts research?" I said, no, that's not research. It's a synthesis.... He's a synthesizer, a popularizer, a teacher really' (interview with a group of geographers, 1971). 'I think that you shouldn't overestimate prestige. Considerations of intellectual merit are much less important (in geography) than academic power as such. Just think of Z, whose thesis was considered by most people to be a bad thesis: he's someone who has much more power in the university than he would have had if it had been based on intellectual merit.... There are more and more organizations; what counts more and more is access to money, to projects, to work funded by the government, etc., and then it isn't automatically someone's intellectual level which counts' (geographer, 1971).

The extent of the semi-institutionalized power which each agent can exercise in each of the positions of power he holds, his 'weight', so to speak, depends on all the attributes of power which he otherwise holds (this is no doubt what is invoked, in this case as in others, by the use of terms of address such as 'President' or 'Dean') and on all the possibilities of exchange which he can derive from his different positions. In other words, each agent imports into each of the secondary institutions the weight which he wields institutionally, but also personally (for example, as a university president or as an elector to that office) as a member of the highest institution to which he belongs and to which, in a hierarchical universe based on competition, the members of the institutions of lower rank that he frequents aspire by definition. Thus we can explain the fact that the members of the Institute, who are divided more or less equally between the two poles of the university field – the 'academic' and the 'scholarly' or 'intellectual' – can exercise on the whole field, and especially on the former, that is the institutional, sector, an immense power of control and censorship. Here too, capital breeds capital, and holding positions conferring social influence determines and justifies holding new positions, themselves invested with all the weight of their combined holders.[16]

That is what enables us to say of all the great university monarchs what Jean-Baptiste Duroselle wrote of Pierre Renouvin: 'We felt that he moved into the key positions as if by some natural necessity, without having intrigued or postulated. We always turned to him in the end.' Once the initial accumulation has been achieved, one only has to manage this acquired wealth wisely: 'In this way, apart from the great number of committees and commissions which took up an important part of his time, he had attained, by the end of the thirties, and he retained more or less continuously until 1964, the three positions which together gave him extensive power over French historiography: direction of the history department at the Sorbonne, presidency of the history commission at the CNRS. . . . He aimed, successfully, to control the quality of the candidates for teaching posts and to exert influence on appointments. As almost all theses were examined in Paris, and because, being after 1938 the most senior modern historian at the Sorbonne, he presided over all the boards of examiners and was invited to the very few important thesis examinations held in the provinces, he knew all the future senior lecturers personally.[17] He got the Consultative Committee to agree that the 'short list' should not contain any more good candidates than the number of vacant posts. Thus no appointments were made by the Ministry of Education without his approval. Moreover, there is no evidence that the Director-General of Higher Education ever failed to take his advice before making an appointment. As he had also controlled the preparation of the thesis – if only through the management of research posts at the CNRS – he in fact possessed an authority which, although unwritten, was preponderant.'[18]

In general, the accumulation of positions controlled is the condition of the exchanges of services between the powerful which enable them to constitute and maintain their clientele: the circulation of services rendered can only be perceived at the level of a group of institutions, and it is rare that they take the visible form of a direct and immediate exchange in which the appointment of one of X's pupils on Y's recommendation to establishment A would be answered by the appointment of one of Y's pupils on X's recommendation to establishment B; the more the networks of positions controlled are extended and diversified – in the institutions of teaching but also of research; in publishers' series and academic reviews but also, at the other pole of the field, in the daily and weekly press, etc. – the longer, the more complicated and the more indecipherable for the uninitiated is the cycle of exchanges. A 'recommendation' by Y of a pupil of X may perhaps be repaid by a book review in a weekly written by a member of X's 'ideological family', after X has drawn their attention to Y's book, taking advantage of an editorial committee meeting, an electoral commission or an electoral support committee. In terms of this logic, we can well understand that the title of *normalien*, which certifies the acquisition of competence but also and above all the acquisition of a disposition towards the academic institution, plays so important a role in the accumulation of power: the social capital represented by Ecole Normale connections when they are duly maintained by sustained exchanges, is one of the sole bases of transdisciplinary solidarity; which explains why it plays a decisive role every time that someone has to obtain and hold positions of university power which are situated beyond the little local fiefs, limited to the scale of a discipline, and even positions of prestige such as those offered by the Collège de France. As social capital of actual or potential connections, the fact of being a *normalien* exercises a multiplier effect on all the social powers held; it is therefore all the more effective in the case of those placed higher up in the hierarchy of these powers.

Because of the fact that the accumulation of academic capital takes up time (which is evident from the fact that the capital held is closely linked with age), the distances, in this space, are measured in time, in temporal gaps, in age differences. It follows that the structure of the field is perceived by the agents in the form of an ideal career – from the Ecole Normale to the Institute, passing through the stages of assistant lecturer, doctoral thesis, promotion from assistant lecturer to lecturer and then a chair at the Sorbonne – against which all other trajectories are objectively measured. The agents tend to associate with each of the major stages of this itinerary, which is also an obstacle race and a competitive examination, a normal age of access, with reference to which one might appear young or old at any (biological) age. In fact, since the positions of power are hierarchized and separated in time, reproduction of the hierarchy supposes a respect for distances, that is respect for the *order of succession*. It is this very order which threatens the *celeritas* of those who want to 'cut corners' (for example, by importing into the university field properties or powers acquired on other terrains), as against *gravitas*, the healthy slowness which people like to feel is in itself a guarantee of reliability (in writing a thesis, for instance) and which is really the most authentic proof of *obsequium*, unconditional respect for the fundamental principles of the established order.[19]

Far from containing the threat of a permanent revolution, the struggle of each against all which this permanent competition stimulates among those who have once entered the race, and who have the competitive dispositions both required and reinforced by the race, contributes by its own logic to the reproduction of the order as a system of temporal distances: on the one hand because the very fact of competing implies and elicits recognition of the common objectives of the competition; on the other hand because the competition is restricted at any one moment to competitors placed at approximately the same point in the race, and because it is arbitrated by those who hold a more advanced position.

If it is clear that all the strategies of domination would be nothing without the structures which render them possible and effective, it is no less evident that the powers conferred by mastery of the strategic positions which give control over the progress of the competitors will only have an effective impact on the new entrants – the assistant lecturers, for example – on condition that they are willing to play the competitive game, and accept its objectives. Moreover, the exercise of academic power presupposes the aptitude and propensity, themselves socially acquired, to exploit the opportunities offered by the field: the capacity to 'have pupils, to place them, to keep them in a relation of dependency' and thus to ensure the basis of a durable power, the fact of 'having well-placed pupils' (geographer, 1971), implies perhaps above all the art of manipulating other people's time, or, more precisely, their career rhythm, their curriculum vitae, to accelerate or defer achievements as different as success in competitive or other examinations, obtaining the doctorate, publishing articles or books, appointment to university posts, etc. And, as a corollary, this art, which is also one of the dimensions of power, is often only exercised with the more or less conscious complicity of the postulant, thus maintained, sometimes to quite an advanced age, in the docile and submissive, even somewhat infantile, attitude which characterizes the good pupil of all eras – in Germany the thesis supervisor is called the *Doktorvater*, the 'doctor's father'.

'As for the lecturers and assistant lecturers, they must often kick their heels a little before getting an article published in a review. . . . In Paris especially, you can keep them waiting a year or two and when they are about to be placed on the LAFMA[20] that can be a nuisance' (geographer, 1971). 'The heads have all the power because they have the power to appoint assistant lecturers. They have the power at two levels: first by choosing assistant lecturers, then by making them pay for this first service. When he is placed on the promotion list, the assistant lecturer ceases to be obligated: so they invent regulations to control nomination to the list; for some heads, there is a certain number of thesis pages to be written; for others, it's a question of diligence' (literature teacher, 1971).

In all the situations where power is hardly or not at all institutionalized,[21] the establishment of *durable* relations of authority and dependency is based on *waiting*, that is, the selfish expectation of a future goal, which lastingly modifies – that is, for the whole period that the expectation lasts – the behaviour of the person who counts on the thing expected; and it is based also on the art of *making someone wait*, in the dual sense of stimulating, encouraging or maintaining hope, through promises or skill in not disappointing, denying or discouraging expectations, at the same time as through an ability to inhibit and restrain impatience, to get people to put up with and accept the delay, the continuing frustration of hopes, of anticipated satisfactions intrinsically suggested behind the promises or encouraging words of the guarantor, but indefinitely postponed, deferred, suspended.

Academic power thus consists in the capacity to influence on the one hand expectations – themselves based partly on a disposition to play the game and on investment in the game, and partly on the objective indeterminacy of the game – and on the other hand objective probabilities – notably by limiting the world of possible competitors. As long as a provincial professor aspires to move to the Sorbonne, or a professor at the Sorbonne or the Collège de France aspires to the Institute, the Institute member or the Sorbonne professor on whom his election depends can dictate his choice of assistant lecturer, count on his vote in an election (in particular, in an election to designate his own successor), or, quite simply, obtain from him reverence and references (the reader will understand that exemplification, which would mitigate the peremptory style of our analysis, is impossible here). Such authority is founded on career expectations: one is only hooked if one is in the pool. But these expectations themselves are not independent of the objective existence of probable futures, neither totally determined nor totally indeterminate. If, for the mechanism to function, it is obviously necessary for several competitors having the same qualifications and belonging to the same academic generation to be in competition for the same posts, their number must be small enough for them to reasonably aspire to the posts on offer and to identify in advance with their holders – something which becomes impossible when the objective probabilities slip below a certain threshold – and yet still numerous enough for them not to have any absolute certainty, which would eliminate the expectation. Within the latitude thus defined, the master adjudicates the race between competitors differentiated by secondary properties (age, sex, graduation from the Ecole Normale Supérieure), reminding them of proprieties and priorities, of promises and precedence ('I will get you on to the promotion list, but not before X'). And the seminars at which each week he welcomes 'pupils' from Poitiers, Rennes or Lille are much closer, in their functions and mechanism, to the great annual meetings organized by the American professors' associations, that is to the logic of the 'academic market-place',[22] than to the research seminar in the German tradition: almost compulsory for those who want to succeed, these meetings of the whole group of the competitors for the coveted posts are no doubt the place where we find inculcated and reinforced, in and through mimetic submission to the master or to more advanced competitors, that ethical relation to scientific work which, more than any other factor, determines the forms and limits of academic production.[23]

TIME AND POWER

Relations of dependency, and their outcome, depend on the strategies of the thesis director, or 'head', themselves linked to his position and his dispositions, and on the strategies of the 'clients', albeit, of course, within the limits imposed on all parties, and of which the most important is doubtless the degree of saturation of the employment market in the discipline considered (the dominators having it all the easier when the market is more saturated, and the competition between the new entrants that much stronger). If we leave aside those professors who, as one informant says, 'provide intellectual stimulus, help with your work and incite you to publish' (linguist, 1971) – no doubt a minority in this area of the university space – we see that the thesis 'heads' who have adjusted to their position, that is who have enough gamesmanship to be able to place their clients, to ensure them a career and thus secure the transmission of power, must achieve an optimum equilibrium between the desire to hold back their 'colts' as long as possible, preventing them from becoming independent or even active rivals (especially for their own clientele) too soon, and the necessity to 'push' them enough so as not to disappoint them, enough to gain their loyalty (preventing them, for instance, from going over to the side of their rivals) and thereby affirm their own power, thus reinforcing their academic prestige and their power of attraction.

But perhaps it will suffice to quote the analysis that a particularly alert informant offers of the comparative strategies of two heads: 'X surrounded himself, at one time, with a lot of people; a lot of the best people wanted to work with X. Did he disappoint them? He didn't push them, except for the ones who were far from him geographically . . ., who weren't his assistant lecturers; these he did push, they were awarded their doctorates and they succeeded very quickly, since Y got tenure at the Sorbonne at the age of 38 or thereabouts. The others he kept on as lecturers. He left them to rot. Someone like R, who was X's assistant lecturer, didn't interest him. Others who were with X became *chargés d'enseignement*,[24] but only when they were over 40. They made the most of May 1968 to get posts at Vincennes. If it hadn't been for Vincennes, they would still be lecturers at the Sorbonne. For this reason none of X's pupils has made it to the top yet, except D. Some stay loyal to him, like Y, but even so. . . . Either they do make it, and they don't stay loyal to X, or they don't make it. There are those who switched their allegiance to Z, who took off without X, who switched to Z when they were ready to submit their theses, and once they had their doctorates he helped them' (geographer, 1971).

There are surely few social worlds where power depends so strongly on belief, where it is so true that, in the words of Hobbes, 'Reputation of power is power'.[25] Thus we cannot entirely understand the phenomena of the concentration of academic power without also taking into consideration the contribution made by the claimants, by way of the strategies which lead them towards the most powerful protectors. These are strategies of the *habitus*, therefore more unconscious than conscious. Just as the master, according to his panegyrist, seemed to accede to the dominant posts 'as if from some natural necessity, without intriguing or postulating', so the most cunning pupils, who are also the most favoured, have no need to calculate opportunities or weigh up chances before offering their gratitude and custom to the most influential masters. It is another example of the way in which capital breeds capital. We can verify in fact that there exists a close relation between the capital of academic power possessed by the different 'heads' and the number and status (measured in terms of academic capital) of their clients – who represent a dimension and a display of their symbolic capital.

The mere number of theses supervised suffices to distinguish the important heads, in the various disciplines. For instance in history the discipline where our data are most reliable:[26] Girard, 57 doctoral theses; Labrousse, 42; Renouvin, 23; Guiral, 22; Perroy, 21; Mollat and Mousnier, 19.[27] Likewise, in Greek: Fernand Robert, 33 doctoral theses (also 3 'complementary' theses and 3 'third-cycle'[28] theses); Mme de Romilly, 21 (plus 4 complementary and 9 third-cycle); Flacelière, 20 (+ 8 complementary); Chantraine, 17 (+ 8 complementary); Mme Harl, 16 (+ 12 third-cycle).[29] Or in philosophy: Ricœur, 10 (+ 4 complementary); Hyppolite, 10 (+ 3 complementary); Schuhl, 10 (+ 3 complementary); Jankélévitch, 7; Wahl, 6 (+ 3 complementary): Gandillac, 6 (+ 7 complementary); Alquié, 5 (+ 1 complementary); Gouhier, 4 (+ 12 complementary); Canguilhem, 4 (+ 4 complementary); Souriau, 4 (+ 2 complementary).[30] We may observe, in all these disciplines, a marked difference between the scholars or the eminent researchers who, especially when they are at the Collège de France, generally supervise only a small number of candidates, and in a very specific field, and the most powerful ordinary professors who supervise a large number of often very different studies.

But it is when we take into account the social status of the candidates that the most significant differences are revealed: indeed, we find grouped around the most powerful heads the candidates endowed with the most effective properties in the field (masculine gender, *agrégation* – and even a high grade in it – the title of *normalien*) and consequently the most endowed with potential 'power' (as their subsequent career clearly shows). Thus it is that in philosophy,[31] where we doubtless find the virtuosos of the system, Jean Hyppolite, himself a *normalien* and at one time Director of the Ecole Normale Supérieure, professor at the Sorbonne and then at the Collège de France, stands out clearly against Paul Ricœur, not a *normalien*, professor at Nanterre (and then in the United States), who, although enjoying, as translator and critic of Husserl, an authority and a renown at least equivalent to those of Hyppolite, known above all as translator and critic of Hegel, and although he can add to this his own work as a phenomenologist and also as philosopher of language and of interpretation, attracts doctoral students of distinctly inferior social status. Hyppolite's 10 registered students are all men, 9 are *agrégés*, 6 are *normaliens*, and, at the time of the enquiry, 6 were at Paris and 4 were already senior lecturers, 2 lecturers, 2 assistant lecturers and 4 seconded to research posts at the CNRS. Of Ricœur's 10 candidates, 8 were men, 8 *agrégés*, nobody was a *normalien*, only two were at Paris, and 5 were lecturers, 3 assistant lecturers, one a senior lecturer, and one a teacher in a Roman Catholic school. This simple sounding none the less allows us clearly to perceive the role and the mechanism of the thesis in the case of a canonical discipline where, through the thesis, the thesis supervisor controls in an absolute fashion access to the only possible career, that of university professor.[32]

The success of a university career depends on the 'choice' of a powerful head who is not necessarily the most famous nor even the most technically competent; thus it is that the most prestigious careers, for the 'philosophers', of the generation which will come to power in the seventies, depended on the registration of a thesis topic with one of the Sorbonne professors of the fifties, who thirty years earlier were attached to Emile Bréhier and Léon Brunschwicg. The effect of specialization, which, by attracting certain of the most 'promising' candidates to a specialist in a clearly defined area of the philosophical space (Schuhl, Guitton, Gouhier or Canguilhem), would seem to counter the process of monopolization, tends in fact to reinforce it: the most general topics are, in fact – according to a hierarchy which is implicit but recognized by everyone – the most prestigious (as witness, among other indices, the fact that the most specialized topics are reserved for the secondary thesis and for the secondary supervisors that the specialists are). We need only look at the details of the list of topics registered with the most attractive 'heads' to see that what is (objectively) expected by the thesis director, with few exceptions, is not a true supervision of research, with advice on methodology or technique, or even philosophical inspiration, but a sort of recognition of status and the freedom that goes with it, and, more unconsciously, supervision of a career, patronage (thus in Hyppolite's case, alongside a small number of topics on Hegel – which are moreover the work of a few eccentrics – we find studies on Leibniz, Nietzsche or Alain, on historical thought in Greece, on the phenomenology of meaning, etc.). In short, the intellectual affinities between the major heads and their clients are much less evident than the social affinities which unite them.

In fact, although they appear to obey two independent principles, the 'choice' of the topic and the choice of a head represent the same dispositions translated into two different logics: the sense of philosophical grandeur which is displayed in the scope of the topics and the distinction of the authors is simultaneously shown in the choice of a 'head' who, through his university post at least as much as through his work, can appear at any given moment as the most philosophical of the philosophy professors, while still being the best placed to ensure for the philosophically ambitious claimant the social conditions of the full exercise of philosophical activity, that is, concretely, a university post. Each of these two 'choices' expresses that sort of sense of inextricably intellectual and social investment which leads the best qualified supplicants towards the most distinguished partners and towards the most prestigious position, to which they can grant access. As with the 'choice' of a marriage partner, the 'choice' of a head is also to some extent a relation of capital to capital: in the grandeur of the head and the topic chosen, the candidate affirms the sense that he has both of his own grandeur and of the grandeur of the various potential heads, something like good or bad intellectual taste (with all its potential effects of *allodoxia*). The head is the chosen one rather than the chooser; and the value of his pupils, who, although they are not exactly his disciples, none the less grant him a form of intellectual recognition, helps to create his value – as he helps to create theirs.[33]

It is through all these mutual 'choices' operated by partners well matched even in the principles behind their choices that the solidarities which are destined to appear as the product of operations of judgement and classification, founded on explicit criteria and express rules, are constituted. Here, as elsewhere, we must beware of interpreting as an effect of the rules, or an effect of deliberate and methodical intention, the regularities whose guiding principles are commonsense inclinations. Objectification, and especially that arising from statistics which aggregate the result of multiple individual strategies, itself produces a theoretical distortion which we have to guard against: it shows up relations between the properties of the agents and their practices, which one might be tempted to read as the result of a cynical calculation of carefully considered self-interest. Such a reading is all the more plausible since this naïvely utilitarian philosophy of (other people's) action is the ordinary basis of everyday polemics, sometimes disguised as science, whose bogus lucidity is often fuelled by resentment.

The boldness or even rashness statutorily granted to some provides the best of justifications and the safest of alibis for the institutional prudence which is incumbent on the greater number. The cult of 'brilliance', through the facilities which it procures, the false boldness which it encourages, the humble and obscure labours which it discourages, is less opposed than it might seem to the prudence of *academica mediocritas*, to its epistemology of suspicion and resentment, to its hatred of intellectual liberty and risk; and it colludes with appeals to 'reliability' (*le sérieux*) and its prudent investments and small profits, to spoil or discourage any thought liable to disturb an order founded on resistance to intellectual liberty or even on a special form of anti-intellectualism. The secret resistance to innovation and to intellectual creativity, the aversion to ideas and to a free and critical spirit, which so often orientate academic judgements, as much at the viva of a doctoral thesis or in critical book reviews as in well-balanced lectures setting off neatly against each other the latest avant-gardes, are no doubt the effect of the recognition granted to an institutionalized thought only on those who implicitly accept the limits assigned by the institution. And nothing helps more than the doctoral thesis to reinforce the dispositions required. This happens through the intermediary of the diffuse control which the patriarchal authority of the 'doctor's father' tends to exercise over all practices, notably over publication, via self-censorship and obligatory reverence towards masters and academic production, and above all via the prolonged relation of dependency in which the thesis maintains the candidate and which most often has no connection with the technical necessities of a true apprenticeship.[34]

To place the emphasis, as people usually do, on the ritual of the viva is, in any case, to disguise the essential point, which consists in the submissive waiting and in the recognition of the academic order which it implies. As we are reminded by the ordinances regulating the examination which, in the Middle Ages, gave access to the status of master in the profession of saddler, there is no master without his master: *nullus assumi debet in magistrum, qui sub magistro non fuerit disciplus.* There is no acknowledged master who does not recognize a master and, through him, the intellectual magistrature of the sacred college of masters who acknowledge him. In short, there is no master who does not recognize the value of the institution and its institutional values which are all rooted in the institutionalized refusal of any non-institutional thought, in the exaltation of academic 'reliability', that instrument of normalization which has all appearances on its side, those of learning and those of morality, although it is often only the instrument of the transformation of individual and collective limits into the choice of scientific virtuousness.

Like all forms of loosely institutionalized power which may not be delegated to representatives,[35] strictly academic power can only be accumulated and maintained at the cost of constant and heavy expenditure of time. The result is, as Weber has already noted, that the acquisition and exercise of administrative power in the university field – that of dean or *recteur* [vice-chancellor], for example – or the unofficial power of an elector to professorships or an influential member of an electoral college, or of commissions and committees of all kinds, tends in fact to compromise the accumulation of a capital of scientific authority and vice versa. Like the accumulation of symbolic capital in a pre-capitalist society, where the objectification of economic and cultural mechanisms is not very advanced, the accumulation of a specific capital of academic authority demands payment in kind, that is, with one's own time, in order to control the network of institutions where academic power is accumulated and exercised and also to enter into the exchanges of which these gatherings are the occasion and where a capital of services rendered is gradually constituted, which is indispensable to the establishment of complicities, alliances and clienteles.

> To convince ourselves of this, we have only to picture the timetable of a typical incarnation of the omnipresent professor: Marcel Durry, who, once appointed professor at the Sorbonne in 1944, will, for thirty-odd years, accumulate administrative duties, presidencies, membership of the highest agencies of 'latinity', as, apparently, he liked to call it. He is the man with all the winning tickets: Director of the Institute of Latin Studies and dean of the Sorbonne, he was for a long time President of the Board of Examiners for the *agrégation* and President of the Consultative Committe, and also Administrator of the Society for Latin Studies – and for a time of the Rome–Athens Association, and a member of the governing body of the Casa Velasquez. 'He is often consulted by the Ministry', but he still finds the time to travel 'all over Europe' and even as far as Constantine or Brazil, where he heads a project.[36] We may find a paradigmatic image of the second-rank head, sub-dean rather than dean, treasurer rather than president, secretary rather than director, but just as devoted and doubtless just as indispensable to the good running of the university, in a summary of the career of Pierre Wuilleumier.[37]

The sacrifice of time implied by participation in these rituals, ceremonies, meetings, and displays is also the most rigorously necessary condition for the accumulation of that particular form of symbolic capital known as a reputation for academic worthiness. Here the recognition accorded by any group in exchange for recognition accorded to the group, to its values, its obligations, its traditions, and the rituals through which it reaffirms its being and its value, is the founding principle of a form of internal authority relatively independent of scientific authority properly speaking. Only a set of monographs would enable us to capture the logic of the exchanges which academics enter into for a thesis viva (the person who asks a colleague to participate in the viva of a thesis which he has supervised commits himself tacitly to offering the return service and therefore enters into a circuit of continuous exchanges), for elections (the person who speaks up in favour of a colleague's candidate earns with this colleague – and his candidate – credit he can make use of on the occasion of another election), for an editorial committee (where analogous mechanisms operate), for a selection committee, etc. It is doubtless because of this that the logic of the accumulation of power takes the form of a viciously circular mechanism of obligations which breed obligations, of a progressive accumulation of powers which attract solicitations that generate more power.

But here we should follow an informant in his description of the most recent state of the university field (around the year 1980), where, with the development of consultative agencies, the logic of the equivalence of time and university power seems to have reached its limit: 'There is a great advantage in belonging to this committee because you are solicited, you are sought out, you become part of a network of contacts – if you play the game – part of a network which helps you to get to know more or less everybody: thus you are invited to sit on specialist faculty boards, or even to give visiting lectures. Once X invited me to L to give a lecture, I made forty or fifty quid out of it. That's not the main thing, but it's worth the trouble if you're looking for a job. For a lecturer finishing off his doctoral thesis, working with these people, even if they're not people he sympathizes with (some of them are elected by the union, others are appointed by a right-wing government), there is objectively, like it or not, a certain something in the fact of belonging to that committee. It's true to such an extent that at each meeting we got into the habit of having lunch out together at a restaurant, lecturers and professors together. . . . There is a considerable advantage in sitting on that committee, because you make a name for yourself; for a lecturer looking for a professorship, once he's finished his thesis, if he has sat on some slightly far-out local committee, in exchange, if they have a post available, the committee of local specialists pre-selects him immediately. That gives you a network of social relations other than through publications, or through strictly intellectual recognition' (sociologist, 1980). In the case of these new-style powers which have developed under the influence of trade-unions and categorial pressure-groups, power is increasingly paid for in time, that is in renouncing the accumulation of a specific capital of authority; and everything leads us to believe that the intensification of categorial struggles has the major effect of reducing the overall time which remains available for scientific research (a result which, without having been intended as such, suits the interests of those who have the least advantage to expect from research proper): 'Seven reports to write, for someone who's got the knack, that's easy, it's a day's work at most. On the other hand, sitting on committees takes ages (a week). That year, we had one session that lasted a week, and one that lasted three and a half days. It's very tiring. In addition there were office sessions, where we had to share out the files among the members of the committee. I was there on behalf of the lecturers. I spent a couple of hours there, or a good half-day. "Ah, so-and-so's thesis supervisor is whatsisname, so we can't have whatsisname." And X also had to spend several half-days at the Ministry because the Ministry works directly with the university presidents, issuing instructions. A president has much more work than your grassroots committee members. . . . One thing that takes up a lot of time, is telephoning other members of the committee. I think it must affect the professors most, not only the members of the committee but also the people living in the provinces, etc. For the union officials, there are letters to write to the union members to keep them informed, there are preparatory meetings (for the union delegates from the SNESup). All in all the time taken up is worth about a month of work, I reckon; in any case, the year I was on it, it was a very hard year. It's nothing compared to the CNRS; there are people who are on the CNRS as well as the CSCU. They spend three months of their year at it' (sociologist, 1980).

Thus nothing could better sum up the set of oppositions established between those situated at the two poles of the university field than the structure of their time-economy (because of the fact that the kind of capital possessed influences the way in which agents allocate their time): on one side, those who invest above all in the work of accumulation and management of academic capital – including their 'personal' work, devoted to a considerable extent to the production of intellectual instruments which are also instruments of specifically academic power, lectures, textbooks, dictionaries, encyclopaedias, etc.; on the other side, those who invest above all in production and, secondarily, in the work of representation which contributes to the accumulation of a symbolic capital of external renown. Indeed, those richest in external prestige could be divided again according to the proportion of their time which they devote to production properly speaking or to the direct promotion of their products (especially working at the academic import–export trade: colloquia, symposia, conferences, reciprocal invitations, etc.) or, again, to all the public activities, especially those of a political nature, which are part of the role of an intellectual, and which, without being necessarily conceived as such, derive to a certain extent from the logic of public relations and advertising (with, for example, frequentation of journalists, production of newspaper articles, participation in petitions or demonstrations, etc.).

It is understandable that academic power is so often independent of specifically scientific capital and the recognition it attracts. As a temporal power in a world which is neither actually nor statutorily destined for that sort of power, it always tends to appear, perhaps even in the eyes of its most confident possessors, as a substitute, or a consolation prize. We can understand, too, the profound ambivalence of the academics who devote themselves to administration towards those who devote themselves, successfully, to research – especially in a university system where institutional loyalty is weak and largely unrewarded.

Everything leads us to believe that an initial or subsequent orientation towards positions of temporal power depends on the dispositions of the *habitus* and on opportunities – to which these dispositions themselves contribute through anticipation and the effect of the 'self-fulfilling prophecy' – of attaining the only officially recognized objectives in the field, that is, scientific success and specifically intellectual prestige. The logic of circular causality which arises between positions and dispositions, between *habitus* and field, means that a poor return on scientific investments can lead to accepting or seeking out non-scientific investments of a substitutional or compensatory type which contribute in their turn to reducing the profit of the scientific investments. It follows that nothing would be more pointless than to try to determine whether the lower intellectual success rate is the determining principle or rather the effect of these negative vocations which lead to positions of academic power or university administration – or again to that particular form of trade-unionism which, in teaching or research, represents an alternative route to temporal success; all the more so since, in more than one case, at least in the period before the 1968 crisis, the university-approved dispositions towards academic culture seemed to lead quite naturally to administrative duties. It is logical that these areas of the university space should be occupied by agents who, being produced for and by the academic institution, have only to follow their natural dispositions in order to produce *ad infinitum* the conditions of reproduction of the institution, starting with the most important: setting limits to cultural needs and aspirations at the same time as encouraging ignorance of those limits, restricting people's vision of the world and canvassing their support for this mutilated vision, which leads people to perceive as universal, under the guise of 'general education', an extremely singular culture.[38] The 'oblates' are always most inclined to think that without the church there is no salvation – especially when they become the high priests of an institution of cultural reproduction which, in consecrating them, consecrates their active and above all passive ignorance of any other cultural world. Victims of their elite status, these deserving, but miraculously lucky, 'survivors'[39] present a curious mixture of arrogance and inadequacy which immediately strikes the foreign observer – such as Leo Spitzer, who on several occasions refers to the 'double autarky, sorbonnard and national' of French Rabelais specialists.[40]

> We would fail to understand the most permanent traits of the French university system if we forgot that its cultural aristocracy, essentially originating in the petty bourgeoisie most implicated in the academic system – the heart of the Sorbonne belongs to sons of primary teachers – is doubtless more lacking than others (the German or English, for example) in everything that provides a heritage of cultural aristocracy, and is deprived of awareness of that lack. The intellectual elitism of the poor is behind the vicious circle of cultural poverty. And there is no need to invoke national character to understand that the combination of egalitarian Jacobinism and academic elitism which are incorporated in the institution of the competitive entrance examination engenders a profoundly ambivalent disposition towards all academic achievement: a collective defence against all objectified hierarchization of performances (which discourages any search for institutionalized indicators of scientific status) can thus be associated with an unequalled enthusiasm for distinguished intellectuals.

The canonical professors of the canonical disciplines originate predominately in the teaching profession, and especially in its lower and middle strata, almost all having passed through *khagne*[41] and the Ecole Normale Supérieure, where again they very often teach and are often married to teachers. They offer to the academic institution which they have chosen because it chose them, and vice versa, a support which, being so totally conditioned, has something total, absolute, unconditional about it. The dialectic of consecration which helps to propel agents towards the places to which their socially constituted dispositions predestine them is fully functional here, and only with the most refined knowledge of sub-linguistic communication could we detect the indices by which, in the procedures of co-optation, the institution recognizes those who recognize it, whether in the case of what is called *le sérieux* (reliability), that is, the inclination to respect academic suggestions or injunctions, or its corollary, 'brilliance', which, often identified with precociousness, that is early success in academic examinations, also measures the precociousness of support for the values of reliability, the most precocious person, in a sense, being the one who grows old at the earliest age.[42]

Strictly academic power is typical of the canonical disciplines, the history of French literature, classics or philosophy, which are closely linked to school syllabuses and examinations and, through them, to secondary school teaching, whose reproduction they directly control by fashioning, through syllabus, lecture and entrance examination topic, the dispositions durably inculcated in the teaching body. Invested with a sort of social magistrature – as witness their active participation in the defence of French language and culture and of the institutions designed to support them – the professors of these disciplines subordinate the essential part of their pedagogical – and 'scientific' – practice to the exigencies of competitive and other examinations.

> This quasi-judicial function is easily seen in the case of the grammarians: exploiting without even realizing it the ambiguity of grammar, which could be understood in either a descriptive or a prescriptive sense, they say both what language is and what it should be: 'The grammarian had a dual role: it was his task on the one hand to enquire into the nature of language, and on the other to teach its norms to the young. As an observer and discoverer, he was a founder of the science of linguistics, but, as professor and legislator, he belonged to the same institution as the priest, the judge or the prince. Just as they founded or administered the codes of religion, law or etiquette, so he established and interpreted the codes of "right" and "proper" language.'[43]

The canonical masters of the canonical disciplines devote a considerable part of their own work to the production of works

whose academic intention is more or less cleverly denied and which
are at once the privileges, often economically fruitful, and the
instruments of cultural power, inasmuch as they are an enterprise in
the prescription of knowledge and the canonization of the legitimate
heritage: these are of course textbooks, books published in the 'Que
Sais-Je' series,[44] and also the innumerable 'survey' series, particularly
flourishing in history, as well as dictionaries, encyclopaedias, etc.[45]
These 'general surveys', often written in collaboration, apart from
providing for the education and gratification of a vast clientele, have,
through the selection they make, a consecration (or hit-parade) effect,
which operates at first on the teaching body and, through it, on
pupils in the different stages of education.[46] Born in the classroom
and destined to return to rest in the classroom, these studies most
often perpetuate an outmoded state of knowledge, instituting and
canonizing problems and debates which only exist and subsist
through the inertia of academically objectified and incorporated
syllabuses. They are the natural prolongation of the great reproductive
teaching which, as legitimate popularization, should inculcate what
'the common opinion of the doctors' deems to be received
and respected wisdom, and thereby establish it as authenticated
knowledge, academically ratified and endorsed, and thus worthy of
being taught and learnt (as opposed to the merely 'fashionable', or
to all the modernist heresies), rather than produce a new or even
heretical body of knowledge, or the ability and inclination to produce
such knowledge.

In a more general fashion, the structural time-lag (greater or lesser
according to the discipline) between research and teaching causes teachers
at all levels to be inclined to find in a defensive neophobia a way to
avoid being outmoded, and it is not uncommon for them to abuse the
monopoly situation afforded by teaching, to adopt a bogus detachment
from the knowledge which they would in any case have had trouble
transmitting: 'As for those who are not at the front line [of current
research], their procedure is to rubbish theories while they transmit
them; they try to mark themselves out from the authors they popularize
by pseudo-criticisms and pseudo-opinions or pseudo-declarations on the
problems and the way they are treated' (linguist, 1971).

Here we would have to attempt a detailed analysis of biographies and
bibliographies, in order, for instance, to relate academic production to
the corresponding activities of reproduction (lectures given, entrance
examinations corrected, etc.), and also examine the functioning of the
allocation of time between research activities and teaching activities, and,

finally, within these categories, determine what is the place assigned to teaching designed to prepare for research properly speaking, and what to teaching designed to produce teachers.[47] Of this last opposition, we can find indicators in the importance that the different institutions and the different professors accord to the *thèse de troisième cycle* ['third-cycle' thesis, a short thesis providing training in research] and to the *agrégation*. Although they no doubt serve very different purposes according to the discipline and, within the same discipline, according to the degree of scientific retraining of the teachers, the 'third-cycle' thesis represents the institutional possibility of escaping the ambition, encouraged by the institutionalized 'state' thesis, to produce the unique, apocalyptic masterpiece, after a solitary effort taking several years, and of finding a mode of expression adapted to the requirements of research, such as the scientific article making an original contribution to a limited topic. And, in fact, we find a decrease in the proportion of state doctoral theses submitted or being prepared and, inversely, a growth in the proportion of third-cycle theses submitted or being prepared as we move from the traditional disciplines to the disciplines open to research (we know that the third-cycle doctorate first developed in the science faculties, where it is tending to supplant the *agrégation*, especially for access to posts in higher education): thus, for example, the proportion of teachers of rank B [lecturer and assistant lecturer] who have not submitted and who are not preparing a third-cycle thesis rises from 40 per cent in sociology to 59.7 per cent in linguistics, to 73.6 per cent in Latin and Greek, to 75.15 per cent in literature (these data, extracted from the 1967 enquiry by the Maison des Sciences de l'Homme on researchers in arts and social science, are confirmed by examination of the list of theses submitted, which shows that the number of third-cycle theses submitted at Paris in 1968 was 32 for sociology, 17 for ethnology, 14 for psychology, 11 for Greek, 3 for English).

The progress of the third-cycle thesis gives a fair idea of the difficulties of institutionalizing new modes of producing and evaluating cultural works. Indeed, it is clear that in this case university mores have once again overcome the prescriptions of law: among other reasons, because a number of professors have shown the low esteem they have for the third-cycle doctorate by giving it away liberally. The third-cycle doctorate, which rewards a research project, is more or less totally devoid of value on the market of the canonical disciplines of the faculties, still dominated by the *agrégation* and its academic exercises, and remains strongly challenged by more traditional diplomas (notably the *agrégation*) even on the social science market. That is one of the factors which cause the institutions most orientated towards research teaching, like the Collège de France and the Ecole Pratique des Hautes Etudes, to be more or less totally deprived of social weight: 'The third cycle is worth absolutely nothing. Look, here's an example: for the last two years the arts students [from the Ecole Normale Supérieure] have been allowed exemption from the *agrégation* [when they wanted to register for research]. What is the result? We were the first to advise the *normaliens* not to claim this dispensation. What would they have gained from it? A third-cycle thesis? But what would they have gained from the third-cycle thesis? Nothing. . . . We have to tell them the truth, and even admit the sordid details, that in the end it all comes down to choosing the right head, we have to reveal something of the way the system works' (literature professor, 1971). 'The best diploma is the *agrégation*. Even the third-cycle thesis is considered inferior, quite plainly' (classics professor, 1971). 'To be an assistant lecturer, the *agrégation* is increasingly vital. In 1968 it seemed on the point of collapse; but now it's healthier than ever: the heads' recruiting policies have restored its importance' (history professor, 1971).

We would understand nothing of the functioning of this temporal power in the cultural order if we failed to realize that, despite everything that separates it from specifically intellectual and scientific prestige, it manages, especially within the limits of its temporal sphere, to gain recognition as a genuine intellectual or scientific authority, and that this allows it to exercise distorting and delaying effects on the domain of research itself. This is because it helps to generate all sorts of acts of obligatory recognition and homage (among which, servile references and reviews are only the most visible) through the effects of authority operated by any legitimate institution, and through the conscious or unconscious deference paid to those people who wield power over coveted positions. And also, more profoundly, because, in the name of a kind of inner submission to the established cultural order, all those who owe a part of their real or estimated value to academic acclaim tend to recognize the legitimacy of the claim to legislate in scientific or intellectual matters, which is made in fact by any temporal power each time that it intervenes in a world where the objectives are intellectual or scientific through control of appointments, funds or, *a fortiori*, validation (by boards of examiners for doctoral theses, for instance).

Doubling up is not entirely unknown, and we find, in the centre of the space, a number of professors who manage to unite and to reconcile the powers of the head, virtually absolute master of all academic destinies, and the authority of the scholar (which is what is often implied by the association of a chair at the Sorbonne with a seminar at the EPHE). The *allodoxia* which finds its objective basis in the fact that, between the two extremes where the two kinds of power would be entirely dissociated, there exist all the intermediary profiles provides support for the individual and collective bad faith without which intellectual or academic life would perhaps be unliveable: it is what enables the old-style thesis supervisor to see himself as a master selected and consulted for his scientific competence alone, at the cost of a little self-deceit backed up by the complicity or indulgence of the passing pupils channelled towards him for reasons of institutional power.

This power over the mechanisms of reproduction, and thereby over the development of the university body, which is at its peak in the medical faculties, is based on control, through co-optation, of access to the university body, on durable relations of production and dependency between the head and his clients, and finally on control of the institutional positions of power, boards of entrance examiners, Consultative Committee, even committees of enquiry.[48] But the surest guarantee of academic order, inextricably social and scientific, doubtless lies in the complex mechanisms whereby promotion towards the summit of the temporally dominant institutions goes hand in hand with progress in academic initiation, marked, in the case of the medical faculties, by successive competitive examinations (which, as one observer notes, postpone until very late true initiation into the scientific methods of the laboratory), or, in the case of the arts faculties, by the long wait for the doctorate, that is, in both cases, by an enforced prolongation of the dispositions which have been acknowledged through the primitive procedures of co-optation, and which hardly encourage heretical breaks with the artfully intertwined knowledge and power of academic orthodoxy.

THE CONSECRATED HERETICS

Those who hold positions in the field diametrically opposed to those of the *lectores*,[49] or lecturers primarily orientated towards the reproduction of culture and of the group of reproducers, have in common their own primary devotion to research, although they also have teaching functions (but generally in academically peripheral institutions like the Collège de France or the Ecole des Hautes Etudes): they are very often at the head of a research team, and are rarely found in positions of university power whose tenure takes up much time, and they supervise fewer theses. They are particularly well represented in the new disciplines, especially ethnology, linguistics and sociology, or in the peripheral disciplines (like Assyriology, Egyptology, Indian studies, Sinology, Islamic or Berber studies, Indian languages and literatures, etc.), or even in the canonical disciplines if using new methods, like economic and social history, and they have a renown which, for some of them at least, considerably transcends the frontiers of the academic field. Accumulating the most prestigious titles of academic recognition (like the Institute, the peak of a long series of relations of dependency), to which they sometimes add those indices of 'intellectual' conse-cration most recognized by the general public (publication in paperback, a mention in the *Larousse* or membership of the French Academy) and positions of power in the intellectual field (participation in the editorial committees of intellectual reviews, direction of publishers' series, etc.), known and acknowledged abroad (as witnessed by the frequency of citations and translations of their works), often writing in a foreign language, these authorities whose names, at least in the cases of those who have founded a school, are associated with various '-isms' have pupils or disciples rather than clients, although their symbolic capital tends to be accompanied, at least in certain cases, by a certain social power.

> The fact that symbolic authority is more often found among specialists of the new sciences should not disguise the fact that these disciplines, through the combination of old-style powers – like the Consultative Committee – and the new powers associated with research which they offer (like the committees allocating posts in research at the CNRS and elsewhere, research funds, etc.), had allowed some 'recycled' heads to achieve a concentration of powers out of all proportion to those of the little academic principalities of the canonical disciplines. The scale of positions being considerably extended, the person who at the same time, through doctoral theses and the Consultative Committee, controlled access to posts in higher education,and, through committees in the CNRS, access to posts in research and an important proportion of funds, possessed unprecedented possibilities of exchange and could thus, directly or indirectly – especially through the control of access to the teaching body – define the whole orientation of a discipline, and were able to do so for a considerable period of time.

If the professors of the Collège de France or the Ecole des Hautes Etudes and the professors of the minor and marginal disciplines of the faculties, or even the most specialized professors of the canonical disciplines (for instance, historians of Christian philosophy) are particularly well represented towards the research pole, it is because they have in common the more or less total avoidance of the constraints which hamper the dominant disciplines of the faculties, and first and foremost those imposed by a syllabus and a large audience, with all the responsibilities and also the prestige and the powers that follow. Free to choose their own lecture topics, they can explore new areas, for the benefit of a small number of future specialists, instead of propounding to a large number of pupils, who are mostly destined to teach, the state of reseach already accomplished (often by others) on topics imposed every year by the syllabuses of entrance and other examinations, and in a spirit which inevitably owes much to the logic of school tests.

> The opposition between the two poles should not be confused with the opposition between the faculties and more prestigious institutions. Even the Collège de France, as well as having specialists who follow the tradition of the eighteenth-century 'private collection', has its contingent (even in the most classic disciplines, such as classical languages) of 'eminent academics' who have followed a classic career-pattern (teaching at Rhétorique Supérieure [preparatory class for *grande école*] and the Sorbonne) and who have added to the ordinary titles of academic excellence a social renown acquired sometimes through journalism.[50] To which we might add that purely academic merit (a good grade at entrance to the Ecole Normale Supérieure and a good grade in the *agrégation*) was at all times an entrance ticket to scholarship by way of the School of Athens and archaeology. For their part the faculties too have in their ranks professors orientated towards research, especially in social science and in minor disciplines, but also in the most specialized sectors of the canonical disciplines, like philosophy or history.

As a corollary, the marginal positions, however prestigious some of them may be, often tend virtually to exclude power over the mechanisms of reproduction. Knowing the characteristics of these posts, we may understand why those who hold them (when they are not entirely estranged from the 'normal' career pattern – as is the case with those of them who were not born in France), without ever being totally alienated from the university order, have almost all accomplished a more or less decisive detour from the 'normal' trajectories which lead to simple reproduction, and from the psychological and social security which these trajectories guarantee.[51]

A typical example of these academic trajectories on the margins of or outside the university is the career of Claude Lévi-Strauss, as he recalls it himself in an interview (revealing in passing that he has always given precedence to research over teaching): 'I retired fifty years to the day after taking up my first post: philosophy teacher at Mont-de-Marsan. Fifty years of public teaching is a very long time. I only stayed in secondary teaching for two and a half years, since I left for Brazil in 1935, for a university post at São Paolo. From that moment on, teaching and research were always very closely connected. For me, teaching has always been a public test-bed – obliging me to articulate my ideas, even if this formulation was provisional or erroneous, with a view to later publication. All the books which I have written were initially expressed orally. . . My career has constantly been interrupted by external factors. My departure for Brazil profoundly changed it. I had absolutely no thought of going there until the opportunity came up. Then the expeditions to the far interior of Brazil completely upset my academic routine. I went back to secondary teaching for a few weeks. But my appointment was rescinded after the [anti-Semite] Vichy government laws. I was lucky to be able to get away to the United States, because of the interest which American colleagues had taken in my early work. So I spent a few years in New York before being recalled to France, as soon as Paris was liberated. I spent only six months in Paris, during the winter of 1944–5. Then I was sent to the United States, as cultural attaché at the embassy. On my return to France, in 1948, I taught at the Musée de l'Homme and at the Ecole des Hautes Etudes. Then in 1959 at the Collège de France. So it was a switchback academic career whose most striking characteristic was no doubt that it was accomplished outside the university system properly speaking' (*Libération*, 2 June 1983).[52] Some of these distinguished marginals, and some of the most eminent, have had difficulties or disagreements with the Sorbonne. And we know that several of the best-known teachers of the Collège de France were for a long time *personae non gratae* at the Sorbonne: thus it is that around 1960 degree candidates could not quote the name of Lévi-Strauss in the presence of Gurvitch or refer to the name of Dumézil in the presence of Heurgon (to restrict ourselves to the examples best known, along with those of Benveniste or Gourou, at the time of the enquiry).

It is doubtless thus, that is, by means of the disposition to take the (relative) gamble implied by any deviation from the canonical curriculum vitae, and likewise from its associated lifestyle and modes of thought, that an intelligible relation with social and geographical origins generally much more privileged than those of ordinary professors can be established: we know, having often observed its effects, the law which requires that the propensity to take risks – in all kinds of investments – is a function of objective security and the confidence which that encourages.[53] Thus it is that the opposition between the professors situated towards the pole of research and cultural production and those professors most orientated towards teaching reproduces within the limits of the university field (as is normal at a time when a particularly large proportion of writers and critics have become part of the professorial body), therefore doubtless in attenuated form, the structural opposition between writers and professors, between the freedom and the audacity of the artist's life and the strict and somewhat circumscribed rigour of *homo academicus*.

That having been said, the professors situated towards the pole of research and of cultural production, like those who are situated at the opposite pole, are distributed in their respective orders of precedence – the Collège de France being to the Ecole des Hautes Etudes, in the first sector, what the Sorbonne is to Nanterre in the other – according to a hierarchy based in both cases on the amount of capital which they possess, scientific or intellectual capital on the one side (membership of the Institute, direction of a laboratory), above all academic capital on the other (membership of the Consultative Committee). This capital is itself strongly linked to the status of *normalien* and to age (as well as to variables such as marital status or place of birth). At the heart of the most academic sector (where the faculty of Nanterre holds the subordinate position), the principles of hierarchization are purely academic, and the hierarchy corresponds simply to the hierarchy of ages but also the few distinctions – such as the title of *normalien* – and of the disciplines, with philosophy and classics at the top and geography at the bottom. At the other pole, the hierarchy is arranged according to symbolic capital between a small number of professors endowed with all the attributes of fame, and the others, much less famous, often linked with the Ecole des Hautes Etudes and the social sciences and also with the intellectual field, especially through the medium of a more or less frequent participation in journalism.[54]

A statistical analysis, which amputates it of those holding dual membership, does not provide a good reconstruction of the position of the 6th section of the Ecole des Hautes Etudes and does not enable us to do justice to the decisive force exercised by this academically minor institute in the university field. This is why in this case we must look at the institution itself, and at the *institutional effect* which it is no doubt alone among French university establishments in exercising. At the time of the enquiry, that is, on the eve of 1968, it was a marginal institution, but prestigious and dynamic.[55] It was distinguished from all the other establishments of higher education through the freedom given it by the absence of the academic servitude of the ordinary faculties (like the preparation for examinations and entrance examinations, especially the *agrégation*) and also through the organizational action of academic and adminis-trative directors entrusted with an ambitious academic and insti-tutional project. At this phase in its history, it included a number of professors officially seconded from other institutions ('visitors') to whom it offered the material and institutional conditions (offices, administrative services and, above all, perhaps, a spirit of openness and enterprise) of a research activity of a new type, often long-term and collective, of which the great enterprises of the Centre for Historical Research constitute the paradigm.

> The first social science 'laboratories' (like the Laboratory of Social Anthropology,[56] the Centre for Historical Research,[57] The Centre for Comparative Research on Ancient Societies,[58] etc.) were not created at the CNRS, nor at the Sorbonne, but at the Ecole des Hautes Etudes, which has gradually equipped itself with the apparatus for collective work: documentation centres, libraries, laboratories of cartography, calculation centres, etc., and with a whole range of publications (seventeen reviews were launched between 1955 and 1970). One of the most important factors in this development which has made this institution the place of innovation in social science *par excellence*, as much in the domain of research as in research training, is doubtless a policy of risky investments based first and foremost on the rational exploitation of the marginality of the institution – with, for example, the concern to do what was not being done elsewhere, to welcome unknown or forgotten disciplines, to prospect for promising researchers, etc.: but also based on the creation of a genuine institutional loyalty, which is exceptional in France;[59] and finally, and above all, an openness to abroad, the 6th section having always been willing to welcome teachers, influences, innovations and even funds from other countries.[60]

Without claiming to characterize in a few sentences a long and slow evolution – linked in particular to the transformations of the Parisian faculties after 1968 and to the correlative improvement of the position of the Ecole des Hautes Etudes – we may at least note that the importance of 'visiting' professors, as much within the team of directors (during the 1960s, the academic council was entirely composed of 'visitors') as among the teaching body, has tended to wane, the administration (president, council, academic council) being recruited nowadays from purely internal candidates. As a result, if the enquiry, because of the fact that it amputates the 6th section of its visiting members, underestimates the weight of this institution in 1967, it gives a fairly accurate picture of what it is tending more and more to become with the passage of time; a very different picture at all events from the image it manages to sustain, owing to the symbolic capital collectively accumulated by the Ecole des Annales, owing to the effect of symbolic contamination still ensured by the presence of prestigious 'visitors' and owing to the effect of public relations, privileged and facilitated by its almost organic links with the press and with publishers: a large proportion of its professors lack the titles and powers of the orthodox university, yet without having won public acclaim or produced scientific work on the scale of the grand masters. There is hardly any property of its members which cannot be described in two opposite ways, in the language of lack – that of its adversaries – or in the language of elective refusal. We could say the same about the pedagogical models (seminars rather than lectures), the diplomas awarded (the School's diploma or the 'third-cycle' thesis rather than the *agrégation*), or even the external renown of the professors, where some will perceive the effect of a dubious compromise with journalism, whereas others will see in it evidence of an opening up to the world and to 'modernity'. This *structural dissonance* is written into the institutional regulations, in terms of the dependency of the Ecole des Hautes Etudes on other faculties (at least until recently) for granting degrees, especially the doctorate, and also in terms of the discrepancy between the two diplomas it awards, the School's diploma, open to students without the *baccalauréat*, and the 'third-cycle' thesis, still not widely recognized on the university market – not to mention the concomitant heterogeneity of the student population.

The heretical traditions of an institution based on a break with academic routine, and structurally inclined towards pedagogical and academic innovation, lead its members to become the most vigorous defenders of all the values of research, of openness to abroad and of academic modernity; but it is also true that they can encourage to the same extent work based on bogus, fictitious and verbal homage to these values, and that they can encourage members to give prestigious excuses for activities which promise the maximum symbolic value for a minimum real cost. Thus it is that, as the institution ages, there is a continuously growing gap between the level of aspiration and the level of achievement, between the ideal representation and the reality of scientific and pedagogical practices. Thus we may no doubt explain why the need to overcome this structural discrepancy is felt ever more strongly by the institution as a whole, as it must conform increasingly to a policy of public relations liable to endanger its autonomy; and also felt by those teachers least certain of realizing the ambition of scientificity and modernity so loudly proclaimed, who must transgress the old academic norms prohibiting all compromise with journalism in order to obtain, outside the institution, and especially in so-called cultural journalism, a symbolic capital of renown partly independent of recognition within the institution. The structural ambiguity of the position of the institution reinforces the dispositions of those who are attracted to this very ambiguity, by offering them the possibility and the freedom to live beyond their intellectual means, on credit, so to speak: this is why it represents the weak point of the university field for the intrusion of journalistic criteria and values.[61] To all the impatient claimants who, against the long production cycle and long-term investment represented by the monumental doctoral thesis (above all for historians), have chosen the short production cycle, whose ultimate example is the article in the daily or weekly press, and have given priority to marketing rather than production, journalism offers both a way out and a short cut: it enables them to overcome rapidly and cheaply the gap between aspirations and opportunities by ensuring them a minor form of the renown granted to great scholars and intellectuals; and it can even, at a certain stage in the evolution of the institution towards heteronomy, become a path to promotion within the institution itself.

COLLUSION BETWEEN OPPONENTS

The conflicts which are rooted and engendered in the structural opposition between the official 'oblates' of the higher-educational 'clergy' and the minor modernist heretics grouped mostly around the Ecole des Hautes Etudes do not exclude a form of complicity and complementarity. These social oppositions, which owe their particular intensity, in the French case, to the fact that the university field has long been dominated by the values of the literary field, are predisposed to function as 'epistemological pairs' which lead people to believe that the world of possibilities is restricted to the two polar positions – which thus prevents them from seeing that each of the two camps finds the better justification of its limits within the limits of the opponent. Here as elsewhere, traditionalism feels free, authorized by the real or supposed boldness of modernism, to entrench itself in submission to routine, and modernism finds in the over-obvious archaism of traditionalism the justification for limited innovations which, exploring facile freedoms, are bound to serve to found a new academic routine (as is illustrated, for instance, by the habit-forming popularity experienced by structuralist semiology in the French teaching system).

> This pincer effect is an exemplary illustration of the constraint which is exercised by the very structure of the field and which remains invisible or unintelligible as long as we perceive the intellectual or academic agents, institutions or currents in isolation, independently of the relations which unite them. To open the way effectively from the sociology of the field as a space of positions, to the sociology of cultural production which we have sketched here, we would have to study the individual trajectories corresponding to the principal positions, in relation to the development of their corresponding production, by proceeding for example to write monographs on significant cases (which our social norms would tend to proscribe, since they would describe our contemporaries).

We should not, indeed, by overemphasizing the differences, or even the oppositions, as the logic of analysis would naturally lead us to do, allow ourselves to forget the solidarities and complicities which are affirmed even in antagonism. The oppositions which divide up the field are neither provisional contradictions preparing for inevitable transcendence towards a superior unity, nor insuperable antinomies. And nothing would be more naïve than to allow the imposition, for instance, of the Manichaean vision which places on the one side 'progress' and 'progressives' and on the other 'reaction' and 'conservatives'. As in the field of power or in the university field taken as a whole, here too there is no absolute domination of a principle of domination, but the rival coexistence of several relatively independent principles of hierarchization. The different powers are both competitive and complementary, that is, in some respects at least, accomplices: they share in each other and owe a part of their symbolic efficiency to the fact that they are never completely exclusive, if only because the temporal power allows those most bereft of intellectual authority to ensure for themselves through the medium of academic constraints – especially the imposition of syllabuses – a more or less tyrannical form of power over people's minds, and because intellectual prestige is not without its very special and generally very circumscribed form of temporal power.

The plurality of rival principles of hierarchization (which is the basis of the struggles for the imposition of a dominant principle of domination) creates a situation where, as in the field of power overall, each field – the field of the arts and social sciences, but also the sub-field of the discipline or, within that, of the specialism – offers innumerable satisfactions which, even when they function as a consolation prize (which is the case, for instance, with positions of temporal power), can be experienced as irreplaceable. Thus there are no doubt very few social worlds which provide as many objective supports for the process of bad faith which leads to the rejection of the inaccessible, or to the choice of the inevitable. Academics (and, more generally, the members of the dominant class) have always been able to afford to be at once infinitely more satisfied (especially with themselves) than we would expect from an analysis of their position in their specific field and in the field of power, and infinitely more dissatisfied (especially with the social world) than we would expect from their relatively privileged position. Perhaps this is because they retain a certain nostalgia for an accumulation of all the forms of domination and all the forms of excellence, without realizing the psychological advantages associated with the plurality of rival taxonomies whose result is that, if one accumulates all the principles of classification, one obtains more or less as many classes as there are individuals, who are thus constituted as incomparable, unique, irreplaceable; and, again, without realizing the effects for their class as a whole of the consequent limitation of competition between individuals. Not that this prevents them acting systematically, whether as individuals, especially in cases of co-optation and of appointment of temporal authorities, or collectively, using corporatist strategies of defence more or less cunningly disguised behind a mask of universalist claims, in such a way as to discourage or prevent the accumulation by the same people of intellectual authority and academic power.

Nothing could show more clearly the structural complicity between the different powers and the different expressions, orthodox or heretical, through which they appear and are legitimated, than the debate in which one of the holders of the monopoly of the legitimate commentary of literary texts, Raymond Picard, was opposed to the spokesman for modernist exegesis, Roland Barthes. In the quasi-experimental situation which is thus created, we can see functioning as a field of conflict, with its two camps mobilized around their champions, the field of forces in which the principle of opposition is defined. It is indeed sufficient to know the positions occupied by the two protagonists in the university field to understand the true principle of the debate which has divided them and which one would seek in vain, as the most acute observers have remarked, in the actual content of their respective declarations, which are simply rationalized retranslations of the oppositions between the posts held, between literary studies and social science, the Sorbonne and the Ecole des Hautes Etudes, etc.

Raymond Picard was well aware of this, for he reproached Roland Barthes with being ignorant of 'the extreme diversity of the methods used in the university' and rejected his right to define the 'new criticism' merely in opposition to 'academic criticism, a dead horse which he has revived so that he can flog it'.[62] And, in fact, the detractors as well as the defenders of this 'new criticism' will identify with it everything which seems opposed to the academic 'establishment': '"new criticism" until then was the Hydra of Lernes. It had an existentialist head, a phenomenological head, a Marxist head, a structuralist head, a psychoanalytic head, etc., according to the ideology invoked by its representatives to guide their "approach" to the literary works.'[63] Roland Barthes explicitly claims this rooting of criticism in social science – sociology, history, psychoanalysis; and his partisans lose no time in denouncing an academic criticism 'which continues to act as if Marx, Freud, Adler, Saussure and Lévi-Strauss had never written'.[64] The spokesman of the 'new criticism' condenses as it were all the social principles of the struggle into one when he asserts that the rules of 'reading' are 'linguistic rules, not philological rules'.[65] This conflict displays a break which had already occurred – more or less the same as the one which was to re-emerge around 1968: in the modernist camp are the writers or critics close to the social sciences and to philosophy (Barthes's partisans reel off a list of people who have in common their position on the fringes of the university institution, sometimes abroad: *Tel Quel*,[66] Jean-

Paul Sartre, Gaston Bachelard, Lucien Goldmann, Georges Poulet, Jean Starobinski, René Girard, Jean-Pierre Richard);[67] in the camp of the 'traditionalists' are the canonical academics, ex-students of the Ecole Normale or of a *khagne*, and conservative journalists, who often graduated from *khagne* or the Ecole Normale, like P.-H. Simon, Thierry Maulnier or Jean Cau.[68] In this quarrel of the Ancients and the Moderns, which creates an enormous uproar in the academic field and the intellectual field (one commentator talks of the 'Dreyfus Affair of the literary world'[69]), the cast-list appears to be drawn up in advance by the logic of the field.

On the side of the institution, the *lector* finds himself obliged to erect as orthodoxy, as explicit profession of faith, the doxa of the doctors, their silent beliefs which have no need for justification: challenged to produce in broad daylight the unconscious thoughts of an institution, he articulates in black and white the truth of his post of humble and pious celebrant of a faith which transcends him. Steeped in the obviousness of his position, he has nothing to propose as method apart from his *ethos*, that is the very dispositions elicited by his position: he is and intends to be 'patient and modest'.[70] Constantly preaching 'prudence',[71] he reminds people of the limits of his function, which thus becomes those of a functionary: he claims to 'be satisfied with editing texts, an essential and difficult work', to 'determine in a reliable way some little fact concerning Racine'.[72] Destined for the dead and deadening work of daily worship, he chooses to *abase* himself in the face of the work which his only right is to 'explain and make lovable'.[73] But, like any delegate, this man of order finds in the humility which earns him the gratitude of his professional body the motive for an extraordinary self-assurance: conscious that he is expressing the ultimate values, which it would be better not to have to publish, of a whole community of belief – 'objectivity', 'good taste', 'clarity', 'common sense' – he finds it scandalous that anyone should question those certitudes which constitute the academic order which has produced him, and he feels the right and the duty to denounce and condemn what appears to him to be the result of impudent imposture and unseemly excess. One of his defenders expresses plainly the ethical horror inspired in the guardians of public decorum by the loose insolence and rash claims of these rather showy pretenders: 'some, I agree, are able to wield authority and obtain consent; others rather to abase themselves before a text, which in any case had no need of them to exist. . . . If I were the *Petit Larousse*, I would define [the two categories] thus: "baroque critic": equal or superior to the creator, and creative in his turn; a reader who adds to the work to complete it, perfect it, transfigure or defigure it. "Classical critic": humble servant of the work."[74] This language, which is that of the church, makes plain the indignation of the clergy in the face of the *hubris* of the immodest *lector*, a minor prophet claiming to supersede the authentic prophet, the *auctor*, usurping the *auctoritas* which the latter alone should enjoy.

And in fact it is indeed a prophetic role that Roland Barthes claims for himself: rejecting the boredom of the inspid 'textual exegesis' offered by the academic institution, which is doomed to repetition and compilation, he adopts the language of politics to denounce the authority usurped by the guardians of the 'literary state';[75] deliberately esoteric, flaunting all the external signs of scientificity, making liberal and often approximate borrowings from the combined lexicons of linguistics, psychoanalysis and anthropology, he proclaims on high his intention to 'subvert'[76] and his bias towards 'modernity'.[77] Through a double break with the humility of the university 'clergy', he sets himself up as a hermeneutic modernist, capable of unlocking the meaning of texts by applying the latest weapons of science, and as a creator able to re-create the work through an interpretation itself instituted as literary work and thus situated beyond the true and the false. Using the tactics of the chameleon, he becomes psychoanalyst, linguist or anthropologist to denounce the Lansonian obscurantism of the Sorbonne, and changes into a writer to claim the right to a peremptory subjectivism against the finicking meanness of scientistic red-tape, and thus wash himself clean of the plebeian crime of positivism.[78] By affirming that he is capable of combining the imagination of a top-flight researcher with the iconoclastic freedom of an avant-garde writer, to annul the sociologically so powerful opposition between the traditions and the previously incompatible functions of Sainte-Beuve and Marcel Proust, the Ecole Normale and the salons, the disabused rigour of science and the inspired amateurism of the literati, he obviously plays both games, trying thus, as has often been attempted since the social success of structural anthropology, to accumulate the benefits of science and the prestige of philosophy or literature. It is as if, in the age of science, the *aggiornamento* could only be accomplished through this kind of homage paid by the vice of belles-lettres to the virtue of science.

To judge the ambiguity of this struggle, it is enough to compare

what, at the end of last century, was the fight for the 'new Sorbonne'
of Durkheim, Lanson, Lavisse or Seignobos against the old literary
Sorbonne and the society critics, then closely associated with it, such
as Lemaître, Faguet or Brunetière, sustained, as was to become
apparent in the case of Agathon, by a whole literary milieu. Over
the issue of Dreyfus as in May 1968, the new sciences, sociology,
psychology, history, are opposed to the old literary disciplines and
more or less according to the same principles, science versus
creativity, collective work versus individual inspiration, international
openness versus national tradition, left versus right.[79] But the
apparent analogies must not disguise the switch which has occurred:
the decadent inheritors of the 'new Sorbonne' are at least as marked
by the rhetorical complacency dear to Agathon as by the scientific
demands of Lanson; as for the semiologists of the sixties, which
their opposition to such an opponent and to his archaic modes of
thought ('l'homme et l'oeuvre'[80] series) situates on the side of scientific
and political 'progressiveness', in fact they are carrying on, with the
help of the cultural press and the student audience which it nourishes,
the old struggle of the literati and the society essayists against the
'scientism', 'positivism' and 'rationalism' of the 'new Sorbonne'. But
this unending struggle between the 'reductive materialism' of the
social sciences, here incarnated in a perfect caricature, is henceforth
achieved in the name of a science which, in the guise of semiology,
or even structural anthropology, claims to be capable of reconciling
the requirements of scientific rigour with the society elegance of
authorial criticism.

THE *AGGIORNAMENTO*

This polemic could have been one of the paradoxical manifestations
of the transformation of the symbolic relations of force which had
previously obtained, within the whole academic system and beyond,
between science and arts, between scientific culture and literary
culture, between the scientific definition and the literary definition
of the 'faculties', in the dual sense of the professorial body and of
a mental capacity or power.[81] Raymond Picard's pamphlet constitutes
the first overt riposte of substance from the old, traditionally
dominant disciplines, directly implicated in reproducing the academic
institutions and culture, against those who, at the cost of a partial

reconversion which helps them claim allegiance both to scientific 'modernity' and to literary elegance, aim to invade the private reserve of the canonical disciplines; and aim to do so by relying on the student public and the educated general public whose requirements or expectations are directly expressed and fashioned by intellectually pretentious journalism, stemming from the convergence between the most intellectual of the journalists and the most journalistic of the intellectuals.

Although they are not really recognized in the traditional definition of teaching as an object of its rivalry, and even less as umpires of the competition, students do none the less play a decisive role in the internal struggles of which the university field is the site, and first and foremost by providing the avant-garde movements – real or supposed – with the minimum contingent of followers and militants that they need to oppose the academic 'establishment'.[82] Thus it is that the growth in the number of students and also of junior lecturers has been the cause of a quantitative growth in the demand for cultural products, and of a qualitative transformation of this demand: it is certain in particular that all the intellectual 'novelties' find their chosen audience among the students of the new disciplines in the arts faculties, intellectuals aspiring to vaguely defined categories of perception and appreciation, given to adopting external signs of the intellectual profession and often inclined to be satisfied with facsimiles of the fashionable sciences – semiology, anthropology, psychoanalysis or Marxology. And this at a time when producers of a new type found in the opportunities offered by this new public (and by publishers wishing to appropriate it) an opportunity to impose a redefinition of the limits of the publishable, to abolish the frontiers between research and belles-lettres or journalism, and to pass off the products of middlebrow culture as authentic avant-garde conquests.

It would not be possible to account for the evolution of the symbolic power relationships within the university field without an analysis of all the processes which led to the weakening of its autonomy and to the growth of the power of external instances of consecration, and especially of cultural journalism, able to guarantee certain producers and certain products a much swifter and wider distribution and publicity than the internal agencies procure even for those that they do consecrate, after their long and slow process of canonization. We would have to analyse under this heading the properties of mixed institutions and agents (university institutes closely connected to the media, like the EHESS; cultural weeklies, like *Le Nouvel Observateur, Le Magazine littéraire, Les Nouvelles littéraires*; reviews of high-quality popularization, like *L'Histoire, Le Débat*, etc.), structurally committed to mixing the genres and blurring the differences between the limited field of production and the field of general production, between journalists and academics or writers, or, more precisely, between the enterprises of short-term cultural production and their annual, swiftly packaged products, which intrepidly approach the biggest problems, hitting any moving target and refusing to bother with references, notes, bibliographies and indexes, and the long-term cultural enterprises and their products, with their restricted circulation, doctoral theses destined, more and more often, to an obscure fate with some university press, or original articles in scientific reviews which are raided with few scruples and less discrimination by the producers of middlebrow culture and high-quality popularization, intermediaries anxious to gain instant profit from their cultural contraband. We would have to reconstruct (but how could we do it without being accused of mounting a police investigation?) all the networks of solidarity and the circuits of exchange, through which the whole set of the agents defined by dual membership and dual identity, journalist-authors and author-journalists, journalist-academics and academic-journalists, tend to validate each other's claims to wield the power of cultural conservation, associating their fellows, as much in their hit parades as within the new agencies of consecration (editorial committees, publishing houses, etc.), through a self-justifying error in perception and appreciation, with the best-known scholars and writers among their peers, for whom they provide success with the general public late in the day, in exchange for the consecration which their presence confers on the essayists.[83] We would have to show the logic of the strategies through which they accumulate this parasitical power of consecration: analyse the exchange which arises – not without the whiff of mutual contempt inevitably implied by mutual exploitation – between consecrated academics or intellectuals, and journalists who consecrate themselves by declaring themselves qualified to consecrate them (a journalistic academic [Catherine Clément] who made her name interviewing Sartre or Lévi-Strauss will find herself thereby invested with the power to consecrate all those whom she allows into the series, starting with her fellows, who will return the favour in another daily or weekly, by consecrating as a legitimate work her essays on structuralism or Lacanian psychoanalysis or her inspired denunciations of totalitarian regimes or ideas); or we should describe the conditions and forms of the transfer on the university market (especially at the EHESS, the point of least resistance to infiltration) of the capital of symbolic power acquired and exercised in the media, or of the cashing in of academic authority on the market of journalism and publishing (by recording, for instance, reviews written by academics of books written by journalists).

To understand the quite singular position of the social sciences, playing the part of a Trojan horse in their struggle to impose a new definition of legitimate culture, we have to reinsert them into the two spaces to which they more or less strictly belong, that of the arts and that of the science faculties. If we take as our indicator the proportion of *normaliens* (and, at least in the arts faculties, the proportion of *agrégés*), we show up a social hierarchy of social origins of the students and also of the professors (in spite of the blurring effects of overselection).

Thus, for instance, if we take as a measure of the value accorded to the different disciplines the proportion of *normaliens* in the whole set of teachers of rank A [professors and senior lecturers] in 1967, we obtain the following hierarchy: philosophy and classical languages, 40 per cent; French, 39 per cent; psychology, 27 per cent; history, 24 per cent; linguistics, 19 per cent; geography, 4 per cent. In the more select population of professors and senior lecturers at the Sorbonne and Nanterre in 1967 we obtain, for German and Greek, 75 per cent; Latin, 66 per cent; philosophy, 60 per cent; minor modern languages – Scandinavian, Russian, etc. – 53 per cent; French, 50 per cent; history, 48 per cent; psychology, 35 per cent; sociology, 30 per cent; English, 22 per cent; Spanish and geography, 10 per cent; Italian and ethnology, 0 per cent – and the hierarchy is more or less the same, but the proportions much lower, among the lecturers and assistant lecturers.

Without entering into the details of the analysis, we may observe that the social sciences assume a doubly subordinate position, both under the hierarchy which is tending more and more to predominate, that of the natural sciences, and under the old hierarchy, today threatened by the rise in natural sciences and scientific values on the cultural stock exchange. Which explains why these disciplines still function as a refuge for bourgeois children with fair-to-middling results.[84] What one might call the *scientific syndrome*, typical of most semiological work and of all the more or less phantasmagorical combinations of the different lexicons of the social sciences, linguistics and psychoanalysis, psychoanalysis and economics, etc., which proliferated in the seventies, can be understood as an attempt by disciplines defined as doubly negative (neither arts nor science) to reverse the situation by inverting the signs, and to aggregate the prestige and profits of literary (or philosophical) avant-gardism with those of scientific avant-gardism, although these had long been considered incompatible, through the miraculous conjunction of the appearance of scientific rigour with the appearance of literary elegance or philosophical profundity. We can understand how the circular structure of domination, which allows disciplines that are doubly subordinate according to traditional criteria simultaneously to dominate from another angle the disciplines that dominate them, only if we realize that it characterizes a critical moment of the historical process which tends to subordinate the citadel of literary culture to scientific culture, which used to be subordinate.

The social success of what is called 'structuralism' can no doubt be explained by the fact that those whom cultural journalism has grouped under this label had in common at least the fact that they seemed to bring a miraculous solution to the contradiction which confronted a whole generation of professors and students, as much in the canonical disciplines most open to the outside world such as philosophy, literature or history as in the social sciences, by enabling them to remain on the level of 'science'. It should be sufficient as proof to analyse the social usage of structural linguistics and of semiology, as much in teaching, where more or less well-digested borrowings from these disciplines have played the part of last rampart against despair – especially for the younger and more modernist professors – as in cultural production, where they have enabled cut-price conversions to be carried out.

The interests which are associated with the position held in the space organized around the opposition between the traditional humanities and the new disciplines with scientific pretensions,

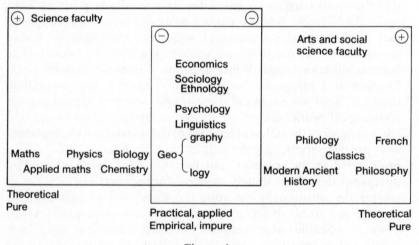

Figure A

linguistics, psychology, sociology, ethnology, even semiology, are always present, even if mostly unconsciously, in the most purely intellectual disputes; and declarations in the domain of theory, method, technique or even style are always social strategies in which powers are affirmed and claimed. No doubt we should be careful not to see a relation of cause and effect in the correlation to be found between the importance of research in a given discipline and the majority of the characteristics attached to the whole of the discipline, not least the dispositions of its teachers towards research; however, even when, as is the case with the social sciences in France, research has at first often been an escape route or a refuge for those excluded from the traditional careers, the appearance within a university discipline of a body of professional researchers, conducting their research as their principal activity, officially recognized and remunerated in organizations especially set up and run to this end (like the CNRS), constitutes in itself a break with the most specific characteristic of the university model – the conflation of the activities of teaching and research – with the result that pedagogical debates and concerns are very often the true motive for publications with scholarly pretensions, and that the most 'personal' research can so often provide material for the classes preparing pupils for academic entrance examinations.

Moreover, when the numerical importance of the researchers grows, the status of the teachers, themselves divided between the products of the old type of appointment and the newcomers, who often display academic and social properties close to those of the researchers,[85] becomes transformed. Through the medium of the institutions germane to the discipline, the committees and commissions entrusted with financing research and appointing new researchers, but also and above all through the institutionalization of the status of the researcher, which tends to constitute academic research and publication as a subjective norm for all practices and relegates pedagogical investment to the second rank, new solidarities and new needs become imperative, countering the effects of membership of the professorial body. Similarly, through new institutionalized modes of production and circulation of cultural works (debating clubs, study groups, symposia, etc.), encouraged by their relation with the bureaucracies, there are new modes of thought and expression, new themes and new modes of conceiving intellectual work and the role of the intellectual, which filter through into the intellectual world. The appearance of a public or private demand for applied research and of an audience of readers attentive to the social usage of the social sciences – higher civil servants and politicians, educators and social workers, advertisers and experts in health, etc. – encourages the success of a new kind of cultural producer, whose presence in the academic field (in the enlarged sense which is increasingly tending to become the norm) constitutes a decisive break with the fundamental principles of academic autonomy, and with the values of disinterestedness, magnanimity and indifference to the sanctions and demands of practice. These academic managers, who are busy seeking funds for their 'laboratories', frequenting committees and commissions to pick up the contracts, information and subsidies necessary for the good running of their enterprise, and organizing symposia designed to publicize their productions as much as to increase their productive capacities, introduce new tasks, often borrowed outright and without preliminary critique from the men of action, and new ways of approaching these tasks. They produce works of a tone and style which combine the neutrality of a positivist account with the blandness of a bureaucratic report, in order to obtain the effect of respectability necessary to cloak the recommendations of the expert with the authority of science.[86]

The claim to bureaucratic reliability which defines the *responsible intellectual* (and especially the committee member of political or union organizations) has indeed as its corollary renunciation of the premise of critical detachment from authority and of the total intellectual ambition which define the social personality of the intellectual (as personified in France by Voltaire, Zola, Gide and Sartre).[87] This new protagonist in the field of cultural conflict finds natural support in a new kind of agency of validation, able to counterbalance, at least politically, the weight of academic or intellectual agencies, the clubs (such as 'Jean Moulin', the 'Prospectives' [Perspectives], the 'Futuribles' [Futurables], etc.) where the most intellectual of the managers and the most managerial of the intellectuals exchange their visions of the world, commissions (especially the commissions of the [state Five-Year] Plan and the commissions of finance and research servicing the planners) where administrative researchers and research administrators agree on the future of science, not to mention the institutions constitutive of the bureaucratic cultural order, like the institutes of political studies or the quasi-official newspaper commentaries, reading which is the evening prayer[88] of the active intellectual.[89]

But, above all, the wage earners of research who proliferate with the development of large, socially and technically differentiated units of production (INSEE, INED, CREDOC, INSERM, etc.) can no longer surround themselves with the charismatic aura which attaches to the traditional writer or professor, small producers exploiting their own independent cultural capital, which tends to be seen as a divine gift.[90] This is all the more the case since the products of the new research work often bear the mark of the conditions in which they were accomplished: these 'reports' and 'accounts', often drafted in haste to meet a deadline, according to the standardized norms of mass production, and, because of the need to justify the funds spent, bound to sacrifice all to a display of the amount of work accomplished – with interminable methodological notes, voluminous appendices, etc. – rather than to an interpretation or a systematization of the results, are just as different from a book or a scientific article as are the most traditional doctoral theses, which are also marked by the social need to have their labour displayed and appreciated, even if they cannot always clearly show what its results are.

In fact, the development of independent institutions of research has reinforced the action of new principles of division which affect every dimension of intellectual life. Unlike those differences which could be observed in an earlier phase in the most academic sector of the academic system, which were produced by the very functioning of the system and were indispensable to its functioning, that is to the reproduction of its hierarchies, the ever more marked differences which separate teachers and researchers, or the products of the old and new style of appointment, tend to substitute, at least in the long run, a plurality of worlds controlled by different laws for the unified world of differences produced by one dominant hierarchical principle.[91]

POSITIONS AND STANCES

Thus we can understand why positions in the university space, such as it may be defined *using exclusively academic criteria and properties*, are so closely linked to 'political' declarations. Indeed, we note that, in a space constructed only from academic properties, the associations and the distances correspond very closely to the 'political' affinities and antagonisms of the conflicts of May 1968 *and after* (thus, for instance, all the signatories of a motion supporting Robert Flacelière hold positions in the university space very close to that of their 'threatened' colleague; similarly, the professors who publicly declared themselves in petitions, announcements, books, etc., for or against the movement of May 1968 hold diametrically opposed positions in the university space, those *for* being situated entirely in the south-west sector of the diagram, those *against* above all in the south-east sector). If this is the case, it is in fact because the propensity of the various professors to associate defence of the teaching community with a defence of the protected market which ensures them a strictly controlled academic public varies with the degree to which the value of their products depends on the stability of the market, or, in other words, with the degree to which their competence – that is, their specific capital – depends on the statutory guarantee conferred by the institution.[92] The violence of the reactions which were provoked, among the most traditionalist teachers in the most traditional disciplines, by the questioning of the academic institution and of the market whose monopoly it guaranteed, is strictly commensurate with the dependency of their production on this market: being often more or less devoid of value beyond the limits of the academic market (they are very little translated abroad), the cultural productions of ordinary professors – not least their lectures – are threatened with devaluation by the crisis which occurs in their institution when new products arrive on the market, products offered by more formalized and powerful disciplines, like linguistics or the social sciences.[93] The fate of philology, a long-established academic discipline, brutally relegated by linguistics to the museum cellars, represents an extreme case of what has happened to the majority of literary disciplines, even the best protected, like the history of literature, classical languages or philosophy.[94] The crisis hit the philologists from the Ecole Normale Supérieure head on, since they had remained totally aloof, on the heights of their statutory certainties, from the evolution of the linguistic sciences and from everything which was happening not only abroad but also in France in marginal institutions like the Ecole des Hautes Etudes and the Collège de France. They suddenly found themselves devalued, then relegated or forced into hazardous reconversions doomed from the start, faced with the intrusion of linguistics, imported and supported by marginals, often not *normaliens*, of provincial origins or the products of 'lesser' disciplines (like modern languages).[95] Through a process which may be noted each time that two positions in a social space change places, whether imperceptibly or abruptly, in due course the previously dominant, who find themselves, unwittingly and in spite of themselves, gradually led into a subordinate position, contribute as it were to their own decline by obeying a sense of statutory grandeur which prohibits them from changing gear and operating the necessary reconversions in time. We are obviously put in mind of the relations between aristocrats and bourgeois at the dawn of capitalism; but we could just as well invoke the elder sons of the 'great' farming families in the Béarn region who were condemned to bachelorhood in the 1950s by their concern to avoid misalliance during a period of crisis on the matrimonial market (a crisis governed, among other factors, by the modification of the relative positions of the small farmer and the minor civil servant). And thus we can understand the bitterness of ENS and *agrégation* graduates of petty-bourgeois or working-class origins who have trusted in once dominant careers and positions, when they discover too late, after a series of changes as imperceptible as the intercontinental drift, that their investments will be only very partially repaid. These consenting victims of academic success, whose consecration led them first to hold a teaching post in secondary education, then, as a result of the expansion of the university, a post of *assistant* [assistant lecturer] or *chargé d'enseignement* [temporary senior lecturer] in a provincial faculty, with all the corresponding consequences, those of provincial isolation, heavy teaching load, etc., now see their unlucky rivals who, at first were relegated to unglamorous positions, promoted because of the transformation of the relation between the canonical disciplines and the new disciplines, in the vanguard of 'research', often with no other qualification than their membership of a fashionable group and with no other virtues in their eyes than the 'cheek' often associated with higher social origins, which enabled them to take the risk of investment in marginal institutions.[96]

4

The Defence of the Corps and the Break in Equilibrium

The representation of ages, and the spaces between them, is relative to the composition of society and its parts, to its needs and capacities. In our old nations, especially before the war, when all the positions were filled, where one could hardly progress except through seniority, everyone had to line up and take his turn, and the young were separated from the old by a solid, impermeable mass, whose density impressed them with the feeling of the stages they had to cover before joining their elders.

M. Halbwachs, Classes sociales et morphologie

The structure of the university field is only, at any moment in time, the state of the power relations between the agents or, more precisely, between the powers they wield in their own right and above all through the institutions to which they belong; positions held in this structure are what motivate strategies aiming to transform it, or to preserve it by modifying or maintaining the relative forces of the different powers, that is, in other words, the systems of equivalence established between the different kinds of capital. But, if it is certain that crises (notably that of May 1968) divide the field along pre-existing lines of fracture, so that all the declarations of the professors on the subject of the academic institution and the social world are motivated in the last analysis by their position within the field, we should not conclude that the outcome of the internal struggles depends only on the forces present and the efficiency of the different fields. The transformations of the social field as a whole affect the university field, especially through the medium of morphological changes, of which the most important is the great increase in the student clientele which is partly responsible for the unequal increases in size of different parts of the teaching body and, thereby, the transformation of the power relations between the faculties and the disciplines and, above all, within each of them, between the different teaching grades.

This is what is confusedly felt by the defenders of the old order: since the change occurs to a considerable extent because of the number of students, who, through the corresponding growth in the demand for teachers, threaten to transform the functioning of the university market and to modify, through the transformation of careers, the equilibrium of forces within the teaching body, they become the defenders of a *numerus clausus* and they work, without orchestration, to defend the professorial body against the effects of inevitable growth. Thus, in order to understand the changes which have occurred in the different faculties in response to the problem posed by the growth in the number of students, we have to take note not only of the specific form taken in each case by the morphological transformation of the population of students, that is the *external variables*, such as the size of the growth when it occurred, its intensity and duration, but also the unique characteristics of the institution facing this transformation, that is *internal variables*, such as the principles controlling appointment and careers in the different faculties and, within them, in the different disciplines.

The huge and rapid rise in the student population, which resulted from the coincidence of the rise in the birth-rate in the years after the war with a general growth in the rate of educational enrolment,[1] led, in the sixties, to a growth in the professorial body all the greater since, at the same time, the teacher–pupil ratio improved strongly, although to different degrees, in all the faculties.[2] The most direct consequence of this process has been a considerable increase in the number of faculty posts available and, at least for some categories of teachers, an accelerated career.

It is remarkable that most of those who have looked at the transformations of the university have seen in the growth of the student population only its numerical effect (either as masses or as 'massification'), as is usually the case – with problems of urbanization, for instance – with spontaneous or semi-scholarly sociology. We no doubt all remember the debates on 'quality or quantity', 'elite or masses', 'masses or quality', which were all the rage with academic journalists and journalistic academics in the sixties. Now we may

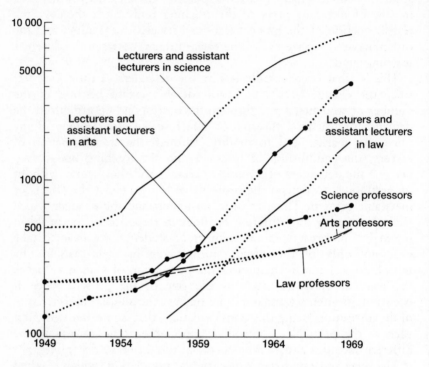

Graph 4 The evolution of the teaching body in the faculties of law, arts
and science

propose as a general law that, apart from the *purely mechanical* effects of *crowding* that the social agents inevitably exercise, in so far as they are endowed with biological bodies and properties occupying space, and the already more specifically social effects of anonymization and 'irresponsibilization' which result from the fact of being 'lost in the crowd', *the action of morphological factors is only ever exercised through the specific logic of each field* which gives their specific form to all these effects. We cannot go mechanically from the growth in *size* of the universities to the growth in complexity of university bureaucracy (which growth is not proven, anyway), or, according to the scholarly stereotype, to the transformation of the 'community' into 'mass' or, even less, of the 'scholar' into 'educational worker'. Similarly, the appearance of a body of academic administrators and the growth of its importance in the academic power structure can be understood only through an analysis of the overall structure of the field, of the struggles which are engaged there and of the benefit which each camp can derive from the effects of the growth in numbers of students and of the different categories of teachers (as can be seen especially clearly in the case of American universities, which, because of their status, are more directly subject to the laws of supply and demand than the French university). That is why the analysis of the effect that the morphological transformations have had on the professorial body, on its vision of the university world and its divisions, is predicated on a *structural history* of the university field which must at least be sketched, within the limits of the available data.

The growth in profitability of academic diplomas resulting from the growth in the offer of employment on the university market is clearly seen in the differences separating the careers open to *normaliens* and *agrégés* at different periods in the history of the teaching system.[3]

The relation between the proportion of former pupils of the Ecole Normale Supérieure who teach in a *lycée* and the proportion of those who teach in a university faculty has become inverted between 1938 and 1969. And the transformation is no doubt much greater than the figures suggest, because the majority of the *normaliens* who teach in *lycées* belong to the earliest matriculation years: in 1969, there were 40 teachers in secondary education for 31 teachers in higher education among the *normaliens* who matriculated between 1920 and 1929; conversely, there were only 23 teachers in secondary education (of whom 5 were in preparatory classes) for 150 teachers in higher education from the matriculation years 1954–59 (that is a ratio of 1 to 6.5). Similarly, despite a growing number of new *agrégés* (there were on average 970 per year between 1965 and 1970, as opposed to 250 between 1945 and 1950), the chances of an arts *agrégé* teaching in higher education rather than in secondary education increased very strongly between 1949 and 1968. And everything seems to suggest that this evolution is even more marked for the holders of scientific diplomas: thus in 1969 only 7.6 per cent of the scientific *normaliens* of the 1945–59 matriculation years taught in secondary schools, as opposed to 46.5 per cent of the scientists of the 1919–30 matriculation years; for the arts graduates, the proportions were 11.6 and 31.7 per cent respectively.

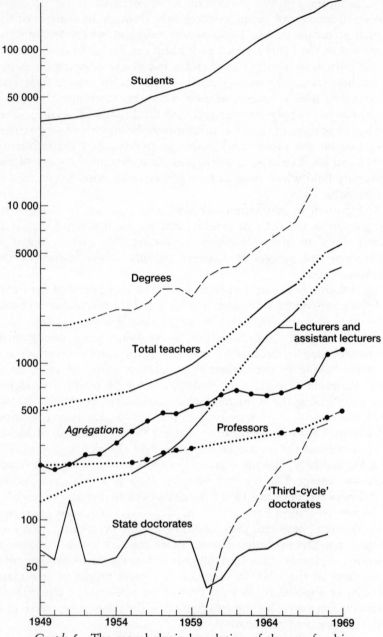

Graph 5 The morphological evolution of the arts faculties

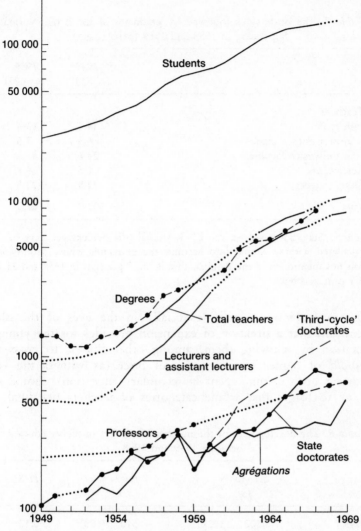

Graph 6 The morphological evolution of the science faculties

Table 7. The professions followed by graduates of the Ecole Normale
Supérieure in 1938 and 1969 (percentages)

	1938 (N=535)	1969 (N=629)
Teachers		
in *lycées*	44.5	16.4
in preparatory classes	6.5	7.5
in university faculties	24.6	46.8
Researchers	1.5	6.8
Other careers	22.9	22.5
Total	100.0	100.0

Source: Statistics based on the ENS Annual (the percentages have been
calculated without taking into account the graduates whose profession
was not mentioned in the Annual, that is, 30.7 per cent in 1938 and 31.7
per cent in 1969)

The over-obvious benefit (especially in the eyes of the older
generation) that a situation of expansion provides for the younger
generation by allowing them, among other things, to cross the
threshold of higher education at cut price (as witness the very
important drop in time spent in secondary education), should not
lead us to forget that whole categories of teachers benefited, to

Table 8. The development of the number of *agrégés* in higher education
between 1949 and 1968

	Secondary [S]		Higher [H][a]		H/S
1949	5,000	(100)[b]	510	(100)[b]	0.10
1960	7,200	(144)	1,100	(217)	0.15
1968	6,020	(120)	4,200	(823)	0.69

[a]Estimated.
[b]Base 100 in 1949.
Sources: Service des Statistiques et de la Conjoncture and A. Prost,
L'Enseignement en France, 1800–1967, Paris, A. Colin, 1968, p. 462.

different degrees, from this favourable conjuncture. Thus the growth in the number of chairs available and the shortage of teachers endowed with the diploma required to hold them (the doctorate) have had the effect of offering to professors and senior lecturers already in posts in the provinces at the time of the expansion much greater opportunities to move into the University of Paris, the apex of all the academic hierarchies, which was until then accessible only to a minority.[4] (Those among the tenured professors of the Paris arts faculty who gained a post after 1960 and who previously held a chair in the provinces are less often *normaliens* or *agrégés* than their older colleagues – that is 34 per cent or 80 per cent respectively, as opposed to 47 per cent or 89 per cent – and, as we have seen, it is the same for professors at the faculty of Nanterre.) Moreover, once we realize that the expansion of the universities had the effect of offering greatly accelerated careers to those of the teachers of intermediate age who gained their doctorate during this period, we can see that this double transformation brought to the highest positions, on the one hand, the highest-ranking second-choice teachers (according to the criteria of excellence pertaining in the previous state of the system), who are most unlikely to feel by this promotion liberated from the traditional values of the corps, and, on the other hand, those teachers of the following generation who adapted most easily or most pliantly to the norms of academic production, in a period of crisis of academic and intellectual paradigms (at least for the arts faculties).

But if, at the level of tenured professors or senior lecturers (rank A posts), a simple upward shift and a brake on the growth required allow a response to the new state of demand without any serious deviation from the old principles of recruitment (we do in fact notice a lowering of the teaching ratio as regards tenured professors, which is particularly marked in the arts faculties) it is not so with the subordinate levels of the teaching body: in this case, the shortage is likely to impose strategies liable to threaten, at least in the long run, the reproduction of the professorial body by constraining the professors to draw more and more widely on the *limited reserve* of candidates traditionally considered as legitimate. However, the different disciplines are distinguished in three fundamental ways: the size of their required teaching ratio, linked to the size of the increase in student numbers; the size of the reserve of *agrégés* at their disposal; and, thirdly, the propensity of tenured professors to draw exclusively on this reserve, a propensity which is mainly a function of their academic diplomas.[5] The new disciplines and the canonical disciplines are strongly opposed enough on these three levels for us to be able to treat them as two different markets – or subfields. Indeed, just as we can explain variations in salary according to regions, branches or professions only if we abandon the hypothesis of a *unified* labour market and thereby refuse to aggregate radically heterogeneous data, in order to research the basic laws of functioning (specific forms of capital and investment, appointment and career norms, procedures for settling disputes, whether institutionalized or not, etc.) specific to the different, relatively autonomous fields – structured spaces of durable relations (between producers themselves, and between producers and their customers) which coexist within the same economic space; similarly, we understand the variations observable not only in careers but, through them, in the practices and representations of the teachers of the different faculties and even the different disciplines, unless we use the hypothesis that these different units constitute so many different markets where formally identical diplomas can have different *values* and procure rates of remuneration which are genuinely *incommensurable* (for instance, in terms of academic 'power' or intellectual prestige). We immediately see that the proportion of *agrégés* among the holders of posts of rank A (and therefore the propensity to retain the *agrégation* as implicit criterion for appointing new entrants) is plainly stronger in the traditional disciplines (97 per cent in classics; 96 per cent in literature, 87 per cent in history) than in the new disciplines (53 per cent in sociology, 50 per cent in psychology) which, having acquired an autonomous existence only by detaching themselves from the old disciplines, like philosophy, and since they are not taught in secondary schools, are alike in having no competitive entrance examination, that is, they have no *agrégés* designated as reserves of manpower.[6] If we add that these new disciplines have grown at a distinctly faster rate than the old disciplines, we can see how they should have experienced norms of recruitment of new teachers quite different from those of the traditional disciplines.[7]

FUNCTIONAL SUBSTITUTIONS

It is by allowing themselves to be guided, as in all practical choices, by a system of implicit criteria, which are none the less approximately hierarchized, that the professors responsible for appointments have worked without any conscious orchestration to defend the social constants of the professorial body. And that has been at the cost of a series of functional substitutions which were all the more incumbent upon them since the reserve of conventional candidates was weaker, or more reduced by previous appointments. They had to renounce, more or less totally according to their discipline (that is, according to the relation between the manpower required and the reserve of legitimate postulants), secondary requirements concerning academic diplomas, sex and age, which they had tacitly involved in their recruiting procedures (and even more rigorously when they belonged to disciplines situated higher up in the academic hierarchy and thus endowed with an abundant reserve of manpower possessing the scarcest properties). Thus, in a discipline like French literature, which occupies a high rank in the university hierarchy and whose very highly selected members are nearly all *agrégés* and to a very great extent *normaliens*, the relative proportion of graduates of the Ecole Normale Supérieure de la rue d'Ulm among the teachers recruited since the beginning of the period of expansion (relatively numerous, since the teaching body doubled between 1963 and 1967 without exhausting a very full reserve of manpower) decreased in favour of former graduates of the Ecole Normale Supérieure de Saint-Cloud (hitherto extremely rare, at least in the canonical disciplines) and, more generally, in favour of the *agrégés* who did not graduate from a *grande école*, at the same time as the proportion of holders of an *agrégation* in classics decreased in favour of holders of an *agrégation* in grammar or in modern literature, traditionally less prestigious.

> Thus in literature there are only 20 per cent of graduates of the Ecole Normale Supérieure de la rue d'Ulm among the teachers recruited after 1960 compared to 34.4 per cent among those who entered before 1960; contrariwise, there are 7.4 per cent of graduates of Saint-Cloud and 65.5 per cent of *agrégés* who are not *normaliens* among the teachers appointed after 1960, against 5.4 per cent and 58 per cent among those who entered before 1960. Among the teachers of classical languages, the proportion of *agrégés* in classics falls from 76 per cent among those who entered their posts before 1960 to 62.5 per cent for those appointed after 1960. Conversely, the proportion of *agrégés* in grammar and modern literature rises from 24 per cent for the teachers appointed before 1960 to 37.5 per cent for the teachers appointed afterwards.

The same concern to expand the professorial body without contributing to its 'deterioration' is also expressed, for the less prestigious disciplines, like classical languages or history, in the recruitment of teachers who are situated at a level in the implicit or explicit hierarchy of academic excellence directly below the level occupied in this hierarchy by the holders of the same posts in the previous academic generation. In a discipline, like geography, which is situated at the bottom of the whole university hierarchy – the proportion of *normaliens* has always been very small and the professors are often ex-pupils of the preparatory classes, mostly lacking diplomas higher than the *agrégation* – the logic of the defence of the professorial body transpires not in the university diplomas of the newly appointed teachers, since, in this case, the *agrégation* constitutes both the lower limit and the upper limit of the reserve, but in feminization, or in a widening of the age range from which the teachers are chosen.

Thus posts of rank B, which had only 15.2 per cent women in 1963, had 23.6 per cent in 1967; moreover, whereas the majority of teachers appointed before 1950 entered higher education before the age of 28, the mode of distribution according to the same criterion for teachers appointed after 1960 is between 30 and 35. If the increase in numbers of women and older candidates is not more marked, it is because the action of the factors which in classical languages and literature reinforce the propensity to privilege the *agrégés* is no doubt weaker in a discipline placed at the bottom of the traditional hierarchy, and which is relatively open to scientific research.

The commonsense strategies which tend to maintain the social homeostasis of the professorial body may well remind us of the matrimonial strategies which, in the case of imbalance in the sex-ratio, cause a change in the modal age of marriage (and above all, perhaps, flexibility around this age) of the individuals belonging to the numerically depleted sex, in order to facilitate a readjustment of the market, enabling the members of each social group to acquire a spouse without compromising on the most pertinent criteria from the viewpoint of matrimonial union, like economic and social status.[8] The same growth in the reserve of manpower which can be obtained at the cost of lowering the age of appointment to posts in higher education can also be ensured by the opposite choice, taking out of secondary education relatively old teachers, or at any rate teachers who have been employed in the career for a long time, who would never have got into higher education, once they had 'missed the boat', if the expansion of the system had not offered them this second chance. If between these two strategies, which are never completely exclusive, the second seems to have triumphed in the more traditional disciplines, that is classical languages and to a lesser degree literature, it is no doubt because the professors of these disciplines are particularly predisposed to experience with special acuity and irritation the concessions imposed by the conjuncture, and to try to minimize their scope by adopting the least risky solution. In addition, they unconsciously tend to reproduce, in a totally different conjuncture, the pattern of their own careers: it is remarkable that a large proportion of assistant lecturers enter faculties at the age when, twenty years earlier, the professors responsible for recruiting them had also spent ten to fifteen years in a *lycée* before entering the faculty, but at a higher grade, usually that of senior lecturer.

In classical languages, 87 per cent of the teachers who acceded to posts as lecturers or assistant lecturers between 1950 and 1960 were younger than 32 at the time of their appointment, as opposed to 59 per cent of those who were appointed to the same posts after 1960, whereas 13 per cent of the former were older than 35, as opposed to 28 per cent of the latter. Similarly, in literature, apart from the fact that the proportion of women of rank B went from 19 per cent in 1963 to 34.6 per cent in 1967, 40 per cent of the teachers who were appointed to rank B posts between 1950 and 1960 were younger than 30 and 27 per cent older than 35 at the time of their appointment, as opposed to 25 per cent and 33 per cent respectively of those who acceded to the same posts after 1960. Conversely, in a subject like history, which holds a position almost identical to that of classical languages as regards both the size of its reserve and its rate of growth, the increase in volume of the reserve has been obtained by lowering the age of appointment to higher education: 50 per cent of the historians who were appointed to posts of rank B between 1950 and 1960 were at least 32, and 30 per cent were over 36 on appointment, as opposed to 57.8 per cent and 23 per cent of those who were appointed to the same posts after 1960.

Although these norms of recruitment are sometimes justified by invoking the 'secondarization' inevitably caused by the increase in numbers of students, the resort to older *agrégés* no doubt constitutes the clearest indicator of the situation of the disciplines where the schism between secondary and higher education is so little marked, as much for methodology as for the knowledge transmitted, that teachers who have spent several years in secondary education can find a place there, and where, with the crisis in the system of teaching and the culture which it is supposed to transmit, the young teachers, even those made to measure, like the *normaliens*, endanger the perpetuation of the system. By choosing either 'old' *agrégés* lacking any heterodox talents, therefore very unlikely to relativize the culture of their masters, and reinforced (provisionally at least) in their support for the system by this last-chance promotion, or by choosing those among the younger *agrégés* whose diplomas and style promise to reproduce the institution, the professors of the classic disciplines also more or less consciously help to prevent a sudden transformation of the mode of reproduction of the producers and consumers of academic products from showing up their competence as obsolescent and devalued. The objective of this recruitment policy is to perpetuate the mode of academic reproduction whose product is the teachers' competence, and perpetuate the market where the products attain their value, the endlessly renewed clientele of the preparatory classes and the *agrégation* candidates. And the absolute privilege bestowed on the *agrégation* above all other criteria is understandable if we realize that it is through the domination of the *agrégation*, the ultimate goal of all lectures and all competitive examinations, that the intellectual norms governing this competition are imposed on all teaching and training at a lower level, whether in the case of preparation for the first degree or even for the writing of a master's degree.

The same logic could not operate in the new disciplines. Lacking a proper reserve, and although they could recruit from the *agrégés* of the canonical disciplines – in philosophy, notably – the tenured professors could not contain the recruitment of subordinate teachers within the limits of the population of *agrégés*: the proportion of *agrégés*, which remains constant among teachers in the arts, decreases strongly after 1960 in all the new disciplines, falling for example from 44.4 per cent of the teachers of psychology recruited before 1960 to 22.8 per cent among those appointed afterwards, and from 71.5 to 42 per cent in the corresponding categories of teachers of sociology. But the main thing is that, in these disciplines, the teachers are dominated numerically, and, at least in some respects, socially too, by the researchers who import and impose dispositions quite different from those which were current in the old university order. No doubt the faculty professors, who retain a considerable importance in the university (at least until 1967, the date of the enquiry), and even, up to a certain point, in the agencies of research appointments, strive to maintain, in the area of professorial appointments, principles which differ little from those of the traditional disciplines (continuing to attract the researchers with better academic qualifications than the category as a whole).[9] It remains the case, however, that there is an ever-increasing gap between the tenured professors and the subordinate teachers or researchers (who, at least in the period 1945–60, are often the product of negative selection within the clientele of the canonical disciplines) and that the divergence is extreme, even within the different statutory categories, to the detriment of methodological consensus.

The diversity of the education, careers and qualifications increases, among teachers in the same discipline, as we move from the traditional disciplines, whose market remains relatively saturated, towards the new disciplines: thus the proportion of teachers of rank B who attended a *khagne* [preparatory class for a *grande école*] decreases progressively as we move from the traditional disciplines (33 per cent in literature, 32 per cent in philosophy, 25 per cent in the ancient languages, 21 per cent in history, 20 per cent in English) to the new disciplines (18.8 per cent in linguistics, 16.3 per cent in psychology, 8.4 per cent in sociology). In these disciplines, the teachers have received, most often in a university faculty, a shorter education, no doubt less academically brilliant (to judge from the rate of distinctions) and quite disparate, as much at the level of individual careers (with the accumulation of credits from different degree courses) as at the collective level: the diversity of qualifications obtained by members of the same discipline and the heterogeneity of the disciplines covered during their education are all the stronger as we move towards the disciplines whose university validation is more recent. Similarly, while the teachers of the traditional disciplines have almost all started their career in secondary school teaching, the teachers of the new disciplines, who to a relatively large extent (all the larger as we move towards the more recently appointed and therefore the younger categories) were appointed direct to a post in higher education and above all research, previously exercised very various activities, which often had no connection with their present profession.

The extreme discordance of academic qualifications or types and levels of education of the specialists in social science is a result of the fact that those responsible for appointments are not able to resort to their traditional mode of recruitment, and yet they are equally unable to benefit from the freedom offered by their independence from secondary education (linked to the absence, until recently, of an *agrégation* and of secondary-schoolteaching careers) in order to elaborate and impose specific criteria and requirements. In the science faculties, partly no doubt because the break is infinitely clearer and sharper, at least in mathematics and physics, between teaching for an *agrégation* class and undertaking scientific research, new criteria of evaluation have been elaborated and imposed, deriving for the most part from research activities, such as the 'third-cycle' thesis, whereas the more exclusively academic qualifications (like the *agrégation*) tended to become useless on the research market and could in any case only produce their maximum benefits in so far as they were associated with scientific qualifications (as is shown by the fact that the number of teachers of rank B and the number of 'third-cycle' theses increase in roughly parallel fashion, while, conversely, the *agrégation* seems to be reduced to its official role as a competitive examination for entrance into secondary school teaching). In the new disciplines in the arts faculties, however, although there is certainly a higher proportion of holders of third-cycle doctorates among those teachers who do not hold the *agrégation*, it is still the case that this diploma is far from constituting a necessary and sufficient condition for appointment to higher education or scientific research: the *agrégation* (not to mention the title of graduate of a *grande école*) is so obviously recognized by those responsible for appointments (and, until 1968, by the committees of the CNRS themselves) that the majority of the *agrégés* who intend to enter research or are already engaged in it are still often exempted from the third-cycle doctorate, which, conversely, is far from being an automatic passport to posts of lecturer or even assistant lecturer – which does not mean, as we have seen, that the fact of possessing neither of these titles is sufficient to prevent appointment to a post in higher education.

> Thus, in a discipline like sociology, where the proportion of teachers who hold or are working on a third-cycle doctorate is relatively large, the proportion of teachers of rank B without a third-cycle doctorate or who are not at least working on one is only 28 per cent against 85 per cent of those who are *agrégés* or graduates of a *grande école*. At all events, less than half (44 per cent of the teachers of rank B who are neither holders of the *agrégation* nor graduates of a *grande école* have submitted a third-cycle thesis – and this, for a considerable proportion among them, despite already holding posts in higher education.

It follows that appointment to the professorial body is subject to arbitrary decisions by the diverse authorities (and especially directors of research groups) whose choices are eventually validated and ratified by the body as a whole;[10] and consequently that chances of appointment to research posts and increasingly, posts in higher education tend to depend at least as much on the scope, diversity and quality of academically profitable social relations (and thereby on place of residence and on social origins) as on academic capital. The absence or incoherence of criteria of recruitment destines the candidates for research posts, who cannot be ignorant of the virtually random nature of the relation between the characteristics displayed by an individual and the objective characteristics of the post, to undertake a quest for employment which is as inevitable (since nothing is impossible) as it is anguished (since nothing is certain) and which can lead them to place themselves under the dependency of some powerful protector or else to try to give themselves additional scarcity value by accumulating the most diverse qualifications.

A CRISIS OF SUCCESSION

The university system in its previous state tended to ensure its own reproduction by producing teachers endowed with fairly stable and homogeneous social and academic characteristics, which were therefore relatively interchangeable over a period of time as well as at any given moment. More precisely, the stability of the system over a period of time supposed that the teachers were endowed, at every hierarchical level, with an academic *habitus*, a veritable *lex insita*, as Leibniz says, an immanent law of the social body which, having become immanent in the biological bodies, causes the individual agents to realize the law of the social body without intentionally or consciously obeying it: in the absence even of any express regulation or any explicit warning, aspirations tend to adjust themselves to the modal *trajectory*, that is the normal trajectory for a given category at a given moment; the holders of a diploma invested with a given value on the academic market only ever actually aspire to posts invested with a scarcity and a value corresponding to the value of their diploma, or, more precisely, they do not feel authorized, or even inclined, to apply for a post when they are younger – or even older – than the average of the holders of such posts possessing qualifications identical to theirs. The good pupil is the one who, adapting to the rhythms of the system, knows when he is late or early, and acts in consequence to keep his distance or reduce it; similarly, the proper professor is the one who, having entered at the right age, always knows when he is too young or too old to apply for or claim a post, a favour or a privilege.

The educational institution, operating as pleasure principle and reality principle, stimulates the *libido sciendi*, and the *libido dominandi* which this conceals, and which is fuelled by competition, but it also assigns them limits, causing the agents to internalize frontiers between what it is legitimate to obtain, even in the field of knowledge, and what it is legitimate to hope for, to desire, to like (thus for a long time there was a frontier between *le primaire* (the elementary) or '*les primaires*' ('elementary people') and *le secondaire* (the secondary)). Such are the paths through which, in a phase of equilibrium, the institution manages, more or less well, to persuade all the agents to stake their investments in the games and objectives which it proposes, so that the frustrations which it inevitably provokes in some people are not transformed into a revolt against the principle of the investment, that is, against the game itself (and the drama of the 'runner up' in the entrance examination to the Ecole Normale de la rue d'Ulm, or the imposture of the graduate of the Ecole Normale de Saint-Cloud, who claim the title of *normalien* as if they had graduated from the ENS de la rue d'Ulm, repeating their failure in their ceaseless attempt to deny it, are there to attest to the fact that the institution manages to exclude in those it excludes the very idea of contesting the principle of exclusion).

We can more easily understand, in the light of these analyses, the disruptive effects that can follow an objective transformation of the temporal structure which constitutes the institution, and of its order, of this *order of succession* which is retranslated, at every moment, into a given correspondence between ages and grades. By choosing, in order to preserve the essentials, to recruit *agrégés* at all costs, even if they are women, or not *normaliens*, or over-age – in terms of the previous norms – the professors acted, without realizing it, as good defenders of the professorial body: we can indeed expect that agents who, having suffered and accepted the oscillatory manoeuvres of the institution, have as their immanent law the law of the institution should modify their expectations in conformity with the opportunities defined by the law of the institution. Thus, in so far as the agencies of education and selection of the professorial body were able to inculcate into all its teachers an intense and durable disposition to recognize the hierarchies and values of that body, the institution would no doubt have been able to master the effects of the growth in the number of students if the lack of a sufficient reserve of manpower had not obliged it to appoint agents who, having escaped from the traditional channels of education, were lacking in this 'internal law'.

The transformation of the practices of recruitment brought into the profession two categories of teachers whereby the institution was led to admit what it had excluded above all, that is, aspirations detached from legitimate expectations: on the one hand those who, although endowed with some of the properties required under the previous mode of recruitment, were destined to discover sooner or later that they had benefited from a false promotion, because of the fact that the post they held was no longer what it had been, as soon as people like themselves could hold it, and that it no longer carried with it the certainty of a career which was formerly tacitly guaranteed to the beneficiaries of this mode of recruitment (as is underlined by the fact that the number of assistant lecturers so greatly exceeds that of the professors, that an ever-increasing proportion of those newly promoted seems objectively destined to remain in the lower ranks of the hierarchy); and on the other hand all those who, lacking the former entrance qualifications and above all the dispositions which were associated with them, were hardly willing to perceive their appointment to a post in higher education as a miraculous ennoblement, if they then had to content themselves with an inferior career. All the conditions were therefore fulfilled for the new entrants furthest from possessing the properties and the dispositions which would previously have guaranteed a career in due course to almost all those who were appointed to a post in higher education, that is as much the *agrégé* in grammar appointed assistant lecturer at 35 as the sociology graduate appointed assistant lecturer at 28, to come to understand that the maintenance of *career norms* (as illustrated by the properties of the tenured professors at the Paris universities at the time of the enquiry) rendered illusory the transgression of the *recruitment norms* from which they had benefited.[11]

In so far as it is not accompanied by any real transformation of the procedures of promotion, the transformation of the mode of recruitment leads thus to a division of the subordinate teachers into two categories of teachers destined for careers as different as their education and the criteria according to which they have been appointed; on the one hand, the assistant lecturers and the lecturers who are destined to obtain the benefits of the career implicitly inherent in their position as it was defined in the previous state of the institution and of the structure of opportunities, and, on the other hand, those who will finish their career in a subordinate position (that of lecturer, at the top of the scale, or, in science, assistant lecturer with tenure). The formal identity of the synchronically defined positions disguises considerable differences, linked to academic capital, between the potential categories which are the true motivation underlying overt attitudes towards the academic system. These differences are revealed in the simple *indicator* of the *slope* of trajectory corresponding to a person's relative precociousness in a post (within the same discipline), always itself associated with the possession of properties which, like those designated by the title of *normalien* or *agrégé*, favour a swifter, and therefore more successful, career. And these differences in potential trajectories themselves correspond to quite different relations with the educational system (and even with the qualifications or the properties which seem to underpin these differences in trajectory). For instance, if the lecturers or assistant lecturers who lack the *agrégation* are more favourable to the abolition of the *agrégation* than are the *agrégés* (74 versus 44 per cent), the *agrégés* are all the more favourable in proportion to their juniority in the grade they hold (for instance, among the assistant lecturers with the *agrégation*, those under 30 are more favourable to the abolition of the *agrégation* than those over 30: 48 per cent as opposed to 42 per cent, the same difference being apparent among the lecturers).[12] This independent attitude to the *agrégation* is understandable if we know that possession of this diploma promises new entrants positions whose value is independent of the possession of the *agrégation*: thus it is that criticism of the *agrégation* competition and the corresponding preparation is found more or less exclusively among those of the *agrégés* who, because of their high position in the academic institution, or their membership of disciplines orientated towards research, are able to impose their worth independently of any reference to the *agrégation*.[13] We can understand in terms of the same logic that the lecturers who have not got the *agrégation*, and who are old for their grade, expect salvation above all from the new structures of university management: for instance, those who are over 35 are more inclined to consider that the powers of the new university structures are insufficient (62 per cent) than lecturers of the same age with the *agrégation* (21 per cent) (we note a similar but much less marked difference among assistant lecturers aged over 30, according to whether they are *agrégés* (45 per cent) or not (40 per cent)). We understand that, contrary to what was thought and written at the time of the crisis of May 1968, the conflict which divided the faculties did not oppose generations understood in the sense of age but *academic generations*, that is agents who, even when they are the same age, have been produced by two different modes of academic 'generation'. Whether they are old and already established or young and destined for a career, the teachers who are the product of the former mode of generation need to maintain in their careers the difference which they were not able to defend at the level of recruitment to the faculty; whether they are already old and provided with the minimal diplomas required under the former mode of recruitment or young and lacking in diplomas, the products of the new mode of recruitment are condemned to discover that only a modification in the laws of the career could grant them access to the advantages that access to the faculties had led them to hope for. And when we know that the laws which are derived retrospectively from the regularity of practices were in no way rules explicitly decreed and consciously applied, and that the claimants were more or less consciously compliant in determining the rhythm of their own promotion, we can understand that such a moment of awareness constitutes in itself an objective change, liable to make the whole mechanism grind to a halt.

A FINALITY WITHOUT ENDS

The statistics which shed light on the immanent logic of the behaviour of a set of agents encourage a whole series of theoretical errors, alternative or simultaneous. We can hardly formulate the statistical data which reveal a pattern, without running the risk of suggesting, through the connotations of ordinary language, a mechanist or finalist philosophy of action, as if it were immanent in things themselves. The most extreme linguistic vigilance, and all the precautionary phrases imaginable, like 'everything leads us to believe that', will not prevent the reader bound by his thinking habits, those of his political views especially, from seeing the effect of a mysterious mechanism or a sort of collective conspiracy in the fact that the different disciplines (a collective subject encouraging both the mechanist and the finalist view of the collectivity) welcomed agents who conformed as closely as possible to the former principles of recruitment (immediately in danger of being perceived as explicit rules), that is as similar as possible to the ideal *normalien* (and graduating near the top of the class), *agrégé* (and with distinction), a man (which goes without saying) and young, meaning 'brilliant'. The most probable reading consists in understanding the results recorded in the statistics as the product of an aggregate of actions based on rational calculation of clearly understood self-interest, or, worse, in supposing the action of those known colloquially as 'mandarins' to be the product of a collective strategy, conscious and organized; and all this without asking what the preconditions for such a *conspiracy* would be: preliminary organization, clear knowledge of the 'rules' obtaining, explicit statement of new rules of procedure, hierarchical structure allowing their application to be imposed, etc. Which question should make us realize that these conditions are obviously not fulfilled, as witness moreover the statistics attesting that the hierarchy of compensatory substitutions – between a woman *agrégé* and an old *agrégé*, who is not necessarily an *agrégé* who graduated a long time ago, which one should be chosen? – has nothing particularly rigorous about it. But, provided that the scientific account has used a (convenient) term such as 'mechanism' (speaking, for instance, of recruitment mechanisms), we might think of the university body as an apparatus able to produce, beyond any conscious or unconscious intervention by the agents, the regulations noted. Demographers, and all those who would like to reduce history to natural history, often succumb to this spontaneous physicalism, which, moreover, does not exclude a kind of finalism: the model of a cybernetic mechanism programmed to record the effects of its own action and react to them is a providential myth invented to account for these mysterious returns to equilibrium which are the delight of conservative scientism. We would then – tempted by language – slip into thinking of the professorial body as an organism inhabited by mysterious homeostatic mechanisms which, beyond any conscious intervention by the agents, would tend to re-establish the endangered equilibrium, the proportion of *agrégés* among the assistant lecturers playing the part of one of these organic constants which 'the wisdom of the body' (as in Cannon's title) aims to maintain. But where would we situate the source of this wisdom, the entelechy which determines and orientates the actions of these agents who act unconsciously and yet who are attuned to the collective ends ultimately most suited to their individual and collective interests?

It is only on condition that we understand them as the product of the combination – irreducible to a simple mechanical aggregation – of the strategies engendered by objectively orchestrated dispositions (*habitus*) that we can account for the statistical regularities of the practices, and the appearance of finality which they generate, without subscribing either to the subjective teleology of a universe of agents rationally orientated towards the same goal – here, the defence of the privileges of the dominant – or to the objective teleology of personified collectivities pursuing their own goals – in this case, the defence of the professorial body.[14] But our minds are so deeply accustomed to think of history in terms of these alternatives that any attempt to transcend them is likely to end up resorting to one or other of the ordinary modes of thought.[15] The slippage is all the more likely since it can only be avoided at the cost of a permanent struggle against ordinary language. Thus it suffices to constitute as subject of a sentence the name of one of those collectivities fashionable in politics, to constitute the designated 'realities' as historical subjects able to posit and realize their own ends ('the People want . . .'). The objective teleology implied by this social anthropomorphism coexists quite happily with a sort of spontaneous individualism, which is also inherent in the *subject-orientated* sentences of ordinary language, which, as in a fictional narrative, incline us to see the individual or collective history as a logical sequence of decisive actions. The sociologist thus finds himself faced with a writing problem very similar to that faced by novelists like Victor Hugo, especially in *Seventeen Ninety-Three*, and above all like Flaubert, when they wished to break with the privileged viewpoint of the 'hero' – say Fabrice at Waterloo in Stendhal's *Charterhouse of Parma* – in order to evoke the 'battlefield in such a way that we can deduce from it the movements and the impressions of any one of the individuals who are involved in it', in Michel Butor's words, and, more generally, in order to 'reveal the historical fields into which the individuals are drawn like iron filings'.[16] We need to escape the mechanist vision which would reduce the agents to simple particles swept up in a magnetic field, by reintroducing not rational subjects working to fulfil their preferences as far as circumstances permit, but socialized agents who, although biologically individuated, are endowed with transindividual dispositions, and therefore tend to generate practices which are objectively orchestrated and more or less adapted to objective requirements, that is irreducible either to the structural forces of the field or to individual dispositions.

A scholarly posture can lead us to misread the logic of the 'choices' of practice which operate most often outside any calculation and without explicitly defined criteria:[17] there would be little more sense in asking a 'head' how he chose his assistant lecturer than in asking him what criteria he used to choose his wife.[18] That does not mean that he hasn't in both cases used practical selection principles, models of perception and appreciation, whose cumulative effects, discovered statistically after the event from among the ensemble of practices of co-optation, have nothing arbitrary about them. What may appear as a sort of collective defence organized by the professorial body is nothing more than the aggregated result of thousands of independent but orchestrated strategies of reproduction, thousands of acts which contribute effectively to the preservation of that body because they are the product of the sort of social conservation instinct that is the *habitus* of the members of a dominant group.

To convince ourselves that the various philosophies of action which are most often used unconsciously in sociological analyses, therefore in uncoordinated fashion, are purely and simply incompatible with the facts, we have only to introduce, as a transition towards a description of the functioning of reality which will challenge the traditional alternatives, that kind of experimental refutation of the finalist vision of individual and collective action [Rational Action Theory] which was provided by the crisis in the old mode of functioning. We know indeed that the crisis of 1968 caused a profound transformation in the logic of the professors' collective action, by substituting a concerted action deliberately orientated towards the preservation of the status quo for a spontaneously orchestrated ensemble of actions inspired by solidarity with an 'elite'. The reactionary mobilization evoked by protest against what was self-evident from the point of view of the dominant, that is, the ordinary university order, tended to transform the diffuse and ungraspable complicity which was the basis of networks founded on an affinity of *habitus*, common memories, Ecole Normale friendships, into an active and institutionalized solidarity, founded on an organization orientated towards support for or restitution of order, the explicitly non-aligned union, the Syndicat Autonome.[19] From that moment on, everything that made up the old order, the intangible liberties and connivances which are shared by people of the same milieu, the respectful familiarity which is *de rigueur* between different generations of the same family, were abolished. Since the task is to take up the defence of something so self-evident that nobody would have thought of having to defend it, we see new personalities appear, often people with administrative responsibilities and defectors from the opposite camp, second-rank figures at all events and thrown into the front line by the retreat of those previously dominant. Thanks to this politicization and professionalization linked to their experience of managing the administrative machine, these anonymous spokesmen, often somewhat despised by the old authorities, 'took things in hand', as the saying goes, setting themselves objectives which could have been attained under the old order only if they were not declared as objectives, and constituting as explicit entrance requirements properties and qualifications which until then had merely been intuited via non-verbalized indices of behaviour or unverifiable rumours of the renown of the Ecole Normale. They enjoyed all the consequences and benefits of the transformation of a select club, whose members don't need to be investigated, into a corporate union. And they contributed thereby to reinforcing the very logic which they claimed to combat: by working to reduce the apparent discrepancy between liberties, to minimize the contradictions, conflicts and rivalry between heads which were dissimulated by the non-conspiratorial consensus on common values, by forcing themselves to offer up the united front of a managerial union against the united front of the unions dominated by subordinate teachers, in short, by giving the consistency of a plan to what was only the more or less coherent effect of the spontaneous orchestration of the *habitus*, they reinforced the break between categories which is the source of the protest against which they intended to struggle, and above all they contributed to destroying one of the main pillars of the old order, ignorance, or, in other words, faith: vagueness has its social function and, as we see with clubs, or with salons in a previous age, the most unimpeachable criteria are those which are the least definable.[20]

A TEMPORAL ORDER

The crisis which has divided the teaching body is a crisis of faith: the statutory barriers, in the event, are sacred frontiers which presuppose recognition. And we cannot understand the crisis without understanding the inner truth of the doxic order with which it breaks, and which this very break renders comprehensible. It is hardly possible to describe the two states of the institution, the organic and the critical, other than in their relation, passing constantly from one to the other, the critical state functioning as a tool of analysis of the organic state. The old mode of recruitment was a form of anticipated co-optation whereby the elders chose not subordinates destined for a subaltern career (since then institutionalized in the guise of the post of lecturer) but their potential peers, likely to be called on one day to succeed them. This is why it was based on a tacit acceptance of a definition of the post and of the conditions of access to the post, that is on selection criteria all the more imperative for being able to function only in an implicit mode, as is appropriate in the case of the election of an 'elite'. It supposed no more than a minimal consensus on the minimal, that is the negative, conditions for access to the profession, or, more precisely, on the limits of the eligible population: because of the fact that everyone agreed, without even having to state it, to accept the value of the criteria which were the foundation of his own value and of the value of his colleagues, such as the title of *normalien* which non-*normaliens* often acknowledge by surrounding themselves with *normaliens*. Nobody dreamed of rejecting or contesting the choice of the other professors in so far as they obeyed these criteria. Thus it is that the synchronic and diachronic homogeneity of the professorial body was based on a harmony among *habitus* which, being produced by identical conditions of selection and training, engender objectively harmonious practices, and especially selection procedures.

If the crisis of the university hierarchies has crystallized around the opposition between professors and lecturers, it is because the latter, and especially the older among them, as typical products of the new mode of recruitment, were condemned, more than the assistant lecturers (especially the younger ones) and the senior lecturers (a kind of professor by anticipation), to feel in all its intensity the contradiction between the promises written into their appointment and the future which was really ensured by the unchanged career procedures. The assistant lecturers who, in the previous state of the institution, were no more numerous than the tenured professors, and who were nearly always *agrégés* and often former graduates of the Ecole Normale Supérieure, were separated only by age, that is by a time-lag, from the professors, from whom they differed as little as possible in every other respect. This difference was at once total and minimal, like that which separates the generations in any social order based on simple reproduction. It was minimal, because the career was more or less completely predictable – which did not prevent agents whose entire academic apprenticeship had led them to interpret their professional progress in terms of the competitive examination from experiencing trajectories which were in fact only separated by infinitesimal differences as if they were unique; and also because the stability of the number of chairs was such that it was necessary and sufficient to wait for one university life-cycle to draw to its close for another to commence. So it was more or less inconceivable that assistant lecturers could even conceive of categorial claims opposed to those of the professors. But, simultaneously, the irreducible time-lag which separated the holders of the various grades established between them an unbridgeable distance: identical except for their separation by one university life-span, professors and assistant lecturers could not become competitors for the same posts, the same functions, the same powers.

Endowed with the same academic titles of nobility, that is with the same essence, the young and the old have merely reached different stages of fulfilment of their essence. The career is merely the time of waiting for the essence to be fulfilled. The assistant lecturer shows promise; the master has realized his promise, he has proved himself.[21] This all contributes to a world without surprises; and helps to exclude the individuals capable of introducing other values, other interests, other criteria in relation to which the old ones would be devalued, disqualified. *Noblesse oblige*: it establishes simultaneously the right of succession and the duties of the successor; it inspires aspirations and assigns them limits; it offers the young an *insurance* which, being of the same order as the assurances offered, implies patience, recognition of the distance and therefore the security of the elders. Indeed it is possible to get the assistant lecturers to resign themselves to have nothing for so long and to such an advanced age, to hold merely subordinate positions in a hierarchy where the intermediate degrees (which moreover are few enough) are defined only negatively through lack of certain attributes attached to higher positions, only because they are guaranteed eventually to have it all, and all at once, to pass without transition from the incompleteness of the assistant lectureship to the plenitude of the professorship, and, by the same token, from the class of impoverished heirs to that of legitimate title-holders. Just as the certainty of the compensations attached to their promised inheritance could lead the elder sons of noble families (or, in certain traditions, peasant families) to accept the sacrifices and servitudes of a prolonged state of tutelage, so the confidence of the rightful heir is, paradoxically, the reason for the resignation of the claimants to the post of professors; and, as we see with the thesis, the constraints of the institutions which contribute to regulate the rhythms of careers can operate only with the complicity of those who suffer them.[22]

The thesis for the state doctorate is, as we have seen, what enables the professors to exercise a lasting control over those aspiring to their succession; it offers a means of protracting for a long period of years the putting to the test which operations of co-optation always imply, at the same time as it enables them lastingly to *hold on* to the aspirants to their succession, thus maintained in a position of dependency (which excludes polemic, criticism or even competition, owing to the rule preventing previous publication). The time-lag between academic generations (between twenty and twenty-five years) being the condition of successful preservation of the order of succession, the duration and preparation of the thesis must take between ten and fifteen years (to which can be added a stay of ten to fifteen years in posts of lecturer, and professor in a provincial university) for this gap to be maintained. And no doubt it is not far-fetched to think that it is the institutional necessities of the successful reproduction of the professorial body which determine the time necessary for the production of the thesis, and, thereby, the very nature of the work involved, its size and scope, rather than the opposite.[23] The fact that the institutional constraints are experienced as an inherent requirement of the task of research and of the thesis itself is one of the results of the misconstrual and the faith which contribute to the accomplishment of institutional necessity. This investment in the work itself, which is all the greater when the candidate feels already consecrated academically, therefore the more compelled to excel, and which can be reinforced by the injunctions or the warnings of the thesis supervisor, tends to compensate for the effects of the dispositions which push the most famous of the postulants towards precociousness.

Legitimate precociousness (as opposed to opportunist haste) is the exception which proves the rule, contributing to a misconstrual of the real logic of the career. It is doubtless no coincidence that it is so often associated with the initiatives of supervisors whose atypical action also tends to mask the general logic. In fact, everything seems to suggest that professors tend to deviate more from the normal propensity to restrain their candidates' impatience, the more they are academically eminent – that is, no doubt, less dependent on statutory distance to maintain their authority. This can be seen through the evidence of a professor (a *normalien*, Henri Gouhier, who was top of his *agrégation* year in the twenties): 'Oh, no, I couldn't submit it [the thesis] earlier, because I already did it early enough, because men like Gilson and Brunschvig, even in those days, had told me: "Don't treat your thesis as your life's work. You need to get your doctorate while you are young, it's the researcher's first piece of work." . . . It was really the intellectual politics of men like Gilson and Brunschvig (who was much older than Gilson) to tell people: "Don't wait till you are forty-five to finish your thesis." That's what they believed. People say: "French theses take much too long", but even in those days really distinguished men advised you, if not to rush it, at least to consider that it wasn't your whole life's work.' We could also invoke the case of Meillet, responsible for a whole series of accelerated careers (among others, those of Benveniste and Chantraine).

But the true regulator is none other than that sort of *sense of legitimate ambition* (for oneself) which leads a person to feel both stimulated and authorized to claim a post as his due, or to do whatever is necessary to obtain one, that sense of the rhythm of university life which cannot be understood otherwise than as the effect of the personal internalization of the structures of probable careers (for the whole of a generation and for a particular individual endowed with particular properties). Everything happens as if the whole set of suitably socialized agents (of which *normaliens* and former pupils of the preparatory classes are the kernel) had an intuition – which does not mean that it is consciously conceptualized – of the network of probable trajectories of the agents of their age (most often reduced to the group of mutual acquaintance constituted by a matriculation year in the Ecole Normale) and could at any moment measure their own past trajectory, and the future trajectory it implies, by that standard of academic normality, and thus evaluate their relative success or failure.[24]

The break in the cycle of simple reproduction which offered every assistant lecturer a future as professor is the cause and, at least partially, the effect of the autonomization of the production of the thesis in relation to the temporal structures of the career. The (at least apparent) upsetting of the space of possible trajectories determined by even a limited growth in the numbers of tenured professors continues no doubt to explain why, treating the doctorate as an internal promotion test, the less academically socialized of the newly appointed assistant lecturers start to produce theses in a much shorter time, thus breaking with the conventions and etiquette which characterized the long patience of the claimants; but it also explains why, at the same time, a considerable number of holders of acknowledged qualifications (those of *normalien* and *agrégé*), who insist on producing according to the rhythm of the old university life-cycle, like those old marine creatures thrown up on the shore which continue to live according to the rhythm of the tide, find themselves in fact deprived, especially when they are not particularly precocious, of the benefit of the expansion of the universities. The dearth of candidates having both unofficial and official qualifications (including the state doctorate) thus allowed those of the newcomers who were readiest to understand the new rules of the game to fill a good proportion of the newly created posts of professor.

THE BREAK IN EQUILIBRIUM

Thus under the effect of a (limited) increase in the opportunities for promotion and above all of a transformation in the dispositions of the agents, linked to a change in conditions of recruitment, the automatic harmony between expectations and probable trajectories, which led people to see as self-evident the order of succession, was broken, and the university order founded on the concordance between internalized temporal structures and objective structures was subjected to two kinds of challenge. On the one hand there was the individual challenge of the new entrants who, lacking the qualifications and the dispositions previously supposed necessary for entrance to the professorial body, refused to observe the delay and circumspection always deemed suitable until then: this is particularly so in the case of the new disciplines, where the abandonment of the old criteria of recruitment was not accompanied by the constitution of a new system of criteria of evaluation of pedagogical and scientific competence; so that the growth of the body of tenured professors here was more beneficial than elsewhere not only to the newcomers bereft of the canonical qualifications who knew how to jump the lights by offering as their entrance fee not a new form of production more suited to the demands of scientificity – for instance, empirically based work stripped of rhetorico-theoretical preconceptions, etc. – but a slimmer, reduced form of the old thesis; it was equally beneficial to the holders of canonical qualifications, which guarantee neither the acquisition of a specific competence nor the dispositions for acquiring it.[25] And on the other hand there was the collective challenge constituted by the simmering or overt protest against university hierarchies thus founded on fundamentally contradictory principles and equally difficult to justify on strictly scientific grounds: the trade-union movement has often been the mouthpiece for all those who feel that they have been cheated of their rightful expectations, whether as beneficiaries of the new appointments who were unable to benefit from the new possibilities offered by the expansion of the corps, or as latecomers under the old mode of recruitment, victims of the *hysteresis* of the *habitus* which leads them to prolong the preparation of a thesis often undertaken late in the day, and rivalled (in the case of the *chargés d'enseignement* (senior lecturers)) by the duties and obligations encoded into their magisterial position obtained by means of an accelerated, but deceptive promotion.

The transformation of the conditions of recruitment of subordinate teachers caused the appearance and affirmation of interests specific to lecturers and assistant lecturers, and, by the same token, the affirmation of the categorial interests of the professors (with the Syndicat Autonome, the non-aligned union); the logic of trade-union 'struggles' tending always to be substituted, at least on formal occasions (like elections to the CNRS or in the faculties' CCUs, for instance), for the logic of patriarchal relations, marked by the liberalism and 'fair play' which were operative as long as the professors and the assistant lecturers stemmed from the same mode of recruitment.[26] At all events, the divisions and mergers based on oppositions between statutory categories (*assistant, maître-assistant, chargé d'enseignement, professeur* – assistant lecturer, lecturer, senior lecturer, professor), often conceived or expressed in terms of a class struggle or a labour dispute, disguise considerable differences, for a similar position, according to the trajectory hoped for; so that the teachers of the intermediate categories are led into fluctuating strategies and alliances and are destined to hesitate between individual salvation and collective salvation according to their practical intuition of their own chances of acceding to the dominant positions.

By breaking the relation of anticipated identification with the masters and their magisterial positions, and ending the complicity of holders and claimants in support of the norms of legitimate promotion, the transformation of the norms of appointment laid the university field open to the combined effects of the old career law and transgression of that law; and it is difficult to see where there might arise any forces capable of imposing in practice the establishment of an order where recruitment and promotion would depend on the sole criteria of pedagogical or scientific productivity and efficiency.

5

The Critical Moment

Since no business could be transacted, a mixture of anxiety and idle curiosity drove everyone outside. As people dressed less carefully the difference between social ranks was less marked, hatred was suppressed and hopes expressed, the crowd was imbued with tolerance. Faces were gleaming with the pride of newly won rights. There was a carnival gaiety, a camp-site spontaneity; nothing could have been more fun than the sight of Paris during those first few days.

The actor's performance excited the crowd, and subversive proposals proliferated.

'No more academics! No more Institute!'

'No more committees!'

'No more baccalauréat!'

'Down with university degrees!'

'Let's keep them,' said Senecal, 'but let them be awarded by universal suffrage, by the People, the only true judge!'

Public thinking was shaken as after some natural disaster. Intelligent people became half-wits for the rest of their lives.

G. Flaubert, Sentimental Education

Limited as they are to the partial and superficial data of biographical experience but motivated by the ambition to judge and explain, most essays devoted to May 1968 remind us of what Poincaré said of Lorentz's theories: 'An explanation was needed, one was found; one can always be found; hypotheses are the commonest of raw materials.'[1] The temptation to multiply tailor-made hypotheses unreasonably is always most tempting for specialists in the social sciences when they are dealing with events, and with critical events at that. Moments when the meaning of the social world hangs in the balance are a challenge, beyond the merely intellectual, for all those whose profession is to read the meaning of the world and who, appearing to formulate a state of affairs, tend to remodel the world in conformity with their desire, thereby producing immediate political impact; which requires their immediate statement, rather than reflection after the battle. The political profits that the interpretation of a social event can procure depend closely on its 'topicality', that is to say the extent to which it provokes interest because it is the object of conflict in clashes of material or symbolic interest (which is the very definition of the *present*, never entirely reducible to immediately available facts and events). As a result, the motivation of most of the differences between cultural productions lies in the markets to which they are (more unconsciously than consciously) destined, the restricted market, within which the producer might have as clients in an extreme case only the set of his competitors, or the general production market.[2] These markets ensure for cultural products (and their authors) material and symbolic profits – that is of sales, of audience, of clientele – and a social profile, a reputation – a good gauge of which is provided by column space in the press – which are extremely unequal, both in size and duration. One of the reasons for the backwardness of the social sciences, constantly threatened with regression into *belles-lettres*, is that the chances of obtaining a purely social success of topical import diminish as one moves away in time from the object studied, that is, with the increase in the time invested in scientific work, a necessary but not a sufficient condition for the scientific quality of the product. The researcher can only arrive after the show, when the lamps are doused and the trestles stacked away, with a performance which has lost all the charms of an *improvisation*. The scientific report, constructed in counterpoint to the questions arising from the immediacy of the event, which are riddles rather than problems, and call for integral and definitive action rather than necessarily partial and arguable analyses, lacks the advantage of the fine clarity of the discourse of good sense, which has no difficulty in being simple, since its premise is to simplify.

Those who pay instant attention to the instant, which, drowned in the event and the emotions it arouses, isolates the critical moment, and thus constitutes it as a totality containing within itself its own explanation, introduce thereby a philosophy of history: they tend to presuppose that there are in history moments which are privileged, in some way more historical than others (we can see a specific case in the eschatological vision, whether the authorized or the revised version, describing revolution as a final term, *telos*, and culminating point, *acme*, and its agents – proletariat, students or others – as a universal, and therefore ultimate, class). The scientific *ambition*, on the other hand, aims to reinsert the extraordinary event into the series of ordinary events within which it finds its explanation. It does so in order to further examine how to locate the singularity of what remains a moment like any other in the historical series, as we can clearly see with all threshold phenomena, qualitative leaps where the continuous addition of ordinary events leads to a singular, extraordinary instant.

Being an intersection of several partly autonomous series of events arising in several fields pregnant with their own specific determinants, a crisis like that of May 1968 – and no doubt any crisis – introduces a visible break in relation to what produced it, although we cannot comprehend it without restoring it to its place in the series of preceding events. As a university crisis transforming itself into a general crisis, it poses the problem of the conditions of the differential extension of the crisis both within the university field and outside it: to explain how a crisis in the mode of reproduction (in its academic dimension) could thus become the principle of a general crisis, we must, knowing the increasingly important contribution that the education system makes to social reproduction, and which makes it an increasingly disputed stake of social struggles,[3] propose a model which allows us to take into account the social effects which the education system has produced, and whose most striking effect is a 'structural downclassing'[4] generating a kind of collective disposition to revolt. But does the model, which permits us, on the basis of an analysis of the structural conditions of the crisis, and without restoring *ad hoc* hypotheses, to understand the logic of the appearance of the crisis in the different areas of the university space, then of the social space where it appeared, also allow us to understand how a *critical state* of the structure occurred in a clearly determined area of the academic field? The probability that the structural factors which underlie critical tension in a particular field will come to engender a situation of crisis, fostering the emergence of extraordinary events (which a normal state of affairs would render unthinkable or, at the very least, 'exceptional' and 'accidental', therefore bereft of social significance and impact), reaches a maximum when a *coincidence* is achieved between the effects of several latent crises of maximum intensity. But what are the specific causes of the coincidence of the local crises and, thereby, of the general crisis as integration rather than simple addition of synchronized crises, and what is the specific effect of this synchronization of different fields which defines the historic event as noteworthy and the situation of general crisis as orchestration of different fields? Paradoxically, it is no doubt only if we reinsert the critical moments into the series where the principle of their intelligibility resides, negating what in a sense makes for their singularity, that we can understand what is the unique criterion of definition of the critical situation, if not as 'creation of unpredictable novelty', as Bergson says, at least as intrusion of the possibility of novelty, in short, as open time where all futures appear possible, and are indeed so to a certain extent, for that very reason.[5]

All these questions, which one might call theoretical, must be thought through as historical questions, which implies that we should work at neutralizing the effects of the socially instituted division between simple description, which, as Hegel remarked in his Preface to *The Phenomenology of Mind*, is ill suited to the 'intrusion' of the concept, and pure 'ratiocination', which is no less resistant to interference from effective reality. But we cannot call into question the best-established principles of the visions and divisions of the scientific process, without running the risk of allowing the products of this attempted break to be misunderstood or pass unnoticed; without seeming to disappoint the exigencies both of theory and of empiricism, and allowing the surest gains of research to escape not merely those who can only recognize theoretical questions when they give rise to dissertations (on power, on politics, etc.), but also those who will be moved to suspicion and reserve by the very effort to treat the series of events unfolded by historical description as if they were the product of different effects – as the physicist says – that is as a singular integration of intelligible sequences of events destined to appear, other things being equal, each time that certain conditions are united.

A SPECIFIC CONTRADICTION

We cannot account for the crisis, or at least for the structural conditions of its appearance and its generalization, without mentioning the principal effects of the increase in the number of pupils, that is, a devaluation of academic diplomas which causes a generalized downclassing,[6] particularly intolerable for the more privileged, and, secondarily, the transformations in the functioning of the education system which result from the morphological and social transformation of the public. The increase in pupils and the concomitant devaluation of educational qualifications (or the educational positions to which they provide access, like the status of student) have affected the whole of an age-group, thus constituted as a relatively unified social generation through this common experience, creating a structural hiatus between the statutory expectations – inherent in the positions and the diplomas which in the previous state of the system really did offer corresponding opportunities – and the opportunities actually provided by these diplomas and positions at the moment we are considering.[7] This hiatus is never greater than when it affects children who come from the dominant class and who have not managed to reconvert their inherited cultural capital into academic capital; and even then their social future does not depend entirely on their academic capital, for the economic or social capital at the disposal of their families allows them to obtain the maximum return for their academic diplomas on the labour market and thus to compensate for their (relative) failure by choosing alternative careers.[8] In short, the specific contradiction in the mode of reproduction in its educational aspects, which can only contribute to the reproduction of its class by eliminating with their consent a number of its members, takes on an increasingly critical form with the growing number of those who see their chances of reproduction threatened and who, refusing to accept their exclusion, find themselves falling back on a protest against the legitimacy of the instrument of their exclusion, which threatens the whole of their class by attacking one of the bases of its perpetuation.

The effects of this devaluation are no doubt more and more fully effective, since they are in no way corrected by the accumulation of social capital, in inverse proportion to the social origins of their holders, other diplomas and positions being equal. At all events, the *tolerance* of these effects also varies according to the same criterion, but in the opposite direction, on the one hand because aspirations tend to diminish as objective opportunities do, and on the other hand because various mechanisms, such as the plurality of markets, tend to disguise the devaluation – some devalued diplomas keep a certain symbolic value in the eyes of the least well provided – and the secondary benefits associated with the rise in the nominal value of the diplomas. The partly illusory rise of the 'miraculously lucky survivors' who attain posts improbable for the members of their class of origin (like the son of a primary teacher who becomes assistant lecturer in science, or the smallholder's son who becomes a teacher in a comprehensive school) at a time when these posts are becoming devalued by a general effect of translation, in other words, downclassed, is fundamentally different, despite the surface analogies, from the more or less obvious decline of the person whose origins are in the dominant class, but who does not manage to acquire diplomas sufficient to maintain his position, such as the doctor's son who becomes a literature student or an instructor in remedial education. It remains the case that, however different they may be, the experiences born of downclassing can help create more or less fantasized alliances between agents holding different positions in social or academic space, or, at the very least, can help create partly orchestrated reactions to the crisis, whose objective concordances it would be wrong to attribute to the effects of 'contagion' alone.

In order to understand the forms which the crisis has evolved within the education system, therefore, it is not sufficient to perceive the growth in the size of the population of the different educational establishments. It is true that specifically morphological phenomena have no doubt exercised important effects, by encouraging the transformation of pedagogical relations and of the whole experience of being a student. But the main thing is that the increase in size of the population of an educational establishment, and above all the concomitant transformation of the social composition of this population, are a function of the position which it occupies actually or potentially in the academic (and social) hierarchy of establishments. Thus it is that the *grandes écoles* (or the *classes préparatoires*) have been much less affected than the university faculties; and, within the latter, the faculties of law and medicine have been much less affected than the science and above all the arts faculties, and, within these latter, the traditional disciplines have been much less affected by the influx of students than the new disciplines, especially psychology and sociology. In other words, the social and academic effects of the increase in numbers are all the more striking in an academic institution (institute, faculty or discipline), the more its position in the hierarchy – and, secondarily, the content of the teaching offered –

predispose it to serve as a refuge for students who, in the previous state of the system, would have been excluded or would have dropped out. To which should be added the fact that the effects specifically linked to the disparity between expectations and objective opportunities are never as powerful as in the de luxe refuges represented by some of these new disciplines, especially sociology for boys and psychology for girls: these ill-defined academic positions, which give access to social positions which in their turn are ill defined, are well designed to allow their occupants to surround themselves and their future with an aura of indeterminacy and vagueness.

The same law which regulates the extension of the crisis within the academic institution also regulates the extension beyond the institution of the crisis specific to the institution: the proportion, among the holders of a social position, of agents belonging to the academic generation affected by the devaluation of academic diplomas, and thus endowed with aspirations maladjusted to the objective likelihood of their accomplishment, explains the differential reactions to the crisis of occupants of different positions in the social space. The crisis whose motives are to be found in the academic system is never entirely equivalent to the crisis of any determined class or fraction of a class: no doubt the protest movement found its most fertile ground in the intellectual fractions, and more especially the regions of social space most apt to welcome agents arriving from the dominant class which the academic system did not recognize; but it could also have evoked sympathy or even complicity within the different fractions of the middle classes, and even in the working or agricultural classes, among those adolescents who, having completed a vocational education, or even a normal, full-length secondary education, were disappointed in the expectations apparently autho- rized by the status of secondary or grammar school pupil (positions all the more prestigious for being rare in the social group of origin), or even *bachelier*.[9]

This is the case, which may serve as a test case, for the holders of a 'Diploma in General Education' or of a 'Certificate of Professional Aptitude', or even of the *baccalauréat* (in 1968 there were several thousands of 'O.S.' [unskilled workmen] who had this diploma), who are channelled into manual professions which attribute low economic and symbolic value to diplomas in general education and even to vocational diplomas, and who therefore find themselves destined to be objectively and/or subjectively downclassed, and the frustration engendered by the experience of the uselessness of the diploma (as in the case of one educated young workman who, condemned to carry out the same work as workmen having no academic diploma or, 'worse', the same work as 'foreigners', concluded: 'I didn't study for four years to end up working a slicing-machine'). The answers to the question (put in 1969 to a representative sample of the working population) whether, in 1968, it would have been preferable for the students 'to come to the factories to discuss with the workers' provide indications as to the social characteristics of those who feel 'concerned' by the crisis in the educational system: the proportion of workers who declare themselves in favour of opening up factories to students is at its peak in the 20–24 age-group and even more so in the 15–19 age-group and among workmen holding a CAP.[10] And it has been noted elsewhere that, among workers (who, unlike members of the dominant class, are increasingly likely to situate themselves further to the left as they grow older), as among the other social categories, participation in demonstrations increases with the level of instruction and in inverse proportion to age.

The effects of the increase in the number of agents receiving education, and of the concomitant devaluation of the diplomas awarded, do not operate automatically, homogeneously, but only take on their meaning as a function of the dispositions of the agents who are affected by them. Thus it is that, against the logic of analysis itself and of the discourse which expresses it, that is, against a tendency to synchronize and universalize what has taken the form of a slow and uneven transformation of minds, we would need to describe the different forms assumed – mainly as a function of social origins and of dispositions correlative to the education system – by the process of adjustment of hopes to opportunities, of aspirations to accomplishments, and in particular the work of disinvestment required in order to accept a lesser success, or a failure.

We must indeed be careful not to forget the important *time-lag* between the first appearance, in the science faculties, of the morphological transformations which are responsible for the tensions between teachers and the downclassing of the students, and, in a very specific sector of the university field, the outbreak of open crises which will later become generalized. This interval corresponds to the time necessary for certain agents to become aware, intermittently, of the transformations which have occurred in the institution and the effects which these transformations have on their present and future condition: that is to say, in the case of the students, the devaluation of academic diplomas and the students' relative or absolute downclassing, and, in the case of the subordinate teachers appointed according to the new criteria, the *de facto* inaccessibility of careers apparently promised to the holders of their positions. And if the work (of mourning) indispensable for them to adjust their expectations to the effects of the morphological evolution is necessarily very long, it is because the agents only perceive a very limited fraction of social space (moreover they perceive it through categories of perception and appreciation which are the product of a previous state of the system) and because they are led by this fact to interpret their own experience, and that of the agents who belong to their world of mutual acquaintance, in an individual rather than a categorial perspective, in such a way that the morphological changes can only appear to them in the shape of a multitude of fragmented experiences, difficult to grasp and interpret as a whole. We should thus take into account in our analysis of this process of transformation of the vision of the future the role of institutions responsible for producing scholarly representations of the social world (like official and unofficial statistical institutes) and for accordingly manipulating the representations of prospects liable to be profitable (like careers advisers, and, more generally, all the agents responsible for providing information on prospects for qualifications and posts).

In the case of 'lucky survivors' such as students (or lecturers) coming from social categories particularly improbable for the posts which they hold, the very fact of being present in these positions, even devalued – and by their very presence – constitutes a form of symbolic remuneration, comparable to a nominal rise in salary in a period of inflation: the *allodoxia* is inherent in the fact that the schemes which they implement to perceive and appreciate their position are the product of an earlier state of the system. In addition, the agents themselves have a psychological stake in becoming party to the mystification of which they are the victims – according to a very common mechanism which persuades people (no doubt all the more so, the less privileged they are) to work at *being satisfied* with what they have and with what they are, to love their fate, however mediocre it may be.[11] In fact, we may doubt whether these representations can ever fully succeed, even with the complicity of a group, and it is probable that the enchanted image always coexists with the realistic representation, the first being tested primarily in competition with immediate *neighbours* (in the social space) and the second in collective claims challenging the *out-group*.

These effects of *dual consciousness* are even more visible in the logic which leads students from the dominant class and poorly endowed with academic capital towards the new disciplines, whose power of attraction lies no doubt largely in the vagueness of the future which they offer and the freedom to defer disinvestment which they allow. Or it may lie in the orientation towards ill-defined professions which are as it were designed to allow students to perpetuate as long as possible, for themselves as much as for others, an indeterminacy of social identity, just like the professions of writer or artist and all the minor occupations of cultural production in former times, or all the new occupations, on the frontiers of the intellectual field and the university or medical field, which have proliferated in direct proportion to the effort to escape from devaluation by producing new professions. Everything leads us to believe that the critical tension is all the stronger, the longer the distance between reality and the representation of the self and of a social future has been maintained, necessitating a greater psychological effort.[12]

We can thus argue, first, that the overt crisis reached its maximum intensity in all the social spaces encouraging the perpetuation of maladjusted expectations; and, secondly, that the places liable to encourage a maladjustment which will have to be drastically revised later are those which, because of the vagueness of the social future which they promise, attract agents with maladjusted expectations and provide them with conditions encouraging the perpetuation of the maladjustment. To verify these hypotheses, we can take as our index of the homogeneity or heterogeneity of a position (faculty, institute, discipline) the dispersal of the corresponding population, either according to social origins or according to educational capital (the options studied or grade awarded in the *baccalauréat*), or, more germane to our hypothesis, according to the relation between social origins and educational capital: indeed, we might suppose that the disparity between these expectations and opportunities increases in all probability in proportion to the increase in the presence of students of high social origins and low educational capital. So we might then determine whether the variations in the degree of social and educational homogeneity according to the sectors of the educational institution correspond to variations in the intensity of the crisis.[13]

Only comparison of the distribution according to social origins and educational capital (and also, secondarily, according to gender, increase in numbers, and place of residence) of the holders (students or lecturers, especially junior ones) of the different positions (*grandes écoles*, faculties, disciplines) in the university field, with variations according to the same variables of the postures adopted by these groups during May 1968, would allow us to verify or to refute the model proposed. At all events, we may establish, from the data available, that there is a correlation between the two series. Although the statistics which show an increase in the relative proportion of middle-class children in educational institutions conflate the populations of different institutions (*lycée*, CEG,[14] etc.), thus masking the mechanisms of educational segregation which tend to maintain a relative social homogeneity of the student population during the period which precedes the crisis, we note a general tendency towards a decrease in the social homogeneity of the student population in the period preceding the crisis: still very strong in the top establishments (such as the *grandes écoles*, the medical faculties, or even the classics sections of grammar schools) or the lowest (such as the CET or the IUT[15]), social, academic and above all what one might call socio-academic homogeneity is generally weak in the institutions, options or disciplines occupying an intermediate position, or at least which have an ambiguous status in the hierarchy of the educational system. Moreover, if (since we have no indices of participation in subversive activities[16]) we agree to take as an indicator of conformity to, or support for the established university order, the rate of participation in the university elections of 1969 – which is, however, an extremely ambiguous indicator, since a high rate of abstention can result either from an explicit refusal to participate, therefore from a genuinely negative stance, or from a feeling of political impotence, as a consequence of a process of dispossession – we note that the proportion of voters is highest in institutes, disciplines or faculties which define themselves clearly in relation to the precise professions to which they lead. These include the medical faculties (68 per cent) and, to a lesser degree, the law faculties (53 per cent) or, at the other extreme of the university hierarchy, the IUTs (77 per cent). Conversely, the proportion of voters is low in the faculties or disciplines leading to professions strongly scattered throughout the social hierarchy: distinctly lower in the arts faculties (42 per cent) and the science faculties (43 per cent) as a whole, it reaches its lowest level in disciplines like sociology (26 per cent) and psychology (45 per cent), which, leading to particularly dispersed and ambiguous professions, are in clear contradistinction to disciplines leading to tenured teaching posts in secondary education, as in French literature (60 per cent), Greek (68 per cent), Latin (58 per cent), history (55 per cent) or geography (54.4 per cent) – with the exception of philosophy, which, because of the prospects it offers, is related to the social sciences, and which has a very low proportion, 20 per cent (*Le Monde*, 13 March 1969).[17] The structure of the breakdown according to faculties and disciplines is the same in the provinces, although participation is generally effective at a higher level, doubtless partly because of the effect of the size of the establishments, noticeable everywhere).[18]

But we cannot completely understand the special role of the new disciplines, notably sociology, in the triggering of the crisis, if we fail to see that these positions are the place of intersection of two latent crises of maximum intensity. At once inferior and indeterminate, the new disciplines in the arts faculties were predisposed to attract above all students from the dominant class with a low level of academic attainment, therefore endowed with expectations strongly maladjusted in relation to their objective chances of social success, and middle-class students relegated from the more prestigious options and threatened with disappointment in their ambitions since they lacked the social capital needed to enhance their devalued diplomas; moreover, as we have seen, these disciplines had to respond to a very rapid growth in the student population by appointing a considerable number of junior teachers weakly integrated into the university institution and liable to resentment because of the contradiction between the elevated expectations resulting from their (more or less) undreamed-of access to higher education and the disappointment of these expectations entailed by their maintenance in the lowest ranks of the university hierarchy.[19]

Just as social and academic heterogeneity seem to account for the attitudes of the students towards the movements of May 1968, so likewise the dispersal of past and above all potential trajectories, and the corresponding tensions between different ranks, seem to be the motivating force behind the different attitudes of the teachers. In order to verify this we have only to make a mental link between the synchronic and diachronic characteristics of the body of teachers of the different disciplines, and their differential participation in the movement of May 1968 or the intensity attained in the conflicts between the teachers of different ranks. But in order to push our demonstration as far as possible we can apply the analysis to the case of teachers of geography and sociology, who, although they both belong to subordinate disciplines, present differences able to explain why they played very different roles both in the movement and in the ensuing struggles over the future of the education system. Whereas the geographers, who are situated at the lowest level of both social and academic hierarchies, present a set of neatly crystallized social and academic characteristics for each rank, the sociologists are distinguished by very marked disparities in these characteristics, especially at the lower levels of the hierarchy: the proportion of *normaliens*, equally weak in ranks A and B (4.5 and 3 per cent) for the geographers, is relatively high (25 per cent) for the sociologists at the top of their hierarchy (very close to the historians, 24 per cent, and the psychologists, 27 per cent) who, moreover, have often moved from philosophy, whereas it is among the lowest (5.5 per cent as opposed to 10 per cent in psychology and 13 per cent in history) for the sociologists at the lower level (rank B), although the proportion of teachers from the dominant classes is nearly as high in these categories as at the higher level (rank A).[20] This double discord (based on an almost chiastic distribution of social and academic qualifications according to rank) between the top and the bottom of the hierarchy is no doubt the most visible expression of a duality of modes of recruitment which results from the structural ambiguity of the discipline at the same time as it reinforces it: sociology, a pretentious discipline, as Georges Canguilhem has said,[21] which situates itself at the top of the hierarchy of the sciences, thus challenging philosophy whose ambitions it claims to fulfil but with the rigour of science, is also a refuge, but a de luxe refuge allowing all those who wish to flaunt grand ambitions in theory, in politics and in political theory the maximum symbolic profit for the cheapest educational entry fee (the link with politics explains that it is for male students of high social origins and mediocre academic success what psychology is for female students endowed with the same properties).[22] We can understand why sociologists and geographers were so clearly marked out, at the heart of the university protest movement, to such an extent that they symbolize, especially in the trade-union movement, the opposition between the 'leftist' tendency and the 'reformist' tendency, between global and 'radical' protest against the university institution and the social world, and 'corporatist' claims placing the accent on teachers' careers or the transformation of the methods and contents of teaching.

To give an immediate impression of the structural affinity between the students and the subordinate teachers of the new disciplines from amongst whom were recruited many of the leaders of May 1968, we have only to present on one side the growth curves between 1950 and 1968 of numbers of pupils in the *grandes écoles* and of the numbers of students in the arts or science faculties, and on the other side those of the tenured professors and of the subordinate teachers (lecturers and assistant lecturers). Whereas the populations of professors and pupils of the several *écoles normales supérieures*, who have distinctly higher chances of becoming professors in higher education than the other students, remain more or less static, the other two populations, those of subordinate teachers and ordinary students, showed a very considerable increase. As a result, the pupils of the *grandes écoles* can *recognize* in their professors (at their preparatory classes or in the faculty) the holders of positions which one day could be theirs; on the contrary, the ordinary students, but also those among the assistant lecturers who, having benefited from the new mode of appointment, do not have the secondary properties (the title of *normalien* or *agrégé*) still needed to proceed to the grade of professor, and who, especially in science and in the new disciplines of the arts faculties, are very close to the students, no doubt feel less inclined to establish with the titular professors the relation of anticipated identification which is doubtless designed to encourage investment, and above all encourages a prolongation of their support of the pedagogical status quo.[23] In other words, the paradoxical relations which have long obtained in science and arts – and which have also become predominant in economics recently – between teachers chosen by the most competitive examinations and the least-selected pupils is now tending to arise between the subordinate teachers, often stemming from the population of ordinary students and excluded in fact from careers leading to positions of professor, and the titular professors, in whom, unlike the legitimate heirs, they cannot see a prefiguration of their own future.[24] In short, the virtual line of fracture passes more and more clearly between the professors on one side, and the lecturers and assistant lecturers on the other, since the latter are usually objectively closer to the students than to the titular professors. This break in the *chain of anticipated identifications*, which were rooted in the order of succession which they tended to reproduce, is of a kind to encourage a sort of secession of agents who, excluded from the race for future prospects which until then had been programmed into their position, are now led to call into question the race itself. And we can no doubt recognize in this a specific realization of a general model of the revolutionary process: the objective break in the circle of expectations and opportunities leads an important fraction of the less subordinate among the subordinate (here the intermediate categories of teachers, elsewhere the petty bourgeoisie) to leave the race, that is to say, the competitive struggle implying acceptance of the rules of the game laid down and the goals proposed by the dominant class, and to take up a struggle which we may call revolutionary in so far as it aims to establish alternative goals and more or less completely to redefine the game and the moves which permit one to win it.

SYNCHRONIZATION

The students and assistant lecturers in sociology thus represent one of the cases of the *coincidence* between the dispositions and the interests of agents occupying homologous positions in different fields which, through the *synchronization* of crises latent in different fields, has made the generalization of the crisis possible. Such convergences, encouraging the harmonization of local crises or conjunctural alliances, could be seen throughout the arts and science faculties, where the disenchantment of an important fraction of the subordinate teachers, facing a difficult post and destined for mutilated careers, met that of the corresponding students, threatened by the downclassing associated with the devaluation of diplomas. Such convergences could also be seen among all those who, in the academic field itself, took part in the protest, and those who, outside the field, held structurally and sometimes functionally homologous positions, like the subordinate representatives of the agencies of cultural production and diffusion.

A regional crisis can extend to other regions of social space and thus become transformed into a general crisis, a *historical event*, when, through the effect of *acceleration* which it produces, it is able to bring about the *coincidence* of events which, given the different *tempo* which each field adopts in its relative autonomy, should normally start or finish in dispersed order or, in other words, succeed each other without necessarily organizing themselves into a unified causal series, such as that which is suggested after the event, with the benefit of illusory hindsight, by the historian's chronology. It follows that the position of the different fields in the general crisis and the behaviour of the corresponding agents will depend, to a considerable extent, on the relation between the social time-scales germane to each of these fields, that is to say between the rhythms with which, in each one of them, the processes generating its specific contradictions are accomplished.

We cannot understand the roles taken in the crisis by the different faculties or disciplines or even by the individuals who appeared as the incarnations of the movement (notably Daniel Cohn-Bendit, a student of sociology at Nanterre, Jacques Sauvageot, leader of the UNEF,[25] and Alain Geismar, lecturer in physics at Paris and general secretary of the

SNESup), unless we realize that, at the moment in objective time when the crisis broke out in the arts faculties, the structural conditions which encouraged its appearance had already been present for more than six years in the science faculties – where the SNESup, which played a decisive role in the generalization of the movement, was very strongly implanted, and had been for some time – whereas they had only just started to appear in the law faculties.

The crisis as conjuncture, that is to say as conjunction of independent causal series, supposes the existence of *worlds* which are separate but which participate in the same *universe* both through their motive forces and through their contingent functioning: the independence of the causal series which 'develop in parallel', as Cournot says, supposes the relative autonomy of the fields; the meeting of these series supposes their relative dependence as regards the fundamental structures – especially the economic ones – which determine the logics of the different fields. It is this independence in dependency which renders the *historical event* possible – societies without history being perhaps societies so undifferentiated that there is no place for the properly historical event which is born at the crossroads of relatively autonomous histories. If we take into account the existence of these worlds 'in each of which', as Cournot goes on to say, 'we may observe a chain of causes and effects developing simultaneously, without having any connection between them, without each exercising on the other any appreciable influence', we can escape from the dilemma which so often traps us between structural history and the history of events (*histoire événementielle*), and gain the means of understanding how the different fields, at once relatively autonomous and structured, but also open, and linked to the same factors, therefore to each other, can proceed to interact to produce a historical event in which are expressed at one and the same time the potentialities objectively inherent in the structure of each of them, and the relatively irreducible developments which are born of their conjunction.

Synchronization as coincidence in the same objective time (as marked by a historical date) of the latent crises germane to each sector of the university field (or, and it amounts to the same thing, the unification of the different fields resulting from the provisional suspension of the mechanisms tending to maintain the relative autonomy of each field) takes agents previously holding homologous positions in different fields, and engages them in the same game with identical positions. The effect of synchronization exercised by the critical events which are at the *chronological* origins of the crisis and which can comprise a portion of accident (imputable to factors external to the field, such as police violence) is only completely exercised if there exists a relationship of *objective orchestration* between the agents experiencing crisis, as their field reaches its critical state, and other agents, endowed with dispositions which are similar, because produced by similar social conditions of existence (*identity of condition*). But, moreover, agents subjected to very different conditions of existence and endowed by this fact with very different, or even divergent, systems of dispositions (*habitus*), yet occupying in the different fields positions structurally homologous to the positions held by the agents in crisis (*homology of position*), can identify rightly or wrongly (*allodoxia*) with the movement or, more simply, seize the opportunity created by the critical break in the ordinary order, to advance their own claims or defend their own interests.

Starting out from the new disciplines in the arts and social science faculties and spreading to the whole of the university field, the crisis found its most propitious terrain in the institutions of production and diffusion of cultural goods for mass-consumption – radio and television organizations, the cinema, the press, advertising or marketing media, opinion poll institutes, youth movements, libraries, etc. – which, also benefiting from their rapid and considerable growth in size and offering a whole range of new positions to the products of the university threatened with downclassing, are a locus of contradictions analogous to those experienced in the academic field: driven by intellectual ambitions which have not always been able to find fulfilment in works able to give access to acknowledged positions in the intellectual field, the new agents of symbolic manipulation are led to live out in a state of unease or resentment the opposition between their own representation of their task as intellectual creation in its own right and the bureaucratic constraints to which they must bend their activity. Their *anti-institutional mood*, constituted essentially in their ambivalent relationship with a university which has not fully recognized them, cannot fail to be recognized in all the forms of protest against cultural hierarchies of which the revolt of the students against their academic institutions no doubt represents the archetypal form. Which is to say that we cannot impute to the sole effects of fashion, nor of 'contamination' (the spreading of the protest has very often been analysed in terms of contagion), the relatedness of themes which were invented and expressed in the sectors furthest away from the 'movement', benefiting from the lifting of taboos which offers an opportunity to reveal social pretensions, or even impulses, often scantily veiled by an appearance of political generalization.[26]

The 'spontaneist' thematics which is the unifying factor behind the 'May ideas', a more or less anarchic combination of fragments of diverse discourses taken out of context, and which is destined above all to reaffirm the founding complicities of emotional communities, functions in what Malinowski calls the 'phatic' mode,[27] that is, as a communication whose only aim is its own act of communication itself or (and it comes to the same thing) the strengthening of the integration of the group.[28] The 'practical *gauchisme*' no doubt owes much less than we had thought to the diffusion of learned ideologies – such as that of Marcuse, elicited more often by the commentators than by the participants – even if, according to the characteristic logic of prophecy, certain spokesmen owed some of their impact and their charisma to their art of bringing into public debate and on to the streets popularized versions of learned doctrines, often reduced to key words and themes which had been until then the preserve of limited exchanges between academics ('repression' and 'repressive', for instance). This semblance of ideological diffusion results in fact from the multiplicity of *simultaneous* but independent, albeit objectively orchestrated, *inventions*, realized at different points of the social space, but in similar conditions, by agents endowed with similar systems of dispositions and, so to speak, the same social *conatus* (by which we mean that combination of dispositions and interests associated with a particular class of social position which inclines agents to strive to reproduce at a constant or an increasing rate the properties constituting their social identity, without even needing to do this deliberately or consciously). Indeed, no ideological production better expresses the specific contradictions and the material or symbolic interests of subordinate intellectuals – actual or potential – of the great bureaucracies of cultural production, whose oldest paradigm is obviously the church, than the thematics developed at that moment, in the most apparently anarchic liberty, according to a small number of common generative schemas such as the oppositions between invention and routine, liberty and repression, transformed forms of the opposition between individual and institution. The typically *heretical* attack on cultural hierarchies and official discourse, which, in a modern variant of the notion of a *universal priesthood*, professes a sort of universal right of spontaneous expression (the right of 'free speech'), has obvious links with the specific interests of the subordinate intellectuals of the great bureaucracies of science and culture: setting 'natural creativity' and 'spontaneity', which each individual contains within him, against socially (that is academically) guaranteed competence is equivalent to using this humanist slogan to denounce the monopoly of cultural legitimation claimed by the educational system, and thereby devalue the competence, certified and legitimated by the academic institution, of agents who, in the name of that competence, occupy the highest echelons of the institutional hierarchy. And moreover we can see the special attraction which this representation of culture exerts on all those who have not managed to obtain social recognition of and reward for their inherited cultural capital.

It is again to the effect of solidarities founded on structural homologies between the holders of positions subordinate in the different fields, and often associated with the experience of a structural downclassing, that we should attribute the extension of the crisis beyond the university field and directly connected fields – without forgetting, of course, the specific action of the trade-union and political machinery, one of whose ordinary functions, as centralized (national) bureaucracies, is precisely to work towards the *controlled generalization* of local movements (through orders for a general strike, for instance). Indeed, since any field tends to organize itself around the opposition between dominant and subordinate positions, there is always a relationship through which the agents of any particular field can join or be included with agents holding a homologous position in another field, however distant in social space this position may be and however different may be the conditions of existence which it offers its tenants and, by the same token, the systems of dispositions with which they are endowed: that is to say that any agent can declare his solidarity with agents holding homologous positions in other fields, but on condition that he does it as if the affinity which linked him to them in this abstract and partial relationship was also valid, if not in all perspectives (which is practically impossible), at least in a set of *decisive* perspectives, especially from the viewpoint of the probability of constituting a mobilized and socially active group. But homology of position must not allow us to forget the difference between the fields, although intellectual, political and artistic history has furnished a number of historic examples of this confusion. We know the representation which the artists and writers of the first half of the nineteenth century, more attentive to their position in the field of power than to their subordinate position in the social field, made of their relation to the 'bourgeoisie' in the most acute phase of their struggle for the conquest of the autonomy of the field of cultural production. But, in a more general way, the sub-field which people belong to (often overlapping the space of mutual acquaintance and social interaction) always tends to produce a *screen effect*: the agents tend to perceive the position which they hold in it more distinctly and, in the case of subordinate agents, more painfully than the position which the sub-field itself occupies in the wider field which encompasses it, and thereby more plainly than their real position in the overall space.

The homology of position between those subordinate in the field of power and those subordinate in the social field as a whole provides a sociological answer to the question of 'consciousness of the outside world' (as Kautsky said), a kind of siphoning off for the benefit of the subordinate of a part of the accumulated social energy. And the situation of being (relatively) dominated to the power of two, which is that of second-rank intellectuals from the viewpoint of the specific criteria of the intellectual field at a given moment, explains their inclination to turn towards reformist or revolutionary movements and frequently to import into them a form of anti-intellectualism, of which Zldanovism, but also the *völkisch* [populist] reaction of conservative-revolutionaries, have been exemplary realizations. We can thus understand that a crisis specific to a field where the opposition between the dominant and the subordinate takes the form of unequal access to the attributes of legitimate cultural competence should tend to give preference to the burgeoning of subversive ideological themes, such as the denunciation of 'mandarin rule' and of all forms of statutary authority founded on academically guaranteed competence. These themes are based on a principle of homology, as resemblance in difference, thus on the partly misunderstood, and thus allow the crises germane to other fields which are divided according to other principles to be analysed in the same perspective. Thus it is that, in most revolutionary movements, the 'relatively' subordinate people that artists and intellectuals are, or, more precisely, the subordinate intellectuals and artists, tend to produce forms of perception, appreciation and expression liable to impress themselves on other subordinate groups through homology of position.

In fact, the reality is more complex: certain oppositions specific to the professional politicians or trade-union militants can indeed find support in homologous oppositions among the subordinate; particularly the opposition found between the permanent workers, more aware and better organized, and the demoralized and demobilized sub-proletariat. Thus it is that the representatives within the labour movement of scientist and authoritarian, that is technocratic, tendencies, most usually holders of a capital of scientific competence (theory, economics, dialectical materialism, etc.), tend to seek their support spontaneously among the most stable and well-integrated proletariat, while the defenders of spontaneist, libertarian positions, often poorer in cultural capital and less given to the practical activities of leader or agitator rather than thinker, tend to become spokesmen for the lowest and least organized fractions of the subordinate, especially the sub-proletariat.

We cannot assign *a priori* limits to the *game of assimilation and dissimilation* through which more or less imaginary solidarity can be established between agents having in common a structural property: the alliances which are engendered in this game can be all the larger for being strongly dependent on the particular conjuncture which gave birth to them and for engaging less strongly the most vital interests of agents who seem to participate only partially and distantly, in their most abstract and most generic social aspect (for example, as human beings subjected to some form or other of domination or violence and at the cost of a more or less total suspension of everything that is associated with any particular conditions of existence). The alliances founded on homology of position – for instance, those which were set up, conjuncturally, between agents occupying subordinate positions in the academic field and agents occupying subordinate positions in the social field taken as a whole – are of this sort: unless they are restricted to the realm of the imaginary, as were a number of meetings dreamed of between the 'intellectuals' and the 'proletariat', they have a greater chance of materializing, and lasting, if the partners whom they mobilize at a distance around vague slogans, abstract manifestos and formal programmes, have less opportunity to enter into direct interaction, to see and speak to each other; indeed, their encounters bring together not abstract individuals, defined only in relation to their position in a determined region of social space, but total persons, all of whose practices, discourse and even simple bodily appearance express divergent and, at least potentially, antagonistic systems of dispositions (*habitus*).

THE CRISIS AS DEVELOPER

In establishing an objective or, in other words, a historical time, that is a time transcending the specific time-scales of each different field, the situation of general crisis renders *practically contemporary*, for a shorter or longer period, agents who, although theoretically contemporaneous, evolved in more or less completely separate social times, each field having its own specific time-scale and history, with its specific dates, events, crises or revolutions, and rhythms of development. Moreover, it renders *contemporary to themselves* agents whose biography is answerable to as many systems of periodization as there are fields in whose different rhythms they share. And the same effect of synchronization which explains the collective logic of the crisis, especially what we perceive as 'politicization', also explains the relation between the individual crises and the collective crises which are their occasion: in encouraging the intersection of discrete social spaces and in bringing together in the minds of agents practices and discourses on which the autonomy of different fields, and the successive deployment of contradictory choices which it authorizes, conferred a practical form of compatibility, the general crisis produces conflicts of legitimacy which often give rise to radical arguments; it imposes agonizing revisions intended to restore unity of direction to their life, at least symbolically.

The principal effect of this synchronization is to compel people to introduce into positions adopted a relative coherence which is not required in ordinary circumstances, that is when the relative autonomy of social spaces and times makes it possible to hold separate positions successively, and to adopt different or divergent attitudes, which are none the less in accordance in each case with the requirements of the position held: the propensity for successive sincerities is inherent in the plurality of social positions (often linked with the plurality of spatial localizations) which increases, as we know, the higher we rise in the social hierarchy. (Therein lies one of the bases of the impression of 'authenticity' given off by holders of subordinate positions, who are socially assigned to a single professional position, which is often defined in very rigid terms, and who are by this fact little equipped with the dispositions necessary for successively holding different positions, all the more so because the dispositions imposed by these unitary conditions of existence find reinforcement in the explicit ethical imperative which favours people who have a 'consistent, 'you know me', etc., sort of character.) In obliging everyone to organize his political position with reference to the position held in a specific field and in that one alone, the crisis tends to substitute a *division* into clearly distinguished *camps* (according to the logic of a civil war) for progressive distribution between two poles, and for all the multiple, partly contradictory memberships which the separation of spaces and times allows to reconcile. Moreover, in forcing us to decide in all things on the basis of a single principle of choice and in thus excluding the evasions and equivocations allowed by multiple frames of reference, it acts as a *developer* and discourages or inhibits the usually tacit rather than explicit concessions ('we let them say what they like', 'we pretend not to notice'), the compromises, concessions or even deals and self-denials which render existence tolerable; by forcing us to choose and to proclaim our choices, by multiplying situations where not to choose is still a manner of choosing, it cuts into the vagueness of relations more or less consciously maintained towards and against all the factors of fission. Repressed feelings and judgements break out into broad daylight, and, in order to describe the effects of synchronization and the inevitable alternative which it imposes, we might use Lanson's words on the Dreyfus case (thereby underlining the general validity of the analysis proposed): 'Each group, each individual, will turn out his pockets, so to speak, and reveal his inmost tendencies.'[29]

This effect is compounded, in the case of a predominantly symbolic crisis, by a radical questioning, requiring a systematic response, which is determined by the appearance in one sector of the milieu of *paradoxical* acts and discourses, what Goffman calls *discrediting events*, liable to shake the doxa on which the normal order relies: these are extraordinary situations, whose paradigm no doubt is the 'general assembly', making manifest on the university campus itself, and sometimes in the presence of the professors, the symbolic reversal of ordinary educational relationships (with the most venerable professors being addressed by their first name), and the practical transgression of the presuppositions normally objectified, and above all unconsciously internalized, in this relationship. Extraordinary actors are revealed by these situations, students suddenly catapulted out of anonymity, obscure trade-union militants, known only to close colleagues, suddenly promoted as political orators or even revolutionary leaders, etc.; finally there are all the dramatic and theatrical questionings of the beliefs and views which ordinary agents have of the ordinary world, such as the symbolic depositions and destitutions of the symbols of economic power (the Stock Exchange) or cultural power (the Odéon theatre or the Hotel Massa[30]) or, at the other extreme, all forms of magical negation of real social relations, with various ceremonies of symbolic *fraternization*.

It is clear that critical discourses and displays can break the doxic relation to the social world which is the effect of a correspondence between objective structures and personally internalized structures only in so far as they objectively encounter a critical state able by its own logic to disconcert the pre-perceptual anticipations and expectations which form the basis of the ahistorical continuity of the perceptions and actions of common sense. If the crisis goes hand in hand with criticism, it is because it introduces a break in duration, because it suspends the ordinary order of succession and the ordinary experience of time as presence in an already present future; in overthrowing in reality or in representation the structure of objective opportunities (for financial or social success, etc.) to which behaviour reputed reasonable is spontaneously adjusted, and which creates social order as a world one can count on, that is, a predictable and calculable world, the crisis tends to undo that sense of placing, both as 'knowing one's place' and as knowing how to place sound investments, which is inseparable from the sense of realities and possibilities which we call sensible. It is the *critical moment* when, breaking with the ordinary experience of time as simple re-enactment of a past or a future inscribed in the past, all things become possible (at least apparently), when future prospects appear really contingent, future events really indeterminate, the moment truly instantaneous, suspended, its consequences unpredicted and unpredictable.

The crisis makes the field (in this instance, the academic field) appear retrospectively in the objective truth of its system of objective patterns, more or less converted (distinctly less, in this case) into explicit rules and regulations, which each agent can and must take into account in order to organize his investments; the objective possibilities immanent in this world are, essentially, attributed in advance and the (objective or personally internalized) capital confers rights of pre-emption on the options, whether positions available for tenure or privileges available for acquisition. It is this temporal structure of the field, as shown in careers, curricula vitae and accumulated honours, which becomes shaken: the uncertainty about the future which the crisis establishes in objective reality itself means that everyone can believe that the processes of reproduction have been interrupted for the time being, and that all futures are possible for all people.

It goes without saying that the *provisional indeterminacy of options* is very differently perceived and appreciated. It engenders more or less 'crazy' hopes in some, notably in all those who hold intermediate positions in the different fields, claimants tempted to project on to the old order, which they continue to recognize implicitly, the new aspirations which it excluded and which become possible once that order is undermined. For those on the contrary who are involved in maintaining and reproducing the status quo, therefore with the 'normal' future of this economy in which they have invested everything, and from the beginning, the sudden appearance of an objective *discontinuity* (of which certain exemplary scenes give a brutally manifest image, thus proving that 'all things are possible' in a world turned upside-down – professors reduced to listening to students, Cohn-Bendit interviewed by Sartre, etc.) seems like *the end of the world*: the reactions of the teachers who are most completely integrated into this social world, which, as long as it was contained within the cyclical time of simple reproduction, was compatible with traditional societies, resemble the despair and the disarray of the elders of such societies when faced with the irruption of modes of life and thought hostile to the deepest axiomatics of their existence.

> Just like old Kabyle peasants speaking of the heretical methods of cultivation practised by the young, they can only express their stupefaction, their incredulity in the face of the *incredible*, the world upside-down, the denial of their most intimate beliefs, of all that they hold most dear: 'On the other hand, but it's difficult to talk about. Is it true? Might it not be lies or slander? I hear that recently some professors were not only driven to refuse to invigilate exams – which could be defensible as such – but to boycott them, to mark them

improperly on purpose. That's what I've heard, but I can't believe it. Professors who did that would no longer be professors. They would ruin any reputation we had left. But above all they would wreck the values on which our professional life is founded, and whose basic tenet is that duty is sacrosanct.'[31] 'The papers and the radio kept repeating during the crisis of May and June that the students and the "professors" said this or did that. It is true that professors in the strict sense of the term did demonstrate alongside students through visceral disgust at the police, but in the vast majority of cases the university teachers who associated themselves with revolutionary students in the pursuit of specific aims were lecturers or assistant lecturers. The public, which was not informed about this, was dumbfounded during the crisis, and continues to wonder how it came about that "professors" participated furiously in demonstrations directed against the "professors".'[32] In fact, these besieged professors took a long time to shake off the sort of 'stupor' they had been cast into by 'the irruption of the barbarians, unconscious of their barbarity'.[33] Having to defend the untouchable, a universe without explicit sanctions or obligations, based on a 'spontaneous consensus' and on 'agreement on self-evident truths',[34] they had no real arguments to speak of. Moreover, how could or should they possibly argue about defending what goes without saying? Thus they only relate their experience as teachers, as if the (awestruck) description of their practice contained the evident proof of its excellence: 'The fact that any education worthy of the name implies intellectual objectivity, and, as a result, a strict political neutrality in the exercise of our profession, is an obvious truth which should not have to be spelt out'.[35] Education is invoked in an almost religious language: the lecture is a moment of grace, a moment of intense communion with the pupils; and the defence of the profession culminates in a proclamation of faith and love: 'I am one of those who love their profession';[36] 'I was proud of my profession and still am';[37] 'I have known the joy of teaching; I have also known the virtues of the university, chief of which is integrity, integrity often taken to extremes. I have to laugh at pupils or students who want to monitor our examination procedures. If only they knew!'[38]

It is clear on the other hand that the teachers are all the more inclined to project themselves into the indeterminate options which are provided by *disrupting events*, to project their fantasies, encouraged by the lifting of taboos, on to the blank screen of the future thus offered, the less they are tied objectively and subjectively, in their present and their future, to the previous state of the system and to the statutory guarantees of their specific competence, the less they have invested in it and the less they expect from it in exchange.

The systems of dispositions and the interests associated with a trajectory and with a position in the university space (faculty, discipline, academic trajectory, social trajectory) are the motive force behind the perception and the appreciation of the critical events, and thereby in practice they mediate the effects of these events themselves.

Added to the effect of symbolic provocation, which, by making the unexpected or the unthinkable suddenly appear, interrupts automatic acceptance of the unquestioned truths of the status quo, there is the effect of all the social techniques of protest or subversion, whether in the case of demonstrations as collective transgression, of sit-ins in privileged spaces or of the intentional misuse of social objects or spaces whose social definition is thereby suspended – theatres, amphitheatres, workshops, factories, etc. – or finally, with the local or the general strike, there is the effect of the suspension of the activities which structure normal existence. The break with temporal rhythms which characterizes the strike does not produce only free, festive leisure time; just as holidays reproduce the effect of synchronization produced by the event which they commemorate, so the strike displays and amplifies the effect of synchronization produced by the crisis; by replacing the time-scales of ordinary existence – multiple time-scales specific to each field and filled with all the events written into its several calendars – with a vague and almost empty time, *common* to the different fields and to the different groups, which, like 'festive' time in Durkheim's description, is defined by the inversion of normal temporality, the strike, through the symbolic effect of its display, materializes and compounds all the actual effects of the crisis.

The effect of synchronization operates fully here: time becomes a *public time*, identical for all, measured by the same markers, by the same presences, which by impinging on everyone simultaneously, makes everyone share the same present. Moreover, just as in festivity everyone is reinforced in his festive dispositions by the display of others' enjoyment, so here everyone becomes revealed to himself, and thus reinforced or legitimated in his malaise or his revolt, by the fact of seeing and hearing expressed the revolt or the malaise of others (which sometimes gives to debates a style of psychodrama or logotherapy). It is still the case that there is never a perfect parallel, and that, behind the appearances of homogeneity which one gets from the speeches of the spokesmen, are hidden divergences in experience and expression. Thus it is for instance that, when the malaise of the students and teachers from social categories previously little represented in the institutions of secondary and especially higher education managed to find expression, thanks to the crisis, and especially in areas of social space where these categories are most represented, as in the small provincial universities, it was possible to see that although the rebellion which it harboured was apparently less radical and universal than that of the Parisian vanguard, which was more inclined to symbolic fraternizations and revolutionary verbalism, it was no doubt more overtly directed at the immense block of silence which props up the academic institution.[39] But the movement unleashed by the aristocratic revolt of the students of bourgeois origins had only a slim chance of bringing to light everything which, in the phase of equilibrium, had been hidden by the spontaneous collusion between the agents and the tacit presuppositions of the institution, which is an effect of the inextricably social and academic selection of individuals possessing dispositions isomorphic to the positions constituting the university space. Indeed, the various official spokesmen of the university student movement or the unions of lecturers (or others) were hardly disposed to express a malaise which had no definition in the phraseology of the political and trade-union establishment, which was ill prepared to perceive and enunciate the specifically cultural dimension of their domination. As for the spontaneous-style speech of the grassroots leaders of the protest movement, it often found its principle – as expressed in slogans like 'Give the Sorbonne to the workers!' or 'Let the workers into the Sorbonne!' – in a magical denial of the factors causing the malaise.

In the case of the majority union of lecturers, the SNESup, the current which is no doubt the closest to the new entrants and the 'gatecrashers' by its social base is also the most directly inspired or controlled by executive organizations more or less totally lacking in open minds or original thoughts on the educational system. The 'leftist' tendency which controls the union between 1966 and 1969 and which, through Alain Geismar, then its general secretary, plays an important role in the May 1968 movement, formulates a global protest against the kind of culture channelled through the educational system, and against hierarchical relations (between heads of department and other staff, between teachers and students), analysed in terms of the model of class relations as 'relations between oppressors and oppressed', and considers the union as an organization for 'struggle against the capitalist system in its university institution'. The opposite tendency, which took over the direction of the union at the extraordinary congress of March 1969,[40] and which is dominated by militants of the Communist Party, intends to concentrate on specifically trade-union issues and places the emphasis of its claims on 'concrete means', reform of lecturers' careers, democratization of access to higher education, 'possibilities of intervention in the councils of the units of education and research'. The almost total absence of any analysis of the functioning and the specific conditions of education, the absolute refusal, justified by the desire to 'consolidate gains', to debate major contradictions – between the conditions affecting the scientific quality of the teachers and their teaching, and conditions affecting democratization, for instance – make this programme tend to use the imperative of 'democratization of access to higher education', a vague and empty slogan, as an ideology justifying the corporatist claims of the junior lecturers who make up the social base of the SNESup. And this was fostered by an amalgam, encouraged by a 'leftist' denunciation of 'mandarins' and 'conservatives', between the university hierarchies – which are not always completely lacking in scientific or technical rationale – and social hierarchies, between the 'democratization' of the population of pupils and the levelling down of the population of lecturers.

PUBLISHED OPINIONS

Through its proliferation of specifically political events, demonstrations, assemblies, meetings, etc., where political declarations, motions, petitions, alliances, manifestos, programmes, etc., are elaborated and professed publicly and collectively, the crisis leads to the constitution of a common political problematic, of a space of formal political attitudes, that is attitudes explicitly formulated and overtly associated with socially situated agents and groups, unions, parties, movements, associations, etc.;[41] from this point on, whether we like it or not, whether we are aware of it or not, we can no longer avoid defining ourselves or being defined in terms of this space of potential positions.[42] Concretely, through all the occasions which oblige us to declare ourselves or to betray ourselves in public, that is to say to 'take sides', whether we like it or not, and whose most exaggerated form is represented by the kind of public confession, whether free or induced, which characterized so many contributions to the assemblies of 1968, in short, through the generalized unveiling of public opinion which it encourages, the political crisis constrains each agent (also pushed in this direction by all the effects already analysed) to generate all his choices from one specifically political principle and to apply this same principle to the perception and the appreciation of the choices of the other agents.[43] By the same token it tends to introduce definitive separations between people who were in agreement until then because they left out, or left implicit through a kind of tacit understanding, the differences which could separate them, especially in political matters. What we call 'politicization' designates the process which leads to the principle of political vision and division tending to prevail over all the others, bringing together people clearly separated by former criteria and distancing people who in their previous existence were quite close in their choices and judgements. Emotional excitement generated by the 'revolt of the lecturers' was thus able to drive certain 'leading academics' to link up, either in signing a petition or more permanently, with 'ordinary professors' for whom they had previously felt nothing but contempt;[44] while links, bound to appear to the other side as unnatural fraternizations, spring up, beyond differences in grade, status and officially recognized competence, between those who communed in the 'spirit of May'. The logic of the classificatory thought which thus tends to predominate persuades everyone to imagine himself as a collective person, speaking with the entire authority of the group, at the same time as investing each individual member of the opposing class with responsibility for the deeds and misdeeds of the ensemble of the group he belongs to: thus the professor debating with his students during a seminar held in May 1968 imagines himself – according to his Memoirs[45] – establishing a dialogue with 'Maoist students' or with 'leftist militants';[46] and thus another group of eminent professors who, at the same time, are working at preparing the principles of a reform of the university, welcome with the attention due to an official body the comments of an unrepresentative science student who occasionally turns up to take part in their discussions.

In ordinary existence, the specifically political principle of choice is only in one sense the *visible continuation* of factors which, like dispositions and interests, are linked to the position (in social space, in the field of power and in the academic field); but, because of its explicit and differential character as taking sides, as partisan choice, a position consciously affirmed and negatively determined by the whole set of the different or contrary positions, it permits the generalized and systematized application of specifically political criteria to the whole set of problems and, notably, to precisely those which only touch on secondary, marginal interests. (This effect of generalization and systematization is obviously all the more 'successful' as the cultural capital is more important and the inclination and the aptitude for *coherence* greater, which placed academics and intellectuals, professionals in these matters, in a privileged position.) Thus it is that the lecturers who favour change in a fundamental issue (for themselves, and also for reproduction of the system), that is, the problem of careers, will be led by their concern to obey the explicit and objectified principle of their established political opinions to take up progressive positions on problems, whether academic ones (such as selective admission to universities) or non-academic ones which do not affect their interests directly.[47] And we can even understand in the same logic those (paradoxical) cases, whose paradigm is that of the aristocrats of the *ancien régime* converted to the new ideas, where the formal constraints of coherence prevail over the influence of their central interests. It is because we can only move from holding social positions to adopting stances on secondary issues, through the mediation of established political opinions (which does not necessarily mean that these are public and advertised), that these positions arising from an explicit principle can threaten (in an entirely theoretical manner, at least ouside times of crisis) the interests inherent in the position. The crisis in the academic field as specific revolution calling directly into question the interests associated with a dominant position in the field cancels out that detachment from specifically academic interests which could be introduced by the relative autonomy of specifically political logic: primary reactions to the crisis clearly have as their principle the position of teachers in the university field, or, more precisely, the degree to which the present and future satisfaction of their specific interests depends on the conservation or subversion of the power relations constitutive of the academic field. If these political attitudes, whose social determinants are thus revealed in broad daylight, can appear as conversions or apostasies, it is because, as long as the university order is not threatened, the taking of sides, especially in the domain of general politics, but also, although within stricter limits, in the specifically academic domain, can be motivated not by the position in the academic field but, especially for the professors closest to the 'intellectual' pole, by their position in the field of power and by the political option which is traditionally attached to the subordinate positions in this field, as the necessary expression of their being and their destiny. The return to the primary interests inherent in the nearest field of membership obliges them to abandon the games which allowed membership at different levels; and a number of positions adopted for or against the May 1968 movement are political rationalizations, necessitated by the effect of politicization, of reactions whose source is not in politics: the situation of philology or linguistics, or even of some particular trend in linguistics, may be detected through apparently purely political commitments – against the Communist Party and the leftists, or with the Communist Party and against the leftists, assimilated, in some particular case, to modernism and thereby to America or Chomskyism – where drives and impulses of individuals or groups determined to defend their social being are often expressed.

THE ILLUSION OF SPONTANEITY

The effect of *context awareness* which results from the global perception of the stances displayed (and which affects agents all the more, as political competence is more strongly attributed to them socially) tends no doubt to reduce the efficiency of the effects of *allodoxia* by rendering less vague, less confused, therefore more readable than in ordinary existence, the relation which is established between the space of political stances and the space of social positions. But it goes without saying that the different types of objectified opinions, demonstrations, slogans, petitions, manifestos, platforms and programmes, which arise in the situation of crisis, are as far removed from so-called 'public' opinion obtained by statistical aggregation of isolated opinions (we know the hostility of political or trade-union organizations to anonymous enquiries) as from the collective opinion which would arise spontaneously from the spontaneous dialectic of individual opinions freely expressed and confronted, in the fusion and effusion of revolutionary enthusiasm. The symbolic production of a time of crisis is neither an arithmetical addition of individual opinions nor a mystical fusion of minds exalted by collective effervescence. It is no different in its principle from what happens in ordinary times through the – often one-directional – exchange between the professional constructors and imposers of definitions of the social world, and those whom they are supposed to speak for – if it weren't for the fact that, as we have seen, the political action of mobilizing the subordinate is reinforced by the crisis and by the effect of 'politicization' which it causes. The myth of the moment of awareness as foundation of the voluntary formation of a group on the basis of common interests consciously perceived, or, in other words, as immediate coincidence of the individual minds of all the members of the theoretical class with the immanent laws of history which constitute them as a group, at the same time as assigning them the ends, both necessary and free, of their action, masks the work of construction of the group and of the collective vision of the world which is accomplished in the construction of common institutions and of a bureaucracy of *plenipotentiaries* entrusted with *representing* a potential group of agents united by affinities of dispositions and interests, and making that group exist as a political force in and through this representation.

This work is doubtless most important in times of crisis, when the meaning of a social world less totalizable than ever vacillates; and, in fact, the political apparatuses and above all the party men, experts in the social techniques of manipulation of groups because of their experience of party machines – even those which constitute almost the whole existence of so many political groupuscules and sects, richer in leaders than militants – are perhaps never more present and active than in these circumstances. In the vast, semi-anonymous assemblies of these critical moments, the mechanisms of competition for the expression and imposition of legitimate opinion, which, like market mechanisms, act 'in spite of anarchy, in and through anarchy', as Engels somewhere says, give an advantage to those with acquired verbal skills and those skilled in appropriating places of speech, and in using techniques producing unanimous, monopolistic meaning and its expression (such as the vote by show of hands or by acclamation of motions or petitions drawn up by a few and often only marginally inspired by the interminable discussions which they are supposed to express, etc.).[48] Paradoxically, the appearance of previously unknown spokesmen and the challenge which they have thrown down to the titular heralds of the major political and above all trade-union organizations have concealed the fact that there is doubtless no situation more favourable to professional public speakers of the political variety than the situations of crisis apparently totally abandoned to the 'spontaneity of the masses'; and, in fact, just as the prophets of ancient Judaism were often defectors from the priestly caste, so the majority of the leaders thrown up by the 'popular ferment' had in fact been trained in the various political organizations, those of the students or the lecturers or the revolutionary 'sects' where a specific competence is acquired, usually comprising a set of linguistic and postural instruments, enabling exploitation and control of the institutionalized places of speech. Ideally we should *evoke* the typical style of the discourse of May, a populist dramatization of 'popular' speech, whose negligent syntax and lax expression mask a formidable rhetorical violence, a soft, relaxed violence, but enveloping and penetrating, especially noticeable in the techniques of interpellation and interruption, of questioning and warning, which allow intervention in and control over the discussion, in the 'knockout' phrases, which blast aside all analytical subtleties, in the obsessional repetition, destined to encourage interruption and questioning, etc.[49] We forget in fact that *freedom of speech*, which was so much discussed during and after May 1968, is always freedom from the speech of others, or rather control of their silence, as was so cruelly demonstrated in those meetings between students and 'workers' where the spokesmen of the former orchestrated the speech and silence of the latter: indeed, faced with the president of a society of *agrégés* with hardly any members speaking in the name of all the *agrégés*, with the secretary of a trade union who commits all his members to policies which have emerged from his particular *habitus* alone or from the contagious influence of the ideal model of the revolutionary leader, or with the ephemeral leader of one day's general assembly who calls for a vote to pass a revolutionary motion in favour of the abolition of diplomas or a reform of the statutes of the university prepared by the corporate imagination of its members, the individuals who are objectively implicated as a result of categorial membership can only offer up a resigned silence, the vain revolt of uncoordinated protest or the sectarian foundation of dissident groups destined to disappear or to discover in their turn the privative effects of delegation.

But there does still exist a sort of incompatibility between situations of crisis and social and political organizations, even those, like the parties of the left or the workers' unions, which must reproduce *in ordinary times* some of the effects of 'politicization' and of mobilization, which the crisis also produces, but in a basically discontinuous and extraordinary way. Thus the *action of representation* which creates the visible existence of the class represented must be based on official institutions, provided with *headquarters* (buildings, offices, secretariats, etc.) and with *permanent staff* who must *continuously*, or with a controlled and regular periodicity, accomplish acts which are destined to maintain the state of mobilization of the group represented and of the group of the representatives (producing tracts, displaying posters, selling news-papers, distributing cards, collecting subscriptions, organizing con-gresses, festivals, meetings and debates, etc.) and who, by exploiting the results of their permanent action, can produce *tailor-made crises*, such as demonstrations, strikes, work stoppages, etc. There is at least the germ of a contradiction between the immanent tendencies of the permanent organization, including those who are involved in it and its reproduction, and the ends which it is supposed to serve: the autarky of an organization which becomes its own self-sufficient end leads it to sacrifice external functions to the internal functions of self-reproduction. Thus we explain the fact that the organizations officially mandated to produce or maintain *critical* states can fail in this function when the crisis is not a controlled effect of their action, and the fact that the crisis thereby contains by the same token a threat to their internal order, if not their very existence.

No doubt the situation of crisis is more favourable than the normal order for a subversion of the space of the spokesmen, that is to say the political field as such. Indeed, however powerful the effect of the social techniques which tend to oppose or control the improvisation of the non-professionals, the latter, reinforced and sustained by the meeting of kindred homologous dispositions, can benefit from the lifting of taboos in order to contribute to what is doubtless the most important and the most durable effect of the crisis: the symbolic revolution as profound transformation of styles of thought and life, and, more particularly, of the whole symbolic dimension of everyday existence. Functioning like a sort of collective ritual of divorce from ordinary routines and attachments, its aim is *metanoia*, spiritual conversion. The crisis leads to countless simultaneous conversions which mutually reinforce and support each other; it transforms the view which the agents normally have of the symbolism of social relations, and especially the hierarchies, highlighting the otherwise strongly repressed political dimension of the most ordinary symbolic practices: formulas of politeness, gestures of deference practised between social ranks, ages or sexes, cosmetic and vestimentary habits, etc. And only the techniques of the *Bildungsroman* could enable us to show how collective crisis and personal crisis provide each other with a mutual opportunity, how political revision is accompanied by personal regeneration, attested by the changes in vestimentary and cosmetic symbolism which consecrate a total commitment to an ethico-political vision of the social world, erected into the principle of a whole lifestyle, private as much as public.

Postscript

The Categories of Professorial Judgement

At the suggestion of the Marxist students' section, Lenin had to give three lectures at the Ecole des Hautes Etudes on the agrarian question, organized in Paris by professors expelled from Russian universities. ... I remember that before the first discussion, Vladimir Ilich was very nervous. But, once on the rostrum, he became quite self-confident, or, at least, appeared to be. Professor Gambarov, who had come to listen to him, told Deutsch quite succinctly what he felt: 'a real professor'. He evidently felt that this was paying him the greatest possible compliment.

Leon Trotsky, My Life

We may admit that practice always implies a process of knowledge far removed from any passive recording, without thereby presenting it as a purely intellectual construction. Practical knowledge is an operation of construction which sets up systems of classifications (taxonomies) in terms of practical functions. These systems organize perception and appreciation, and provide a structure for practice. Produced by the practice of successive generations, in given types of conditions of existence, these schemata of perception, appreciation and action which are acquired through practice, and set in motion on a practical level, without acceding to explicit representation, function as practical operators through which the objective structures which produce them tend to reproduce themselves in the various practices.

The practical taxonomies, instruments of knowledge and communication which are the condition of the establishment of meaning and of a consensus of meaning, exercise their *structuring* efficacity only in so far as they are themselves *structured*. Which does not mean that they are answerable to a strictly *internal* analysis ('structural', 'componential' or other), which, by tearing them artificially away from their conditions of production and use, prevents itself from understanding their social function. In order to demonstrate this, it should suffice to submit to analysis not one or another of the exotic *curiosities* which distance neutralizes – terminologies of kinship, classifications of plants or diseases – but the classifications which the professors produce every day, as much in their judgements on their actual or potential pupils or colleagues as in their specific productions (textbooks, theses and scholarly works) and in all their practice. Indeed, it is more difficult in this case to bracket out the social functions of the deeply buried system of classification which lies behind all these academic classifications, and the social classifications which they determine or legitimate.

PROFESSORIAL JURISPRUDENCE

The analysis of an exceptional document, that is the set of individual files kept for four successive years by a philosophy professor in a *première supérieure* in Paris, should allow direct verification of the hypotheses already formulated to account for the implicit criteria of professorial judgement in its traditional form:[1] the taxonomies which are revealed by the ritual formulas of the evidence for professorial judgement ('progress reports') and which, we may suppose, structure professorial judgement as much as they express it, can be set in relation to the numerical sanctions (the marks) and the social origins of the pupils who are the object of these two forms of evaluation.

At this level of the academic career, and since the objective is to evaluate pupils who are for the most part destined to constitute the elite of the professors, the operations of classification are *operations of co-optation*. Invested with a function analogous to that which is incumbent upon *strategies of succession* in other milieux, they are doubtless the place where it is easiest to grasp the organizing principles of the teaching system as a whole, that is, not only the selection procedures which produce, among other things, the properties of the professorial body, but also the true hierarchy of the properties being reproduced, and thus the fundamental 'options' of the system reproduced.

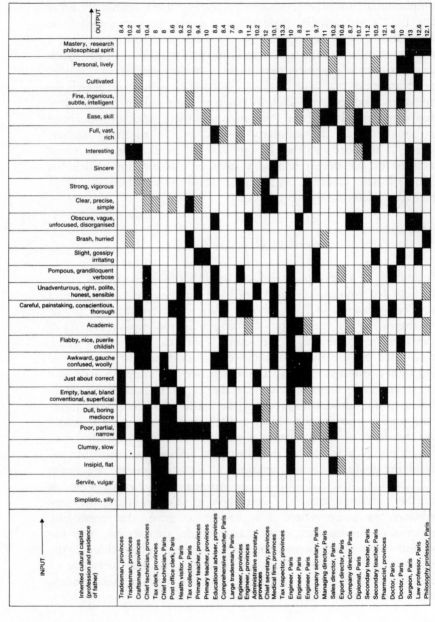

Classification 1 Classificatory machine no. 1: from social classification to academic classification

Thus we shall find at work *academic forms of classification* which, like the 'primitive forms of classification' mentioned by Durkheim and Mauss, are essentially transmitted in and through practice, beyond any specifically pedagogical intention. These forms of thought, expression and appreciation owe their specific logic to the fact that, being produced and reproduced by the academic system, they are the product of the transformation imposed by the specific logic of the university field on the forms which organize the dominant thought and expression.

The construction of the diagram

We had at our disposal 154 individual pupils' files from a girls' *première supérieure* in Paris.[2] In these documents, established in the 1960s, we find on the one hand a record of the date of birth, the profession and address of the parents and the secondary school attended, and, on the other hand, the *marks* (five or six exercises marked for each pupil) awarded for their written work and oral contributions, along with supporting remarks. Given the nature of this material, it is understandable that it was not possible to obtain similar information for other classes and determine rigorously what the object studied owes to the specific characteristics of the institution, of its (female) population and of the professor. Everything seems to guarantee, however, that *the principles of classification used are universally valid.*

1 Having first of all established, through a diagonalization of the data (according to the principles proposed by Jacques Bertin in his *Sémiologie graphique*), a hierarchy of epithets (from the most pejorative to the most appreciative) and a hierarchy of social origins, linked by a simple and clearly visible relation, and having noted that the hierarchy according to social origins was very close to that obtainable *a priori* by taking as criterion the cultural capital of the family, we ordered the pupils of one of the years studied *according to the importance of the cultural capital* which they had inherited from their families (or, in other words, according to their closeness to or distance from the educational system, relying, in the absence of more precise criteria, on the profession and the place of residence (Parisian or provincial) of the parents). Thus we progress from the pupils whose origins are in the middle classes to the pupils

from the upper classes, and, among the latter, from the (relatively) least endowed with cultural capital (managers and executives) to the richest (university professors), the liberal professions holding an intermediate position.

2 Each line of the diagram represents *the universe of judgements liable to be made on a pupil* by the professor: we ordered the adjectives, arranged into twenty-seven classes, from the most pejorative to the most appreciative (grouping in the same class adjectives of related significance which are used in association with each other). We have marked with a *black square* the presence of one of the adjectives of the class considered in the professor's remarks on a given pupil; with a *shaded square* the case where the epithet is accompanied by a nuance or restriction or meaning (for instance, 'fluent but nervous delivery' [*élocution aisée mais saccadée*], 'conscientious but servile' [*de l'application mais servile*], 'incomplete but correct and well argued'; [*partiel mais juste et bien conduit*], 'thin and unexciting, but well organized' [*forme diffuse et plate, mais de l'organisation*]).

3 We placed on the far right of the diagram the *average of all the marks* obtained during the year by each pupil.

We can see straight away that the black squares form approximately a diagonal: the most favourable epithets appear more and more frequently as the social origins of the pupils rise. We may also note that the average marks rise, as we rise in the social hierarchy, that is, the frequency of commendatory judgements rises. Everything seems to indicate that Parisian origins constitute an extra advantage, the Parisian girls, given the same social origins, always obtaining a slightly higher rate of select epithets – despite the fact that the provincial girls are, at this level of career and in a preparatory class reserved for the academic elite, highly overselected. The pupils from the middle classes (who make up more than half the group of those with marks situated between 7.5 and 10 and who are totally absent from the small group with marks over 12) are the prime target of negative judgements – and of the most negative among them, such as 'simplistic' [*simplet*], 'servile' [*servile*] or 'vulgar'[*vulgaire*]. It should suffice to group the epithets which they seem to elicit to see how the bourgeois image of the petty bourgeois as a lesser bourgeois is composed: 'poor' [*pauvre*], 'narrow' [*étroit*], 'mediocre' [*médiocre*], 'just about correct' [*correct sans plus*], 'awkward' [*maladroit*], 'clumsy' [*gauche*], 'confused' [*confus*], etc. Even the virtues which are attributed to them are negative too: 'academic' [*scolaire*], 'painstaking' [*soigneux*], 'careful' [*attentif*], 'conscientious' [*sérieux*], 'methodical' [*méthodique*], 'cautious' [*timide*], 'polite' [*sage*], 'honest' [*honnête*], 'sensible' [*raisonnable*]. On occasions that their rarer qualities, like 'lucidity' [*clarté*], 'strength' [*fermeté*], 'finesse' [*finesse*], 'subtlety' [*subtilité*], 'intelligence' [*intelligence*] or 'culture' [*culture*], are acknowledged, it is almost always with reservations (note, for example, comment 1b in the synoptic table, chosen for its ideal-typical character). The pupils whose origins are in the least culturally rich fraction of the dominant classes entirely escape the most insulting comments, and the pejorative labels which they earn are often qualified; they receive the most appreciative epithets but still very often expressed with reservations. As for the pupils from the fractions of the dominant class with the richest cultural capital, they almost entirely avoid the most negative judgements, even in their euphemistic forms, as they do the petty-bourgeois virtues, and they most often find themselves granted the most sophisticated qualities.

In fact the mode of classification adopted tends to minimize the differences between the classes. The great dispersal of the distribution of the adjectives which hold a median position in the taxonomy is not entirely imputable to the effect of this position nor even to the effect of the grouping of different adjectives, however close. It lies no doubt essentially in the fact that the same adjective can enter into different *combinations* and thereby receive very different meanings: this is the case in particular with epithets like 'thorough' [*solide*], which associated with 'painstaking' [*soigneux*] and 'careful' [*attentif*], may be only a euphemistic way of acknowledging the merits of impeccable petty-bourgeois mediocrity (which is admirably expressed in the 'just about' [sans plus] of 'just about correct' [*correct sans plus*]), whereas, combined with 'intelligent' [*intelligent*] or 'subtle' [*subtil*], it may express the perfect synthesis of academic virtues.

Moreover, we note that, where the marks are the same or equivalent, the remarks are all the more severe and more brutally expressed, less euphemistic, as the social origins of the pupils decrease. To get a concrete idea of this effect, we need only read in the synoptic table the judgements made on pupils of different social origins who have obtained similar marks (that is, situated on the same line, for instance 1b, 2b, 3b). We can see that the *judgemental evidence* seems more strongly linked to social origins than the *mark* in which they are expressed; this is no doubt because they betray more directly the professor's representation of her pupils, using her extraneous knowledge of their *bodily 'hexis'*, and her evaluation of this in terms of criteria quite alien to those which are explicitly recognized in the technical definition of the performance demanded.

The professorial judgement is in fact generally based on a whole collection of disparate criteria, never clarified, hierarchized or systematized, which the professor derives from academic exercises, or from the physical person of their authors. 'Handwriting', which is sometimes explicitly mentioned, when its 'ugliness' [*laideur*] or 'puerility' [*puérilité*] is striking, is perceived with reference to a practical taxonomy of writings which is far from being socially neutral, and which is organized around oppositions such as 'distinguished' [*distinguée*] and 'intellectual' [*intellectuelle*] or 'puerile' [*puérile*] and 'vulgar' [*vulgaire*]. 'Appearance' [*présentation*], which is only rarely mentioned, is also apprehended through a socially marked grid: excessive negligence and meticulous care (childish underlining in bright colours) are equally condemned. 'Style' and 'general culture' are explicitly taken into consideration, but to differing degrees and with varying criteria according to discipline (for instance, in philosophy and French).

We can see that specialized culture – which, in the specific case of philosophical authors, implies mastery of the technical vocabulary of philosophy, aptitude in constructing an argument and making rigorous demonstrations, etc. – in fact accounts for only a minority of the comments. The 'external' criteria, most often implicit and even rejected by the institution, have even greater importance in the remarks on oral work, since the criteria already mentioned are compounded with all those concerning speech, and, more specifically, *accent, elocution and diction*, which are the surest, because the most indelible, marks of social and geographical origins, *the style of the spoken language*, which can differ radically from written style, and finally and above all the *bodily 'hexis'*, manners and behaviour, which are often designated, very directly, in the remarks.

Thus there is no doubt that the judgements which claim to apply to *the whole person* take into account not only physical appearance as such, which is always socially marked (through indices such as weight, complexion, facial features) but also the *socially processed body* (with clothes, jewellery, make-up and above all manners and behaviour) which is perceived through socially constituted taxonomies, and thus read as the *sign* of the quality and value of the person. (Because of the poor quality of the photos attached to the files, we had to abandon our intention of showing the relation between the adjectives used and the perception that the professor might have of the pupils through their physical appearance.) The bodily *hexis* is the principal prop of a class judgement which fails to recognize itself as such: it is as if a concrete intuition of the properties of the body, grasped and designated as properties of the person, motivated the global perception and appreciation of the intellectual and moral qualities.

We can see the diagram as the model of a machine which, from an input of socially classified products, produces academically classified products. But this would be to overlook the essential feature of the operation of transformation which it effects: in fact, this machine ensures a very close correspondence between the classification at entry and the classification at exit, without ever (officially) knowing or acknowledging the principles and criteria of the social classification. This means that the official, specifically academic, taxonomy, which is objectified in the form of a series of adjectives, fulfils a dual and contradictory function: it allows the operation of a social classification while simultaneously masking it; it serves at once as relay and screen between the classification at entry, which is overtly social, and the classification at exit, which claims to be exclusively academic. In short, it functions according to a logic of *negation* [*Verneinung*]: it does what it does in forms tending to show that it is not doing them.

The taxonomy which expresses and structures academic perception is a neutralized and misconstruable, that is to say euphemized, form of the dominant taxonomy:[3] it is organized according to the hierarchy of 'inferior' (lower-class) qualities – servility [*servilité*], vulgarity [*vulgarité*], clumsiness [*lourdeur*], slowness [*lenteur*], poverty [*pauvreté*], etc.; 'medium' (petty-bourgeois) qualities – pettiness [*petitesse*], narrowness [*étroitesse*], mediocrity [*médiocrité*], accuracy [*correction*], conscientiousness [*sérieux*], etc.; and 'superior' qualities – sincerity [*sincérité*], expansiveness [*ampleur*], richness [*richesse*], facility [*aisance*], expertise [*savoir-faire*], finesse [*finesse*], ingenuity [*ingéniosité*], subtlety [*subtilité*], intelligence [*intelligence*], culture [*culture*], etc. Apart from a few adjectives which can designate properties of the academic exercise ('incomplete' [*partiel*], 'sketchy' [*sommaire*], 'confused' [*confus*], 'rambling' [*diffus*], 'methodical'

Table 9. Synoptic table of some professorial epithets

Average mark	1 Middle classes	Fractions of the upper classes	
		2 Poorest in cultural capital	3 Richest in cultural capital
a between 8 and 10	*Father chief technician, Paris* Silly, mediocre, allusive, badly organized, a series of disconnected points. Summary correct but servile. Absolutely insipid. Some good (second-hand?) points but thin and unfocused.	*Father engineer, mother secretary, Paris region* Confused; some philosophical flotsam for the sake of effect, but no research, purely academic work. Disorganized, vivacious, fluent but nervous delivery. Disorganized, patchy knowledge, worse than lack of knowledge. Some ideas, but very badly developed. Satisfactory work. Better.	*Father doctor, Paris* Some knowledge, but uses philosophical concepts for their stylistic effect: hollow rhetoric. Otherwise shows evidence of learning and organization. Servile summary. Some knowledge, and clarity of expression, but no direct analysis. Some good points, but not well developed, heteroclite quotations.
b between 10 and 12	*Father craftsman (carpenter), mother postal worker, provinces* Not stupid but rather childish, incomplete, awkward but interesting, some culture. Knowledge misapplied; strong views, but very one-sided.	*Father assistant export director, Paris* Rich, long, fairly correct, rather verbose, however. Conscientious, thoughtful, embarrassed, gets bogged down in problems.	*Father teacher of physics and chemistry, mother teacher of natural science, Paris region* Precise, scrupulous, clear but somewhat narrow. Some foolish blunders, but some qualities.

Sincere, conscientious, rather shy; good use of German.

Same comment: awkward but sincere, conscientious, good examples.

c
12 and over

Woolly and dull in form, but not disorganized, quite well constructed survey of the topic, handwriting untidy, with words crossed out.

Fairly good: conscientious, but fails to define clearly enough.

Flabby and somewhat foolish, with some good points.

Misuses and misunderstands terms.

Father senior administrative executive, mother primary teacher, provinces

Good, some culture and thought, fairly well written, sometimes tries to move beyond limits of her knowledge.

Fairly good.

Interesting and confident.

Precise, irritating: some conviction, some sophistry.

Fine, fairly well written, not always very accurate.

Father surgeon, Paris

Interesting but disorganized.

Very vigorous and well argued: conclusion a trifle too mystical, but sincerely philosophical.

Very personal and well developed, but badly written.

Vigorous, fairly well written.

Interesting but obscure, badly expressed.

We have recorded here all the professor's remarks on the files of a few pupils, together with their average mark. The number of remarks recorded for each pupil is different, since the professor did not add a commentary after the mark for each piece of written or oral work.

[*méthodique*], 'obscure' [*obscur*], 'vague' [*vague*], 'nebulous' [*flou*], 'disorganized' [*désordonné*], 'clear' [*clair*], 'precise' [*précis*], 'simple' [*simple*]), almost all of the adjectives used designate *personal qualities*, as if the professor felt authorized by the conventions of academic narrative to judge, like a literary critic or art critic, not the pupil's technical aptitude to conform to rigorously defined technical norms, but a general, and moreover undefinable, disposition, a unique combination of lucidity, firmness and strength, of sincerity, facility and expertise, of finesse, subtlety and ingenuity.

The very vagueness and nebulousness of the adjectives, which, like the adjectives used in the appreciation of a work of art, are the equivalent of *interjections* which convey virtually no information (except about a state of mind), suffice to bear witness to the fact that the qualities which they designate would remain imperceptible and indiscernible for anyone who was not already familiar, on a practical level, with the systems of classification which are written into ordinary language. Thus we would not understand the 'vague, emotive meaning' of the word *vulgar* [*vulgaire*] ('totally lacking distinction, betraying crude taste, independently of social class', as the *Robert* dictionary defines it), if we did not take into account the primary, primitive meaning, which is overtly situated in the social domain: 'of mediocre and low condition and taste, of ordinary thought, as opposed to those of the elite . . . ; proper to the lowest levels of society'. Working as an ideology in a state of practice, producing logical effects which are inseparable from political effects, the academic taxonomy entails an implicit definition of excellence which, by constituting as excellent the qualities possessed by those who are socially dominant, consecrates their manner of being and their lifestyle.

The homology between the structures of the educational system (hierarchy of disciplines, of sections, etc.) and the mental structures of the agents (professorial taxonomies) is the source of the functioning of the *consecration of the social order* which the education system performs behind its mask of neutrality. It is indeed through the medium of this system of classification that the academic system establishes a correspondence between the social properties of the agents and academic positions themselves hierarchized according to the order of teaching (primary, secondary, higher), according to the establishment or the section (*grandes écoles* or faculties, superior sections or inferior sections[4]), and, for the teachers, according to their grade and to the location of their establishment (Paris or the provinces). This allotment of agents to hierarchized academic positions constitutes in its turn another mediation between social class and academic class. But this mechanism can only function if the homology remains hidden and if the taxonomy which in practice expresses and structures perception uses the most socially neutral antitheses of the dominant taxonomy ('brilliant'/'dull' [*brillant/ terne*], 'graceful'/'clumsy' [*léger/lourd*], etc.) or euphemized forms of these antitheses: 'clumsy' [*lourd*] thus yields to 'laboured' [*lourdaud*] or 'clearly constructed' [*charpenté*] or 'painstaking' [*appuyé*], 'simple' [*simple*] to 'simplistic' [*simplet*], 'graceful' [*léger*] to 'easy to read' [*qui se lit bien*], apparently pejorative forms, but in fact attenuated by the gruff, paternalistic benevolence which they betray.

The manifest brutality of some epithets – which would not be permissible in ordinary usage: where 'servile' [*servile*], for example, would be replaced by 'humble' [*humble*] (as in 'humble occupation') or 'modest' [*modeste*] (as in 'modest conditions') – should not deceive us: the academic excuse which maintains that the judgement is applied to a piece of work and not its author, the fact that these are adolescents who may still improve, and who therefore may be treated more roughly and frankly (cf. 'nice [*gentil*], puerile [*puéril*], childish' [*enfantin*]), the situation of correction and sanction which authorizes the infliction of a symbolic punishment as in other times and other places physical punishment was inflicted, the tradition of strictness and discipline which all the 'elite schools' have in common ('per ardua ad astra'), none of these suffices to explain the complacency and freedom in symbolic aggression observable in all examination situations. It is the academic field as such, functioning as if it were censored, which makes it unthinkable, as much for those pronouncing them as for those who are their object, to decipher the social significance of the judgements, which are thus reduced to simple gestures in the unreal and unrealistic ritual of academic initiation, just like any other collective anathema. Academic neutrality is indeed no more than this extraordinary collective negation which, for instance, allows the professor, in the name of the authority delegated to her/him by the academic institution, to condemn as academic' [*scolaire*] those productions and expressions which are merely what the academic institution requires, and merely what it produces from pupils whose only mode of acquisition is their academic training. This negation is produced in and through each individual professor who attributes marks to pupils as a function of an academic perception of their academic expression (dissertations written, papers read out, etc.) and of their whole personality: what is judged is an academically qualified product, a 'dull' [*terne*] script, a 'just about acceptable' [*passable sans plus*] paper, and so on; never a petty bourgeois. The negation is reproduced in and through each of the pupils who, because s/he perceives her/himself as s/he is perceived, that is as 'dull' [*terne*], 'lacking philosophical talent' [*peu doué pour la philosophie*], concentrates on Latin prose composition or on geography.

Is this to say that the collective misconstrual is only the result of aggregating a number of individual denials? In fact, it is the whole structure of a field organized and divided according to the very classifications that it is supposed to produce (faculty and *grandes écoles*, disciplines, sections, etc.) which is expressed either in the taxonomy operated by the practical operations of classification and very regularly used, although it is *never explicitly codified*, each time that a classification has to be expressed (marks for homework, end-of-term grades, etc.). As a *neutralized form* of the dominant taxonomy which is produced by and for the functioning of a relatively autonomous field, and which raises to a second degree of neutrality the taxonomies of ordinary language, academic language helps to make possible the functioning of mechanisms which can only operate by persuading agents to adopt their logic, which supposes that these objectives are offered to the agents in a misconstruable form.

Reproducing in transposed form the social division of labour in its own organizational divisions, the educational system operates classifications which are first of all expressed in the attribution of academic classes (classes, sections, etc.) and later of social classes. It is no doubt through the medium of the successive *classifications* which have made them what they are, from the viewpoint of the academic taxonomy, that the classified products of the academic system, pupils or professors, have acquired, to varying degrees according to their position in these structures, their practical mastery of classificatory systems, adjusted circumstancially to objective classes, which allow them to classify everything – starting with themselves – according to academic taxonomies, and which function within each one of them – in all good faith and genuine belief – as a machine for transforming social classifications into academic classifications, as recognized-yet-misconstrued social classifications. As objective structures which have become mental structures through a process of apprenticeship which is accomplished through a world organized according to its structures and submitted to sanctions formulated in a language also structured according to the same oppositions, the academic taxonomies classify according to the logic of the structures whose product they are. Because they find constant confirmation in a social world organized in accordance with the same principles, they are deployed with the feeling of obviousness which characterizes doxic experience of the social world, and its underside of the unthought and the unthinkable.

The agents entrusted with the operations of classification can fulfil their function of social classification only because this is performed *in the guise* of an operation of academic classification, that is, through a specifically academic taxonomy. They successfully perform what they (objectively) have to do only because they *believe* that they are doing something different from what they are actually doing; because they are actually doing something different from what they believe they are doing; and because they *believe* in what they *believe* they are doing. As mystified mystifiers, they are the *first victims* of the operations which they perform. It is because they think that they are operating a purely academic or even specifically 'philosophical' classification, because they think that they are issuing certificates for charismatic qualities ('the philosophical mind' [*esprit philosophique*], etc.), that the system is able to perform a genuine *distortion of the meaning* of their practices, persuading them to do what they would not do deliberately for 'all the money in the world'. It is also because they believe that they are making a strictly academic judgement that the social judgement which is masked by the euphemistic implications of academic (or, more specifically, philosophical) language can produce its characteristic effect: by persuading those who are its objects that this judgement applies to the pupil or the philosophical apprentice within them, to their 'persona' or their 'intelligence', and never in any instance to their social personage or, more crudely, to themselves as sons of professors or shopkeepers, the academic judgement elicits a recognition – in fact a misconstrual – which would no doubt not be elicited by the social judgement of which it is a euphemized form. The transmutation of social truth into academic truth (from 'you are a petty bourgeois' to 'you work hard but lack brilliance' [*vous étes travailleur mais pas brillant*]) is not a simple game of writing of no consequence but an operation of social alchemy which confers on words their symbolic efficiency, their power to have a lasting effect on practice. A proposition, which in its untransformed guise ('you come from a working-class family') or even at a higher level of transformation ('you are vulgar') would lack all symbolic effectiveness and which would even be liable to incite rebellion against the institution and its personnel (if such an appellation were even 'imaginable', as people would say, 'from the mouth of a professor'), becomes acceptable and accepted, admitted and personally internalized, in the *misconstruable form* imposed on it by the specific censorship of the social field ('I have no philosophical talent' [*je ne suis pas doué pour la philo*]). The academic taxonomy of academic qualities (offered as an index of human excellence) intervenes between each agent and his 'vocation'. It is this taxonomy which, for instance, directs orientation towards one discipline or section rather than another, entailed in advance by the academic verdict ('I'm really keen on geography' [*j'aime beaucoup la géo*]).

In order to disentangle ourselves from discoursing on the power of discourse, we have, as we see, to relate language to the social conditions of its production and use, and, unless we accept in the social order the equivalent of magical power, we must seek beyond words, in the mechanisms of production of these words and the people who emit and receive them, the motive force of a power which a certain way of using words allows us to mobilize. Conventional usage of conventional language is only one of the conditions of effectiveness of symbolic power, and a condition which works only under certain conditions. We only ever preach to the converted. The power of the academic euphemism is absolute only when it works on agents selected in such a way that the social and academic conditions of their production dispose them to recognize it absolutely.

EUPHEMISM IN ACADEMIC RHETORIC

The truth of euphemism is revealed in the use made of it by professorial rhetoric any time that an unfavourable judgement has to be delivered within the limits of academic etiquette and/or prudence. In book reviews or references, reports on theses, or panegyrics pronounced in favour of candidates for co-optation, speeches intended for equals able to read between the lines and understand the unspoken, the paean can subvert itself by dealing in 'subordinate' and 'minimal' qualities (in the following quotations: 'conscientious and hardworking' [*sérieuse et travailleuse*], 'intellectual honesty' [*honnêteté intellectuelle*], 'unassuming' [*discrète*] which imply the absence of the complementary category ('brilliant' [*brillant*], etc.) or which use transparent devices to signal their own conventional and circumstantial nature ('honourable' [*aux alentours de la moyenne*], 'encouraging prospect' [*encourageant pour l'avenir*], 'the further effort necessary' [*après un nouvel effort*], 'rather too dependent on secondary material' [*un peu trop près des fiches*]).

References for (rejected) candidates, September 1972:

> I have known Miss X from the start of her university studies: she has always impressed me as an extremely conscientious and hardworking student. On several occasions she asked me to mark her work for the *agrégation*, and her marks were honourable. This is an encouraging prospect. For this reason, I trust that she will be able to make the further effort necessary for success in the *agrégation*.

> Miss X wrote her master's thesis under my supervision in 1970–1; this dissertation studied the idea of nobility in Euripides' theatre and was awarded a mark of 15 out of 20 (*cum laude* [*mention bien*]). It was an extremely conscientious piece of work, carefully researched and showing considerable intellectual honesty. Its only fault was that it remained rather too dependent on secondary material, and lacked an original overview. I can attest to Miss X's qualities, which lead me to believe that she has the ability to be a worthwhile *agrégation* candidate, despite her first, unsuccessful attempt. I would like her to be able to prepare the *agrégation* under favourable conditions. I should add that she is both hardworking and unassuming, which may well help your assessment.

The academic dialectic of recognition and misconstrual attains its most accomplished form when the structure of the system of categories of perception and thought, which organize the expressions of academic judgement and this judgement itself, is in perfect harmony with the structure of the contents which the academic system is entrusted with transmitting, as is the case with literary or philosophical culture in its academic form. In cases where philosophical discourse is reduced to what is often offered in philosophy classes as ethics or psychology, the harmony is more or less perfect between the structure of the discourse transmitted and the structures of perception and appreciation that the academic field imposes on the emitters as well as the receivers of the discourse. We can see, for instance, the elective affinity which unites the system of representations and values objectively written into the academic taxonomy and the Heideggerian discourse on 'the ordinary' or 'everyday chatter' when, reduced to its most simple expression, that is to its objective truth, for the purposes of academic communication, it is limited to the aristocratic affirmation of the distance of the thinker from the 'vulgar' and from 'common sense' which is behind the professorial philosophy of philosophy and the facile enthusiasm it engenders in adolescents.[5] Starting with the transposition produced by the expression of the dominant vision of the social world in the esoteric language of traditional philosophy, the *oblique legitimation* comes full circle with the academic enterprise of exoterization of the esoteric. With the legitimate divulgation for a small number of legitimate addresses (which makes *all* the difference between teaching and mere 'popularization') of a more or less simplified version (and explicitly given as such) of the esoteric form of the official vision of the social world, the circular circulation which defines religious alchemy finds its end and fulfilment. The effect of *autonomization* and, thereby, of *legitimation* produced by the work of euphemization and esoterization required by the censorship implicit in the specific laws of a relatively autonomous field of production like the philosophical field (or, more generally, the religious field, the artistic field, etc.) is not cancelled out by the reverse operation of the exoterization of the esoteric discourse. The distinguished and the vulgar, the rare and the common, are no longer what they are, euphemized but still over-transparent expressions of class interests, when, after their orbit through the heavens of the philosophical idea, they return in the neither 'common' nor yet quite bourgeois style of what is 'personal' and what is 'general', 'authentic' and 'inauthentic', *Eigentlichkeit* and *Uneigentlichkeit*, according to the degree of initiation of the master and his disciples.

ACADEMIC ETHICS AND THE JUDGEMENT OF PEERS

In the following diagram, the first analysis of the obituary notices published in *L'Annuaire de l'Association amicale des anciens élèves de l'Ecole Normale Supérieure* for the years 1962, 1963, 1964 and 1965, we have ranked the thirty-four 'old boys' whose social origins were indicated in the notices according to the importance of their original cultural and social capital as far as they can be evaluated from the available information, that is, chiefly, the profession of the father and, if applicable, of the mother, the place of residence of the parents at the time of birth, and more or less precise indications of the cultural atmosphere of the family.

The alumni studied were for the most part born around 1880–90 and were in employment between 1905 and 1955. The result is that the image of the *normalien* evoked by the obituary writers corresponds to a relatively old state of the system. From a check which was only possible after this analysis had been carried out, we note that the former pupils whose social origins are not recorded in the notices do not differ significantly in this respect from the population studied (six are from the middle classes, five from the upper classes, and for another five there is no information available) and the epithets applied to them follow exactly the same laws as those revealed by this analysis (an archival search has even allowed us to discover very close correlation between the academic reports which remain on file and those contained in the obituaries). Moreover, the former pupils who are the object of an obituary notice do not seem to be any different from the whole set of deceased pupils except perhaps for their devotion to the *école*. Thus it seems that the life members are rather more numerous among those who are the object of an obituary notice than among the others. Finally, everything seems to indicate that the relation between the author and the object of the obituary notice is not arbitrary, and that in general they share the same origins, discipline and type of career, roughly defined.

As in the case of pupils of the preparatory classes, this classification is obviously not entirely free of all arbitrariness, in particular in respect of pupils whose origins are in the upper petty bourgeoisie and the bourgeoisie: the paucity of information available is not the only problem (we do not always know the rank of officers, nor even their training – Saint-Cyr or Polytechnique, for instance; we do not always know the exact status of professors; we do not know the size of industrial and commercial firms, etc.); a social history of the structure of the dominant class and of the development of the different professions within this structure is the precondition (to which all studies of 'social mobility' are blissfully blind) of any rigorous analysis of social trajectories (and, *a fortiori*, of any

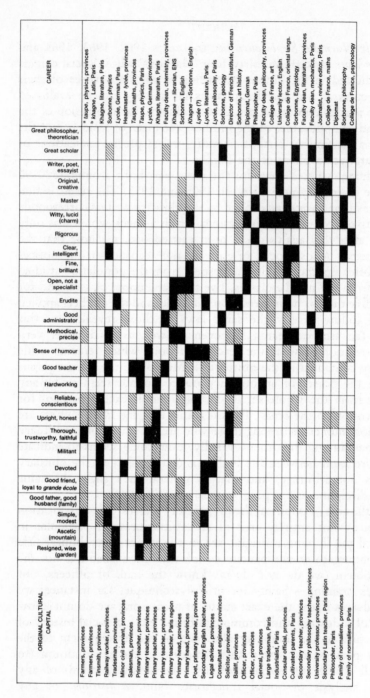

Classification 2 Classificatory machine no. 2: from academic classification to social classification

[a] *Taupe* = preparatory class (science). [Tr.] [b] *Khâgne* = preparatory class (arts). [Tr.]

establishment of any linear hierarchy, such as the one attempted here
for the purposes of our analysis). Furthermore, it is extremely
difficult to evaluate the relative importance of the professional
situation of the family and its place of residence: everything leads
us to believe that at this very high career level, where the
qualities associated with the university image of excellence are most
imperatively required, the opposition between Parisian origins and
provincial origins (reinforced by the difference between the people
from the south of France and those from the north, which remains
ingrained in their *habitus* in the form of different *accents*) plays a
decisive role.[6]

After scrutinizing about ten years' issues of the Annual, and
establishing twenty-six classes of epithets, we marked with a black
square (without ever exceeding ten notations) the qualities (usually
evoked by adjectives) which appeared to be endowed with the
greatest relative importance in the notices considered (because, in
the longer notices, they were evoked more than once, or, in the
shorter ones, they were underlined by the vigour or emphasis of the
expression used: for instance, 'of the race of great philosophers' [*de
la race des grands philosophes*]; 'a great figure in French science' [*une
grande figure de la science française*]). The final judgement which
the group makes on one of its members through the medium of a
duly mandated spokesman (the elegy is incumbent upon a friend
from the same matriculation year, and it is only in case of dire
necessity that it is entrusted to anyone else, usually a pupil, but
always a normalien, as in the boards of examiners for the Ecole
Normale entrance examination) is always the result of a collective
labour whose trace sometimes appears when the author compiles or
integrates information given by different people. The author of the
obituary notice obviously takes into account the point attained at
the end of the university career, which can, in some cases, correct
the 'first impression', often resumed in the evocation of a bodily
hexis and an accent: that is to say that it is not possible to suppose
that between the system of epithets and the final social achievement
there is a relation that is perfectly identical with that established
between social origins, academic reports and grades. In fact, what
the obituary restores, as does the professorial report at a different
stage of the career, is the academically constituted social representation
of the person, which is the principle behind all academic operations
of appreciation and co-optation: it is through the mediation and *in*

the guise of this representation – in which the academically constituted representation of the bodily *hexis* plays a decisive part – that social origins have their impact, although they are never taken as such to form a basis for judgement (indeed, it is significant that, despite the conventions of the biographical genre, it is missing from many of the obituaries – in this case, sixteen out of fifty – and that their closest academic colleagues often say that they were obliged to undertake specific research in order to be able to reveal this information).

If the discourse entrusted with evoking *the departed* gives such prominence to the description of their physical appearance, it is because this functions not only as a kind of remembrance, but also as a palpable *analogon* for the whole person, as revealed at the first meeting:

> His whole being gave one the impression that he lived in a body only because one is forced to do so, even if one is not too sure what to do with it. His elongated neck supported a head which was pleasant but odd, being almost always tilted to one side or the other. He had a bland, fair complexion, typical of the delicate child, cared for, or even pampered, by anxious women past their prime, enormous, vaguely nautical eyes, of an indefinable shade of blue, a nose if not quite imperial, at least most classical, and a splendidly developed, although not disproportionate, brow.[7]

And if the general intuition expressed in this portrait supports the evocation of the intellectual and moral qualities of the man so effectively, it is because the bodily *hexis* provides the system of indices through which class origins are *recognized-yet-misconstrued*: 'finely distinguished' [*fine distinction*], 'poetic' [*un poète*], 'unique qualities partly concealed by an expressive shyness' [*qualités si originales et partiellement dissimulées par une timidité communicative*], 'a delicate, emotive intelligence' [*esprit ombrageux et sensible*]. Similarly, the enumeration of virtues attributed to another character ('professional stamina' [*puissance de travail*], 'varied and productive scientific activity' [*activité scientifique variée et féconde*], 'dedication' [*dévouement*], 'great intellectual honesty' [*grande honnêteté intellectuelle*], 'prodigious but discreet activity' [*prodigieuse et discrète activité*], 'tough, hardworking, cheerful and kind' [*robuste, laborieux, souriant et bon*]) is only a long paraphrase of the scattered notations which evoke his *hexis*: 'a cast-iron constitution in a sportsman's body' [*une santé de fer dans un corps athlétique*], 'healthy and energetic lover of life' [*vigoureux gaillard*].[8]

The system of adjectives used maps out the *world of professorial virtues*, which, like the university careers to which they grant access, are hierarchized. The truth of this world, which, in itself, tends to be closed in upon itself, would be completely revealed only by comparison with other worlds of virtues, associated with other positions in the field of power (we intend to work towards capturing the variants of the dominant ethics which correspond to the different fractions of the dominant class, by making a comparative analysis of a whole set of celebratory discourses – funeral elegies, welcoming speeches, etc – in which different groups celebrate each other by celebrating one of their members). At all events, we quite palpably set limits to a taxonomy which takes itself to be universal when we note that it turns out to be totally absent in the description and praise of the virtues of those *normaliens* who left the university sector – the two diplomats, whose elegy is entrusted to other famous defectors: we enter a world of discourse ('devotion to his country' [*dévouement à son pays*], 'a career entirely devoted to the service of the state' [*carrière vouée au service exclusif de l'État*]) which introduces an entirely different world, antagonistic or even antinomial ('no vocation for teaching' [*pas la vocation de l'enseignement*], 'felt limited by the musty atmosphere of the classroom' [*se trouvant à l'étroit dans le cadre vieillot d'une classe*], 'all his aspirations led him towards wider horizons' [*toutes ses aspirations l'entraînaient vers de plus larges horizons*]), that of the senior civil service or bourgeois big business.

We see that the system of academic classification (captured here in the adjectives used in the funeral elegy) has not ceased to function throughout the university career as a hidden instrument of social classification: it is remarkable that, among all the 'old boys', who are both formally equal and really rendered equal – as far as academic criteria are concerned – by the effect of overselection, the academic system has continued to establish, as a function of the very same criteria which enabled their election to the status of *normalien*, the hierarchies directly displayed in university careers. Everything indeed happens as if the *normaliens* were being promised academic careers very closely proportionate to their social origins in an academic space very rigorously organized according to institution (from the Collège de France to the *lycée*), place of residence (from Paris to the small provincial town) and discipline (from philosophy to modern languages and from maths to chemistry). Out of the fifteen 'old boys' of working- or middle-class origins, twelve became teachers in secondary education or professors in advanced secondary education (*khagne* and *taupe* [preparatory classes for the *grandes écoles*]) and only three became professors in higher education, but in disciplines considered professionally inferior (modern languages, chemistry, physics) and/ or in the provinces; on the contrary, out of the nineteen 'old boys' from the upper classes, only two became teachers in secondary education, whereas two became diplomats, two others became writers and thirteen became professors in higher education, mostly in Paris, and four of them at the Collège de France.

We must beware of establishing a mechanical causal relation between social origins and academic success: as classified products, professors never cease classifying themselves and each other in terms of academic taxonomies – in a permanent self-appraisal where 'ambitions' and self-esteem are inseparably defined; in other words, their 'aspirations' and 'career decisions' anticipate the judgements that the academic system will pass on their ambitions. In this sense, the obituary notices are only superficially deceptive when they praise the modesty of those who have sacrificed 'a brilliant career' in the university or in Paris to provincial and family delights: so involved is the dialectic linking objective opportunities to aspirations that it is useless to try to distinguish the objective determinisms from the subjective determination. The provincials didn't want a Paris which didn't want them; the secondary teachers rejected the university as much as it excluded them. Any successful socialization tends to persuade agents to collaborate with their own destiny.

The minutest choices (registering a thesis topic or not, sooner or later, on one author rather than another, with this or that supervisor, etc.), which map out an itinerary leading to positions assigned in advance, already constitute so many contributions to the work of disinvestment which will end, at the cost of a few pirouettes of self-deception, in *amor fati*, that sinister virtue praised in obituary notices. The relative independence of the different principles of hierarchization (institution, place of residence, discipline) produces a scrambling effect which contributes very strongly to facilitating the work of disinvestment, allowing us to convert failure into refusal and to come to terms with abandoned hopes: the teacher of philosophy in a Parisian *lycée* has no trouble convincing himself, as long as he writes for the intellectual weeklies or reviews, that he has little to envy the professor of English in a provincial university. And vice versa. Thus it is that the work of a celebration which is imposed by the laws of the obituary genre gives a reasonably fair idea of the work of mourning by means of which those who believed themselves 'destined for the highest achievements' can always repair their own self-esteem.

The classifications produced by academic taxonomies are linked by relations which are never purely logical because these taxonomies tend to reproduce the structure of the objective relations of the social universe which produces them in the first place. In the case in point, the hierarchy observed in the universe of professorial virtues, that is, in the world of ways of realizing academic excellence, corresponds very closely to the hierarchy of possible careers, that is, to the hierarchy of educational institutions. Everything happens as if, within this world of hierarchized qualities which the professorial body recognizes as its own by recognizing them in its best members, each agent found himself objectively situated by the quality of his virtues. The series of adjectives recorded map out the field of professorial qualities, from the minimal qualities, expected of any 'educator of youth' – domestic virtues of the good father and the good husband or professorial virtues in their most elementary form, dedication to one's pupils or professional integrity – right up to the supreme qualities, implying a negation of the negative aspect of the more ordinary virtues, but which never goes as far as negating the positive principles behind these virtues (the great philosopher is also praised for his qualities as family man and his dedication to the Ecole Normale).[9]

It is the same system of classification which continues to function throughout an academic *career*, which is a strange obstacle race where everyone classifies and everyone is classified, the best classified becoming the best classifiers of those who enter the race. This is always the case from the entrance examination to the Ecole Normale to the *agrégation*, from the *agrégation* to the doctorate, from the doctorate to the Sorbonne, and from the Sorbonne to the Institute, the winning post, where those best classified in all the competitions rule *de facto* over all the operations of classification by controlling access to the agency of classification of the level immediately below, which in its turn controls the next, and so on. This process of external regulation which is set in motion throughout the institutional hierarchy – the academic anxious to improve his classification having to appear respectful of the classifications in force, as much in his statements as in his academic practice – only reinforces the effects of the adaptable, conformist dispositions which have been selected and inculcated through all the previous operations of classification.

Obituary notices – particularly those published in the *Annuaire de l'Association amicale des anciens élèves de l'Ecole Normale Supérieure* – are first-rate documents for an analysis of university values. In the last judgement made by the group on one of its deceased members, they still display the principles of classification which determined his assimilation to the group. It is hardly surprising if, in this last examination, the 'absent friends' find themselves classified as they were always classified during their lifetimes, that is, as a function of subtly hierarchized academic qualities which, at this final point of their career, still maintain an immediately visible relation with social origins. In the most obscure, minor provincial teachers, the minimal qualities are detected, those of the good teacher, most often associated with those of the good father and husband. Then come the lower intellectual qualities, conscientious-ness, erudition, integrity, or superior qualities applied to inferior activities, like translations, critical editions, those rather 'educational' works which the educational system, as we know, never fully acknowledges. Beyond these minor virtues of the humble servants of culture are the qualities which distinguish academics able to demonstrate their excellence by transgressing the limits of the academic definition of excellence: the supreme homage, which, through the medium of someone (academically) close to him, the group awards to the person who fulfils its ideal of excellence, is paid by allowing him that transcendence of academic categories which is always catered for in academic classification.

We can see an illustration of this in these three obituary notices taken from the *Annuaire de l'Association amicale des anciens élèves de l'Ecole Normale Supérieure.*[10]

Paul SUCHER
Born at Versailles, 10 January 1886
Father: tradesman
Teacher of German in a *lycée* in the provinces

After his [master's] thesis on Hoffmann, his many translations are witness to the ease, elegance and accuracy with which he could transpose a text, while his long introductions always decanted the essence of a literary problem, however potentially embroiled and controversial.

. . . Sucher could easily have written an excellent doctoral thesis which would have gained him a university post, to the delight of his former teachers, I doubt whether he was inhibited by any problems – these he would easily have resolved; nor by the demands of the labour or erudition, which he was quite capable of accomplishing with skill and pleasure when he wanted to. His inner life was sufficient: reading, meditation, travel, long cross-country walks or cycle-rides, spectacular Alpine views discovered by dint of the climber's muscular efforts, a peaceful family life founded in 1926 with his marriage to one of our colleagues in the state school system, were sufficient to animate and enrich his existence, to his heart's content.

Roger PONS
Born at Equeurdreville, 28 August 1905
Mother: primary teacher. Grandparents: farmers
Literature professor for preparatory classes at Lycée Louis-le-Grand [Paris].

The explanation of his unique success must be sought in his perpetual self-abnegation. Roger Pons was a distinguished humanist who put himself at the service of a text or an author, striving, whether for Pascal or for Diderot, for Claudel or for Gide, to allow them to be understood and appreciated according to their own lights, without taking their place, without trying to catch them out, in a spirit of simplicity and enthusiasm. As a scrupulous *agrégation* examiner, and an inspector of schools, Roger Pons was always a teacher, and one who put his experience and knowledge at the disposal of teaching and teachers. . . . Roger Pons was a prolific writer, and, in the briefest notes as in the most handsomely developed essay, he wrote with infinite care, as a perfectionist in detail and accuracy, and an unfailingly vigorous, lucid and moving stylist. And yet this careful craftsman who constantly made artefacts that would be useful for others, who was entirely dedicated to his profession, his friendships and his duties, was finally betrayed by destiny: he produced only the introduction, only the preliminaries and the outlines of the great ethical and critical work that he had within him. His academic asceticism allied with a Christian humility prevented him (for virtue may perchance be cruel and destructive) from saying the most important, the most personal things, which are everywhere implicit in his writings but nowhere explicitly expressed.

Maurice MERLEAU-PONTY
Born Rochefort-sur-mer, 1908
Father: artillery officer
Member of the board of examiners of the entrance examination for the Ecole Normale Supérieure
Professor of philosophy at the Collège de France

I can clearly remember now how he used to be then, with his reserved manner, his way of listening so attentively, his apt but somewhat enigmatic replies, punctuated with periods of silence; there was something aristocratic in him, a distance, which still left room for profundity of friendship. . . . Maurice Merleau-Ponty was one of the race of great philosophers; in some ways he was the successor of Alain and Bergson, in another he was close to J.-P. Sartre, and, like him, he had felt the influence of Husserl and Heidegger.

Thus it is through reference to the structure of this field of the qualities offered objectively to every *normalien* embarking upon a professorial career that we may objectively define the *social value* of the virtues attributed to each of them. In the same way, the series of posts available, which in the sample studied range from teacher of modern languages in a *lycée* in the provinces to professor of philosophy at the Collège de France, defines the field of possible trajectories, for a given cohort of *normaliens*,[11] the space of possibilities, to which the initial indifferentiation of careers gives a feeling of lived reality, and in relation to which the social value of the individual careers is objectively defined (the value which provides the objective foundation of the experience of success or failure). It follows that the virtues and the careers indiscriminately praised by the obituary notices are the object of a twofold perception and appreciation. Grasped in themselves and for themselves, the lower virtues, minimal but also indispensable, elementary and banal but also primordial components of the academic definition of excellence, are the object of an absolute and unconditional recognition, the absence of these qualities being sufficient to jeopardize membership of the group. But on the one hand one can never entirely forget the truth of academic asceticism, making a virtue out of necessity, and the entirely negative form of academic excellence which is reduced to this asceticism; these simple, modest lives, composed entirely of wisdom and inner serenity, of rectitude and dedication, the oft-praised virtues of the man who 'cultivates his own garden', dons his rucksack to go mountaineering, and looks after his children, cannot help appearing for what they are as soon as they are situated in the field of possible careers. The lower virtues, and also the middling virtues, already more specific and less exclusively moral, such as the pedagogical skills, lucidity, fluency, coherence [*clarté, aisance, méthode*], or the lower intellectual qualities, erudition (memory), precision [*érudition (mémoire), précision*], are never more than *subordinate virtues*, mutilated forms of the dominant virtues which can attain their full value only when they are associated with the dominant virtues, which offer atonement and salvation for their traces of laborious effort and mean scholarship: erudition is fully valued only if it is 'cloaked in elegance' [*parée d'élégance*], and the scholar is really recognized only if he is 'not a prisoner of his specialization' [*pas enfermé dans sa spécialité*]. Gradually taking over the whole space of the elegies as the higher virtues become rarer, the moral virtues can only be what allows us to accept the limits of intellectual virtues in a world which places these virtues at its peak. There, too, the most cynical truth is always detectable beneath the most dithyrambic incantation: it is indeed significant that these panegyrics almost always associate the subordinate virtues with the virtues of resignation which allow people to accept an inferior position without succumbing to the resentment which is the normal counterpoint to frustrated over-investment, these virtues being the refusal of honours, moral rectitude, modesty, discretion. And the obscure toilers have on their side the utter complicity of a professional body which honours modesty and disdain for honours when, exchanging positive for negative in a characteristic strategy of reversal, they attempt to transform their obscurity into a positive choice of virtue, and thus to cast into disrepute or suspicion the inevitably ill-gotten prestige of over-glittering glory.[12]

The resignation and wisdom praised by the official memorialists find an objective grounding in the relative autonomy enjoyed by the different teaching orders within a globally hierarchized field. Each of these sub-fields offers a mode of fulfilment specific to the ambition of the highest career which is implied in membership of the class of *normaliens* (as the right to pre-empt the field of opportunities) in the guise of a career at least subjectively incomparable to any other: it is the *agrégé* teaching philosophy in a small provincial *lycée*, who wins the respect of his less qualified colleagues through the simplicity of his manners and the entirely philosophical wisdom of his lifestyle; it is the professor of a *khagne* or a *taupe*, basking in the absolute adoration of successive generations of claimants to the title of *normalien* who include him in their idolatrous vision of the Ecole Normale and who, through their high academic quality, make him participate in a world of academic dignity superior even to that of the university (cf. the case of [the philosopher] Alain); and so on, at every level.

Two examples will speak for a thousand others:

> Another day, taking a lorryload of compost to Saint-André, dressed for the occasion, he stopped halfway along the winding road to sit on a bench to enjoy the view and smoke a cigarette, to relax for a moment. Along came a city family, on holiday, who came and sat down next to him. The father pointed out the beauty of the view and the countryside to his children, and quoted a line from Virgil's *Georgics* in Latin for their benefit. Passeron stood up, recited the rest of the verse, and climbed back on to his lorry, leaving the tourists open-mouthed with admiration for the farmers of the county of Nice, who know Virgil, and by heart![13]

> It was then that he discovered that he had been preceded by a German who had hurriedly published his results. . . . This discovery left him profoundly discouraged and somewhat bemused, and, despite all the encouragement that he received, he asked to go back into scondary teaching. . . . In the town of La Flèche as well as at its school he lived rather unobtrusively, interested only in his family, on the fringes of official life, and yet he was very well known and greatly esteemed in the town. For he knew how to be of service, and always discreetly, when the occasion arose. . . . This extreme modesty and lack of ambition (he never sought favours) characterized the 35 years he spent at La Flèche until his retirement.[14]

Thus every *normalien* participates, to differing degrees, in this world of virtues to which the *normaliens* attribute quite naturally the epithet *normalien* (a *normalien* sense of humour): in that unique combination of the intellectual and moral virtues in which the 'elite' of the professorial body sees its own reflection, and which underpin its belief that it constitutes both a moral and an intellectual elite, the full position of this body in social space is expressed. Holding a temporally dominant position (in relation to artists) in a subordinate fraction of the dominant class, professors constitute a sort of upper petty bourgeoisie committed to an *ethical and intellectual aristocratism*. The dispositions which characterize the professors specifically as opposed to the 'bourgeoisie' (the dominant fraction) and the 'artists' (the temporally subordinate fraction of the subordinate fraction) are explained by the fact that they are situated halfway up each of the two hierarchies into which the fractions of the dominant class fall, the hierarchy of economic and political power and the hierarchy of intellectual authority and prestige: too 'bourgeois' in the eyes of the writers and artists, from whom they are separated by their living conditions and lifestyle, too 'intellectual' in the eyes of the 'bourgeoisie', whose lifestyle they cannot wholly share (except in the realm of cultural consumption), they can only find compensation for their double half-failure in an aristocratic resignation or in the satisfactions associated with domestic life, which are encouraged by their living conditions, by the dispositions linked to their social career and by their concomitant matrimonial strategies.[15] Through their domestic virtues, through the aristocratic asceticism which underlies their lifestyle, and which forms a last rampart of self-esteem when all other principles of legitimation have disappeared, and also through their support for society and the hierarchy of values of society illustrated by that sort of spirit of 'public service' [*service public*] and 'dedication' [*dévouement*], often rewarded by decorations, which leads to administrative careers, the professors are closer to the senior civil service than to the intellectuals and artists whose praises they sing. The dual truth of this professorial body, which cannot fulfil the values it recognizes and preaches without sacrificing those which correspond to its real function, can be read in the assessment made by the Vice-Chancellor of the University of Lille on [the novelist] Jules Romains, when he was a young philosophy teacher in a *lycée*: 'A cultivated, original mind, perhaps rather distracted by his literary ambitions, which are of course quite justified' [*esprit cultivé, original, peut-être un peu distrait par ses ambitions littéraires, d'ailleurs fort légitimes*].[16]

This contradiction is inherent in the very definition of the post and is reproduced by the social characteristics of the agents. The only people who have any chance of overcoming it are those who realize the proclaimed ideal of intellectual excellence, but by moving outside the university field (or settling in 'free territories' inside it like the Collège de France). Even more than the twin intellectual and temporal renunciation, which their subordinate position in a temporally subordinate universe imposes on the lower levels of the professorial body, it is the temporal demi-consecration of the intermediate categories which reveals the truth of professorial asceticism and disdain for honours, in a symbolic reversal of their dispossession: those who realize the intellectual ideal within the limits of the university, thus reaching this kind of inferior form (in terms of the very criteria which they recognize) of the intellectual glory which can be obtained from the university field; and those (often the same people) who take hold of and come to terms with the powers offered by the world of powerlessness, recognizing thus the dual ambition which is inherent in their double half-failure.

The professorial schemata of perception and appreciation thus function as generative schemata which structure their whole practice, and in particular the production of that specific category of cultural products constituted by specifically academic works: courses, textbooks or doctoral theses. Indeed, we find the equivalent in the order of intellectual virtues of the contradictions encountered in the order of moral qualities, if we analyse what these productions can owe to the social conditions of their production and use, and in particular to the contradiction between the imperative of culture and eclecticism, in the encyclopaedic tradition, and the imperative of originality: this contradiction is inherent within the very objectives of an *enterprise of cultural production for the purposes of reproduction* which, because of this, always comprises a proportion of simple reproduction (increasingly weak and above all increasingly dissimulated as we go from the inferior forms, like the textbook, to the superior, like doctoral theses, encyclopaedias, monographs, dictionaries, etc.). But the dispositions constitutive of the *academica mediocritas*, this cult of the virtues of moderation and even-handedness in things intellectual which implies the refusal of all kinds of excess, even in questions of intelligence and originality, are no doubt inherent in the intermediate position, of double negation, which the academic holds between the artist and the bourgeois.

The secondary teachers had not written any books (except for one of them, who had published translations); the literary production of the professors of preparatory classes was almost exclusively composed of manuals, and other kinds of educational textbook. 'These works, which are well thought out and clearly written, are always accurate summaries, and excellent aids for pupils' [*Ces livres, bien conçus et clairement écrits, sont, quand ils paraissent, de précises mises au point et d'excellents outils pour les élèves*].[17] As for the production of the higher civil servants of the education system, general inspectors, or vice-chancellors, we can apply to it the terms that are used to characterize the work of Hardy, a faculty dean: 'But the great task, for Hardy, as soon as he arrived in Dakar, was to provide their educational system with the textbooks and other works necessary to put into operation the various study programmes. Hardy set the example, showed the way, launched the series. He published educational works ranging from the textbook or the didactic exposition to the work of provisional synthesis.'[18] The majority of professors in higher education had produced theses and works of synthesis ('A genuinely successful work of luminous synthesis and vast but discreet erudition' [*Une vraie réussite de synthèse lumineuse et de vaste érudition discrète*]);[19] very occasionally novels, 'original' [*originaux*] essays written with 'wit', 'finesse', 'charm', 'lucidity' [*esprit, finesse, charme, lucidité*]. The 'work' [*œuvre*] proper, in the sense given to the word by the intellectual milieu, or the 'great work' [*grande oeuvre*], is mentioned only in connection with the professors of the Collège de France.

The schemata of perception and appreciation unearthed by sociological analysis of obituary notices may also be detected in academic readings of Epicurus and Spinoza, of Racine or Flaubert, of Hegel or Marx. The works whose conservation and consecration are incumbent on the educational system are thus continually reproduced at the cost of a distortion all the greater, as the schemata which engendered the works are the further removed from those applied to them by the *authorized interpreters*, convinced that their highest ambition should be to read them through 'spectacles tinted with their whole outlook', as Weber said,[20] and thus create them in their own image. These generic dispositions are in fact made specific by the position held by each reader in the university field. We see, for instance, what the most common reading of the classical texts (O Epicurean garden!) may owe to the virtues of provincial gardeners, and what ordinary and extraordinary interpretations of Heidegger may owe to that aristocratic asceticism which, on forest path or mountain pass, flees the flabby, vulgar crowds or their concrete *analogon*, the continually renewed (bad) pupils who have to be endlessly saved from the temptations of society in order to inculcate in them the recognition of true value.

Appendix I

The Sources Used

1 DEMOGRAPHIC INDICATORS AND INDICATORS OF ECONOMIC AND SOCIAL CAPITAL, INHERITED AND ACQUIRED

The information on the age, birthplace, marital status, number of children, place of residence, socio-professional category of father and decorations has been collected through systematic scrutiny of the *Annales de l'Université de Paris*, a termly review published by the Sorbonne until December 1968, which gives a detailed curriculum vitae for every professor appointed to Paris, a list of publications and work in progress, details of their foreign visits, information on French or foreign honours awarded, at the same time as a 'chronicle' containing valuable details of 'university life', contacts with higher administration, and university ceremonies. (We found some useful details in the biographical files of the Paris City Library.) We also checked *Who's Who in France 1970* (and, where necessary, earlier years); various biographical dictionaries, including the *International Who's Who 1971–1973*, the *Nouveau dictionnaire national des contemporains 1962*, the *Dictionary of International Biography 1971* and *Africanistes spécialistes des sciences sociales 1963*. (I hardly need say that the collection of this source material is in itself a long and difficult piece of research and that some parts of it, often the most valuable, like the *Annales de l'Université de Paris*, were only discovered at the last moment.) But above all, in order to refine and check the published information, we resorted to data provided by administrative enquiries (concentrating especially on the arts and science professors, who were the least well represented in the other sources). Among all these complementary sources, the most valuable were no doubt the 'Enquiry into the scientists' and above all the

'Enquiry into researchers in arts, social science, economics, politics and legal history', undertaken with our assistance in 1963–64 and 1967–68 by the Service of Scientific Exchanges and Information of the Maison des Sciences de l'Homme, in order to draw up a directory of researchers; if, in spite of a very high rate of response, 80 per cent overall, it suffers from the faults inherent in any enquiry by correspondence, this enquiry has the dual merit of providing *very full* information, particularly on university careers and publications, and also on social origins, for the *whole* of the teaching body – albeit with rates of representation which decrease in proportion to position in the hierarchy. We also drew some information from answers to the national consultation by the Association d'Etudes pour l'Expansion de la Recherche Scientifique in 1969; from the enquiry of the Association des Ecrivains Scientifiques de France of 1968 and of the writers of the Pen Club for 1973. Another extremely valuable source was the obituary notices published after 1970 in the old students annuals of the *grandes écoles* and various professional reviews: thus we checked the *Annuaire de l'Association amicale des anciens élèves de l'Ecole Normale Supérieure* from 1970 to 1980; the *Revue des études latines* from 1970 to 1980; the *Bulletin de l'Association Guillaume Budé* from 1970 to 1980; the *Revue d'études grecques* from 1970 to 1980; the *Revue d'études italiennes* from 1970 to 1980; and also accounts of sessions at the Académie des Inscriptions et Belles Lettres from 1970 to 1980. And finally we consulted the special files kept on outstanding personalities by the newspaper *Le Monde*.

As a last resort, when the information could not be obtained either by these means or from reliable informants, we carried out some complementary enquiries on the people concerned, either through an in-depth interview at home or over the telephone. The collation of these various sources often enabled us to refine, or even to correct, some piece of information or other which the biographical dictionaries gave as certain. Thus, for instance, one professor's father, who, according to *Who's Who*, was a 'viticulturist', was in fact a 'vineyard owner, with a degree in law'; the father of another, given as 'professor', was a 'primary teacher, with the *brevet supérieur;*[1] the fathers of others were not 'tradesman' or 'civil servant', but 'senior executive in a textile factory' or 'post-office clerk'. In another case, we managed to learn from direct questioning that a 'business adviser', at first classified under 'big business', was in fact a humble solicitor's clerk who had set up a private consultancy to give personal advice to individual small businessmen. In general, the articles in the biographical dictionaries, dictated by the individuals themselves, or at least checked by them, show a systematic bias towards the *maximum indeterminacy* (the editors of *Who's Who* say that they have problems obtaining answers, and that they often take it upon themselves to suggest a euphemistic compromise of the 'civil servant' variety). This strategy, which seems very common, except in a few special cases of ostentatious origins, tends to minimize social differences (and therefore the weight of social origins in the analysis). Apart from the ordinary refusal to be categorized which is expressed in the search for the most vague and all-embracing category, the concern to shape one's own image, by modifying if necessary one's own origins, therefore one's career and one's merits, leads in different cases to giving a starting-point higher or lower than it actually was (thus for a moment we thought of codifying these discrepancies and their orientation, to try to calculate the logic behind them). All of this gives rise to extremely difficult problems of codification: apart from the fact that a rigorous code could only be established on the basis of a rigorous and complete knowledge of what was the structure of the professions for the generation of the fathers of the professors who are themselves distributed over two (biological) generations, the information available is very unequal, so that the codes finally used are always liable to be too precise for the less well-documented cases (which leads to over-codification – in the case, for instance, of trying to distinguish between different categories of engineers or tradesmen) or too general for the best-documented cases (which leads to under-codification and a loss of information).

As far as religion is concerned, we have classified as Jewish or Protestant (the minority religions) everyone with such origins, without taking into account the intensity of their religious practice, whereas for the Catholics (the majority religion) we have distinguished between overt Catholics, designated by their membership of organs linked to the church and noted in the *Annuaire catholique de France* 1967 (and whose composition we were able incidentally to study[2]) or their participation in activities or organs (reviews, associations, etc.) of overt Catholic persuasion (such as the Catholic Centre for French Intellectuals)). For the Jews, we relied on the *Guide juif de France 1971*, and, for both Jews and Protestants, we consulted reliable informants (priests, rabbis, directors of religious associations, etc.). We also consulted the *Annuaire Châteaudun* on *mouvements confessionnels* [religious movements]. Although we did everything we could to minimize the risks of error (especially in not considering any information certain unless confirmed by more than one person), we cannot be completely sure of having entirely succeeded.

2 INDICATORS OF CULTURAL CAPITAL,
INHERITED OR ACQUIRED

The sources of biographical information already mentioned above (biographical dictionaries, complementary enquiries, obituary notices, informants, interviews) have provided information on the studies carried out into the secondary cycle (type of establishment attended, public or private, Parisian or provincial) and into higher education (at Paris or in the provinces, partly abroad or not, in a university or at a *grande école*), which often had to be supplemented, because of the fact, for instance, of the frequent confusion between the establishment attended for secondary studies and the establishment preparing entrance to the *grandes écoles*. In addition, in order to check on membership of a *grande école*, we consulted the lists of former pupils published by the annuals of the *grandes écoles* (*Annuaire de l'Association amicale des anciens élèves de l'Ecole Normale Supérieure d'Ulm, Annuaire par promotions de l'Ecole Normale Supérieure de Sèvres, Annuaire de l'Association des anciens élèves de l'Ecole Normale Supérieure de Saint-Cloud, Annuaire de l'Association amicale des anciennes élèves de l'Ecole Normale Supérieure de Fontenay-aux-Roses, Annuaire des anciens de Sciences-po, Annuaire des Ponts et Chaussées, HEC Annuaire officiel, Anciens élèves de l'Ecole Polytechnique, Annuaire des Mines, Annuaire de l'Association des anciens élèves de l'Ecole Centrale des Arts et Manufactures*). Attendance at a *grande école* has a very variable value among the different faculties: if attendance at the Ecole Normale Supérieure, for instance, is very important within the arts faculties, it is something quite different again within the science faculties, where the Ecole Normale Supérieure is rivalled by other *grandes écoles*, like the Ecole Polytechnique, the Ecole des Mines or the Ecole Centrale; it is almost without significance within the law faculties, where attendance at the Institute of Political Studies, relatively common, and at the Ecole Nationale d'Administration, predominates, although the latter is rarer in the arts faculties than attendance at the Ecole Normale Supérieure. Finally, it has no significance at all in the medical faculties.

Thus it seemed necessary to examine a more uniformly significant criterion of academic success, success in the *concours général*. It would no doubt have been more satisfactory to be able to note the professors who were entered for the *concours général* in one or several subjects during their penultimate or final year in school, but, since we don't have an exhaustive list of candidates, we have only been able to note the successful candidates. For this we consulted the *Annuaire de l'Association des lauréats du concours général* for 1974, and, as this annual only recorded members of the association (and not all the winners of the competition), we consulted all the previous years of the annual that we could find, as well as the periodical bulletins of the association, in order to try to find as many as possible of the temporary members. It is still the case, no doubt, that the proportion of prizewinners in the *concours général* is underestimated here.

Further criteria liable to give an indication of academic success or precociousness (both aspects often being closely linked) were examined without our being able to use them. This is the case for all the information linked to the great trials which punctuate university life; the *agrégation* and the state doctorate, the *internat* and the *agrégation* for medicine. We noted for the whole of the sample, thanks to the files of the Ministry of Education, qualifications obtained (*agrégé*, doctor, *interne*), the age at which they were obtained and the examination classification. But the information gathered remains incommensurate between the different faculties. For instance, if, in very general terms, we may treat the state doctorate for artists and scientists as equivalent to the *agrégation* for jurists and medics, we cannot for all that assimilate them, as we would be tempted to do, to such an extent as to make a direct comparison of the ages at which these different diplomas were obtained; or again, even when there is a similarity in the structures, as there is between the arts and science faculties, there are institutional effects which explain why the state doctorate is submitted earlier in science than in the arts.

We will mention just for the record other lines of research, followed for a while and then abandoned, attempting to detail the educational capital of the professors of the sample. Thus the fact of having passed two *baccalauréats* or two first degrees represents a sure index of success at school and university, but it was impossible to verify it systematically for the whole sample. Similarly, at the other extreme of the university career, the age of appointment to the exceptional class (grade E) is a good indicator of professional success, but it only affects a limited number of academics in the sample. Thus, although the information was available in this case (unlike the information on two *baccalauréats* or two degrees) and scrupulously recorded, we resigned ourselves to leaving it out. Thus we had to decide, in more than one case, not to codify and utilize very significant data, because they were available only for too small or too unevenly distributed a proportion of the population.

3 INDICATORS OF CAPITAL OF UNIVERSITY POWER

Membership of the Universities Consultative Committee was established by consulting the *Annuaire de l'Education nationale, 1968* (sections on arts, science, medical science, law and economics) which publishes lists of members elected or appointed in 1966, the SNESup 'Memento' of 1 May 1971 which gives a list of members of the CCU for 1969, and finally *Les Universités et la recherche scientifique*, a case-study by the SNESup, supplement no. 60 of the *Bulletin du SNESup*, December 1975, which gives a list of members of the CCU in 1975. We codified the number of mentions.

An examination of the composition of the Higher Council for Higher Education and of the Council for Higher Education led us to discard them as indicators. In the first case, indeed, out of the 106 members of the Higher Council for Higher Education, according to the *Annuaire de l'Education nationale 1968*, only 16 have a connection with higher education (including 7 for all the Parisian faculties); in the second case, more than half of the 63 members of the Council for Higher Education figure in this council either as members representing the Administration (N = 19) or as representatives of diverse associations and organizations, like the Interministerial Committee for Medical Studies or the National Federation of Pupil Associations of *grandes écoles* (N = 13), and the proportion of Parisian professors among the elected members (N = 31) is very low.

Since academic power can be exercised also within the framework of the various university institutions, we noted, in the *Annuaire de l'Education nationale 1968* and in the *Annales de l'Université de Paris*, the professors who exercised functions of responsibility in their institution, whether they were, at one time or another, members of the Council of the University of Paris, dean, sub-dean, faculty assessor, director of a faculty or university institute, director of a university scientific college, a university literary college or a university law and economics college, dean of a CHU,[3] director of an an IUT, etc., or whether they were at some time director of a school like the Ecole des Chartes [School of Palaeography], the School of the Louvre, of Athens, of Rome, of Physics and Chemistry, of Oriental Languages, or director of an Ecole Normale Supérieure, etc.

The fact of being a member of the Institute (of the Académie des Inscriptions et Belles Lettres, of the Academy of Science, or the Academy of Moral Philosophy and Political Science) or of the National Academy of Medicine confers particular credit and thereby reinforces the power associated with the function. The members of the Institute have been noted thanks to the *Annuaire de l'Institut de France* and the members of the National Academy of Medicine with the *Annuaire de l'Education nationale 1968*. We abandoned attempts at codifying membership of other academies and learned societies, since we were not able to ascertain the true value of these very diverse and dispersed institutions without a preliminary enquiry. It is the same with professional distinctions, information which could easily be gathered by following, for example, the 'Distinctions et nominations' section of the *Courrier du CNRS*: these distinctions have too unequal a value for them to be purely and simply recorded without giving details. Only honorary doctorates (*docteur honoris causa*) from foreign universities have been noted, and then only for the arts professors of the limited sample who, being more highly selected, had a better chance of appearing in biographical dictionaries.

Finally, in the case of the enquiry into arts professors alone, we noted membership of boards of examiners for the *agrégation* and the entrance examination to the Ecole Normale Supérieure de la rue d'Ulm. We consulted lists of *agrégation* boards of examiners between 1959 and 1980 and boards of examiners for the entrance examination for the ENS from 1961 to 1981 (arts). It appeared on this occasion that the membership of these boards by professors in higher education started to decrease from the beginning of the sixties and that these positions seemed to have lost a little of their value. In addition, we tried to discover which arts professors were members of editorial committees of academic reviews: thus we studied the composition of editorial committees of the social science reviews published by Presses Universitaires de France in 1970, that is forty-one reviews, and by the Ecole Pratique des Hautes Etudes in 1969, that is eight reviews.

4 INDICATORS OF CAPITAL OF SCIENTIFIC POWER AND PRESTIGE

The links which tie professors in higher education to the Centre Nationale de la Recherche Scientifique (CNRS) represent the principal indicators chosen to measure their scientific prestige. Membership of the Directorate and of the different sections of the National Committee for Scientific Research has been noted for the years 1963, 1967 and 1971, by consulting the lists of members of the Directorate and the Committee published by the CNRS. We measured the frequency of mention of the same names in the three lists and distinguished between members of a section according to whether they had been appointed or elected. But we decided not to take this information into account in our analysis: law and medicine are in fact much less orientated towards the CNRS than are the arts and above all the sciences. Similarly, we were unable to codify properties like the presidency of a committee or a board of examiners, which are the prerogative of a small number of professors, who are in any case already characterized by the proliferation of positions of this kind which they hold.

Direction of a CNRS laboratory seemed to constitute a much more reliable index of scientific prestige than the direction of a 'research team' without further detail. Indeed, the direction of a team may only designate an administrative responsibility, by virtue of office and seniority. We consulted the pamphlets published by the CNRS, *Services et laboratoires 1968*, *Les Formations de recherche* (1972 and 1973) and the *Annuaire de l'Education nationale 1968*. However, we should bear in mind that the proportion of professors who are simultaneously laboratory directors is underestimated, and in all strictness, we should have introduced the laboratory directors at the CNAM, the Museum National, the Collège de France, etc.

But that would have introduced options whose relevance and completeness would have been impossible to guarantee.

For the medal of the CNRS, we went through the lists of gold, silver and bronze medals awarded by the CNRS from 1962 to 1972.

The measure of attendance at scientific conferences was obtained by checking the annuals published by the different institutions for the years 1969 to 1971, and showing, with an account of the year's teaching, the scientific activity of each of the professors: conferences, visiting lectures, scientific visits and publications. We thought of taking into account topics taught in lectures and seminars; but it seemed difficult, with only the title to judge from, to define indisputably separate and above all qualitatively neutral categories of teaching.

Teaching in an institution other than the home institution was also considered, distinguishing, among the extra teaching, between teaching done for the 'intellectual schools' and that done for 'establishment schools'. By 'intellectual schools' we mean the Ecoles Normales Supérieures d'Ulm, de Sèvres, de Saint-Cloud and de Fontenay, and schools like the Ecole des Chartes [Palaeography], the Ecole du Louvre, the Ecole des Langues Orientales and the Ecole des Beaux-Arts. The information was taken from the *Annuaire de l'Education nationale 1968* (for the Ecole Nationale des Chartes, the Ecole Nationale des Langues Orientales Vivantes, the Ecoles Normales Supérieures d'Ulm, de Sèvres, de Saint-Cloud and de Fontenay, the Ecole du Louvre and the Ecole Normale Supérieure des Beaux-Arts) and in the lists of teachers published by the schools. We abandoned the idea of codifying the number of hours of extra teaching, which is a good indicator of orientation towards teaching rather than research, since we were not able to be sure in each case of the total number of lectures given.

As regards scientific production, there would not have been much point in using sources which were vague and often partial (such as questionnaires destined for the composition of annuals) to count the number of books or articles published. We would have had to examine the frequency of publication, the number of pages, and above all the editor or the review in which they appeared, in order to take into account the hierarchy of collections and reviews, which is different for each discipline. It seemed preferable to examine the number of books translated into foreign languages (which we should also have differentiated), excluding articles and taking as a base the

Library of Congress (from 1942 to 1952) and the National Union Catalog (from 1953 to 1967): thus we noted, for each author in the sample, the number of translations registered by the Library of Congress, in whatever language. It is obvious that by proceeding in this way we favoured translations into English at the expense of authors whose works figure in the Library of Congress catalogue in their own native (French) language (which is the case above all for works on law); apart from the fact that, by purely and simply adding up the number of translations, we counted more than once works which appeared in the catalogue under translations in various languages.

The *Social Sciences Citation Index, 1970 Annual* enabled us to obtain an equally sure indicator of scientific prestige (albeit limited to the social sciences), although affected by the same bias as the number of translations. We had, at an earlier stage of our research, constituted an index of celebrity in the intellectual field by establishing a list of names of intellectuals and writer ranked according to the frequency of their mention in the hit parades published during the three years 1972–74 by *L'Express*. But this method still had its weak points, for the hit parade in question was based on success in bookshop sales. So we decided to count for each individual in the sample the number of mentions in the *Citation Index* for the year 1970. Although the selected set of international social science reviews on which the counts are based is a fairly representative section of scientific production in the field, it no doubt has certain defects: first, citations in books, for example, are excluded; secondly, the citations noted are of very different kinds, from intentional citations of scientific import to simple reviews which may well be purely routine and perhaps complaisant; finally, because of the fact that the citations are recorded by an American institute, the Philadelphia Institute for Scientific Information, and because the number of American reviews scrutinized is vastly preponderant (57 per cent), the disciplines most orientated towards American science, that is sociology or psychology more than philology or ancient history, for example, and in each discipline the professors most concerned with their distribution in the United States, are privileged.

We also tried to take into account professional visits abroad, and especially to the United States. For this, we scrutinized the list of French award-holders for the Franco-American Committee (Fulbright scholarships) from 1960–1 to 1972–3 (professors, researchers, students). But, strictly speaking, we should have introduced secondary variables, such as the length of stay, and above all the place, since American universities are strongly hierarchized.

Direction of doctoral theses is doubtless also one of the most powerful and reliable indicators of academic power. We had to abandon the idea of using it, because it was not possible to obtain homogeneous information for all disciplines. Since we were not able to gain access to the central filing system for theses – despite repeated requests – we attempted to collate the few lists available, but it appeared that they did not exist for all disciplines and were extremely disparate. Thus the list available for philosophy (*Répertoire raisonné des sujets en cours de doctorats d'Etat – lettres et sciences humaines – inscrits en France, 1965–juillet 1970*) refers to these registered between 1965 and 1970, preventing us from calculating the registration capital of each professor – which we might suspect to be all the greater depending on how long he has held his post, that is, how precocious he is. In history, the available sources (*Liste des thèses d'histoire contemporaine déposées dans les facultés de lettres de France métropolitaine*, as of 1 October 1966 and drawn up at the request of the Association of French University Professors of Modern History) record all theses in preparation, but do not come any nearer to enabling us to define the registration capital, that is the clientele, of each professor, since even theses of professors still in service are omitted once they have been successfully completed and submitted. More generally, the number of students registered is a very imperfect measure of the capital of a professor: on the one hand, because registration has an entirely different significance for a French student as opposed to a foreign student who will not invest his qualification in the French market; on the other hand, because we would have to take into account the social weight of the different students registered and how 'realistic' their registration is.

5 INDICATORS OF INTELLECTUAL CELEBRITY

The fact of being published in a paperback or mass-market series constitutes an indication of the relations of the professors to the general public. Thus we scrutinized a series of publishers' catalogues proposing series of this kind: Armand Colin, Les Belles Lettres, Gallimard (for the 'Idées' series), Presses Universitaires de France (for the 'Que Sais-Je?' series), Seuil (for the 'Points' series), Denoël (for the 'Médiations' series) and Klincksieck.

We also measured participation in television broadcasts, another indicator of relations with the general public. We scrutinized the review *Télé-Sept-Jours* over four years (1969, 1970, 1971, 1972), distinguishing between direct participation in a broadcast and indirect participation (as the object of study, for instance). Of course, we would have liked to be able to introduce finer distinctions, especially between different broadcasts: is the prestige conferred by participation in a medical or scientific broadcast of the same nature as that procured by participation in a literary debate? It is certain that participation in a television broadcast has a different status according to whether one consults, say, a law professor on a newly introduced electoral reform, that is, on a quasi-technical point, or whether one questions a historian on his conception of history.

The publication of an article in *Le Monde* has also been selected as an indicator of intellectual prestige and access to the general public. We scrutinized the following sections of *Le Monde* – 'Le Monde des Arts', 'Le Monde des Sciences', 'Le Monde de l'Economie', 'Le Monde des Loisirs', 'Le Monde des Livres' – for three years (1968, 1970, 1971) and the 'Tribune libre' and 'Libres opinions' columns of *Le Monde* for the same years. In order to assess the contribution that the professors of the sample made to intellectual reviews and weeklies, we noted articles published during the same three years in *Les Temps modernes, Esprit, Critique, La Pensée, La Nouvelle Critique, Le Nouvel Observateur, La Quinzaine littéraire, Le Figaro litteraire, La Nouvelle Revue Française, Tel Quel, La Revue des deux mondes, La Nef, Preuves, L'Arc, Contrepoint, Futuribles*, distinguishing between substantive articles, book reviews, interviews and participation in debates.

What all these indicators (publication in mass-market series, participation in television broadcasts, contribution to *Le Monde* or to intellectual reviews) have in common is that they affect the different disciplines very unequally and that they privilege the arts professors at the expense of the others.

Moreover, we extended this research in the specific case of the literature professors. First of all, we drew up lists of intellectuals (of first and second rank), basing our selection, as we have explained above, on the hit parades published in the press. In the interests of greater rigour, we preferred to fall back on an indicator that was both more reliable and more discriminatory, contributions to the *Nouvel Observateur* in 1975 and 1977 (according to the lists published by Louis Pinto, in 'Les affinités électives – les amis du *Nouvel Observateur* comme "groupe ouvert"', *Actes de la recherche en sciences sociales*, 36–7, 1981, pp. 105–124, and especially pp. 116 and 118). We also codified for the literature professors the fact of being mentioned in the 1968 *Petit Larousse* and of belonging to the Académie Française.

6 INDICATORS OF CAPITAL OF POLITICAL OR ECONOMIC POWER

The extra teaching undertaken by professors in higher education, in institutes like the ENA or the National Foundation for Political Science, but also in the scientific *grandes écoles*, like the Ecole Polytechnique, the Ecole des Mines and the Ecole des Ponts et Chaussées, etc., has been treated as an indicator of capital of external power. For this we consulted the *Annuaire de l'Education nationale 1968* (for the Ecole Polytechnique, the Ecole Nationale Supérieure des Mines, the Ecole Nationale Supérieure des Télécommunications and the Ecole Nationale des PTT) and the lists issued by the institutes themselves.

We also sought to discover the relations which the professors of the sample entertained with public bodies, by identifying which of them had participated at any time in their careers in a minister's cabinet,[4] as technical adviser for instance, or in the Constitutional Council, in the Economic and Social Council, the State Council or the Financial Inspectorate. For this we referred, when the information was not already given by *Who's Who*, to the series of *Bottins administratifs* and to the *Annuaire Châteaudun* devoted to presidential and ministerial cabinets (April 1973), to higher administration – where members of ministers' study groups and working parties are recorded (January 1973) – and to members of parliament (April 1973). Participation in the commissions of the 6th [Five-Year] Plan was established by examining the report on the deliberations of the commissions of the Plan published by the Commissariat of the Plan in December 1969. We also examined the lists of members of the Economic and Social Council – only to find that professors from the sample were too uncommon here to justify use of this criterion.

7 INDICATORS OF POLITICAL DISPOSITIONS

We tried to construct a cumulative index of political membership by using *overt* public declarations, that is, signatures of support given and published on different political occasions. Thus we scrutinized on the one hand the list of signatories of the 'Appeal for the abrogation of the decree dissolving the [Trotskyite] Communist League, for the immediate liberation of Alain Krivine and Pierre Rousset', published in *Le Monde* on 8–9 July 1973; the list of the '7,000 French academics and researchers [who] oppose fascism in Chile', a notice distributed by the SNESup–SNCS and dated 11 October 1973; and, finally, various lists of support for the candidature of François Mitterrand published by *Le Monde* for the presidential elections of 1974 (appeals by economists, the Friends of Israel, artists, writers, intellectuals, Resistance veterans, jurists, doctors, etc.).

In addition, we scrutinized lists of support for the candidature of Valéry Giscard d'Estaing published in *Le Monde* for the presidential elections of 1974 (appeals by personalities in the artistic, literary, scientific and sporting worlds, and by the university committee of support of the candidature of Valéry Giscard d'Estaing); and the list of support for the creation of an association to support 'the silent majority', published in *Le Monde* on 26 February 1970. On investigation, it appeared preferable to note only signatures in support of François Mitterrand and of Valéry Giscard d'Estaing (the construction of a cumulative index of public declarations in support of left-wing or right-wing causes introduced many imponderables for only a small gain in information).

One of the great moral debates of the seventies focused on the new laws on abortion. Here, too, an analysis of public declarations, that is signatures collected in support of or in opposition to these laws, allowed us to measure the liberal or conservative dispositions of academics. We scrutinized: the list of signatories of the 'Declaration against the liberalization of abortion', published by the Association of Jurists for the Respect of Life (N = 3,500), by the Association of Doctors for the Respect of Life (N = 12,000) and by teachers, researchers and university professors (N = 432), in June 1973; the Manifesto of 390 Doctors in Favour of Abortion, in February 1973; the Charter for the Study of Abortion, in February 1973.

In the second analysis, we treated as an index of academic traditionalism the fact of supporting Robert Flacelière, the director of the Ecole Normale Supérieure, who had offered his resignation to the Minister of Education (cf. *Le Monde* of 3 April 1971).

We also envisaged noting which academics had written in *Le Monde* during the months of May, June and July 1968, or published a book on the events of 1968. But in this case the raw record gave only the unrefined information that they had made a statement; we would have had to give details each time of the contents of their contribution in order to characterize the positions adopted, and that was more a question of content analysis, with all its nuances, than of a necessarily simplified codification. We also had to decide not to record which academics were candidates for university elections, since we were unable to obtain the lists of candidates presented by the unions. Moreover, in the perspective that we chose, all the university elections were important – including the internal elections specific to each university – and not only those which lead to the constitution of the essential organs of the university structure, like the CNESER[5] or the Comité National de la Recherche Scientifique.[6] But these data are practically impossible to obtain.

Participation in the three conferences which were held, first in Caen in November 1966, secondly in Amiens in 1968 and thirdly in Paris in 1973, and whose object was a critical reflection on the education system, can provide a good index of reformist dispositions. Thus we scrutinized the lists of participants in these three conferences – to find that academics of rank A, in all universities, represented not more than roughly 5 per cent of the whole: which means that this criterion, if it is pertinent for comparison between different universities, taking all categories together, cannot be used within the faculty of arts and social science alone.

We also relied, especially for an analysis of opinions on the university and its transformations, on scrutiny of the enquiry into the education system, carried out in 1969 at the request of the Association d'Etudes pour l'Expansion de la Recherche Scientifique (AEERS).[7] The questionnaire comprised twenty questions on the planning of the academic year, on the teaching situation, on changes in teaching content, pedagogic method and university organization, on relations between teachers, parents and pupils or students, on the powers of different categories of agents, on functions required of the school (vocational preparation, inculcation of moral education, etc.), on politics in schools, on raising the school-leaving age, on subsidies for private schools, etc.

It would also have given added significance if we could have obtained data on the union affiliation of the academics of the sample. Although the SNESup and the SGEN dealt favourably with our request, their files turned out to be difficult to use: they include everyone who has subscribed at least once in his life, and the information recorded (especially the rank) seems most often to correspond to the university post held at the moment of joining. If the breakdown according to faculty for the two unions seems reliable, it is not so with the breakdown according to rank or teaching institution.

Appendix 2.1

The Morphological Transformations of the Faculties

Table 10a LAW

	Professors	Senior lecturers	Lecturers and assistant lecturers	Total teachers	Ratio $\dfrac{Rank\ B}{Rank\ A}$	Ratio $\dfrac{Assistant\ lecturers}{Professors}$	Number of students	Overall staff–student ratio	Staff–Student ratio for rank A (professors and senior lecturers)	Staff–student ratio for rank B (lecturers and assistant lecturers)
1949	222	41		263			39 056	1/148	1/148	
1950	—	—		—			38 665	—	—	
1951	—	—		—			39 364	—	—	
1952[a]	263	76		339			41 309	1/122	1/122	
1953	—	—		—			41 368	—	—	

Year										
1954	—	—	—	—	—	—	40 322	—	—	—
1955	242	91	70	403	0.2	0.3	37 029	1/92	1/111	1/528
1956	244	113	89	446	0.25	0.4	37 476	1/84	1/105	1/421
1957	261	130	131	522	0.3	—	35 171	1/67	1/90	1/268
1958	268	146	158	572	0.4	—	34 229	1/60	1/83	1/216
1959	274	170	195	639	0.45	—	34 171	1/53	1/77	1/175
1960	477		240	717	0.5	—	36 521	1/51	1/77	1/152
1961	—	—	—	—	—	—	42 721	—	—	—
1962	—	—	—	—	—	—	50 318	—	—	—
1963	581		528	1 109	0.9	—	61 851	1/56	1/106	1/117
1964	596		640	1 236	1.1	—	74 267	1/60	1 124	1/116
1965	356	298	776	1 430	1.1	1.5	86 733	1/60	1/132	1/112
1966	365	317	864	1 546	1.3	1.6	99 664	1/64	1/146	1/115
1967	—	—	—	—	—	—	113 144	—	—	—
1968	439	413	1 492	2 344	1.7	2.4	126 696	1/54	1/149	1/85
1969	490	490	1 792	2 772	1.8	2.6	131 628	1/47	1/134	1/73

aFor the year 1952, the numbers of teachers (especially professors) seem high. It has not proved possible to verify the statistical data (unpublished document of the University Statistics Bureau).

Table 10b SCIENCE

	Professors	Senior lecturers	Lecturers, research directors, assistant lecturers	Total teachers	Ratio $\dfrac{\text{Rank B}}{\text{Rank A}}$	Ratio $\dfrac{\text{Assistant lecturers}}{\text{Professors}}$	Number of students[a]	Overall staff–student ratio	Staff–student ratio for rank A	Staff–student ratio for rank B
1949	225	194	509	928	1.2	1.4	25 306	1/27	1/60	1/50
1950	—	—	—	—	—	—	26 981	—	—	—
1951	—	—	—	—	—	—	28 200	—	—	—
1952	297	208	502	1 007	1.0	—	30 683	1/30	1/61	1/61

Year										
1953	—	—	—	—	—	—	—	—	—	—
1954	—	523	626	1 149	1.2	—	32 493	1/31	1/69	1/58
1955	249	303	954	1 406	1.5	2.5	36 102	1/28	1/71	1/46
1956	264	346	984	1 594	1.6	2.6	39 283	1/28	1/74	1/46
1957	312	417	1 196	1 925	1.6	—	45 147	1/28	1/74	1/45
1958	334	475	1 472	2 281	1.8	—	54 337	1/27	1/76	1/42
1959	364	559	1 930	2 853	2.3	—	61 725	1/23	1/71	1/34
1960	—	1 068	2 564	3 632	2.4	—	65 506	1/19	1/65	1/27
1961	—	—	—	—	—	—	69 978	—	—	—
1962	—	—	—	—	—	—	76 453	—	—	—
1963	—	1 376	4 731	6 107	3.4	—	89 882	1/17	1/75	1/22
1964	—	1 484	5 417	6 901	3.65	—	104 060	1/16	1/76	1/21
1965	560	1 024	6 188	7 772	3.9	7.0	113 084	1/16	1/79	1/20
1966	583	1 111	6 580	8 274	3.9	7.1	125 552	1/16	1/76	1/20
1967	—	—	—	—	—	—	129 413	—	—	—
						136 791			
1968	660	1 463	8 166	10 289	3.8	7.6	147 458	1/14	1/66	1/17
1969	696	1 534	8 519	10 749	3.8	7.3		—	—	—

[a]The numbers of students in science are overestimated; in fact we should exclude from the science students those students enrolled for the CPEM (N = 30,090 in 1969), and formerly for the PCB (N = 5,980 in 1960).[1]

Table 10c ARTS

	Professors	Senior lecturers	Lecturers and assistant lecturers	Total teachers	Ratio $\dfrac{\text{Rank B}}{\text{Rank A}}$	Ratio $\dfrac{\text{Assistant lecturers}}{\text{Professors}}$	Number of students	Overall staff–student ratio	Staff–student ratio for rank A	Staff–student ratio for rank B
1949	224	155	132	511	0.35	0.6	35 279	1/69	1/93	1/267
1950	—	—	—	—	—	—	36 265	—	—	—
1951	—	—	—	—	—	—	36 956	—	—	—
1952	293	238	177	708	0.3	—	38 947	1/55	1/73	1/220
1953	—	—	—	—	—	—	39 700	—	—	—
1954	—	—	—	—	—	—	41 339	—	—	—

Year										
1955	231	241	199	671	0.4	0.9	42 930	1/64	1/91	1/216
1956	242	265	228	735	0.45	0.95	48 606	1/66	1/96	1/213
1957	266	288	255	809	0.5	—	51 372	1/64	1/93	1/201
1958	276	298	302	876	0.5	—	55 653	1/64	1/97	1/184
1959	285	318	371	974	0.6	—	59 265	1/61	1/98	1/160
1960	653		497	1 150	0.8	—	66 814	1/58	1/102	1/134
1961	—	—	—	—	—	—	78 092	—	—	—
1962	—	—	—	—	—	—	93 032	—	—	—
1963	832		1 138	1 970	1.3	—	107 455	1/55	1/129	1/94
1964	903		1 493	2 396	1.65	—	122 972	1/51	1/136	1/82
1965	362	622	1 646	2 730	1.7	3.0	137 008	1/50	1/139	1/78
1966	373	674	2 139	3 186	2.0	3.6	158 657	1/50	1/151	1/74
1967	—	—	—	—	—	—	170 976	—	—	—
1968	450	984	3 699	5 133	2.5	4.8	196 144	1/38	1/137	1/53
1969	492	1 119	4 171	5 782	2.5	5.0	208 515	1/36	1/129	1/50

Sources: For the teachers, Ministry of Education, University Statistics Bureau, Direction of Higher Education, Service of Statistics and Conjuncture (unpublished documents), *Rapport général de la commission de l'équipement scolaire, universitaire et sportif, 1962–1965*; for the students, *Informations statistiques*, also *Statistiques des enseignants.*

Appendix 2.2

The Morphological Transformations
of the Disciplines

Table 11a

	Estimated number of agrégés produced between 1927 and 1967[b]		Number of agrégés in the lycées in 1967–8[c]		Estimated number of normaliens produced by the ENS rue d'Ulm between 1923 and 1963[de]	Number of teachers in arts and social science faculties[f]		Rate of increase 1963–7	Number of professors[f]		Number of senior lecturers[f]		Number of temporary senior lecturers		Number of lecturers[f]		Number of assistant lecturers[f]		Rate of increase in rank A posts 1963–7	Rate of increase in rank B posts 1963–7
	M	F	M	F	F	1963	1967		1963	1967	1963	1967	1963	1967	1963	1967	1963	1967		
French[a]	1 549	1 249	1 090	1 371	570	338	675	200	90	110	11	13	35	66	62	154	140	332	139	242
Classical languages[a]	817	439				179	300	168	61	72	6	12	24	30	30	69	58	117	126	211

History	1 606	918	570	604	175	310	527	170	116	128	16	18	26	58	56	144	96	179	129	212
Geography						179	337	188	54	62	7	23	8	19	46	88	64	145	151	211
English	1 021	830	385	489	110	218	517	237	38	44	4	12	20	43	37	118	119	300	159	268
Philosophy	673	295	220	185	240	124	227	183	49	55	5	15	5	18	30	67	35	72	149	214
Linguistics						34	85	250	12	21	1	2	8	12	2	12	11	38	167	385
Psychology						77	221	325	23	21	3	8	4	22	24	59	23	111	170	362
Sociology						34	98	288	7	10	—	7	3	16	8	26	16	39	330	270

[a] The figures on this line concern the *agrégation* in literature, for French, and the *agrégation* in grammar, for classical languages, in so far as the majority of teachers of French hold the *agrégation* in literature and the majority of teachers of classical languages the *agrégation* in grammar.

[b] *Source: L'Agrégation*, official bulletin of the Société des Agrégés, as well as, for the period 1927–39, *Les Agrégés*, termly bulletin of the Société des Agrégés. We did not take into account the calculations of the number of *agrégés* now in employment if we reduced the numbers by about 15 per cent, corresponding to the estimated proportion of deceased.

[c] *Source:* Ministry of Education, Central Service of Statistics and Conjuncture.

[d] Statistics established from the *Annuaire de l'Association amicale des anciens élèves de l'Ecole Normale Supérieure.*

[e] The figure for English does not include anglicists alone, but refers to the whole number of *normaliens* who took modern languages.

[f] Statistics established from the *Bulletin du Syndicat autonome de l'enseignement supérieur.*

Table 11b

Measure	Category / Year	French
Ratio[a]: Number of CNRS researchers / Number of teachers		5.8
Proportion of third-cycle doctorates submitted and passed	B	8.6
	A	1.5
Proportion of third-cycle doctorates registered for rank B posts		16.1
Proportion of women in 1967	B	34.6
	A	8.0
Proportion of women in 1963	B	19
	A	7
Proportion of doctorates registered or passed, for rank B posts		95.2
Proportion of agrégés	B	93.8
	A	95.8
Proportion of former preparatory class pupils not graduates of any grande école	B	6.6
	A	8.3
Proportion of graduates of ENS Saint-Cloud	B	7.4
	A	6.8
Proportion of graduates of ENS Ulm and ENS Sèvres	B	19
	A	39
Ratio: Assistant lecturers / Tenured professors	1967	1.3
	1963	1.5
Ratio: Temporary senior lecturers / Tenured professors	1967	0.60
	1963	0.39

Classical languages	0.39	0.42	0.9	1.6	40	18	1.8	4.1	3.3	3.2	96.8	97.8	89	6.0	24.3	9.5	28.4	20.9	1.8	5.5	12.6
History	0.22	0.45	0.8	1.4	23.9	12.8	4.4	5.4	3.5	3.0	86.7	90.2	94.1	2.8	11.4	5.0	17.8	31	3.5	19	22.9
Geography	0.15	0.31	1.2	2.3	4.4	2.7	11.8	8.4	1.5	0.7	89.7	91.0	87.6	6.5	15.2	8.0	23.6	20.5	5.9	13.5	12.4
English	0.53	0.98	3.1	6.8	12.5	5.8	6.3	11.2	14.6	3.2	98.0	96.8	88.4	9.7	28.8	13.1	35.2	16.5	2.2	1.1	—
Philosophy	0.10	0.33	0.7	1.3	40.7	23.9	—	4.2	3.4	4.2	86.7	86.1	90.1	14	10	13	18	13.5	3.5	13.5	31.2
Linguistics	0.67	0.57	0.9	1.8	19	6.2	2.7	12.6	—	—	86.7	74.4	76.6	—	30.4	8.6	33.8	27.4	6.6	13	71.7
Psychology	0.17	1.05	1.0	5.3	26.9	10.0	—	5.0	7.7	1.3	50	20.5	38	5.5	24	3.4	29.6	53.0	19.2	22	45.7
Sociology	0.43	1.60	2.3	3.9	25.0	5.6	—	2.8	—	—	52.6	19.4	22.9	—	—	—	18.5	25.7	13.2	34.3	108

aStatistics established from the *Rapport national de conjoncture scientifique*, by the CNRS.

Appendix 3

The Hit Parade of French Intellectuals, or Who is to Judge the Legitimacy of the Judges?

The hit parades published from time to time by the daily or weekly press – for instance, at the end of a decade, using the pretext of summing up the previous ten years – are, alongside symbolic attacks like prophesying the end of a supposedly dominant current of thought (Marxism, existentialism, structuralism, etc.) or the start of a new tendency ('post-structuralism', the 'new philosophers', etc.), the most typical of the strategies orientated more unconsciously than consciously towards the imposition of a vision of the intellectual world, of its divisions and hierarchies: following a common procedure in the political world, the wishes, expectations and hopes of a group of intellectual interests ('let's get rid of X', 'I can't wait for the end of X') are disguised beneath the impeccable veneer of a description ('X is over') or a prediction by a well-informed observer. When these interpretative or predictive judgements are presented in the guise of prophetic beliefs, whether proffered by the partly chiefly concerned, or projected into the field of the press by some self-appointed impresario or other, a minor member of the group, a client or trusty servant, the attack has a weak symbolic effect (although naïvety, and the force of conviction it suggests, may provide a form of credit); an efficacity inversely proportional in any case to the knowledge that the receivers have of the interests at stake (therefore of their social and spatial proximity as regards the game and the stakes). The suspicion of indecency, which, despite the tradition of the manifesto and of the right to exhibitionism historically won by artists, attaches to naïve displays of the specific interests of a group or an individual claiming self-legitimation (following the paradigm of Napoleon crowning himself), is in danger of disappearing entirely with social techniques such as the hit parade of intellectuals (cf. the review *Lire*, 68, April 1981): first, because the size of the enquiry (the review talks of a 'referendum') gives a collective basis, and thus the appearance of validation by consensus, to the judgement; then, more subtly, because the collective subject of this judgement seems coextensive with the object judged, thus producing the appearance of perfect self-sufficiency.

In fact this hit parade represents a sort of experiment *in vitro* allowing us to observe processes of evaluation which would otherwise be very difficult to objectify. Having both the list of the 'elect' and the list of the judges, we immediately discover in the latter the principle of the former: as hybrid or mongrel characters defying common taxonomies, writer-journalists and journalist-writers, who are very numerous among those classified by the review as journalists, writers or even teacher-writers, are very strongly represented as much among the judges as in the hit parade which their cumulative judgement has produced (whereas a number of the best-known authorities, for instance all the writers published by Minuit, from Beckett to Simon, including Pinget and Robbe-Grillet, are absent from the list of judges, and, with the exception of Beckett and Marguerite Duras, from the hit parade – and without our being able to suppose that they had conspired to refuse to answer to this; and similarly for the philosophers).[1] The privilege accorded in the hit parade to those intellectuals who have strong 'media muscle', as certain editors would say, and who are also well placed in the hit parade of bestsellers (such as Roger Garaudy, André Glucksmann and Bernard-Henry Lévy),[2] also has its source in the list of the judges: the list of the elect has been predetermined by determining the principle of election of the electors, themselves predisposed to elect according to the principle of their election. Thus we have a first effect of misconstrual, which contributes to the (unintentional) symbolic efficiency of the hit-parade technique, a genuine social invention, obtained by transferring to the intellectual field a procedure common in other domains (for songs, restaurants or politics): the misunderstanding over the social composition of the group of judges encourages the reader to *accept as* a verdict of intellectuals on intellectuals what is in fact the view which a set of judges dominated by intellectual-journalists and journalist-intellectuals has of the intellectual world. But this effect of *allodoxia*, which is reinforced by every commentary – for example, by highlighting the judgements formulated by the few authors figuring in the hit parade who agreed to reply – is present throughout the procedure, and in the very project of the inventors of the technique who tend, for instance, to conceptualize the intellectual field by analogy with the political field – which leads them among other things to introduce the question of 'successors'. Of all the mechanisms which caused the initiators of the enquiry and the respondents to produce unintentionally what could appear to be the expression of a collective intention – that of imposing on the field of limited production, the place of production for producers, the norms of production and consumption of cultural products against which the field was constituted – one of the most powerful is in fact *allodoxia*, as a misunderstanding leading us to take one thing for another, in all good faith, taking a telegenic essay-writer [Bernard-Henri Lévy] as a pretender to the 'succession' of the author of *Being and Nothingness* and the *Critique of Dialectical Reason* [Jean-Paul Sartre], and taking a journalist who writes books which journalists discuss because he discusses books in the newspapers for a writer to be discussed. The indeterminateness of the things to be classified, in this world where journalists write books and writers write articles and where publishers attempt to persuade journalists – especially when they write about books – to write books for them, is only equalled by the uncertainty of the systems of classification, and we can understand why the editors of *Lire* go somewhat astray when they try to classify their classifiers: we can guess that Jean Cau, Jean-Claude Canova, Catherine Clément, Jean-Marie Domenach, Paul Guth, Pierre Nora or Paul Thibaud (among others) couldn't have been very pleased to see themselves placed in the category of journalists, alongside Jean Farran, Jacques Goddet or Louis Pauwels, while Madeleine Chapsal, Jacques Lanzmann, Bernard-Henri Lévy or Roger Stéphane (among others) were classified with the writers, and while so many regular (and in some cases regularly remunerated) contributors to Parisian dailies or weeklies were placed among the teacher-writers.

But the uncertainty of the systems of classification which the intermediate intellectuals deploy is itself a direct expression of the position which these unclassifiable classifiers hold in the classifications, as well as a direct expression of related interests, such as a complaisant fascination for the petty side of 'great men' or an unconscious inclination to confuse hierarchies, to approach the unapproachable by approaching their *alter ego*. Placed in a median position between the field of restricted production and the field of general production, the journalist-intellectuals and the intellectual-journalists most often lack the means (and above all the time) to make distinctions which in any case it is not in their interest to operate: since they work unconsciously to negate the divisions which diminish them, they tend quite naturally to juxtapose in their preferences the great scholars, whose fame is such that their absence would disqualify the voter (Lévi-Strauss, Dumézil, Braudel, Jacob), and the most journalistic intellectuals or the most intellectual journalists. The often eccentric juxtapositions which result from this have the effect of ensuring the *consecration through contagion* of the whole category of those midway between the writer and the journalist. This effect operates first of all on the journalists themselves, who ask for nothing better, thus reinforcing the tendency for the two orders to become confused.[3]

We would no doubt expect the sociologist to confirm the scientific status of his discipline or, more simply, his own dignity as a scientist, to criticize this hit parade and contrast it with rigorous procedures that could detect a really 'objective' hierarchy. In fact, it would be easy to find in the most socially accepted scientific practice the strict equivalent of the hit parade, whether in the case of the 'snowball' sampling procedures most often used in enquiries into the 'elites' or, more simply, in the case of so-called operational definitions which define questions which are not at all clearly defined in reality – like that of deciding boundaries – before any enquiry has taken place – 'what I call an intellectual . . .' – thus anticipating the result of the enquiry by the very delineation of the population it is applied to.[4] But, in addition, if he yielded to his instinctive defence mechanisms against 'unfair competition', the sociologist would deprive himself of vital information, which becomes available as soon as we take the trouble to identify the question – a scientifically valid one, in this case – which the heretical enquiry *actually* answers. The intellectual hit parade represents a sort of artificial reconstruction, and thus one easier to observe, of the process which is constantly at work in the field of cultural production and which elaborates and defines one of the most powerful representations (because objectified and widely broadcast) of the hierarchy of intellectual values. This process, which is no doubt also equivalent to a *judicial procedure* or, in other words, a process of marking up prices (as verdicts of the market), is accomplished through 'informal' exchanges of private and sometimes confidential judgements ('don't say I said so, but so-and-so's book is absolute rubbish') between journalists, between writer-journalists and journalist-writers, but also through the *public verdicts* of book reviews, critical works, invitations to broadcast on radio or television, and finally the hit parades, ratings and rankings, not to mention the more traditional acts of institutional consecration, like appointment to an academy, which, essentially, only ratify the whole set of these verdicts, etc. It follows that the hit parade published by the review *Lire* is a good measure of *one* view of the intellectual world, the one held by all the people who, while being culturally subordinate, have in common their ability to impose their view (for a period): ('men and women', *Lire* tells us, 'who through their professional activity themselves exercise influence over the circulation of ideas and are holders of a certain cultural power').

Apart from providing a good measure of *a high journalistic profile*, this hit parade allows us to ask which factors contribute to determining it. It goes without saying that this newsworthiness (the same thing would apply to what American universities call the *visibility* of a professor and, more generally, of all social reality) is defined in the relation between the thing seen – in the case in point, the work and above all the *author* – and the categories of perception and appreciation liable to be applied to them by the population concerned – in the case in point, the journalists or, more precisely, the writer-journalists and journalist-writers (we know, for instance, that a work can go *unnoticed* by its contemporaries and be later *rediscovered* by a posterity endowed with perceptual categories and interests allowing them to 'tell the difference', to escape indifference and force the perceived world away from its lack of discrimination).

In order to understand everything which helps to determine the subjective aspect of the act of perception, we need to take into account, as well as the statutory propensity to *allodoxia*, the whole of the social conditions of production of the 'judges', notably their present and especially their future relations with the educational system, as well as the institutional conditions within which their verdicts are elaborated and delivered: and especially all the effects of the field which cause journalists to spend more time reading each other than reading the books that they feel *bound* to mention because the others have mentioned them (it's the same process for political 'events'); but also the urgency, the *hurry* of journalists, which along with the press itself, constantly behind the journalists, who are themselves readers of the press, prevents reading and analysis in depth, and tends to make immediate readability one of the prerequisites tacitly required of cultural productions, excluding the 'discovery' of works and authors of low readability and profile (as witness the almost total absence in the hit parade of either the literary avant-garde or that of the social sciences).

Moreover, in order to understand the objective aspect of the relation in which a 'high journalistic profile' – or 'media muscle' – is defined, we would have to take into account the characteristics of works and above all dispositions of authors, more or less inclined to be seen and approved by journalists by maintaining with them relations based on the affinity of the *habitus* or on condescending self-interest.[5] These dispositions, socially constituted and therefore variable according to social trajectories and positions held in the field of production, can receive different expressions according to whatever, at the moment in question, contributes to the dominant definition of the intellectual positions. And it is certain that a 'high journalistic profile', itself linked to the frequency of intervention outside the field of limited production (or the university field), notably in politics (through petitions or demonstrations, etc.), is nowadays a major component of the definition of the intellectual such as it has progressively become constituted in France, from Zola to Sartre. It follows that a propensity to act the role of the intellectual in public implies, through a correlative propensity to comply with journalistic requests (which varies with 'profile', itself partly dependent on the propensity to be seen and approved), a form of *dependency* on the journalistic field (very noticeable in the construction of the social character of Sartre), therefore a form of *recognition* of the legitimacy of the verdicts.

THE VERDICT ACCORDING TO *LIRE*

'Do we still have any intellectual masters? Like Gide, Camus and Sartre? *Lire* put the question to several hundred writers, journalists, teachers, students, politicians, etc. The question was this:

"Who are the three French-speaking intellectuals, living today, whose writings seem to you to have the profoundest influence on the development of ideas, literature, art, science, etc.?"

There was a mass of replies, but admitting uncertainty, and providing a plebiscite for nobody – although recognizing the influence of Lévi-Strauss, Aron and Foucault.'

1 Claude Lévi-Strauss	101
2 Raymond Aron	84
3 Michel Foucault	83
4 Jacques Lacan	51
5 Simone de Beauvoir	46
6 Marguerite Yourcenar	32
7 Fernand Braudel (historian)	27
8 Michel Tournier (novelist)	24
9 Bernard-Henri Lévy (philosopher)	22
9 Henri Michaux (poet)	22
11 François Jacob (biologist)	21
12 Samuel Beckett (dramatist and novelist)	20
12 Emmanuel Le Roy Ladurie (historian)	20
14 René Girard (philosopher)	18
15 Louis Aragon (poet, novelist and politician)	17
15 Henri Laborit (biologist)	17
15 Edgar Morin (sociologist and philosopher)	17
18 E. M. Cioran (essayist and moralist)	16
18 Eugène Ionesco (dramatist)	16
20 Marguerite Duras (novelist and film director)	15
20 Roger Garaudy (philosopher and politican)	15
20 Louis Leprince-Ringuet (physicist)	15
20 Michel Serres (philosopher)	15
24 Julien Gracq (novelist)	14
24 Philippe Sollers (novelist)	14
26 Louis Althusser (philosopher)	12
26 Claire Brétécher (cartoonist)	12
26 René Char (poet)	12
26 Gilles Deleuze (philosopher)	12
26 Georges Duby (historian)	12
26 Vladimir Jankélévitch (philosopher)	12
26 J. M. G. Le Clézio (novelist)	12
26 Alfred Sauvy (economist)	12
34 Georges Dumézil (historian of religion)	11
34 Jean-Luc Godard (film director)	11
36 Jean Bernard (doctor)	10
36 Pierre Boulez (composer, orchestral conductor)	10

36 Pierre Bourdieu (sociologist) 10
36 Albert Cohen (novelist) 10
36 André Glucksmann (philosopher) 10
36 René Huyghe (art historian) 10
36 Léopold Sedar Senghor (poet and politician) 10

(*Lire*, 68, April 1981, pp. 38–9)

THE JUDGES

The question was sent to 600 people. By 11 March, 448 had replied. We wish to express our gratitude to them. These are their names:

ACADEMICIANS
Members of the Académie Française, the Académie des Sciences Morales et Politiques, the Académie Royale Belge de Langue et de Littérature Française, and the Académie Goncourt:

Ferdinand Alquié, Hervé Bazin, Jean Bernard, Bernard Chenot, Jean Dutourd, Jean-Jacques Gautier, Jean Guitton, René Huygue, Jean Laloy, Armand Lanoux, Suzanne Lilar, Félicien Marceau, François Nourissier, Jean d'Ormesson, Karl Popper, Maurice Rheims, Robert Sabatier, Maurice Schumann, Georges Sion, Michel Tournier, Henri Troyat.

WRITERS
ADG, Henri Amoureux, Christine Arnothy, Jean-Paul Aron, Dominique Aury, François-Régis Bastide, Tahar Ben Jelloun, Jean-Marie Benoist, Yves Berger, Daniel Boulanger, Jeanne Bourin, Chantal Chawaf, François Caradec, Marie Cardinal, Jean Carrière, Madeleine Chapsal, Edmonde Charles-Roux, François Clément, Georges Conchon, Jean-Louis Curtis, Conrad Detrez, Géneviève Dormann, Jean Ellenstein, Pierre Emmanuel, Alain Finkielkraut, Viviane Forrester, Max Gallo, François Georges, Alain Gerber, Roger Grenier, Benoîte Groult, Gérard Guégan, Eugène Guillevic, Bertrand de Jouvenal, Hubert Juin, Marcel Jullian, Jacques Lanzmann, Edmée de la Rochefoucauld, Bernard-Henri Lévy, Raymond Lévy, Jacques-Patrick Manchette, Diane de Margerie, Renée Massip, Gabriel Matzneff, Claude Mauriac, Patrick Modiano, Yves Navarre, Eric Ollivier, Hélène Parmelin, René-Victor Pilhes, Suzanne Prou, Pierre-Jean Rémy, Jean-Claude Renard, Alain Rey, Christine de Rivoyre, Denis Roche, Dominique Rolin, Claude Roy, Michel de Saint-Pierre, Jorge

Semprun, Philippe Sollers, Roger Stéphane, René Tavernier, Georges Thinès, Henri Vincenot, Kenneth White.

TEACHER-WRITERS

Paul-Laurent Assoun, Jacques Attali, Elizabeth Badinter, Blandine Barret-Kriegel, Raymond Boudon, Louis-Jean Calvet, Hélène Carrère d'Encausse, François Châtelet, Anne-Marie Dardigna, Jean Denizet, Georges Duby, Jean Duvignaud, Jacques Ellul, Marc Ferro, François Furet, Alfred Grosser, Marie-Françoise Hans, Albert Jacquard, Raymond Jean, Julia Kristeva, Yves Lacoste, Jacques Le Goff, Emmanuel Le Roy Ladurie, Erik Orsenna, Daniel Oster, Mona Ozouf, Régine Pernoud, Catherine Rihoit, Maxime Rodinson, Alfred Sauvy, Martine Ségalen, Lucien Sfez, Louis-Vincent Thomas, Pierre Vidal-Nacquet.

TEACHERS

Teachers in higher, secondary and primary education from Paris and the provinces:

Aline Baldinger, Claude Bellier, Christian Bonnet, Alain Boyer, Josette Chazal, Jean Colmez, Jean-Pierre Cuvillier, M. Davy, L. Dugué, M. Dupuis, Jacques Fierain, Pierre Fontaney, Alain Fredaigue, Françoise Gadet, Claude-Louis Gallien, Nadine Gallifret-Grangeon, Jeanine Gombert, Lucienne Guillet, Henri Guitton, Ibram Harari, Simone Helfer, Michel Hervé, Dominique Janicaud, Jo Landormy, Rosine Lapresle, Mme Geneviève Laurent-Fabre, André Lebrun, Jean-Marie Levesque, Pierre Mathey, Jean-Michel Muglioni, Jim Pichot, Jacqueline Puysegur, Jean-Bruno Renard, Pierre Rigoulot, Jacques Rivelaygues, Michel Rouche, J.-C. Royet, Lélia Sennhenn, Philippe Sussel, M. Tourlières, Jean Touzot, Pierre Verdier, Patrick Vignolles.

STUDENTS

Students and sixth-form pupils from Paris and the provinces:

Véronique Angella, Corinne d'Argis, Gilles Basterra, Gisèle Berkman, Catherine Bernard, Agnès Besnier, Corinne Bilhannic, Laurent Collobert, Christophe Daniel, Marcelle Delhomme, Pierre Desesquelles, Bruno Dive, Jean-Baptiste Divry, Isabelle Duperrier, M. Teboul, Catherine Gaillot, Anne Garreta, Agnès Guiniot, Lydie Herbelot, Julie Jézéquel, Catherine Jouffre, Y. Le Marrec, Anne-Paul Lozac'hmeur, Isabelle Mavian, Isabelle Mercier, Eric Morillon, Pascale Perdereau, Isabelle Philippe, John-David Ragan, Joseph Raguin, Nathalie Richard, Blandine Rivière, F. Sportiche, François Tourlière.

BOOK TRADE
Publishers, booksellers and librarians:

Pierre Angoulvent, Dominique Autié, André Balland, Christian de Bartillat, M. Beaudiguez, Marie-Thérèse Bouley, Christian Bourgois, Jean Callens, Jean-Baptiste Daelman, Henri Desmars, Vladimir Dimitrijevic, Yves Dubé, Anne-Marie Duchesne, Marie-Madeleine Erlevint, M. Gasguel, Gérald Gassiot-Talabot, Jean Goasguen, Gérald Grunberg, Jean Hamelin, Georges Lambrichs, Jean-Claude Lattès, Mlle Lavocat, Françoise Mourgue Molines, Simone Mussard, Paul Otchakovsky-Laurens, Pierre Pain, Geneviève Patte, Jean-Luc Pidoux-Payot, Jacques Plaine, Jean-Pierre Ramsay, Charles Ronsac, Albert Ronsin, M. Teulé, Louis Vitalis.

PRESS
Newspaper and review editors, literary critics, correspondents of foreign newspapers appointed to Paris, etc. It should be noted that many of the journalists are also writers.

Pierre Ajame, Jacques-Pierre Amette, Georges Anex, Yvan Audouard, René Andrieu, Robert Baguet, Barthélemy, Guy Bechtel, Edward Behr, Pierre Bénichou, Alain de Benoist, Jean Barial, Jean Boissonnat, Henry Bonnier, André Bourin, Pierre Breton, André Brincourt, Jean-Jacques Brochier, José de Broucker, Alain Buhler, Robert Boutheau, Jean Cau, Jean-Claude Casanova, Cavanna, Jean Chalon, Claude Cherki, Catherine Clément, Jean Clémentin, Claude-Michel Cluny, Françoise de Camberousse, Annie Copperman, James de Coquet, Jacques Cordy, Jean Daniel, Jean-Marie Domenach, Françoise Ducout, Guy Dumur, Jean-Pierre Enard, Jean-Louis Ezine, Jean Farran, Jacques Fauvet, André Fontaine, Jean-Jacques Gabut, Matthieu Galey, Jean-Louis Gauthier, Annick Geille, André Géraud, Paul Giannoli, Jacques Goddet, Léon-Gabriel Gros, Paul Guth, Danièle Heymann, Claude Imbert, Roland Jaccard, Jean-François Josselin, Janick Jossin, Jean-François Kahn, Konk, Serge Koster, Jean-Claude Lamy, Pierre Lepape, collectif *Libération*, Richard Liscia, Rene Mauriès, Georges Montaron, Pierre Nora, Jean-Paul Ollivier, Jacques Paugam, Louis Pauwels, Bernard Pellegrin, Bertrand Poirot-Delpech, Anne Pons, Marguerite Puhl-Demange, Marcel Raymond, Jean-François Revel, Angelo Rinaldi, Louis-Bernard Robitaille, Jean-Daniel Roob, Pierrette Rosset, Guy Rouzet, François Salvaing, Claude Servan-Schreiber, Maurice Siegel, Nadine Speller-Lefevre, Paul Thibaud, Olivier Todd, Bernardo Vulli, Eliane Victor, René Virgo, Wolinski, André Wurmser, Françoise Xenakis.

BROADCASTING

Laure Adler, André Arnaud, José Artur, André Asséo, Maurice Audran, Claude Barma, Jean de Beer, Gabriel de Broglie, Jacques Chancel, Jacques Chapus, Georges Charbonnier, François Chatel, Pierre Desgraupes, Alain Duhamel, Jean-Pierre Elkabbach, Freddy Eytan, Jean Ferniot, François Gonnet, Philippe Labro, Xavier Larère, Jacques Legris, Ivan Levaï, Noël Mamère, Claude Mettra, Jean Montalbetti, Etienne Mougeotte, Jacques Paoli, Luce Perrot, Claude Jean-Philippe, Patrick Poivre d'Arvor, Jacques Rigaud, Philippe Saint-Germain, Anne Sinclair, Georges Suffert, Jean-Pierre Tison, Alain Venstein, Jean-Daniel Verhaeghe, Roger Vrigny, Pierre Wiehn, Jean-Didier Wolfromm.

ARTS AND PERFORMING ARTS

Actors, directors, musicians, painters, architects, directors of cultural centres, etc.:

Geneviève Bailac, Michel Bouquet, Antoine Bourseiller, André Bruyère, César, Paul Chemetov, Coluche, Jacques Darolles, Yves Deschamps, Pierre Dux, André Feller, Léo Ferré, Edwige Feuillère, Guy Foissy, Jean-Jacques Fouché, Raymond Gérôme, Didier Guilland, Michel Guy, Elisabeth Huppert, Francis Huster, Fabien Jannelle, Bernard Lefort, Maurice Leroux, Marcel Maréchal, Mathieu, Sylvia Monfort, Yves Montand, Jean Morlock, Claude Parent, Gilbert Pellissier, François Périer, Michel Piccoli, Michel Polac, Roland Poquet, Jean-Pierre Pottier, Paul Puaux, Dominique Quehec, Alain Sarfati, Pierre Schaeffer, Nicolas Shoffer, Simone Signoret, Pierre Soulages, Jacques Toja, Victor Vasarely.

POLITICIANS

Christian Beullac, Huguette Bouchardeau, Jacques Chirac, Gaston Defferre, Françoise Gaspard, Pascal Gauchon, Valéry Giscard d'Estaing, Arlette Laguiller, Brice Lalonde, Jean-Philippe Lecat, Jacques Médecin, Pierre Mendès-France, Edgard Pisani, Jean-Marie Poirier.

OTHER CATEGORIES

Religion
The Reverend Father Bro, Josy Eisenberg, the Very Reverend Paul Poupard, the Grand Rabbi Sirat.

Advertising
Bernard Brochand, Lucien Elia, Marcel Germon, Pierre Lemonnier, Maurice Lévy, J. Séguéla.

Foreign cultural attachés appointed to Paris

Bernardino Osio, Charlotte Sow, Bryan Swingler

French cultural attachés appointed abroad
G. Coste, Gilbert Erouart, Christian Morieux.

Ten replies were sent anonymously.

(*Lire*, 68, April 1981)

Everything leads us to believe that this hit parade would doubtless have been even further from what would be obtained using a list of judges more strictly restricted to those producing [culture] for other producers, notably what one normally calls the avant-garde (whose blatant absence from the list of judges becomes easier to understand), if the field of journalism, even and above all cultural journalism, were not still dominated by the restricted field [of cultural production] and its specific principles of perception and appreciation, and if the judges did not have a partial knowledge of the institutionalized *signs* or the informal and diffuse manifestations of the hierarchy tacitly and confusedly admitted within the field of production for producers, and if they did not also have a vague awareness of the law which tends to make any classificatory utterance liable to betray the position of its author in the series classified. Cultural products are provided with labels (for instance, the professional titles granted to the elect: 'philosopher' or 'sociologist'), with *brands* and quality-control tickets representing genuine institutional guarantees (institutional membership, publisher, series, preface-writer, etc.) which orientate and predetermine people's judgement. Here we see one of the most common properties of perception of the social world: what the agents have to perceive is, at each moment, the product of earlier anticipations and acts or expressions destined to display them (which means, for instance, that the likelihood of seeing oneself enclosed in the magical circle of perceptions, endlessly confirmed and reinforced by an objectivity resulting from the objectification of similarly structured subjectivities, no doubt tends to increase in proportion to the symbolic power possessed).

The inclination of journalists to impose a definition of the intellectual closer to their inclinations, that is closer to their productive and interpretative capacities, is thus counterbalanced by their concern to affirm their membership of the circle of true judges.[6] Since they cannot achieve a radical subversion of the scale of values, it is only by according a favourable bias to the most journalistic of intellectuals that the journalists can affirm their membership of an enlarged intellectual field and their right to judge the less journalistic intellectuals, of whom they must none the less quote the most notable, on pain of being excluded from the intellectual game. We can thus easily understand the eminent place conferred on Raymond Aron: more than the lucidity that he showed towards the Soviet Union, which was natural enough given his political options, and which was offset by so many blind spots, it is no doubt his status as the honorary intellectual conscience of journalist-intellectuals and intellectual-journalists which explains that some people, encouraged by the growth in the control of journalism over the intellectual field,[7] thought for a moment that they saw the figure of a great intellectual in this top journalist consecrated by the university, universally known for that anti-intellectual classic, *L'Opium des intellectuels*, and so often celebrated for his clarity and good sense, which the journalists in their incipient anti-intellectualism like to contrast with the obscurity and irresponsibility of the intellectuals.[8]

Thus the strategy of the balance sheet – individual or collective – of which the hit parade constitutes the culminating achievement, tends to substitute for the classificatory acts arising from random daily encounters, and the *unwritten classifications* which are constantly formulated and constantly questioned in the field, the visible, published, public, almost official reality of a classification which, although it is the expression of a vision peculiar to a specific and culturally subordinate sector of the field of cultural production, is endowed with all the appearances of objectivity. It gives a fair idea of the action accomplished day after day, week after week, without any need to orchestrate or to conspire, by all those who replied to the questionnaire published by *Lire* and others like it. Thus, after the social significance of the hit parade, we now discover the meaning of the questions which underlie its production: the issue at stake is perhaps less the list of intellectuals crowned than the list of judges who have the *competence* to elect them and who, most significantly, are published alongside the hit parade of the '42 top intellectuals'. As in the hit parade of hit parades published by *Les Nouvelles littéraires*, where the ordinary judges show off by showing their hit parade for the decade, the publication of this list of judges, of this *album judicum*, as the Romans used to say, shows up the symbolic violence through which a new principle of legitimation claims legitimacy.

The question of the definition of the intellectual, or, rather, of specifically intellectual work, is inseparable from the question of defining the population which can be allowed to participate in this definition. The true objective of the struggle which is engaged at the heart of the field of cultural production, and whose underlying mechanisms are laid bare by the anodyne game of the review *Lire*, is in fact the attribution of the right to judge in the matter of cultural production. It is nearly always in the name of an increase in the population of the judges that such acts of violence against the autonomy of the different fields of production for producers are accomplished, starting with the scientific field: whether it claims allegiance to the 'people' in order to condemn a production which is the product of the internal requirements of an autonomous field – in biology as much as in poetry or in sociology – or, in an entirely different register, allegiance to the ability to 'make a good impression on television' or to 'journalistic readability', constituted as a measure of all cultural value, the anti-intellectualism which flourishes spontaneously among journalists and, more widely, among the dequalified producers who are obliged to produce to order, and which can find the most diverse forms of expression and justification – with notably all the varieties of populist feeling, from *völkisch* [populist] on the far right to Zhdanovist on the far left – constitutes a permanent threat to those who have the historically won *privilege* of producing to meet a demand that they themselves have produced.[9] Thus it is not pure chance that this hit parade, apparently orientated towards the establishment of hierarchies, has as its main effect the abolition of the ever-uncertain and ever-threatened boundaries between those of the producers who, being directly subject to demand, have their problematic imposed from the outside, and those who, because of the specific form of the rivalry between them, are able to create a demand which can anticipate any social demand.

It is not the sociologist's role to set himself up as the judge of the judges, and of their right to judge. He merely points out that this right is the object of conflicts whose logic he analyses. Because of the fact that the hierarchies are not strongly codified or objectified in norms or in forms, the question of which agencies can ultimately legitimize the agencies of legitimation, which is asked in any field, is asked more visibly in the field of cultural production: the extreme insecurity which is born of the uncertainty of the assets acquired tends to confer a particular violence on the symbolic struggle of each against all, and on all the acts of jurisprudence both innumerable and infinitesimal – gossip bordering on vilification, calumny, homicidal 'witticisms', ruinous rumours – of which the unwritten rankings based on a necessarily tacit consensus of those ranked highest in these tacit rankings are but the sum total of these unquantifiable equations.[10] It is still the case, however, that the autonomy of the field is affirmed, as we can clearly see in the test case of the natural sciences – but things are not so different in painting or in poetry – through the fact that people win these struggles only if they use all the weapons, and only those, which have been accumulated in the whole *specific* history of the previous struggles. Afterwards, according to their skill in using these arms, the various competitors are very unequally inclined to strive for autonomy, for a strengthening of the boundaries which prevent the irruption of external principles of evaluation, or, on the contrary, to strive for a more or less cynical alliance with external forces and notably with all the hybrid characters of equivocal judgement who, by setting themselves up individually or collectively as judges, work to dispossess the most autonomous producers of the right of deciding which tribunal they would grant the competence to judge them.

Appendix 4

The Analyses of Correspondences

1 THE FOUR FACULTIES

Main variables (we have noted in parentheses the number of possibilities when it is higher than two): Académie Française; *Bottin mondain*; [socio-professional] category of father (20); *concours général*: CNRS commissions (presence at the three most recent); paperback series; Caen or Amiens conferences (at least one of the two); conferences (frequency) (10); Universities Consultative Committee; director of UER (since 1968); law discipline (4); arts discipline (9); medical discipline (3); science discipline (3); faculty dean; children (number of) (5); teaching in intellectual *grandes écoles*; teaching in establishment *grandes écoles*; secondary schooling (public or private) (4); faculty (4); *grande école* (9); CNRS laboratory (director); place of higher education (3); CNRS medal; *Le Monde* (writing for); birth (year of) (10); place of birth (in which region) (3); Order of Merit; public bodies (participation in); Plan (commision of the 6th); sex; translations (3); television (appearances on); *Who's Who* (mention in).

We treated as illustrative variables: place of birth (unreliable, and redundant with region of birth); place of residence; matrimonial status (redundant with number of children); the title of doctor *honoris causa* (unreliable); institution of secondary education (unreliable, and redundant with region of birth); support for Giscard and for Mitterrand; the *agrégation* (insufficient information); membership of the SNESup, the Legion of Honour; and the Academic Palms.

2 THE FACULTY OF ARTS AND SOCIAL SCIENCES

Main variables: Collège de France; Sorbonne; Nanterre; EPHE 6th section; EPHE 4th and 5th sections; joint post with EPHE 6th section; joint post with EPHE 4th and 5th sections; joint post with CNRS directorship; joint post with oriental languages; joint post with teaching at ENS; joint post with other prestigious establishment; the Institute; discipline (8); date of birth (7); category of father (13); *Who's Who* (mention in); *normalien* ; *agrégation* board of examiners; Universities Consultative Committee; Council of Higher Education; CNRS commission 1967 and 1963; ministerial cabinet or government Plan; director of research team; region of birth (10); children (number of) (8); Legion of Honour; Order of Merit; establishment attended for *grande école* entrance (6); residential neighbourhood (9); Academic Palms; Académie Française, *Larousse 1968*; *Le Nouvel Observateur* (writes for); television (6); 'Que Sais-Je?' series (published in) (6); 'Idées', 'Points', 'Médiations' series (published in) (4); intellectual reviews (editorial committee of); ENS entrance examination board; translations (3); citations (number of mentions in the *Citation Index*) (3).

We treated as illustrative variables: place of birth (unreliable, and redundant with region of birth); matrimonial status (redundant with number of children); the *agrégation* (insufficient and unreliable information); the title of honorary doctor (*docteur honoris causa*) (unreliable); establishment attended for secondary education (unreliable, and redundant with region of birth); support for Giscard, for Mitterrand or for Flacelière.

LIST OF PROFESSORS

Collège de France

Bataillon (Marcel)
Benveniste (Emile)
Berque (Jacques)
Blin (Georges)
Braudel (Fernand)
Courcelle (Pierre)

Duby (Georges)
Dumézil (Georges)
Dupont-Sommer (André)
Duval (Paul-Marie)
Filliozat (Jean)
Grabar (André)

Guéroult (Martial)
Hambis (Louis)
Hyppolite (Jean)
Labat (René)
Laoust (Henri)
Lecoy (Félix)
Lemerle (Paul)
Lévi-Strauss (Claude)

Minder (Robert)
Perroux (François)
Pottier (Bernard)
Puech (Henri-Charles)
Revah (Israël-Salvator)
Robert (Louis)
Sauvy (Alfred)
Schaeffer (Claude)

Sorbonne

Alquié (Ferdinand)
Antoine (Gérald)
Aron (Raymond)
Bachelard (Suzanne)
Bacquet (Paul)
Balandier (Georges)
Barbut (Marc)
Bastide (Roger)
Beaujeu-Garnier (Jacqueline)
Belaval (Yvon)
Bertaux (Pierre)
Birot (Pierre)
Boudon (Raymond)
Bourricaud (François)
Boyancé (Pierre)
Canguilhem (Georges)
Castex (Pierre-Georges)
Cazeneuve (Jean)
Chailley (Jacques)
Chamoux (François)
Chantraine (Pierre)
Chastel (André)
Collart (Jean)
Culioli (Antoine)
Daux (Georges)
David (Claude)
Deloffre (Frédéric)
Demargne (Pierre)

Dollfus (Olivier)
Dresch (Jean)
Droz (Jacques)
Duroselle (Jean-Baptiste)
Durry (Jeanne)
Durry (Marcel)
Etiemble (René)
Fabre (Jean)
Favier (Jean)
Flacelière (Robert)
Fontaine (Jacques)
Fourquet (Jean)
Fraisse (Paul)
Frappier (Jean)
Frechet (Jacques)
George (Pierre)
Girard (Louis)
Gouhier (Henri)
Grandjard (Henri)
Gravier (Maurice)
Grimal (Pierre)
Guénée (Bernard)
Guitton (Jean)
Heurgon (Jacques)
Jullian (René)
Lacombe (Olivier)
Lagache (Daniel)
Landré (Louis)

Las Vergnas (Raymond)
Lebègue (Raymond)
Leclant (Jean)
Leroi-Gourhan (André)
Malaurie (Jean)
Marrou (Henri-Irénée)
Martinet (André)
Minard (Armand)
Mirambel (André)
Mollat du Jourdin (Michel)
Monbeig (Pierre)
Mousnier (Roland)
Oléron (Pierre)
Pellat (Charles)
Perpillou (Aimé)
Perret (Jacques)
Perrot (Jean-Charles)
Perroy (Edouard)
Picard (Raymond)

Poirier (René)
Polin (Raymond)
Pomeau (René)
Portal (Roger)
Renucci (Paul)
Ricatte (Robert)
Ritz (Jean-Georges)
Robert (Fernand)
Robichez (Jacques)
de Romilly (Jacqueline)
Saulnier (Verdun-Louis)
Schuhl (Pierre-Maxime)
Souriau (Etienne)
Stoetzel (Jean)
Tapié (Victor)
Van Effenterre (Henri)
Wagner (Léon)
Wuilleumier (Pierre)
Zink (Georges)

Faculty of Nanterre

André (Jacques)
Anzieu (Didier)
Beaujeu (Jean)
Dufrenne (Mikel)
Duméry (Henry)
Foucault (Michel)
Grappin (Pierre)

Irigoin (Jean-Marie)
Micha (Alexandre)
Rémond (René)
Ricœur (Paul)
Touraine (Alain)
Vallet (Georges)

EPHE 6th section and ENS

Althusser (Louis)
Barrère (Alain)
Barthes (Roland)
Bourdieu (Pierre)
Chombart de Lauwe (Paul-Henry)
Condominas (Georges)
Cot (Pierre)

Derrida (Jacques)
Fourastié (Jean)
Friedmann (Georges)
Glenisson (Jean)
James (Emile)
Labrousse (Ernest)
Le Bras (Gabriel)

Le Goff (Jacques)
Le Roy Ladurie (Emmanuel)
Malinvaud (Edmond)
Marchal (Jean)
Meyerson (Ignace)
Meyriat (Jean)

Morazé (Charles)
Moscovici (Serge)
Piattier (André)
Roncayolo (Marcel)
Rouquet la Garrigue (Victor)
Vernant (Jean-Pierre)

EPHE 4th and 5th sections

Bazin (Louis)
Beaujouan (Guy)
Caquot (Albert)
de Dainville (François)
Festugière (Jean)

Fleury (Michel)
Guiart (Jean)
Lejeune (Michel)
Vignaux (Paul)

Note: In order to indicate the principal appointment of professors attached to more than one of the institutions selected for the population studied, the commonly admitted social hierarchy of institutions has been followed – for example, assigning to the Collège de France or the Sorbonne those who belong *both* to the Collège de France or the Sorbonne *and* to the Ecole Pratique des Hautes Etudes (see above, pp. 75–6).

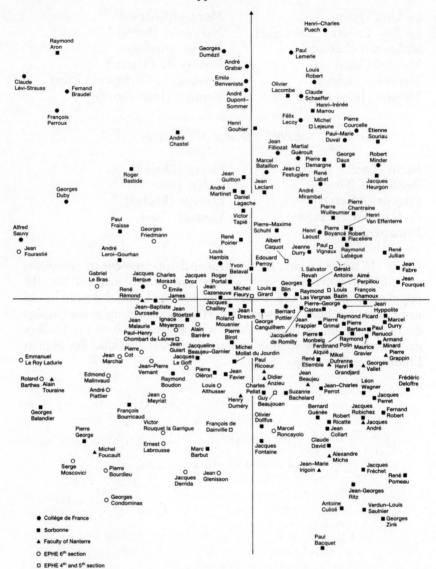

Graph 7 The space of the arts and social science faculties: analysis of correspondences: plane of the first and second axes of inertia – individuals

Notes

PREFACE TO THE ENGLISH EDITION

1 P. Bourdieu, 'Célibat et condition paysanne', *Etudes rurales*, April–September 1962, pp. 32–136.
2 The repudiation is of the Chicago school type of sociology of professions. [Tr.]
3 Because of this, the authors find themselves reduced (more or less completely, depending on the readers' information) to the works bearing their name and are stripped of all the social properties associated with their position in their field of origin, that is, the most institutionalized dimension of their authority and their symbolic capital (although prefaces written by authors placed within the field may serve, if necessary, to effect the transfer necessary to restore their endangered symbolic capital . . .). The freedom which is thus left to the reader's judgement is quite relative because of the fact that the effects of authority can continue to operate through the medium of the solidarity obtaining between holders of homologous positions in different national scientific fields, and in particular between the dominant, who can profit from the power which they exercise over the circulation of translations and the agencies of consecration in order to operate international transfers of academic power and also to control the access to the national market of products liable to threaten their own production. On the other hand, this relative freedom has as its counterpart the danger of misunderstanding and *allodoxia* which is entailed by ignorance of the context: thus it is, for instance, that some essayists come to eclipse the stars of the first magnitude from whom they borrow the very source of their radiance.
4 There is no lack of sociologists, historians or anthropologists who, unable to adopt towards their own world the detached scrutiny of the foreigner, will find in this book, which is the product of a methodical effort to achieve this scrutiny without losing the benefits of familiarity,

an opportunity to reinforce their native confidence in their own world – as expressed in all naïvety in certain studies of France and its universities by foreign authors. The paradigm of this sociology which enthrones ethnocentrism as method (and which can be the product of émigrés needing to justify, in their own eyes, the fact that they have emigrated) is a work by Terry Clark which measures the French university against a set of arbitrary criteria which are no more than the idealized traits of the American university (cf. T. Clark, *Prophets and Patrons: The French University and the Emergence of the Social Science*, Cambridge, Mass., Harvard University Press, 1973).

5 At each point of the analysis, as regards, for instance, the distance between the academic field and political or economic power – which, it would seem, is (or at least was) for historical reasons greater than in any other country – one ought to examine what is variable and what is invariant and try to discover in the variations of the parameters used for the model the sources of the variations observed in reality.

6 I think that the strategy adopted on this point by the translator, to give carefully chosen English or American equivalents for the words designating specific institutions, while retaining the French words in parentheses, should render this work of transposition easier.

7 Simone de Beauvoir, 'La Pensée de droite aujourd'hui', *Les Temps modernes*, nos 112–13 and 114–15, 1985, pp. 1539–75 and 2219–61. [Tr.]

8 The University of Vincennes, created after 1968, crystallized the new intellectual lifestyle and established within the university itself, thereby greatly scandalizing the defenders of the old university, a version of intellectual life which in other times would have been relegated to intellectual reviews or bohemian cafés.

9 Since I am conscious that the analysis of the academic field which is presented in this book would lose a great deal of the interest which it can offer all those who are interested in the cultural production of France over the last twenty years if they were unable to make out the space of the works and the tendencies whose shadows loom behind the space of the positions, I have decided to spell out the names of the academics studied instead of leaving them in the semi-anonymity of their initials as I had done in the French edition in order to avoid the effects of denunciation or of over-interpretation which, with the passage of time (twenty years after the study) and the distance gained by the foreign observer, should today be attenuated.

10 'L'Homme est mort' was a phrase of Foucault's in *Les Mots et les choses*, Paris, 1966 (*The Order of Things*, London, 1970). [Tr.]

11 Cf. P. Bourdieu, *Distinction: A Social Critique of the Judgement of Taste*, trans. R. Nice, Cambridge, Mass., Harvard University Press, 1984, pp. 494ff.

12 'Oblates': see note 31 to chapter 2. [Tr.]

13 It is a singularity absolutely analogous to that of the nineteenth-century academic institution entrusted with training and consecrating painters, and, particularly, the extraordinary concentration in the hands of the great dignitaries of the Academy of the power of consecration and, thereby, access to the market, which goes a long way towards explaining why the revolution which gave birth to modern painting, with Manet and impressionism, appeared in France earlier than elsewhere.

14 One tends to forget that the student revolt of May 1968 was triggered by a clash between students and the academic authorities over freedom of access to female students' accommodation.

15 These 'minor heresiarchs' are Jean Baudrillard, Jean-François Lyotard, among others. [Tr.]

Chapter 1 A 'Book for Burning'?

1 I became fully conscious of this problem when several of my early readers asked me to 'give examples', in the case of analyses from which I had deliberately excluded all 'anecdotal' information, however familiar to 'usually well-informed sources' – the very information that journalists or popular essayists are most eager to reveal.

2 *Habitus* is a system of shared social dispositions and cognitive structures which generates perceptions, appreciations and actions. Cf. P. Bourdieu, *Outline of a Theory of Practice*, Cambridge, 1978. [Tr.]

3 Cf. C. C. Gillespie, *Science and Policy in France at the End of the Old Régime*, Princeton, Princeton University Press, 1980, pp. 290–330.

4 Among others, we could quote the most recent representative of this tendency, Hervé Couteau-Bégarie, whose analyses of the *Ecole des Annales* betray quite ingenuously the repressed violence elicited by intellectual rejection reinforced by provincialism: 'Thus the new historians presented a *coherent project*, ideologically *adapted* to the audience it was designed for. . . . It is this expansion which explains the success of the new historians. They were then able to *mount an attack* on publishers and the media *in order* to obtain what Régis Debray calls "social visibility" ' (H. Couteau-Bégarie, *Le Phénomène nouvelle histoire*, Paris, Economia, 1983, pp. 247 and 248).

5 Bernard Pivot, host of the weekly television show *Apostrophes*, devoted to literary and cultural discussion, was criticized by Régis Debray, presidential adviser, and author of a book denouncing intellectuals, *Les Scribes*, in a notorious interview. Cf. also H. Hamon et P. Rotmann, *Les Intellocrates. Expédition en Haute Intelligentsia*, Paris, Ramsay, 1981. [Tr.]

6 The Ecole Pratique des Hautes Etudes is a research institute for social science, not integrated into the main university system. [Tr.]

7 *Le Nouvel Observateur* is an authoritative yet glossy left-wing political and cultural weekly magazine. [Tr.]

8 J. Bouveresse, *Le Philosophe chez les autophages*, Paris, Minuit, 1984, pp. 93ff.

9 In a kind of symbolic *auto-da-fé*, probably not deliberately orchestrated, all the Viennese newspapers observed the strictest silence about *Die Fackel* throughout Karl Kraus's lifetime.

10 We know that *The Interpretation of Dreams*, which Freud considered his most important scientific work, conceals, beneath the manifest logic of the scientific treatise, a latent discourse in which Freud, through a series of personal dreams, undertakes an analysis of his inextricably tangled relationships with his father, with politics and with the university. Cf. especially Carl E. Schorske, *Fin de Siècle Vienna: Politics and Culture*, New York, Alfred A. Knopf, 1980, pp. 181–207.

11 The reader will find below, in chapter 3, a detailed description of the process of construction of this population. The characteristics of the representative sample which was used as a basis for the analysis of the ensemble of the faculties (except pharmacy) are described in chapter 2. The sources used in these two surveys are described in appendix 1.

12 The Conseil Consultatif des Universités (CCU), the Universities Consultative Committee, is the official organization advising government on university policy and controlling appointments of tenured professors. [Tr.]

13 The *agrégation* is a competitive examination originally designed to provide select recruitment to tenured teaching posts in secondary education, but was already in the period discussed by Bourdieu frequently a passport to teaching in higher education. [Tr.]

14 I cannot regret strongly enough not having kept a *research diary* which would have shown, better than any declaration, the role of empirical work in the progressive accomplishment of the break with first-hand experience. But a reading of the list of sources used (see appendix 1) should at least give an idea of the work of controlled recollection which is the motivating difference between ordinary experience and scholarly experience.

15 The INSEE (Institut National de la Statistique et des Etudes Economiques) is the National Institute for Statistical and Economic Surveys. [Tr.]

16 *Concours* are competitive examinations for a limited number of places, especially for candidates wishing to study at a *grande école*. Students admitted to a *grande école* have their fees paid and receive a generous grant. The *grandes écoles* are strongly contrasted to the ordinary French universities, where any student with the *baccalauréat* (18-plus school-

leaving certificate) may enrol. The *grandes écoles* include the Ecole Normale Supérieure (ENS) for teachers, the Ecole Polytechnique and the Ecole Centrale for engineers, the Ecole Nationale d'Administration for higher civil servants, and the Ecole des Hautes Etudes Commerciales (HEC) for business managers. These *grandes écoles* are roughly equivalent to Oxford and Cambridge in the UK or the 'Ivy League' universities in the USA. [Tr.]

17 We should undertake an extended critique of the effect of naturalization, which is particularly active in demography, since it bestows on certain parameters (age, sex or even matrimonial status), and on studies which manipulate them without any other form of testing, the appearance of absolute 'objectivity'. In more general terms, and yet without expecting to discourage the compulsive repetition of studies tending to reduce history to biological or geographical or similar kinds of nature, it would be worth describing the form which this effect of dehistoricization takes in each of the social sciences, from ethnology, when it pays homage to verbal analogies with the natural sciences, to history itself when it seeks in the 'motionless history' of the soil and the climate that substance whose historical movements are supposed to be merely contingent features.

18 We cannot exclude the possibility that scientific analysis itself might exercise a theoretical effect sufficient to transform the ordinary vision of the field.

19 A *normalien* is a student or graduate of the Ecole Normale Supérieure, a *grande école* which originally trained elite teachers for the *agrégation* and titular posts in secondary teaching, but it now tends to produce university teachers. [Tr.]

20 An *agrégé* is a holder of the *agrégation*. Both titles are commonly considered an intellectual honour, independently of the posts then obtained. [Tr.]

21 A. W. Gouldner, 'Cosmopolitans and locals: toward an analysis of latent social rules', *Administrative Science Quarterly*, 2 December 1957, pp. 281–307.

22 B. Clark, 'Faculty organization and authority', in T. F. Lunsford (ed.), *The Study of Academic Administration*, Boulder, Colorado, Western Interstate Commission for Higher Education, 1963, pp. 37–51, and 'Faculty cultures', in *The Study of Campus Culture*, Boulder, Colorado, Western Interstate Commission for Higher Education, 1963.

23 J. W. Gustad, 'Community consensus and conflict', *The Educational Record*, Fall 1966.

24 L. Wittgenstein, *Philosophical Remarks*, Oxford, Blackwell, 1975, p. 181, quoted by J. Bouveresse, *Le Mythe de l'intériorité*, Paris, Minuit, 1976.

25 We will restrict ourselves to these rather unrealistic cases, which are too 'pure', since we cannot study individual cases, which would inevitably seem to be tendentious character assassinations, although only these would allow us to demonstrate the most typical strategies of this rhetoric of self-legitimation and show that the generic and specific characteristics of the position occupied both in the university field and in the specialized sub-field are expressed there, usually in a highly euphemistic manner, which is none the less perfectly transparent to people in the know.

26 Historicist or sociological relativism, which invokes the insertion of the research worker in the social world in order to question his ability to accede to a transhistorical truth, nearly always ignores insertion in the scientific field, and the correlative interests, thus denying itself any possibility of control over what is the specific mediation through which all determinisms operate.

27 Cf. R. Boudon, 'L'intellectuel et ses publics: les singularités françaises', in J.-D. Reynaud and Y. Grafmeyer (eds), *Français qui êtes-vous'?*, Paris, Documentation Française, 1981, pp. 464–80.

28 The fact that the principal argument sustaining this discourse – the French hierarchy is different from the international hierarchy, the international hierarchy is the only scientific one, therefore the French hierarchy is non-scientific – remains latent even in a text of scientific pretensions shows one of the fundamental properties of the most characteristic polemical procedures used in struggles within the intellectual field: exploiting a bias shared by a whole group, the strategies of defamation aiming to ruin the symbolic credit of competitors proceed by more or less slanderous *insinuations* which would not usually survive being made completely explicit.

29 P. Bourdieu, 'Le Marché des biens symboliques', *L'Année sociologique*, 22, 1971, pp. 49–126.

30 This struggle may not be apparent as such, and a particular agent or group of agents may threaten the credit of other members of the field by their very existence (for example, by imposing new modes of thought and expression, and criteria of evaluation favourable to their own productions), without setting themselves up consciously as rivals, even less as enemies, and without resorting to strategies deliberately directed against them.

31 We ought to analyse the procedures of spontaneous semiotics and statistics through which a practical intuition of positions occupied in the distribution of specific capital is constituted, and especially the deciphering and calculating of the spontaneous or institutionalized indices of positions occupied; and also the mechanisms of inhibition or denial of truth, such as all forms of mutual-admiration society, as well as all compensation and substitution strategies, such as university trade-unionism and politics,

which offer favourable ground for the strategies of dual identity and dual language favoured by the use of infinitely extensible 'concepts' such as 'workers', or the transfer of words and modes of thought borrowed from working-class conflicts.

32 One of the factors permitting the scrambling of hierarchies is the division into disciplines and, within these, into specializations which, although hierarchized, offer autonomous hierarchies.

33 L'Institut de France, the French Institute, comprises the Académie Française and the other academies for arts and sciences. [Tr.]

34 The CNRS (Centre National de la Recherche Scientifique, the National Centre for Scientific Research), is the official organization funding research posts and laboratories. It is more powerful and influential in most cases than the research effort of individual university departments. [Tr.]

35 A *vacataire* is a researcher on a temporary contract, as opposed to full-time, tenured staff, or staff seconded on full pay from university posts. [Tr.]

36 Ignorance of this fundamental Weberian distinction is not limited to the layman, as we can see from the fact that 'sociologists' can reproach the analysis of cultural practices with recording *the fact* of the lesser legitimacy or the illegitimacy of the subordinate classes (for a criticism of this error, see P. Bourdieu, J.-C. Chamboredon and J.-C. Passeron, *Le Métier de sociologue*, Paris, Mouton, 1968, p. 76).

37 The Collège de France is a prestigious institute of higher education, founded by François I in 1530; it provides public lectures and seminars, but is not integrated in the main university system (no examinations are set and no diplomas are awarded). [Tr.]

38 On all these points, the reader may consult, apart from the classic debate among logicians on the proper name and operators of individuation (Russell, Gardiner, Quine, Strawson, etc.) and the reflections of Lévi-Strauss in *The Savage Mind*, the excellent analysis of J.-C. Pariente, *Le Langage et l'individuel*, Paris, Colin, 1973.

39 We might thus contrast the *agent*, defined by the finite set of properties operative within the field, with the pre-constructed *individual*.

40 On the role of spatio-temporal relations in the identification of individuals, see P. F. Strawson, *Individuals: An Essay in Descriptive Metaphysics*, London, Methuen, 1959.

41 Raymond Polin and Frédéric Deloffre are philosophy and philology professors at the Sorbonne noted for their strongly conservative stance in 1968 and after. [Tr.]

42 We could also return to the problem of exemplification: doesn't the choice of Lévi-Strauss as an example of the constructed class of 'great masters', defined by the occupation of a determined area of the

constructed space, demolish the whole enterprise of construction, by encouraging or authorizing the reader to reintroduce the properties of the empirical individual? But the choice of an empirical individual chosen at random would be no more significant. Nor would the choice of the individual most saturated with the typical properties of the constructed population, which would no doubt represent the least disadvantageous realization of the notion of the 'ideal type'.

43 If I was not afraid of indulging in narcissistic complacency, I would evoke the question of contamination of the researcher's doxic viewpoint by his epistemic viewpoint. Or the problems posed practically by belonging to the empirical space which we try to subject to observation: feelings of betrayal, of disloyal manipulation (seeing without being seen), which admit and invite rejection, anguish at confrontation and fear of *bodily* contact, 'face to face' ('We keep bumping into Mr Siegfried Löwy', said Karl Kraus), etc. [Kraus refers to Löwy as the archetype of the fashionable journalist. (Tr.)]

44 Cf. C. Lévi-Strauss, *The Savage Mind*, London, Weidenfeld and Nicolson, 1968.

45 I would merely remind anyone who considers this *analysis* to be a personal vision how much room is taken up, quite logically in a world dominated by *symbolic capital*, by all the strategies aiming to amass *credit* or reduce the credit of others (calumny, disparagement, slander, eulogy, criticism in the various senses of the word).

46 It can happen that the most 'synoptic' concept can be associated with an empirical viewpoint (as in the case of the *petty bourgeoisie*). The break between epistemic usage and ordinary usage is then especially urgent.

47 On polyonomy as it is methodically used in *Don Quixote* to express the plurality of possible viewpoints on the person, see L. Spitzer, 'Linguistic perspectivism in the Don Quixote', *Linguistics and Literary History*, New York, Russell & Russell, 1962.

48 J. R. Searle, *Speech Acts*, Cambridge, Cambridge University Press, 1969. The history of art and literature themselves, where each new system of conventions shows up the relative truth, that is, the arbitrariness of the previous system of conventions, parallels the work of novelists like Alain Robbe-Grillet and Robert Pinget (especially in *L'Apocryphe*), who, by pointing out what was false in the contract between the novelist and the reader, and especially in the coexistence of declared fiction and a search for the impression of reality, establish fiction as fiction, including the fiction of a reality where its fiction is truly constructed.

49 To say that only a scientific criterion can challenge scientific work will tempt the defenders of essay-writing to cry 'terrorism'. And the sociologist will thus see himself accused of being either too weak, and too easy to refute, or too strong, and irrefutable.

50 This does not signify that a strictly 'literary' research cannot find a scientific justification. Thus, as Bateson remarks on the subject of the ethnologist, the evocative power of style constitutes one of the unsurpassable forms of scientific achievement when it has to objectify the relevant features of a social configuration and thereby to reveal the principles of the systematic appraisal of a historic necessity: when the historian of the Middle Ages [Georges Duby] evokes, through the power of language itself, the isolation and the desolation of the peasants who take refuge in oases of cleared land, who are prey to all sorts of terror, he is attempting above all to reproduce for the reader, in and through words capable of producing an impression of reality, the renewal of vision which he had to operate, against the screen-concepts and the intellectual reflex actions, to arrive at a correct understanding of the strangeness of Carolingian culture. We could say as much of the sociologist who may have to alternate the awkward machinery of conceptualization, inseparable from the construction of the object, with the search for stylistic effects designed to recapture the constructed and unitary experience of a lifestyle or of a way of thinking.

51 See E. Benveniste, *Problèmes de linguistique générale*, Paris, Gallimard, 1966, pp. 239, 242, 245, 249.

52 A UER (*unité d'enseignement et de recherche*) is an education and research unit. After the university reforms of 1969, universities, which had been large, loose agglomerations of a small number of powerful faculties, were reorganized into a greater number of smaller, semi-independent UERs. [Tr.]

53 It is clear that the redefinition of subordinate posts and their concomitant pedagogical interests must be set in the context not only of the transformation of the social and scholarly characteristics of the teachers but also of the profound modifications of the conditions of service of their careers, which have been caused by the transformation of the number and social status of their student public, in such a way that a description of the job and its representation, like the one which we shall propose below, which for the purposes of comparison and comprehension inevitably uses the previous state of the system as reference, tends to exaggerate signs of inadaptation and describe unfavourably the practices and the interests elicited by the new demand.

54 L. Wittgenstein, *Philosophical Remarks*, Oxford, Blackwell, 1975, p. 58.

Chapter 2 The Conflict of the Faculties

1 On the structure of the field of power as a space of the positions of power occupied, according to their different kinds of capital, by the various fractions of the dominant class, with at one pole the economically subordinate but culturally dominant fractions (artists, intellectuals,

professors of arts and science) and at the other pole the economically dominant but culturally subordinate fractions (managers or executives of the public and private sector), see P. Bourdieu, *Distinction*, tr. R. Nice, Cambridge, Mass., Harvard University Press, 1984; and, for a more detailed analysis of the temporally dominant sector of the field of power, see also P. Bourdieu and M. de Saint-Martin, 'Le patronat', *Actes de la recherche en sciences sociales*, 20–1, March–April 1978, pp. 3–82.

2 Everything leads us to suppose that the schism between academics and independent writers or intellectuals is much less marked than between the wars, or at the end of the nineteenth century, because of the fact that it has to some extent moved into the heart of the university field, since the university has opened its doors to writer-professors or journalist-professors as a result of the growth of the professorial body linked to the expansion of the student population and the concomitant changes in recruitment procedures. A structural history and a comparative sociology of the university field should concentrate especially on these variations at different moments and in different societies of the social distance between the two fields (which can be measured by different indices, such as the number of movements from one field to another, the frequency of simultaneous tenure of positions in both fields, the social distance – in terms of academic origins, etc. – between the two populations, the frequency of meetings, institutionalized or otherwise, etc.), and the social effects which can be related, in the two fields, to these variations.

3 A. Girard, *La Réussite sociale en France, ses caractères, ses lois, ses effets*, Paris, Presses Universitaires de France, 1961, pp. 158–9. No one is more aware than I am of the insufficiency of the statistical bases of this comparison. But it seems to me that, in this case as in others, the need to take into account everything which the milieu being analysed owes to its position in a surrounding space is an urgent obligation, and that it is better to mark at least roughly the position occupied by the university field in the field of power and in the social field overall, rather than ignorantly record its effects in an analysis whose superficial correctness is only a result of the deceptive limits of a faultily constructed object.

4 As the editors of this *Directory* observe, this work gives the state of the teaching body in 1966, because of the time lag in recording new appointments. As for the 1970 *Directory*, it now only gives, for each university establishment, a list of *unités d'enseignement et de recherche* (UER), with the names of their directors. We therefore resorted to lists obtained from the ministry for the year 1970 which allowed us to check the sample and take into account appointments made between 1966 and

the time of the enquiry. (All through the analysis – even when it applied to a more recent period – we took care to preserve the terms which were in use in 1967, such as 'faculty', since replaced by 'university', or 'dean', replaced by 'Director of UER'.)

5 A comparison between professors of the different faculties should take into account the rate of growth of the populations of teachers (and students) since the 1950s. The various faculties are not, if we may say so, at the same stage of evolution: whereas the science faculties had their period of maximum growth around the years 1955–60 and started to retrench around 1970, the arts faculties only started to recruit teachers heavily after 1960 and the law faculties around 1965. It follows that the same diplomas do not always have the same value in the different faculties. For instance, in 1968, the science faculties were in a phase of retrenchment, appointment to a full lectureship being made only after a relatively long period (six to seven years), whereas in the arts, where expansion was continuing, the waiting period was shorter (this is no doubt partly explicable by the fact that assistant lecturers in the arts did not have tenure; contrary to assistant lecturers in science, they could only be retained through promotion to the post of lecturer). In a similar way, conditions of access to the post of professor were no doubt very unevenly affected by the effects of the growth of the teaching body.

6 Rather than multiply examples of the rather monotonous argument used by the professors interviewed to rebut political or trade-union questions, we will fall back on quoting one professor from the faculty of medicine who spells out the principle quite plainly: 'I assure you that I have not . . . I don't think I'm avoiding the issue, but I don't think that you can classify me, I'm unclassifiable, anyway, because I never wanted to join any party. . . . You know, I think it was Jean Guitton who said that . . . "There are people whose commitment is to remain uncommitted".' But, rather than such attacks on the questionnaire, it is this reply from a professor known to belong to the Communist Party that we must quote, because it presents overtly the scientific and ethical principles which led us to note only those political opinions which were publicly displayed: 'I have said that I will not reply to these enquiries. My opinions are public knowledge. I don't hide them. But I will not reply to the enquiry. I repeat, I will not reply to this enquiry.' (There is a truly fascinating account of reactions to a – somewhat indefensible – questionnaire by E. C. Ladd and S. M. Lipsett on American professors in the work of S. Lang, *The File*, New York, Heidelberg and Berlin, Springer-Verlag, 1981.)

7 The *Bottin mondain* is the French (high) society directory. [Tr.]

8 We analysed, for the faculties of science and medicine alone (where we had at our disposal the information for 58 and 97 per cent of the

samples), more detailed information on the family of origin (father's qualifications, mother's profession and qualifications, profession and qualifications of paternal and maternal grandfathers and grandmothers) and on the present family (profession and qualifications of spouse).

9 A *lycée* is the equivalent of a British grammar school or American state high school. In France as in Britain, opting out of the state education system in favour of private schooling generally supposes an upper-class income. But in France motivation is also frequently religious. Most private schools are Roman Catholic, in overt opposition to the constitutionally non-confessional state system. [Tr.]

10 The *concours général* is a nationwide competition where the best pupils in the *baccalauréat* (18-plus school-leaving certificate) have their examination scripts judged for a national prize in each subject. [Tr.]

11 Only part of the information gathered on this point was usable in the comparative study of professors of the different faculties, since the syllabuses, the competitive examinations, the examinations and the qualifications are profoundly non-comparable and can only be used for purposes of comparison within each faculty, for instance, between disciplines (although these comparisons themselves are rendered difficult, in many cases, by the relative incompatibility of the disciplines and also by the small size of the numbers involved in the sample). Among the data not used, we could mention, for instance, for arts and science, the establishment attended to study for the competitive entrance examination to the ENS or for a degree, the rank obtained in the entrance competition and age on entry, age on passing the *agrégation*, age when appointed assistant lecturer, when appointed professor, when obtaining doctorate, etc., or, for medicine, age when appointed junior hospital doctor and examination grade, age when appointed resident hospital doctor and examination grade, age when appointed assistant, consultant, professor, status as clinical head (major or minor, young or old, etc.), which no doubt constitutes a decisive element of specific social capital and whose choice seems to depend considerably on inherited social capital.

12 Without using it in our analysis, we were able to examine membership of the Council for Higher Education, the University council, and general editorship of series for the Presses Universitaires de France.

13 We also examined membership of foreign academies, honorary doctorates (and, for the arts faculties, the number of books and articles published). We had to reject an item as apparently simple as the number of articles or books published (to avoid comparing the non-comparable, ignoring the differences separating their objects, their methods, their results, the productions of the different categories of producers, according to generation, faculty, subject, etc.).

14 The Académie Française (French Academy) was founded by Richelieu

in 1634 and is an elite body of only forty distinguished literary figures. [Tr.]

15 The *Petit Larousse* is a household reference dictionary, including brief biographical notes on famous people. [Tr.]

16 We could not use the 'intellectual' prizes, extremely numerous and disparate, which could not be satisfactorily codified without a preliminary study.

17 Government ministers in France are free to appoint their own specialist advisers, who need not be civil servants. [Tr.]

18 ENA, the Ecole Nationale d'Administration (National School for Administration), is a *grande école* which, like Sciences Po., recruits postgraduate students through its competitive entrance examination, rather than undergraduates; the ENA trains higher state officials. The HEC, the Ecole des Hautes Etudes Commerciales (another *grande école*), is France's top business school. The Ecole Polytechnique is the most prestigious engineering school. Its origins were military, but now it mainly supplies the upper echelons of industrial and business management. *Ecoles intellectuelles* and *écoles du pouvoir* are intellectual schools and establishment schools. This is Bourdieu's own classification of the *grandes écoles* into those serving the academic field (the ENS) and those serving the field of power (the ENA, HEC, Polytechnique, Centrale, etc.). [Tr.]

19 We did not use membership of the Economic and Social Council, which was too infrequent.

20 The structure of the different institutions of higher education distributed according to the social or academic characteristics of the students or pupils which frequent them correspond quite exactly, in all cases where verification is possible, to the structure of the same institutions distributed according to the social and the academic characteristics of the teachers and lecturers: thus it is that the students more often have their origins in the dominant class or, within that class, in the economically more privileged fractions, such as industrialists and liberal professions, in the faculties of medicine and law than in the arts and science faculties. Moreover, we know that the faculties of medicine and law lead to professions of a higher rank in the economic hierarchy than the science and arts faculties, whose products are to a large extent destined to teach. We could build a rich epistemological and social commentary around the fact that it is sufficient to substitute the socio-logical order, that is to say university institute of technology (IUT), science, arts, law, medicine, pharmacy, for the order habitually adopted in official statistics: law, arts, science, medicine, pharmacy, IUT, and to proceed to an analogous operation on the level of the socio-professional categories, those two ordered in spite of common sense, in order to perceive a

more or less constant structure in the distributions (the rare discordances then assuming remarkable prominence) (cf. Ministère de l'Education Nationale, Service Central de la Statistique et de la Conjoncture, 'Les étudiants dans les universités, année scolaire 1967–68', *Statistiques des enseignements, tableaux et informations*, 5–2, 67–8, March 1968).

21 *Fondamentalistes* ('fundamentalists') are non-clinical medical staff engaged in pure research. [Tr.]

22 The data collected for a proportion (58 per cent) of professors of science and for the professors of medicine allow us to suppose that the hierarchy would be the same if we took into account the profession of the grandparents, paternal and maternal, or, because of the tendency towards homogamy, the professional status of the wife, with, for the arts and science faculties, a high percentage of teachers and, on the other side, a high percentage of doctors and non-working wives.

23 The Ecole Normale d'Instituteurs is a teacher-training college for primary schoolteachers; entrance is competitive. [Tr.]

24 Everything seems to indicate that the subjective and objective significance of declared membership of the Roman Catholic Church varies in frequency according to the whole of the faculty or the discipline and, secondarily, according to the more or less scientific and 'modernist' content of the discipline.

25 On this point as on so many others, whole monographs would be needed in order to determine the proportion of their salary in their global income, and the nature of their supplementary resources, which are themselves obviously connected to the structure of their *time-economy*. As regards university potential, extra lessons can be a source of considerable income, as can the royalties on bestselling textbooks (whose variations should be studied from faculty to faculty). None the less, the indirect *bonuses* must increase substantially as one moves from science to medicine.

26 Academic posts in France correspond roughly as follows to Anglo-Saxon ones:

FRANCE	UK	USA
professeur	professor	professor and chairman
maître de conférences	senior lecturer	professor
maître-assistant	lecturer	associate professor
assistant	assistant lecturer	assistant professor

[Tr.]

27 Cf. J. Nettelbeck, *Le Recrutement des professeurs d'université*, Paris, Maison des Sciences de l'Homme, 1979, roneotyped, pp. 80ff (statistical appendix).

28 On the financial consequences, as regards the sum of salary acquired during a whole career, and disparities between careers, cf. A. Tiano, *Les Traitements des fonctionnaires*, Paris, Genin, 1957, especially pp. 172ff.

29 The data collected for science and medicine allow us to suppose that the proportion of top grades in the *baccalauréat* follows the same pattern.

30 Sciences, Po, the Institut des Sciences Politiques; recruiting only postgraduates. Graduation usually ensures a top administrative post. [Tr.]

31 The original meaning of 'oblate' is a child from a poor family entrusted to a religious foundation to be trained for the priesthood. Bourdieu borrows the religious term to suggest the intensity of institutional loyalty felt by the teacher of humble origins who owes his whole education, culture, training and career to the state educational system. [Tr.]

32 We ought to analyse, for instance, the veritable Kula cycle shown in the exchange of visiting cards at the New Year among professors of medicine. [On the Kula cycle, 'where the armshells always go round in one direction and the necklaces in the other', see P. Bourdieu, *Reproduction*, tr. R. Nice, London, Sage, 1977, p. 112. (Tr.)]

33 Many law professors exercise functions as experts or consultants with public or private bodies, national (Ministry of Justice, for instance) or international (UNESCO), or as official delegates of government agencies (in international conferences, Common Market committees, the International Labour Organization, the United Nations, etc.). For example: 'I was the French government delegate to the conference at The Hague. . . . Now I am on a Common Market committee in Brussels every two months which is concerned with harmonizing all European legislation. Last year at the Ministry of Justice I was on a committee which was revising the statutes on nationality. Now I am still on the Brussels committee. For several years I was one of the experts on the committee of the International Labour Organization. . . .There are conferences. I am a member of the Institute of International Law' (a professor from the Paris law faculty).

34 Homais and Bournisien, characters in Flaubert's *Madame Bovary*, are a pretentious, positivistic pharmacist and a naïve, ignorant priest. [Tr.]

35 It is impossible to record all the consequences – most often prejudicial to the real progress of research – of the universalization of the model of the natural sciences under the combined influences of the organizational and technological models of these sciences and the bureaucratic logic which have led a body of research administrators, disposed by their training and their specific interests to a strictly technocratic vision, to know and acknowledge only 'projects' designed on the model of the natural sciences; thus it is that we have seen the accumulation of a whole series of vast, big-budget enterprises, using 'the latest technology' and

substantial contingents of the 'unskilled workmen' of research, dedicated to the fragmentary tasks which alone can be engendered by the programmes arising from the alliance of technocrats totally ignorant of the sciences they claim to administer or even direct, with researchers dispossessed enough to allow themselves to have the objects and objectives of their study imposed by a 'social need' elaborated in confused 'think-tank' sessions of committees, commissions and other assemblies of scientifically irresponsible 'scientific authorities'.

36 The same is true of professors of law, and, in many cases, of arts professors. Professors of law especially often identify research with *personal* work, linked to their teaching: 'I have no official functions as regards research, so the question is irrelevant. . . . The research one can carry out in present conditions remains a purely individual research which one does for oneself and at one's own expense. . . . I cannot dissociate teaching from research. All pedagogical activity implies research and all research leads inevitably sooner or later to pedagogical activity. . . . Everything we do, in very difficult circumstances, is immediately absorbed pedagogically and we are absolutely unable to distance ourselves enough to make any long-term preparation for research' (professor of public law, Paris).

37 This is true for all the faculties, the effect of contamination which academic power exercises over the representation of scientific authority being no doubt the greater, the less autonomous and formalized is the academic competence.

38 Nettelbeck, *Le Recrutement des professeurs d'université*, p. 44.

39 In the case of law, the candidates for the *agrégation* competitive examination are recruited from an intimate group of doctoral students, part-time assistants and assistant lecturers, that is to say from the people who have been able to make themselves known (cf. Nettelbeck, *Le Recrutement des professeurs d'université*, p. 25). In the case of medicine, the protection of a 'head' was an absolute condition of success – which meant that the competitive examination itself was often a pure fiction. This was the case in the *agrégation*, for instance, according to one of the professors questioned: 'Between you and me, it was a competitive examination for which we had absolutely no respect. We treated it as a free supplement, because you just had to know the examiners. So you only entered for it if your "head" was on the board of examiners. Between an *agrégé* and a hospital surgeon without the *agrégation*, there was no difference. . . . The *agrégation* wasn't a diploma, or, rather, it was a diploma, but there was no problem obtaining it' (a professor at the Paris medical faculty).

40 For *illusio*, see P. Bourdieu, *Outline of a Theory of Practice*, tr. R. Nice, Cambridge, 1978. [Tr.]

41 'Oh, there are doctors in my family on all sides. We really are a great medical family. My father was a doctor; of my four uncles, three were doctors. Of my eight cousins, there are at least four or five who are doctors, I haven't counted. My brother isn't a doctor, but he's a dentist, he's a professor at the Paris dental school. Truly, when we have a family reunion, *it's like a faculty committee*' (a professor at the Paris medical faculty).

42 J. Rivero, 'La Formation et le recrutement des professeurs des facultés de droit françaises', *Doctrina, Revista de derecho, jurisprudencia y administración* (Uruguay), 59, 1962, pp. 249–61. Jean Rivero was tenured professor of administrative law and director of the lecture course for the *agrégation* in public law at the Paris law faculty.

43 *Internes* are 'resident hospital doctors' and *externes* are 'junior hospital doctors'. Both posts were available to students who had completed their theoretical medical studies. Since the *interne* competition creamed off the best students, the *externe* posts were considered second best. [Tr.]

44 It has often been noted how important rhetoric, or even eloquence, is in the competitive examination for resident hospital doctors (cf. J. Hamburger, *Conseil aux étudiants en médecine de mon service*, Paris, Flammarion, 1963, pp. 9–10).

45 Everything leads us to suppose that this relation between the degree of objectification of the specific capital necessary for the production and the commercialization of the products and the differential chances of the new entrants, therefore of the entrance hurdles, can be seen in all the fields, starting with the economic field properly speaking. (Thus it is no coincidence that, within the field of cultural production, it is in the theatre sector, and especially that of the bourgeois theatre, that the greatest professional heredity could be found throughout the nineteenth century.)

46 We cannot entirely account for the opposition between a science subject and an arts subject without seeing that scientific practices are involved in the specifically social process of objectification and institutionalization: I refer, of course, to the role of writing as instrumental in the break with the mimetic immediacy of thought expressed orally, or to the role of all the formal symbolisms, especially logical or mathematical, which bring to their fruition the effects of objectification through writing, by substituting for intuition, even if geometrical, the autonomous logic of symbolism and its own evidence, 'the blind evidence' in the words of Leibniz, which arises from the symbols themselves (Leibniz also called it *evidentia ex terminis*). It is clear that such progress in objectification of methods of thought is always accomplished in and through the social forms which it presupposes and which it brings to fruition (dialectics, from which logic derives, being for instance indissociable from institutionalized

discussion, a kind of tournament between two adversaries in the presence of the public); and we could distinguish between subjects according to the degree of rationalization and formalization of the forms of communication which they employ.

47 We could use the same model to describe the relations between law and economics as established at the end of a progress towards self-sufficiency which released economics from the status of a series of ancillary disciplines (cf. L. Le Van-Lemesle, 'L'Economie politique à la conquête d'une légitimité (1896–1937)', *Actes de la recherche en sciences sociales*, 1983, 47–8, pp. 113–17).

48 This opposition is perfectly homologous to that established, in another field, between the engineer and the architect: in this case, the arts man can invoke the unavoidable exigencies of art (and secondarily of the art of living, that is to say of 'Man') to counter the inhuman and unaesthetic constraints of technique.

49 We hardly need hint at the specifically scientific repercussions of the hierarchy which arose between chairs, and which destined certain research chairs (such as the chair of bacteriology) to be merely holding positions for aspirants to a more prestigious clinical chair (for all these points, see the fine study by H. Jamous, *Contribution à une sociologie de la décision: la réforme des études médicales et les études hospitalières*, Paris, CES, 1967).

50 Cf. I. Kant, *Le Conflit des facultés*, Paris, Vrin, 1953, pp. 14–15, 28 and 37. The partial validity of the Kantian description leads us to ask what are the invariants in the university field, and suggests the need for a systematic comparison of the different national traditions in different periods.

51 Quoted by M. Foucault, *Naissance de la clinique: une archéologie du regard medical*, Paris, Presses Universitaires de France, 1963.

52 It is no coincidence that the law faculty has been so slow to renounce the external signs of statutory authority, the ermine and the gown being the indispensable instruments of the *work of representation* and display of authority of the texts and their interpreters which is an integral part of the very exercise of their function, that is, the act of producing law.

53 An important part of so-called theoretical work in philosophy, literature or law consists in trying to ground in reason notions in '-ism' (Marxism, naturalism or liberalism) which, as we shall see below for structuralism, are principally, if not exclusively, founded in social necessity.

54 We can see that the particular nature of its object, which it has in common, in its phenomenal definition, with the juridical subjects, places sociology in a quite special position: if it does happen that the opinion of scholars becomes an orthodoxy here, it is more often fated to be greatly dispersed because of the absence of strict academic and especially

social control over entrants to the profession and the correlative diversity of the social and academic origins of those producing the opinion.

55 In the university committee of support for the candidature of Valéry Giscard d'Estaing [when Giscard was standing for election as President of the Republic (Tr.)] (*Le Quotidien de Paris*, 17 May 1974), the professors of medicine, and of law and economics, were very strongly represented, especially in Paris: that is, respectively 28 and 18 out of 64 (as opposed to 10 from the arts and none from science) in Paris, and 18 and 14 out of 47 (opposed to 8 from the arts and 7 from science) in the provinces (in Paris, there were in addition five members of the Institute and one professor from the CNAM). The different lists of support for François Mitterrand do not allow so precise an estimate because of the fact that the titles, when they are given, are too vague. But the arts and science faculties were strongly represented.

56 When we consider public attitudes as more 'true' – or 'sincere' – than private opinions, such as those confided to friends, we forget how much these public demonstrations can be automatic, even *obligatory* – without necessarily being less 'sincere' – as when, for instance, they are part of a role being played, or a social identity being defended, etc. We might, in this perspective, analyse the influence that the general opinion concerning the 'true' opinion of an agent – 'X is left-wing' – can exercise, in different circumstances, on public expressions of opinion, since these may be motivated by the intention of confirming or denying this opinion.

57 The error of perception which makes professors from the arts faculties appear predominantly left-wing allows professors from these faculties who declare themselves publicly to be right-wing – and these are relatively rare, or at least were so before 1968 – to seem to themselves as well as to others rather heroic heretics, whereas, as we saw in May 1968, and if we except the general disapproval caused by any public expression of opinion or by journalistic compromise, they have the support of the great majority of their colleagues.

58 Trade-union membership in France is generally lower than in the UK. Moreover, there is often a choice of two or three different unions in each profession, the difference being defined by wider political sympathies. The SNESup (Syndicat National de l'Enseignement Supérieur) is the union for lecturers and professors of the 'traditional' left, tending to sympathize with the communist party, the SGEN (Syndicat Général de l'Enseigne-ment National) is the more radical-left alternative. Thus membership of the SNESup or the SGEN suggests varying degrees of overt left-wing sympathies, and membership of the Syndicat Autonome ('non-aligned union') may be seen as an overtly right-wing stance. [Tr.]

59 The AEERS (Association d'Etude pour l'Expansion de la Recherche Scientifique) is a study group for the expansion of scientific research. [Tr.]

60 An opposition of the same kind can be observed, at the heart of the arts faculty, between sociology and the canonical subjects which it may take as its object (as in the sociology of education) or whose object it may take (as in the sociology of art, literature or philosophy).

61 This note was drafted with the help of Marie-Ange Schiltz. For further details, see J.-P. Benzécri et al., *L'Analyse des données, vol. 2: L'Analyse des correspondances*, Paris, Dunod, 1973; P. Cibois, *L'Analyse factorielle*, Que Sais-Je?, no. 2095, Paris, Presses Universitaires de France, 1984; L. Lebart, A. Morineau and K. Warwick, *Multivariate Descriptive Statistical Analysis: Correspondence Analysis and Related Techniques for Large Matrices*, New York, Wiley, 1984. [The note, which has been written especially for the English edition of *Homo Academicus*, explains the method used to construct the three-dimensional model developed from Bourdieu's data. Different planes of this diagram are shown on pages 50, 80, 82 and 276 of the present edition. [Tr.]]

Chapter 3 Types of Capital and Forms of Power

1 No doubt all the greater, because of the expansion of the teaching body, for absorbing a large number of writers, journalist-writers and writer-journalists.

2 The faculties which, on a surface level, can be treated as homogeneous ensembles in terms of their objective relations as rivals can also, without contradiction, appear at another level of analysis as fields which are themselves subject to differences of different kinds.

3 We decided not to select direction of a laboratory as one of the properties determining belonging: it is in fact very difficult to distinguish the cases where this title is a statutory attribute of the professor, as often in the faculties or even, in more than one case, at the Ecole des Hautes Etudes, and the cases where it implies the effective direction of a real research team; so that we cannot treat it as an index of university power, nor as an index of scientificity or of being engaged in research.

4 Because of the fact that information available tends to diminish as renown diminishes, this selection procedure also has the practical advantage of facilitating research by limiting the proportion studied to the fraction of the base population most represented in the written sources. But we see what can be gained in rigour by limiting this population through explicit and specific (that is, pertinent) criteria, instead of allowing the limits of the population studied to be imposed by the limits of available documentation, as do for example all those who rely on sources like *Who's Who* (thus the proportion of professors studied who are mentioned in *Who's Who* is unequally linked to the different kinds of academic power – partly because mention in *Who's Who* is rejected by some of the most prestigious researchers, because it indicates 'society' consecration).

5 The journalist-professors are distinguished from journalists, and in particular from cultural journalists, who have an effect *on* the university field, by the fact that they can use *within* the university field itself the power that access to journalism gives them, with all its correlative profits. (Thus, to be strictly logical, we should have chosen this criterion, whose importance continues to increase, if only to enable us to account for certain university careers, especially at the 6th section of the Ecole des Hautes Etudes, and to account for the development of this institution as a whole.)

6 The enquiry underestimates specifically academic power because of the fact that, in more than one case, we were unable to take into account the *intensity* of the power associated with the possession of the attribute treated as indicator (for example, the status of president of a committee of the CNRS or the CCU, etc.) or the *duration* of the possession of this power: positions held in the same place, those of the great university heads who have dominated a whole discipline for many years, are no doubt less clearly distinguished in the analysis than in reality. On the other hand, we have not always been able to obtain, for the whole population, the most obviously pertinent information, such as the number of theses directed and the social status of the doctoral students (although we were able to verify, for some disciplines, that these indicators co-vary with indices of academic power). Finally, the introduction of supplementary principles of verification was inhibited by the fact that each one (for instance, the opposition between those published by Les Belles Lettres and those published by Klincksieck) concerned only a tiny sector of the field.

7 Among the factors of uncertainty, as much over whom to include in the population studied as over how to determine the position held within the field, one of the most important is the unequal wealth of information possessed depending on the quality of the sources: those who are known from seven or eight different sources are likely, other things being equal, to seem endowed with more properties than those who are only known from *Who's Who* and complementary sources of a lesser quality. Another factor is the often deliberate imprecision over the father's profession: this uncertainty particularly affects the categories of executives and traders (we had to abandon distinctions between middle and senior management and between small shopkeepers and larger traders) and even the category of teachers (the break is often unclear between teachers in secondary and teachers in higher education).

8 Whatever we may say of the effects of fashion, academic or intellectual prestige is much more stable than academic power, which is more closely linked with the *position* and less to its holder. (We know, however – and it is one of the most revealing characteristics of this field which claims to recognize only scientific values -- that there is no such thing, or hardly any such thing, as a genuine institutional criterion of scientific value.)

9 As far as the collection of information is concerned, we resorted to the same procedures and the same sources as in the case of the representative sample of the professors of the four faculties. With this difference, that we did not select participation in the conferences of Caen and Amiens and the religion of the family of origin, because of the fact that the positions marked enabled us to characterize only an insignificant fraction of the population; and, on the other hand, we added all the information on careers and positions of internal power which, on this scale, took on their full significance.

10 A similar analysis of the academic and non-academic factors of success for the whole set of the faculties encounters several obstacles: first, the indices of academic capital are not at all comparable (qualifications like the *agrégation* or the doctorate having very different values in the different faculties), and there exists no universal standard which would have the same role as the title of *normalien* does in the arts and science faculties; second, the differentiation of powers is not everywhere as clear as in the arts and does not operate everywhere according to the same principles. It remains the case, as we have seen, that geographical and social origins seem closely linked in all of the faculties to differences in success which can be perceived through the application of common criteria (external renown, scientific consecration, etc.)

11 We could no doubt link this opposition, inherent both in institutions and in personal dispositions, to the distinction established by Elga Reuter and Pierre Tripier between two forms of scientific production: on the one hand the 'minimizers', who aim to minimize the risks by producing works conforming in their objects and methods to the prevailing norms (such as the state doctorate) and, on the other hand, the 'professionals', who are usually attached to research institutions, and produce short works, making a swift scientific contribution (cf. E. Reuter et P. Tripier, 'Travail et creativité dans un marché interne: le cas du système français de recherche universitaire', *Sociologie du travail*, July–September 1980, pp. 241–56).

12 It is remarkable that the structure of relations described here is maintained as such, despite all the distortions, when one neutralizes – treating them as illustrative variables – the institutions belonged to, Collège de France, Sorbonne, EPHE 4th and 5th sections, 6th section, Nanterre.

13 See *Lire*, 68, April 1981, pp. 38–51.

14 The almost total exclusion of the non-university world, which is often affirmed as an elective refusal to compromise with society, is doubtless only a way of assuming an exclusion more or less cruelly felt in proportion to the increasing importance of journalism in intellectual life. Apart from evidence from holders of journalistic power (cf. the declaration by Mona Ozouf in C. Sales, 'L'intelligentsia, visite aux artisans de la culture', *Le Monde de l'éducation*, February 1976, p. 8),

we can invoke admissions such as this one by a Paris professor of philosophy, who, after declaring that one should 'keep a great distance between journalism and philosophical research', deplored the fact that, despite all his efforts, he had never managed to have an article published in *Le Monde*.

15 'One element of power is supervision of the theses which lead to appointment as lecturer and assistant lecturer. It is an essential means of action' (historian, 1971 – we have not been able, in this as in other cases, to give indications situating our informants more precisely in the space of the positions, without running the risk of betraying their anonymity).

16 The metaphor of 'social weight' perfectly expresses the logic of the field, the very logic that the analysis of correspondences allows to be reconstituted through a mathematical operation analogous to that which consists in seeking the axes of inertia of a system of weighted points.

17 The concentration in Paris of all the important state doctoral theses (that is, eleven theses in modern history that had obtained a 'very honourable' mention [*summum cum laude* (USA), or first class (UK)] between November 1939 and December 1948 inclusive – according to J.-B. Duroselle) gives total control over the recruitment of tenured staff.

18 To these positions, Pierre Renouvin finally added those of dean of the faculty of arts in Paris, and president of the Fondation Nationale des Sciences Politiques (cf. the obituary notice on Pierre Renouvin by J.-B. Duroselle, in *Revue d'histoire moderne et contemporaine*, 22, October–December 1975, pp. 497–507).

19 This is why, as I shall show, the crisis in relations between the old and the new entrants arises from a break in the harmony which used to obtain, for the great majority of new entrants, between the personally internalized structures of expectation (waiting) and the objective structures (likely trajectories), a break which is influenced simultaneously by the effects of a transformation of the structure of probabilities of promotion and of a modification in the dispositions of the agents. In such a conjuncture, the 'old' and the 'young' feel 'out of phase', the former seeing careerist ambition in what is experienced as a normal claim, and the latter seeing mandarinal conservatism in what is felt to be an appeal for ethical standards.

20 The LAFMA (Liste d'Aptitude à la Fonction de Maître-Assistant) is the waiting-list for *assistants* (assistant lecturers) nominated for promotion to posts of *maître-assistant* (lecturer). Vacant lectureships are filled from this list in order. During the period studied by Bourdieu there was a bottleneck, with more qualified candidates than vacancies. [Tr.]

21 While less institutionalized than bureaucratic power as it is exercised in public or private enterprise, power over the agencies of reproduction of the university body is much more institutionalized than the power of

consecration which is current in the field of cultural production. It is much less institutionalized, however, in the arts faculties than in the medical faculties, where the heads have at their disposal a whole series of institutionalized instruments of control, such as all the successive competitive examinations (junior hospital doctor, resident hospital doctor, assistant, *agrégation*, etc.).

22 Cf. T. Caplow and R. J. McGee, *The Academic Marketplace*, New York, Doubleday, 1965 (1st edn, 1958), p. 99.

23 The same logic can be seen at work in the private studios which in the nineteenth century prepared painters for the Prix de Rome. Everything was done to keep the pupils up to an advanced age in a state of absolute subordination to the master (there was, for example, a whole series of stages through which they had to pass – drawing from engraving, then from plaster casts, then from live models, painting, etc., at a speed determined by the master). Quite old people could be held back at the drawing stage. Nobody could tell how long they might have to spend at any particular stage. In a studio like that of Delaroche, famous for its success in the competition, only the most hardy could survive the discouragement induced by the manœuvres and intrigues (cf. A. Boime, *The Academy and French Painting in the Nineteenth Century*, London, Phaidon, 1971, and J. Lethève, *La Vie quotidienne des artistes français au XIXe siècle*, Paris, Hachette, 1968).

24 *Chargés d'enseignement* hold posts at the appropriate level of professor or senior lecturer, created where no titular post of professor was available. [Tr.]

25 Cf. Hobbes, *Leviathan*, ch. 10, 'Power'. [Tr.]

26 These calculations are based on the *Liste des thèses d'histoire contemporaine déposées dans les facultés de lettres de France métropolitaine, arrêtée au 1er octobre 1966* (N = 756, of which 347 state doctoral theses, 60 'complementary' theses, 271 'third cycle' theses and 78 'university' theses), a list drawn up at the request of the Association of Contemporary History Professors of the French History Faculties. A description of this document may be found in J.-B. Duroselle, 'Les thèses d'histoire contemporaine. Aires cultivées et zones en friche', *Revue d'histoire moderne et contemporaine*, January–March 1967, pp. 71–7.

27 This hierarchy, which is hardly different if we add 'complementary' theses, is modified quite profoundly if we take into consideration the ensemble of theses supervised, including 'third-cycle' theses (and *a fortiori* if we consider only these theses). Although Girard, Duroselle, Mollat and Perroy are still in the top ten and still in the same order, we note the entry of Rémond and Reinhardt and afterwards a whole group of professors from the Ecole des Sciences Politiques and the Ecole des Hautes Etudes. This gap is even more evident if we consider the

supervision of 'third-cycle' theses alone: Rémond (Nanterre, Sciences Po.), 44; Vilar (Sorbonne, EPHE), 20; Reinhardt (Sorbonne, Sciences Po.) 18; Chesnaux (EPHE), 14; Gagniagé (Sorbonne) and Grosser (Science Po.), 14; Lavau (Sciences Po.), 12; Hurtig (Sciences Po.), Lhuillier (Strasbourg), Touchard (Sciences Po.), 10 (the significance of these totals is limited by the fact that some professors – here, those of Sciences Po. – may also supervise theses registered in other disciplines, and therefore not counted).

28 At the time of the enquiry, lecturers and professors were expected to research for a *doctorat d'Etat* (state doctorate), which involved completing a vast principal thesis, as well as a smaller, complementary thesis, after a decade or even more of research. The *doctorat de troisième cycle* (third-cycle doctorate) was introduced in the late 1950s to provide a quicker type of research training for students, involving a short thesis to be written within about three years, before appointment to a teaching post. As Bourdieu's analysis shows, the philosophies behind the two doctorates were divergent. Since the French edition of *Homo Academicus* was published, the French government has decided to reform the system by phasing out the two existing doctorates and replacing them with a single *nouveau doctorat*. For the moment (1988) there are thus temporarily *three* doctorates in operation. [Tr.]

29 These calculations are based on a list, classified according to supervisors of theses (completed and passed) which were noted in an enquiry into researchers by the Maison des Sciences de l'Homme: the totals therefore underestimate the proportion of theses supervised, in comparison with the *Liste des travaux en grec, en latin* (Association des Professeurs de Langues Anciennes de l'Enseignement Supérieure, June 1971), all the more since not all the researchers or professors in a particular discipline answered the enquiry; but they do give a more accurate gauge than the lists of theses registered between any two relatively close dates, both of the number of theses supervised overall by each professor and of the social capital that they represent, since they note those theses intended to be realistically operative in the French academic market.

30 This list, which is based on the enquiry of the Maison des Sciences de l'Homme in 1967, calls for the same remarks as the list of theses in Greek studies. It is certain, in particular, that it underestimates the overall number of candidates: for instance, Henri Gouhier declares in an interview that he had a permanent number of 50–80 postgraduate students and that he participated in about fifteen vivas every year; another, less popular, professor says that, at the time of the enquiry, he had between 25 and 30 postgraduate students, whether candidates for the 'state' doctorate or for the 'third-cycle' doctorate, and that he participated in five or six vivas. The census of theses registered at the

Sorbonne for the years 1965 to 1968 inclusive (*Répertoire raisonné des sujets en cours des doctorats d'Etat – lettres et sciences humaines – inscrits en France, 1965–1970*, University of Paris X-Nanterre and Centre de Documentation Sciences Humaines) leads to a slightly different list, which is understandable, since it provides a better picture of the attraction of the different heads over a limited period of time than of the capital in clientele that they have accumulated in the course of their careers (thus Hyppolite, who entered the Collège de France in 1961 regresses, whereas Souriau and Wahl, who retired, disappear). A rigorous analysis would have to distinguish between academic generations – which do not coincide with biological generations and which mean that professors of the same biological age but who were appointed to the Sorbonne at different ages may be quite non-comparable as regards the number and status of their clientele; and also because the most powerful are often those who, having reached positions of power when they were young, have been in power longest.

31 Using the list of theses in philosophy already cited (theses registered and classified according to topic studied), we redistributed the theses between the different supervisors and attributed to each thesis the known characteristics of its author (as taken from the enquiry of the Maison des Sciences de l'Homme on researchers).

32 The comparison between the candidates of Ernest Labrousse, Director of Studies at the Ecole des Hautes Etudes as well as professor at the Sorbonne (or even Pierre Vilar, also a member of both institutions), and those of Louis Girard, professor at the Sorbonne, who was for a long time president of the CCU, shows us that things are different when the canonical university (as is the case in history) no longer has the monopoly of possible careers, because of the opportunities offered by other institutions such as the Ecole des Hautes Etudes or Sciences Po. While the pupils of Louis Girard have mostly had obscure careers or have made a name for themselves outside the university, like Louis Mermaz [socialist politician], Jean Ellenstein [ex-communist and historian] or Louis Mexandeau [socialist politician], a number of Ernest Labrousse's pupils have become some of the most prestigious historians of their generation and a large proportion of them have followed a career in the Ecole des Hautes Etudes (or at Vincennes).

33 We can understand in this light the obligatory elegy by the successor in honour of his predecessor, and its contents, inextricably mingling declarations of gratitude to the 'head' with professions of intellectual recognition of the 'master'.

34 It goes without saying that social necessity can only operate by disguising itself beneath a veneer of technical necessity. So the double bind linking the two necessities tends to become the rule, with the connivance of both parties, and constitutes one of the major obstacles to the institution

of genuine contracts of *apprenticeship* freely consented to, in which the constraints and controls imposed aim to prepare for their own disappearance, by providing the instruments of labour which are the condition of genuine intellectual liberty.

35 We shall see that power in an institution of cultural production or reproduction implies a specifically cultural form of authority, a sort of *institutional charisma*.

36 Cf. J. Heurgon, obituary notice of Marcel Durry, *Bulletin de l'association Guillaume Budé*, 1, 1978, pp. 1–3, and P. Grimal, *Revue d'études latines*, 55, 1977, pp. 28–32.

37 F. Robert, *Bulletin de l'association Guillaume Budé*, 1, March 1980, pp. 1–4, and P. Grimal, *Revue d'études latines*, 5, 1979, pp. 29–31.

38 In this perspective, it is impossible to overestimate the importance of the *syllabuses* which play a determining role in the conditioning of the clientele – students and future masters – by defining the world of *academically profitable* bodies of knowledge and by thus contributing to produce and reproduce *syllabuses of thought*.

39 In the phrase 'les miraculés du mérite' Bourdieu links the idea of a meritocratic elite with the idea of privileged escape from otherwise certain social disaster. *Un miraculé* is commonly a miraculously lucky survivor of some normally fatal accident. [Tr.]

40 L. Spitzer, *Etudes de style*, preface by J. Starobinski, Paris, Gallimard, 1970, p. 165, n. 26, and p. 159, no. 2.

41 Candidates for entrance to a *grande école* spend as much as two years after the *baccalauréat* cramming for the *grandes écoles* entrance examination in a *classe préparatoire*, which is to be found only at a few of the most prestigious *lycées*. The arts class is a *khagne*, the science class a *taupe*. [Tr.]

42 This is no doubt even truer in the faculties of law or medicine, where an air of reliability, as an index of support for the values of bourgeois normality, is all the more strongly required since the opposition between brilliance and respectability is not pertinent, and since the most brilliant are also the most reliable, showing most clearly and quickly their support for the traditions of the community (this precocious reliability does not, however, exclude controlled and statutory debauch, that is, ritually limited in social time and space, quite the contrary).

43 E. Haugen, *Language Conflict and Language Planning*, Cambridge, Mass., Harvard University Press, 1966, p. 4.

44 'Que Sais-Je?' is a Penguin-type paperback series providing introductory guides to, or surveys of, different areas of knowledge, over the whole range of the arts and sciences. [Tr.]

45 We know the links existing between the Presses Universitaires de France and professors at the Sorbonne, *ex officio* general editors of the major series, which publish subsidized theses and works of synthesis socially

approved by institutional authority. (We ought to analyse in terms of the same logic the functions and the ambiguous role of the university presses (Ateliers d'Imprimerie Universitaire).)

46 At the other pole of the field, the hit-parade effect operates through the medium of the papers and above all the cultural weeklies, which allow direct access, in certain conjunctures, to the student public.

47 It would have been interesting to measure the intensity of orientation towards teaching by counting the number of 'extra' teaching hours in the 'home' institution or elsewhere: all the indications are that, the nearer we move towards the pole of the 'reproducers', the more frequently we encounter those able to garner considerable economic profit by an often very economic proliferation, intellectually speaking, of lectures on the same entrance examination syllabus, especially for the *agrégation*, at the Sorbonne, at the Ecole Normal Supérieure, at the Ecole Sévigne, etc.

48 On the power bases in the faculties of medicine, see especially H. Jamous, *Contribution à une sociologie de la décision*, Paris, CES, 1967, pp. 108–11.

49 This medieval Latin term for lecturers (literally 'readers') indicates their role as unquestioning broadcasters of received dogma. [Tr.]

50 The proportion of 'eminent academics' has, it seems, increased since 1968 as a result of the reconciliation, provoked by the crisis, between great scholars and grand orators, until then strongly opposed.

51 Given the extreme closure of the canonical university to everything alien to it, the marginal institutions, and especially the Ecole des Hautes Etudes, have been the refuge for German émigrés between the wars and émigrés from eastern Europe after 1945.

52 We could also invoke the case of Georges Dumézil, whose career developed to a considerable extent abroad and entirely outside the canonical university.

53 If we find religious specialists (for instance Festugière, a historian of Greek religion) among the most eminent specialists, it is no doubt because their academic vocation is linked to the ethico-religious dispositions of minorities who had to justify their place within the lay university through the excellence of their research (the presence of 'survivors' originating in the subordinate classes should perhaps be understood in terms of the same logic); as for left-wing Roman Catholics, like Marrou, their presence in academically advanced positions is explained by the fact that they have had to assert themselves both against the dominant lay tradition and against the majority Roman Catholic position which is to be found towards the pole of belles-lettres (Heurgon, Courcelles, etc.) and towards the pole of the 'humanist' reaction against the republican tradition (Roman Catholic censorship here taking the form of a literary censorship appealing to etiquette and elegance).

54 The more we move towards the pole of research, the more we see an increase in the likelihood of a gap between specifically symbolic capital and academic status, some of the most prestigious intellectuals holding quite minor university posts (as, at the time of the enquiry, Louis Althusser, Roland Barthes or Michel Foucault).

55 Director, Fernand Braudel. [Tr.]

56 Director, Claude Lévi-Strauss. [Tr.]

57 Director, Fernand Braudel. [Tr.]

58 Director, Jean-Pierre Vernant. [Tr.]

59 If the principal originality of the Ecole des Hautes Etudes, that is, the decisive contribution which it has brought to the development of genuine research in the social sciences, is minimized, it is also because the enquiry grasps it at a moment when its most successful investments have already brought in substantial profits, but which are often attributed to other institutions (notably the Collège de France).

60 Relations with foreign countries, and especially the United States, are one of the most powerful principles of differentiation between agents, disciplines and institutions, and by the same token one of the most contentious stakes of the symbolic struggles for recognition. The 6th section of the Ecole des Hautes Etudes is one of the high spots of academic 'internationalism'; it has been the centre of importation of a number of academic novelties and also one of the most important centres of exportation abroad (especially in the domain of history and semiology).

61 The Ecole des Hautes Etudes in social science has thus become the focus of exchanges between the university field and the field of journalism. Those, like François Furet, who possess both power over a university institution, that is over posts and careers, and power over the press and publishing, are able to accumulate and exercise a considerable symbolic power through a circuit of very complex exchanges between goods which are current in the academic field, such as posts, promotion, and the services current in the journalistic field, such as book reviews and celebratory articles.

62 R. Picard, *Nouvelle critique ou nouvelle imposture*, Paris, Pauvert, 1965, p. 84; and *Le Monde*, 14 and 28 March, 4 and 11 April 1964.

63 J. Piatier, 'La "nouvelle critique" est-elle une imposture?', *Le Monde*, 23 October 1965.

64 J. Bloch-Michel, 'Barthes–Picard: troisième round', *Le Nouvel Observateur*, 30 March–5 April 1966.

65 R. Barthes, *Critique et vérité*, Paris, Seuil, 1966, p. 53.

66 *Tel Quel* is an intellectual review combining literary structuralism with ultra-left politics. [Tr.]

67 *Le Monde*, 5 February 1966. Others add Mauron or Rousset.

68 A list of articles in favour of Raymond Picard may be found in Barthes, *Critique et vérité*, p. 10, n. 1.

69 R. Matignon, 'Le Maintien de l'ordre', *L'Express*, 2–8 May 1986.
70 Picard, *Nouvelle critique ou nouvelle imposture*, p. 69.
71 Ibid., p. 72.
72 Ibid., pp. 78–9.
73 R. Picard, 'Un nihilisme confortable', *Le Nouvel Observateur*, 13–19 April 1964.
74 E. Guitton, *Le Monde*, 13 November 1965.
75 Barthes, *Critique et vérité*, p. 13.
76 Ibid., p. 14.
77 'How can we deny Pascal, Racine and Mallarmé the insight which might be granted them by social science, psychoanalysis, Marxism and sociology? How, in the days of abstract painting and quantum physics, can we leave criticism with only those tools which it had at its disposal in the days of Galileo and Philippe de Champaigne?' (R. Matignon, *L'Express*, 2–8 May 1966).
78 'When we read Raymond Picard, we sometimes feel as if we are sitting an examination for the *baccalauréat*' (J. Duvignaud, *Le Nouvel Observateur*, 3–9 November 1965).
79 Cf. C. Charle, *La Crise littéraire à l'époque du naturalisme*, Paris, Pens, 1970, pp. 157ff, and A. Compagnon, *La Troisième République des lettres*, Paris, 1983.
80 'L'homme et l'œuvre' ('The man and his work') are series of literary monographs providing students' guides to major authors, based on a traditional biographical and descriptive approach. [Tr.]
81 The opposition between the modernist defenders of scientific culture who find allies among senior civil servants and scientific administrators, privileged purveyors of technocratic modernism and holders of a new power, different both from the power of production and the power of reproduction, and the traditionalist defenders of literary culture, must not disguise the emergence of a third pole, that of economico-political culture, whose importance tends to grow in proportion to its increase in symbolic efficiency in the political field. (Analysis of replies to the national enquiry of the AEERS on the university shows that the pure technocratic position, which would subordinate all the functioning of the academic system to imperatives of productivity, is practically not represented in the professorial body, but that there is a substantial contingent of professors, especially in the science faculties, who agree with the top state executives in hoping for a kind of scientific rationalization. Their concern to see scarce scientific resources increased and concentrated coincides with the technocrats' desire to rationalize the use of scientific resources.)
82 This student public has no doubt played a decisive role, right through the nineteenth century, in the progress of the intellectual and artistic field towards autonomy (in relation to the academic authorities in

particular) by providing 'avant-garde' production with what only 'bourgeois art' enjoyed, that is a public large enough to justify the development and the functioning of specific instances of production and diffusion (which is clear enough in the case of avant-garde cinema) and thereby contributing to making the intellectual field close in on itself. It remains true that the same recourse to a public outside the field can serve just as easily to form the basis of real innovations as to legitimize incompetence and conservatism (as, for example, in the resort to politicization, which has often been used, even in painting, as an excuse for incompetence or failure).

83 Cf. appendix 3.

84 The social sciences are also a refuge for some of the specialists of the 'hard' sciences, often inclined to pay compulsory homage to their original milieu, which still dominates them, by making a critical and pejorative representation of the social sciences, whose specific logic they often have difficulty mastering; and all the while using their specific capital to threaten social science with a sort of methodological censorship, which often enough lacks any grounding in the real logic of science.

85 Cf. chapter 4 below.

86 The appearance of this new market has transformed the distribution of opportunities among the professors themselves, especially in geography, and in sociology. This was noted by one observer, conscious that new criteria of appreciation and new capacities were henceforth at issue: 'There are more and more organizations: what counts is access to money, to travel subsidies, to work funded by the Ministry, by the District, by the Paris regional council, etc., and then it isn't necessarily the intellectual level which counts in attributing the money' (geographer, 1972).

87 For an ideal-typical expression of the *claim* for a new definition of the intellectual, see M. Crozier, 'La Révolution culturelle', *Daedalus*, December 1963.

88 The authoritative centre-left newspaper *Le Monde* is published in the evening, instead of in the morning with the other French daily papers. [Tr.]

89 It is certain that the rise of the ENA at the expense of the ENS has contributed considerably to this transformation of the dominant representation of the intellectual.

90 Among the imperceptible transformations which only statistics can reveal, one of the most important is the considerable growth in the number of salary-earning producers, which is linked to the development of radio, television and public and private research organizations, that is to the intellectual craftsman.

91 As regards sharing time between teaching and research, there is a very marked opposition between the two extreme poles represented by on the one hand the professors of the canonical disciplines of the arts

faculties (or, at a pinch, the professors of the preparatory classes for the *grandes écoles*) and on the other hand the professors and researchers in social science who can devote themselves more completely to research. The same kind of opposition can be found as regards the relation between training received and professional practice: the perfect continuity which characterizes the academic and professional career of professors of *khagne* and *taupe* and, almost to the same extent, those of professors of literature and language, is opposed to the more or less total discontinuity which is displayed (and sometimes deliberately underlined, in an effort to display their conversion and their rejection) in the case of the social science researchers (cf. below, chapter 4).

92 The differential dependency of the different species of academic capital on the academic market may also be very easily seen on the occasion of emigration to a foreign country: the loss in value which affects all academically guaranteed cultural capital seems to affect more strongly those kinds most directly linked to the specificities of a national academic institution, like literary history or law.

93 The effect of statutory monopoly is never so clearly seen as at the time of the individual crises which are occasioned by retirement: the end of the most tyrannical reign has often been marked by a sudden collapse in the exchange rate of these compulsory authors.

94 The relations between philosophy and social science obey the same logic, with the difference that a fraction of the 'philosophers' managed to escape the common destiny (as also, it is true, did a – minute – fraction of 'grammarians') at the cost of more or less bold reconversion strategies, tending among other things to 'found', to 'conceptualize' or to annex the social sciences – especially structuralism – and thus to save at least the appearance of their former ambition and dominance. The fate of those who have remained faithful to the old definition of their post is all the more difficult. The social sciences, and especially ethnology and sociology, which in the fifties appeared as soft options, somewhat despised by those who were able to follow the royal way of the Ecole Normale and the *agrégation*, may now appear to them as offering an intolerable threat to philosophy and, in any case, as capable of usurping the imperial position always claimed by this discipline.

95 [For example, A. Martinet. (Tr.)] Of the philologist whose name remains associated with the most ferocious resistance to the movement of May 1968 [Frédéric Deloffre], an informer says: 'He was a pure product of what used to be called the "grammatical" *agrégation*; his thesis was a thesis on lexicography or lexicology. . . . He is a person who . . . well, it was he who said it . . . he was very proud to have been the top student of his graduation year [at the Ecole Normale] and to pass his doctorate and he had deliberately chosen that kind of specialization. In

fact, grammar was for him less an object of study than a career objective. He has said it over and over again. Just as he boasted of not preparing his lectures' (classics, 1971).

96 We need to bear these analyses in mind in order to understand the desperate, and in a certain sense pathetic, reactions, when confronted with the movement of May 1968, of these major or minor holders of cultural shares which were suddenly devalued like tsarist bonds after the Soviet Revolution (cf. chapter 5).

Chapter 4 The Defence of the Corps and the Break in Equilibrium

1 Since we cannot reproduce here the analysis of the factors of the increase in schooling, we can but refer to P. Bourdieu, 'Classement, déclassement, reclassement', *Actes de recherche en sciences sociales*, 24, November 1978, pp. 2–22, and *Distinction*, tr. R. Nice, Cambridge, Mass., Harvard University Press, 1984.

2 See appendix 2 for the data on the morphological transformations of the student population; of the professorial body (by rank), the staff/student ratio and the inter-rank ratio (rank A/rank B) in the various faculties between 1949 and 1969.

3 If, in the case of the analysis of the long-term fluctuations in the overall value of academic diplomas, we have chosen to study the social destiny of *normaliens* from two different matriculation years, it is because the title of graduate of the Ecole Normale Supérieure (as opposed to the various *agrégations* and *a fortiori* the various bachelor's degrees) doubtless provides the academic qualification whose value is most constant in the various markets where it is negotiable, that is in the various academic sub-markets and even in the external markets (although to a lesser degree, because of the devaluation incurred by competition from ENA).

4 In the arts faculties, the number of professors or the number of doctorates varies very little between 1949 and 1969, while the number of lecturers and assistant lecturers increases very rapidly, especially after 1959. Moreover, the number of third-cycle theses increases at a very fast rate, although the *agrégation* continues to hold a central place.

5 The analyses which follow are based on statistical data taken from the enquiry (already used above) which was carried out in 1967–8 by the Maison des Sciences de l'Homme. Initially conceived for the preparation of an Annual Directory, this enquiry had been designed from the start in such a way as to be an object of scientific enquiry, and M. Jean Viet, director of the project, gave us the opportunity to help draw up the questionnaire and insert a set of detailed questions on social origins.

Although it attracted a very high rate of reply (reaching around 80 per cent overall, and varying between 86 per cent in history and 67 per cent in literary studies), this enquiry suffers from the defects inherent in any enquiry by correspondence. If we know, as we have been able to verify elsewhere, that the propensity to reply varies as a function of the degree of identification, that the authorities had set themselves as prime objective an exhaustive census of the researchers and teachers at the top of the hierarchy, and finally that the identification of the teachers of rank B is both more difficult and less reliable, we can understand that the teachers of rank B are slightly underrepresented in all disciplines, as is revealed by a systematic comparison of the structures of the population sampled and the structures of the whole population of teachers in higher education. According to the same logic, people from the provinces and women appear somewhat underrepresented in relation to Parisians and men.

6 Thus sociology, which only found a place in the arts faculties in the framework of a degree certificate in philosophy (certificate in ethics and sociology) and whose teaching body was distinguished from that of philosophy neither by its mode of recruitment nor by the style of its research, becomes independent in 1958, with the creation of a degree in sociology, at the very moment when the largest cohorts of students enter the faculties.

7 See appendix 2.2.

8 Analysing the disturbances in the matrimonial market following the First World War, Halbwachs shows how 'the extremely strong reduction (by nearly a quarter) of the male population (reaching maturity between 1900 and 1915) including, by the end of the war, age categories from 23 to 38' had as its consequence 'to raise the young in the age-scale (and perhaps to lower the older by a few rungs)' (cf. M. Halbwachs, 'La nuptialité en France pendant et depuis la guerre', repr. in *Classes sociales et morphologie*, Paris, Minuit, 1972, pp. 231–74).

9 Thus we see that those research workers in sociology who left research to enter higher education have a higher level of training than those who stayed in research: 46 per cent of the researchers of rank B who became teachers are *agrégés* or graduates of the ENS, whereas the whole set of researchers of rank B has only 9.5 per cent of *agrégés* or graduates of the ENS. Similarly, for rank A, the proportion of *agrégés* or graduates of the ENS is respectively 50 per cent for the research workers who went into teaching and 21 per cent for the whole set of research workers.

10 As we have seen, in recent times, with the massive integration of the 'hors-statut' (that is, 'statusless' temporary, unqualified staff).

11 This gap between the forced transformation of the principles of recruitment and the preservation of the principles of promotion is

doubtless a very general phenomenon, which can be observed every time that a professional body aims to defend itself against the threat introduced by the quality and quantity of new entrants: for example, in the case of the personnel of municipal libraries (cf. B. Seibel, *Bibliothèque municipale et animation*, Paris, Dalloz, 1983, p. 95).

12 These statistical data are taken from an analysis of the replies to the national consultation carried out in 1969 by the Association d'Etudes pour l'Expansion de la Recherche Scientifique (on this enquiry, see appendix 1, pp. 241–2).

13 In a more general fashion, this enquiry shows that the teachers are all the more indifferent to a property (Latin, the *agrégation*, the *grandes écoles*) as their present standing depends less on that property, even if that standing has only been acquired thanks to the initial possession of this property.

14 I need hardly add that, having long denounced what I call *pessimistic functionalism* and, with the notion of the *habitus*, having provided a means of accounting for the appearance of objective teleology presented by certain collectivities, I in no way recognize myself in some of the labels, like those of 'sociologism', 'totalitarian realism' or 'hyperfunctionalism', which are sometimes applied to me (cf. F. Bourricaud, 'Contre le sociologisme: une critique et des propositions', *Revue française de sociologie*, 16, 1975, supplement, pp. 583–603, and R. Boudon, *Effets pervers et ordre social*, Paris, PUF, 1977, or more recently, I. Elster).

15 I am thinking, for instance, of the (incidentally very sympathetic) review of one of my books which said: 'This [linguistic] competence resembles an amount of capital, remunerated with prestige and power. Its holders *defend* it as one protects a market, and *supervise* the linguistic capital to *keep* it unequally shared. *It is important that,* over ordinary language, there *should reign* an erudite language, difficult of access, susceptible only of being written, published, quoted as an example.'

16 M. Butor, *Répertoire*, vol. 2, Paris, Minuit, pp. 214 and 228.

17 This error inherent in the scholarly posture is compounded when the scientific enquiry tries to comprehend in an artificial situation the acts of classification and criteria utilized.

18 'Who asked you to enter higher education? – Things don't present themselves in such a clear fashion. When I was a student at the Ecole Normale, the director was called M. Bouglé. He had sympathized with me and asked me to prepare a thesis. That is why he called on me to work with him for three years as assistant lecturer at the Ecole. That is what stimulated my career. At that time, access to posts in higher education was difficult' (philosophy professor, 1972).

19 We can recognize the conservative orientation of the Syndicat Autonome (non-aligned union) without thereby conferring a patent of progressive-

ness on the SNESup or on the SGEN, this whole analysis having the result of showing up what is hidden by the published oppositions.

20 P. Bourdieu, *La Distinction*, p. 182.

21 This is clear enough in the enquiry into power in the arts faculties which establishes (cf. above, chapter 3) that the distribution of the different powers is closely linked to age (which is easy to understand, since, being applied to a population defined by a minimal possession of powers, it confronts the really powerful with the potentially powerful): the young have the factors of power (the Ecole Normale, etc.) but they do not yet have all its attributes and benefits.

22 All these efforts were no doubt compounded in the small provincial faculties where, because of the small number of teachers, the members of rank B often assumed the same pedagogical functions as the tenured professors (teaching *agrégation* and CAPES classes, supervising masters' degree theses), reinforcing the not-unambiguous propensity towards advance identification with a professorial post. In general, we would have to analyse in greater detail this other principle of division of the field, that formed by the opposition between Paris and the provinces (the two populations we have analysed are strictly Parisian): although, as far as we know, the hierarchy of the cities corresponds roughly to the implicit hierarchy of the faculties, and although centralization makes Paris the ideal conclusion to any successful career, membership of a local society can give rise to specific and not negligible powers, and each provincial faculty has its *academic dignitaries* who, although unknown or discounted in national or international circles, participate in the agencies of local power (planning organizations, regional committees, municipal councils, etc.).

23 'Do you think that you should have submitted your thesis earlier? – In terms of my career, it was impossible . . . in terms of the state of readiness of the thesis . . . on the other hand, I think I could have' (history professor, 1972). And most of the professors questioned reply negatively to the question, even when they have gone on beyond what is considered as the *normal duration* (one arts professor who devoted fourteen years to preparing his thesis deploring only too long a wait between his viva and publication).

24 'Well, we must admit that a delay of ten years, since I took the *agrégation* in 1936 and finished my thesis at the beginning of 1947, is normal for a state thesis, it's normal in the arts, that's what we expect. . . . I haven't calculatd the statistics, but, after all, it isn't a thing you can rush. Ten years, in my opinion, is a reasonable time-scale' (Greek professor, 1972).

25 If they are striking through their exceptional character, the accelerated careers of the outsiders are hardly apparent statistically. Everywhere the *normaliens* and the *agrégés* have careers more rapid than the other

categories of teachers, and this gap is stronger in the social sciences (where they are fewer) than in the other disciplines: thus, in sociology, only 10 per cent of the graduates of the ENS with rank B posts are 36 or over as opposed to 23 per cent of the *agrégés* not from the ENS and 36 per cent with an ordinary university degree, whereas in the arts 41 per cent of the graduates of the ENS with rank B posts are 36 or over, against 65 per cent of the *agrégés* and 67 per cent of the faculty graduates.

26 We would have to analyse all the changes in the representations and the practices which this situation has caused, such as the appearance of forms of bargaining and compromise between categories (rank A and rank B) or between unions on the Universities Consultative Committee or on the CNRS, etc.

Chapter 5 The Critical Moment

1 H. Poincaré *Congrès de physique de 1900*, vol. 1, 1900, p. 22, quoted by G. J. Holton, *Thematic Origins of Scientific Thought*, Cambridge, Mass., Harvard University Press, 1973.

2 On the subject of this contrast, see P. Bourdieu, 'Le marché des biens symboliques', *L'Année sociologique*, 22, 1971, pp. 49–126.

3 Because of the fact that the educational system tends to become the official means of apportioning the right to hold a steadily growing number of positions, and one of the means of preservation or transformation of the structure of class relations through the mediation of the maintenance or change in the number and (social) status of the holders of positions in this structure, the number of individual or collective agents (parents' associations, administration, managing directors, etc.) who are interested in its functioning and claim to modify it, because they expect it to provide satisfaction of their interests, is tending to increase. We can see indications of this process in the extension of parents' associations to the middle classes, in the creation of a new type of common association whose action is directed principally at the education system, in the presence of specific pressure groups – such as those organizing the congresses of Caen, Amiens and Orleans – uniting managers, technocrats and teachers (and, secondarily, in the place reserved for problems of education in the newspapers, which all today have their 'specialist', if not a group of them, or even the proportion of questions devoted to these problems in opinion polls).

4 Cf. P. Bourdieu, *Distinction*, tr. R. Nice, Cambridge, Mass., Harvard University Press, 1984, p. 138. [Tr.]

5 These reflections and interrogations can, it seems, be used to explain any crisis (or revolution). If we fail to perceive the logic of the different fields as such, are we not tempted either to posit as self-evident the

unity of revolutionary events or on the contrary to treat different local crises as successive moments corresponding to different groups (aristocratic, parliamentary or peasant revolution, etc.), driven by the different motors of a cumulative series of separate crises liable in the last resort to be subjected to separate explanations? If every revolution actually encloses several interconnected revolutions and thus refers us back to several causal systems, should we not in addition ask what are the causes and effects of the integration of the specific crises, etc?

6 On this point and especially on the specifically *statistical* logic of academic reproduction and on the unifying effects of the common experience of devaluation, see P. Bourdieu, 'Classement, déclassement, reclassement', *Actes de la recherche en sciences sociales*, 24 November 1968, p. 223, and *Distinction*.

7 Thus we see that all the (numerous) explanations of the crisis of May 1968 along the lines of the conflict of generations (in the ordinary sense) have been deceived by appearances. I note in addition that the devaluation of diplomas had completely different effects according to the social origins of the agents concerned.

8 Among the reasons which limit the validity of the analogy of inflation – to which I resorted in a previous phase of my work (cf. P. Bourdieu, *L'Inflation des titres scolaires*, roneotyped, Montreal, 1973) – there is the fact that the agents can counter this devaluation with individual or collective strategies, such as those which consist in producing *new markets* able to enhance their diplomas (creating new professions) or to more or less completely modify the criteria defining the right to hold the dominant positions and, concomitantly, defining the structure of these positions within the field of power.

9 A *bachelier* is a holder of the *baccalauréat* (equivalent to GCE A level, and still a sufficient guarantee of university entrance in most disciplines except medicine), i.e. a successful school-leaver. [Tr.]

10 [The CAP (*certificat d'aptitude professionnelle*), the professional aptitude certificate, is awarded after technical training and/or apprenticeship. (Tr.)] Cf. G. Adam, F. Bon, J. Capdevielle and R. Mouriaux, *L'Ouvrier français en 1970*, Paris, A. Colin, 1970, pp. 223–4.

11 Many interactions, and even more or less durable social relations, have as their principle an objective reinforcement of those defence mechanisms of which our visions of the social world are always an element (albeit to very variable degrees).

12 The return to reality, a genuine *return of the social repressed* (which has nothing to do with what is normally understood by a 'sudden realization'), and the collapse of the defences long opposed to the discovery of the objective truth of the position held, can take the form of a crisis whose violence is no doubt all the greater for having been so long deferred (cf. the 'mid-life crisis'), and which can find in the collective crisis a trigger

and an opportunity to express itself in a more or less sublimated form (as witness all the cases of moral or political conversion associated with the crisis of May 1968).

13 This model does not allow us an exact understanding of individual reactions to the crisis: these depend on dispositional variables linked to social origins, on positional variables linked to the position of the discipline and the individual's position within the discipline (university status and intellectual prestige), and on conjunctural variables, especially the intensity of the crisis and of the criticism of the university institution, which depends on the discipline (and on its Parisian or provincial location) and on the positions adopted most frequently by agents of the same rank or status.

14 A CEG (*collège d'enseignement général*) is a comprehensive secondary school (non-selective, unstreamed, as opposed to the *lycée*, entry to which is reserved for the most academically successful pupils). [Tr.]

15 A CET (*collège d'enseignement technique*) is a technical school for non-academic pupils; an IUT (*institut universitaire de technologie*) is a university institute of technology, providing specialist higher education in science and technology to about second-year university level. [Tr.]

16 Historians of the future will perhaps find in police archives the information necessary to test the model.

17 To those who would see an exception in the role which a number of students of the Ecole Normale Supérieure held in subversive movements, before and during May 1968, it should suffice to recall that the period 1960–70 was marked by a decline in the academic position of the Ecole Normale and also, no doubt, in the social positions offered to its graduates – despite the increase in the appointment of *normaliens* in the faculties – which coincides with a rise in the social origins of the pupils. Thus the proportion of sons of members of the liberal professions, engineers and senior managers rose from 38 per cent between 1958 and 1965, to 42 per cent between 1966 and 1973, and 43.3 per cent between 1974 and 1977 for the ENS de la rue d'Ulm, from 14 per cent between 1956 and 1965, to 28 per cent between 1966 and 1973, and 32.2 per cent between 1974 and 1979 for the ENS de Saint-Cloud (J. N. Luc and A. Barbé, *Histoire de l'Ecole Normale Supérieure de Saint-Cloud*, Paris, Presses de la FNSP, 1982, table 10, p. 254, and table 6, p. 248).

18 It seems in general that the crisis took on quite different forms in the small faculties in the provinces, where the size of the student populations concerned and the 'reserves' of political leaders were less significant, and where, as we have seen, the relations between the grades were qualitatively very different.

19 The two processes which thus find themselves *synchronized* have their *raison d'être* (at least partially) outside the field, the first in the whole set of factors determining the general expansion of access to secondary

and higher education and the differential distribution of pupils of different social origins between the faculties and the disciplines; the second in the relationships between the different sectors of the university field and the labour market or, in other words, between the different diplomas and posts offered on the labour market at the moment under consideration, with the effects of differential 'devaluation' which affect those same diplomas and, more or less strongly according to their inherited social capital, their different owners.

20 In the majority of disciplines, the researchers are of higher social origins than the teachers: 58 per cent of the researchers in sociology, 52 per cent of the researchers in psychology and 56.5 per cent of the researchers in geography are from the upper classes, as opposed to 50, 40 and 40.5 per cent of the teachers in the same discipline. This is a comprehensible phenomenon, since the chances nowadays of gaining access to a career in research depend fundamentally on the possibility of maintaining oneself in the situation of a student or research assistant (which, despite grants and vacations, supposes economic dispositions and means reserved in fact for the more privileged) long enough to become established in a research unit (thanks to connections, which are also unevenly distributed) or to gain the support of an influential 'head'.

21 Cf. G. Canguilhem, *Idéologie et rationalité dans l'histoire des sciences de la vie*, Paris, Vrin, 1977, pp. 33–45.

22 We can see that the peculiar intensity of conflicts in the field of sociology is no doubt due above all to the dispersed nature of the professional body, and that we can in no case interpret this, as has often been done, as an index of a lesser degree of scientificity in the discipline.

23 We have shown how certain assistant lecturers in the science faculties are led to move closer towards their students and to abandon their magisterial role, in order to escape from the difficulties which are caused for them by their rivalry with the professors and the *normaliens*, whose 'threat' is often mentioned in the interviews, even though they too may be simply assistant lecturers like themselves (P. Bourdieu, 'Epreuve scolaire et consécration sociale, les classes préparatoires aux grandes écoles', *Actes de la recherche en sciences sociales*, 39, September 1981, pp. 3–70).

24 J.-Y. Caro, 'Formation à la recherche économique: scénario pour une réforme', *Revue économique*, 34, 4 July 1983, pp. 673–90.

25 The UNEF (Union National des Etudiants de France) is a left-wing students' union, generally sympathizing with the Communist Party. [Tr.]

26 Since we can reveal here neither the ethnological data noted in the field, which are inevitably partial and disorganized – because of the practical impossibility of totalization – nor a narrative constructed from observations and eyewitness accounts, we can only refer the reader who wants

an evocation of the atmosphere to the pages which Flaubert devotes to the 1848 Revolution in *Sentimental Education* and especially to the subject of the practices whose *principle* is given above, the circuit of 'clubs' where 'systems of public happiness' are elaborated and where 'subversive motions' abound ('Down with academies! Down with the Institute!', etc.).

27 Cf. B. B. Malinovski, 'The problem of meaning in primitive languages', supplement 1, in C. K. Ogden and I. A. Richards, *The Meaning of Meaning: Study of the Influence upon Thought and of the Science of Symbolism*, London, Routledge & Kegan Paul, 1923, 10th edn, 1960, pp. 315ff: 'There can be no doubt that we have here a new type of linguistic use – phatic communion I am tempted to call it, actuated by the demon of terminological invention – a type of speech in which ties of union are created by a mere exchange of words.' [Tr.]

28 This is one of the reasons why political work, contrary to such naïvely utilitarian theories such as those proposed by Olson in *La Logique de l'action collective* (and whose success after 1968, notes Albert Hirschman with a certain cruelty, was no doubt due to the fact that it tended to show the impossibility of movements like May 1968), whether undertaken by the party militant in ordinary times or by demonstrators on exceptional occasions, can be its own end and its own reward: the very efforts of the struggle, not to mention the joys of militant solidarity or the feeling of duty accomplished or even of the real or imaginary experience of being able to transform the world, constitute in themselves so many indubitable satisfactions (cf. A. O. Hirschman, *Shifting Involvements: Private Interest and Public Action*, Oxford, Oxford University Press, 1982.

29 Lanson, *Histoire de la littérature française*, Paris, 1901, 7th edn, p. 1091, quoted by A. Compagnon, *La Troisième République des lettres, de Flaubert à Proust*, Paris, Seuil, 1983, p. 71.

30 The Hôtel Massa, the headquarters of the Société des Gens de Lettres (Writers' Society), was occupied in 1968 by a group of minor writers. The Odéon, one of France's national theatres, directed by the famous actor Jean-Louis Barrault, was occupied by students in 1968, who used it as a forum for public political debate. [Tr.]

31 J. de Romilly, *Nous autres professeurs*, Paris, Fayard, 1969, p. 20.

32 F. Robert, *Un Mandarin prend la parole*, Paris, Presses Universitaires de France, 1970, p. 48.

33 R. Aron, *La Révolution introuvable*, Paris, Fayard, 1968, p. 13.

34 Cf. ibid., pp. 13, 45, 56.

35 De Romilly, *Nous autres professeurs*, p. 14.

36 Ibid., p. 9.

37 Ibid., p. 8.

38 Ibid., p. 15.

39 Symbolically subordinate within the university institution, these 'gate-crashers' have expressed only very partially the questions which they put by the very fact of their presence, and the disturbance which they feel in the face of a system transformed by the very effect of their presence and their disturbance (as is clearly seen in the extreme case of children of immigrants, who put the questions most radically excluded from the normally functioning institution).

40 Cf. F. Gaussen, 'L'opposition proche du PC renverse la direction "gauchiste" du SNESup', *Le Monde*, 18 March 1969.

41 This public display of the space of opinions takes to its maximum intensity the effect produced by public opinion polls when, through techniques as apparently innocent as the presentation of a scale of opinions or of an ensemble of pre-existing responses to a determined question, they impose an explicit problematic, that is to say a space of formal political attitudes.

42 The situation is a constant one for politicians (or, to a lesser degree, for intellectuals), *public men* continually sentenced to *public, published* and advertised opinion, therefore constrained to align all their opinions and their practices with their declared position in the political arena and to repress into *secrecy* any *private opinions* likely to contradict the political attitudes officially linked with the positions and with the groups which they speak for – which implies a strongly censored and euphemistic language.

43 One of the consequences of these analyses is to show up the naïvety of the question of 'true' opinion: opinion is defined each time in the unique relation between an expressive disposition and a market situation. And we could set ourselves the task of establishing, for each agent or class of agents, a *political profile* corresponding to the opinions they might profess (on each one of the questions politically constituted at the moment considered) as a function of the specific laws (of censorship especially) of the market considered (the enquiry situation itself is one of these markets, situated towards the pole of officialdom); and to determine according to which characteristics of the agent the *distance* between public opinions and private opinions varies.

44 It should suffice, to give universal relevance to these analyses, to remember the remark of Proust's Duchess of Guermantes on some salon 'which used to be so charming', that one finds 'all the people one spent one's life avoiding, simply because they happen to be against Dreyfus, and even others, of whom one has not even heard' (M. Proust, *A la recherche du temps perdu*, vol. 2, Paris, Gallimard (La Pléiade), 1954, p. 238).

45 Raymond Aron. [Tr.]

46 Here again, as at each point of this analysis, we may refer to Proust: 'Monsieur de Norpois put these questions to Bloch with a vehemence which, although it intimidated my comrade, flattered him as well; for

the ambassador *seemed to address in him a whole party*, to interrogate Bloch as if he had received the confidences of this party and could assume responsibility for the decisions which would be taken. "If you refused to back down," continued Monsieur de Norpois, without waiting for Bloch's *collective reply*, "if, before the very ink on the decree which instituted the revision procedure had time to dry, obeying who knows what insidious instructions, you refused to back down, and confirmed the sterile opposition which some take to be the *ultima ratio* of politics, if you retired to your tents and burnt your boats, it would be in your own worst interest' (Proust, *A la recherche du temps perdu*, vol. 2, pp. 245–6).

47 In the period immediately following the crisis, the degree to which university problems are perceived as political problems, needing to be formulated and resolved in political terms, instead of remaining in the domain of the unquestioned, varies according to the faculties, the link between opinions on the university and political opinions (what we call 'politicization') being strengthened as we move from the faculties of medicine or law to the faculties of science and arts (enquiry by the AEERS, in 1969).

48 It has not been sufficiently noted that most of the 'May writings' are anonymous or signed with acronyms which fail to identify individual authors. The possibilities of analysis are thereby considerably reduced: one would have to be a true believer in the omnipotence of internalist analysis to hope to understand properly such writings, of which neither the authors nor the social conditions of production and reception can be characterized. This is no doubt true of many writings produced in similar circumstances.

49 An analysis of these *dual* systems of dispositions, with their ambiguous and unavowed ambition, would help us better understand the later success, in the press, in publishing, in public relations, in marketing and even in capitalist business, of many of the leaders of May 1968.

Postscript: The Categories of Professorial Judgement

This study was carried out with the help of Monique de Saint-Martin.

1 Cf. P. Bourdieu and M. de Saint-Martin, 'L'excellence scolaire et les valeurs du système d'enseignement français', *Annales*, 25, 1, January–February 1970, pp. 147–75.

2 A *première supérieure* is a preparatory class (*khagne* or *taupe*) for a *grande école*. [Tr.]

3 This practical taxonomy is revealed with particular clarity in the discourse devoted to the celebration of works of art and, more generally, the celebration of all the exclusive properties of the dominant class (cf. P.

Bourdieu, 'Les fractions de la classe dominante et les modes d'appréciation de l'œuvre d'art', *Information sur les sciences sociales*, 13, 3, pp. 7–32.

4 Corresponding to 'pure' or 'applied' options in the *baccalauréat*. [Tr.]

5 We will willingly accept Lacan's argument that 'Chamfort's formula, "that we can bet on the fact that any public idea, any agreed convention, is foolish, for it has attracted the majority", will certainly appeal to all those who think they escape its laws, that is, precisely, the majority' (J. Lacan, *Ecrits*, Paris, Seuil, 1966, p. 21). As long as we add: the majority of those treated by the social and academic system as an elite.

6 The only accents ever mentioned in the obituaries are accents deviating from the norm, and, among them, 'southern' accents: 'His rough Pyrenean accent, with rolled r's and double consonants' (obituary on G. Rumeau, born at Arbeost, Hautes Pyrénées, son of a primary teacher, *Annuaire ENS*, 1962, p. 42); 'A strong voice, unperturbed by its regional resonance' (notice on A. Montserrat, born at Castres, Tarn, *Annuaire ENS*, 1963, p. 51).

7 Obituary notice on Robert Francillon, *Annuaire ENS*, 1974, p. 46.

8 Obituary notice on Louis Reau, *Annuaire ENS*, 1962, p. 29.

9 It is relatively arbitrary to dissociate the human qualities of the professors from their intellectual qualities, so great is professorial endogamy. From the enquiry which we carried out in 1964 on the matrimonial strategies of six matriculation years (1948–53) of literary *normaliens* (N = 155, that is, a rate of reply of 83 per cent), it appears that among the married *normaliens* who represent 85 per cent of the whole set, 59 per cent married a teacher, 58 per cent of the men who married a teacher married an *agrégée*, 49 per cent of the men who married an *agrégée* married a graduate of the Ecole Normale Supérieure de Sèvres (as for the others, their wives have intellectual professions in 4 per cent of the cases, are middle-ranking executives in 2 per cent of the cases, have no profession at the time of the enquiry in 28 per cent of the cases). We can hardly overemphasize the degree to which this kind of matrimonial strategy contributes to the closing in upon itself of the overprotected world of the academic.

10 *Annuaire ENS*, 1962, pp. 36–7, 52–3, 38·9, 54–5.

11 This series is a good empirical indicator of the market value of the title of *normalien*, and it is from a more or less exact knowledge of the 'exchange rate' of the diploma that is expressed in it that is constituted the subjective vision of the field of opportunities which defines the aspirations and expectations of a given moment in time. On the relation between career and field of opportunities, see P. Bourdieu, 'Avenir de classe et causalité du probable', *Revue française de sociologie*, 15, 1, January–March 1971, pp. 3–12, especially p. 11.

12 Never praised as a value worth pursuing in its own right, obscurity can only be recognized in the guise of the positive virtues which it is

supposed to imply, the disdain for honours and the renunciation of non-academic success. As witness this phrase, flung twenty years ago by a Sorbonne professor at the head of a candidate known outside the milieu for his essays and journalism: 'You are not unknown enough.'

13 Obituary notice on Jacques-Henri Passeron, *Annuaire ENS*, 1974, p. 120.

14 Obituary notice on Paul Blassel, *Annuaire ENS*, 1962, p. 41.

15 The analysis of a sample of academics and writers or artists mentioned in *Who's Who in France* (1969–70 editions) shows a group of systematic differences between these two populations. The academics are characterized by a much higher average number of children (2.39) than the writers and artists (1.56), a lower proportion of the unmarried or divorced (0.9 and 0.9 per cent respectively as opposed to 16.6 and 10.7 per cent), a much higher proportion of decorations (65.1 per cent of the academics have the Legion of Honour as opposed to 39.2 per cent of the intellectuals).

16 Obituary notice on Jules Romains, *Annuaire ENS*, 1974, p. 43.

17 Obituary notice on Guillaume Rumeau, professor of physics in a preparatory class, *Annuaire ENS*, 1962.

18 *Annuaire ENS*, 1965, p. 38.

19 Obituary notice on Aurélien Digeon, *Annuaire ENS*, 1963, p. 58.

20 M. Weber, *The Protestant Ethic and the Spirit of Capitalism*, 2nd edn, London, George Allen and Unwin, 1976.

Appendix 1 The Sources Used

1 The *brevet supérieur* is the lower school certificate for those leaving at age 15 instead of staying on to take the *baccalauréat* at 18. [Tr.]

2 Cf. P. Bourdieu and M. de Saint-Martin, 'La Sainte Famille: L'Episcopat français dans le champ du pouvoir', *Actes de la recherche en sciences sociales*, 44–5, November 1982, pp. 2–53.

3 A CHU (*centre hospitalier universitaire*) is a university clinical school. [Tr.]

4 Each French government minister has his own 'cabinet' of civil servants and/or experts to advise him. [Tr.]

5 The CNESER is the Conseil National de l'Enseignement Supérieur de la Recherche. [Tr.]

6 The National Committee for Scientific Research. [Tr.]

7 The Study Group for the Expansion of Scientific Research. [Tr.]

Appendix 2 The Morphological Transformations of the Faculties and The Morphological Transformations of the Disciplines

The complete set of data can be found in P. Bourdieu, L. Botanski and P. Maldidier, 'La défense du corps', *Information sur les sciences sociales*, 10, 4, 1971, pp. 54–86.

1 The CPEM, the *certificat de préparation aux études medicales,* and the PCB (*Physique, Chimie, Biologie*), the preliminary certificate for medical studies in physics, chemistry and biology, are diplomas enabling students after the first year of general scientific studies at university to specialize in medical studies. [Tr.]

Appendix 3 The Hit Parade of French Intellectuals

1 Of the 448 'judges', we may identify, if we rely on the classificatory system used by *Lire*, 132 'journalists' (92 for the 'written press', 40 for 'radio and television'), 66 writers', 34 with 'professions in the book trade' (publishers, booksellers, etc.), 34 'teacher-writers', 21 'academicians' (to which should be added 44 with professions in the 'arts and performing arts', 14 'politicians', 43 'teachers', 34 'students' and 16 'various'). In fact, the first four categories (which represent nearly two-thirds of the 'judges') include a very high proportion of hybrid characters, who escape the classification proposed: the authors who are classified with the 'journalists' have nearly all written at least one book and, according to this criterion, could be put in the category of 'writers'. This is pointed out by the creators of the classification, who omit on the other hand to note that the majority of authors classified under 'writers' also have more or less permanent and institutionalized links with the daily or weekly press. This difference in treatment shows the hierarchy tacitly established between the two 'conditions': one should apologize to the 'writers' whom one reduces to the status of 'journalist'; one has no need to apologize for promoting a journalist to the status of writer. As for the 'teacher-writers', nearly half of them could just as easily be classified in the category (not used by *Lire*) of 'journalist-academics' which, while it hardly existed thirty years ago, is now very rich, and we could also put in it some of the authors who, although their main source of income is teaching, have been classified by *Lire* among the 'journalists' (we have not attempted here to present lists of proper names, to avoid giving our demonstration the appearance of a denunciation).

2 In the list of the 'bestsellers of the last seven years [Giscard's term as President]' drawn up by the weekly *L'Express* in March 1981 according

to the number of weeks in the list of weekly bestsellers, Roger Garaudy comes in thirteenth place for *Appel aux vivants* – after Jakez Hélias, Peyrefitte (for *Le Mal français*), Schwartzenberg, Viansson-Ponté, R. Moody, Peyrefitte (for *Quand la Chine se réveillera*), Emilie Carles, Dr Roger Dalet, Lapierre-Collins, Murray Kendall, Pisar, Solzenitsyn, Troyat, de Closets – and in eleventh place for *Parole d'homme*; Bernard-Henri Lévy comes in twentieth place, for his *Testament de Dieu*, and Glucksmann in twenty-first for *Les Maîtres penseurs*. The bestseller effect is particularly noticeable, as we see, in the domain of the social sciences and philosophy, no doubt because the frontier between works of research and essays is vaguer there, at least in the eyes of the journalists and the general public (whom they help to orientate): none of the novelists, poets or men of the theatre quoted in the hit parade published by *Lire* appears in the list of bestselling novels. Further down the list, we find more works that Janick Jossin (*L'Express*, 18 April 1981) calls 'unexpected bestsellers' (for instance, *Montaillou* by Emmanuel Le Roy Ladurie, *Plaidoyer pour une Europe décadente* by Raymond Aron or *Fragments d'un discours amoureux* by Roland Barthes). Janick Jossin also cites, for the novel, Michel Tournier, Marguerite Yourcenar, J. M. G. Le Clézio, Julien Gracq.

3 As a result of competition between the different organs of the press, each cultural journalist tends to act as 'taste-maker' for all the other journalists. Moreover, some institutions provide journalists with *objectified criteria*: 'Throughout this seven-year period, French literature has followed the movements of these two semi-official barometers that the television broadcast "Apostrophes" and the list of bestsellers in *L'Express* have become' Jossin, *L'Express*, 18 April 1981). Thus it is that there tends to arise a hierarchy of intellectuals specific to journalists and a special category of intellectuals-for-the-media (the *Lire* hit parade recording as it were the product of an action of which it itself represents the most accomplished form).

4 All the unwitting question–begging that it is possible to deploy (predetermined definition, implicitly biased sample, etc.) may be found in Charles Kadushin's book, which has all the social gloss required to make it a classic of 'empirical' sociology for intellectuals (cf. C. Kadushin, *The American Intellectual Elite*, Boston, Little Brown and Co., 1974).

5 One of the main differences between the viewpoint of contemporaries and the viewpoint of posterity lies no doubt in the fact that contemporaries have a (variable) knowledge of the authors, of their physical person, and also of everything implied by contemporaneity, gossip, rumour, personal mythology. And this *intuitus personae* which constitutes one of principles of our primary perception and appreciation of authors (more than the works, no doubt little read by those whose profession it is to speak about them in the press) and of the difference from later

perception and appreciation, more directly and exclusively based on *reading* the work, is very difficult to reconstitute through eyewitness accounts (for instance, notes on the speech accents of nineteenth-century painters or writers, on their bodily *hexis*, their appearance and behaviour, etc., are very rare and always associated with exceptional cases).

6 Thus it is probable that the bias in favour of journalist-intellectuals or writers with 'media muscle' would have been even more marked if a longer list had been asked for, leaving greater scope for the strategy of pandemic infiltration.

7 The hit parade of intellectuals, which, unlike the enquiry by Huret in 1881, which attempted only to record the opinions of writers on writers, is the product of an explicit intention to judge and classify, and the privilege which it grants to the most 'mediagenic' authors, are only some indications of the growth of this control: suffice it to add the institutional weight that the journalist-intellectuals have acquired within an academic institution such as the Ecole Pratique des Hautes Etudes or the very fact that the 'cultural journalists' of the major dailies and weeklies, armed with only the authority conferred on them by their supposed power to procure fame beyond the field of publishing and the press and their real ability to produce within the limits of their field, especially in publishing houses, can collectively affirm their claim legitimately to judge works (generically called 'essays') whose examination and criticism was in former times reserved for the scientific field and learned reviews (cf. *Les Nouvelles littéraires*, 3–9 January 1980).

8 It is remarkable, as has been noted by those responsible for the enquiry themselves, that Aron is 'the name cited by those who would prefer to cite nobody' (J. Jaubert, *Lire*, 68, April 1981, p. 45): 'My good man, there no longer are any influential intellectuals, except, at a pinch, Raymond Aron' (Yves Berger), 'apart from Raymond Aron' (Alain Buhler), 'Aron, if you think really hard', says Annie Copperman, who adds: 'The media have taken over.' This is corroborated by Jacques Lanzmann when he cites 'Bernard-Henri Lévy, whose really original and penetrating ideas are backed up by fine telegenic features.' It all looks as if, by crowning the most anti-intellectual intellectual, the intention was to dethrone intellectuals as such or, better, negate them – an intention which is also expressed in the urgency of journalists of all persuasions to declare that Sartre has no successor, or again in the propensity to welcome defenders of the different forms of irrationalism, of which we hardly need ask whether they have encouraged the submission of the intellectual field to the problems and the procedures of journalism, or whether they have caused it, so certain is it that they are linked to the creation of a new social definition of the 'intellectual', making rational exploitation of the 'media', with everything that implies, one of the conditions of the ability to dominate the intellectual field.

9 For an exemplary analysis, which is easy to transpose, see M. Goldman, *Literary Dissent in Communist China*, Cambridge, Mass., Harvard University Press, 1967.

10 We know that certain ethnologists have observed that accusations of sorcery appear in social worlds where relations are at once ill defined and competitive, and where tensions between rivals cannot be otherwise resolved (cf. M. Douglas (ed.), *Witchcraft, Confessions and Accusations*, London, Tavistock, 1970).

Index

Index by Justyn Balinski